PLOWED UNDER

PLOWED UNDER

FOOD POLICY PROTESTS AND PERFORMANCE IN NEW DEAL AMERICA

ANN FOLINO WHITE

INDIANA UNIVERSITY PRESS *Bloomington & Indianapolis*

This book is a publication of

INDIANA UNIVERSITY PRESS
Office of Scholarly Publishing
Herman B Wells Library 350
1320 East 10th Street
Bloomington, Indiana 47405 USA

iupress.indiana.edu

Telephone   800-842-6796
Fax   812-855-7931

Manufactured in the
United States of America

Library of Congress
Cataloging-in-Publication Data

White, Ann Folino.
  Plowed under : food policy protests and
performance in new deal America / Ann
Folino White.
      pages cm
  Includes bibliographical references and
index.
  ISBN 978-0-253-01540-2 (pb : alk. paper)
— ISBN 978-0-253-01537-2 (cl : alk.
paper) — ISBN 978-0-253-01538-9 (eb)
  1. Agriculture and state—United States
—History—20th century. 2. Protest
movements—United States—History
—20th century. 3. New Deal, 1933–1939.
I. Title.
  HD1761.W427 2014
  338.1'97309043—dc23

                                2014022234

1 2 3 4 5   20 19 18 17 16 15

For Marc and June

CONTENTS

ACKNOWLEDGMENTS

I RECEIVED GENEROUS FINANCIAL SUPPORT FROM MICHIGAN State University for the completion of this book, including a research leave sponsored by the Residential College in the Arts and Humanities, an Interdisciplinary Research Incubator Grant from the College of Arts and Letters, and a Humanities and Arts Research Program subvention from the Office of the Vice President for Research and Graduate Studies. Funding from the College of Arts and Letters–Undergraduate Research Initiative supported Magdalena Kopacz's translations for this book; Ms. Kopacz also gave freely to me important insights into her hometown of Hamtramck, Michigan, for which I am very appreciative. The College of Arts and Letters, the Residential College in the Arts and Humanities, and the Honors College supported David Clauson as my research assistant throughout the four years of his undergraduate education; David's remarkable intellect and tireless assistance made this book better.

I am also thankful to the American Theatre and Drama Society for the Publishing Subvention Award and to the American Society for Theater Research, the Alice Berline Kaplan Center for the Humanities, and the graduate school at Northwestern University for grants that supported my research. Thanks to Jarod Roll and Don Binkowski for sharing research and to Hannah Tesman and Matthew Campbell and Whitney Minter for opening their homes to me during research trips. Thanks also to Indiana University Press's reviewers for their deep engagement with my work and to the editorial and production staff for their thoroughness and responsiveness throughout this process.

Many thanks to the faculty of the Interdisciplinary PhD in Theatre and Drama Program at Northwestern University, particularly Robert Launay, Nancy MacLean, Susan Manning, and Sandra L. Richards. My graduate cohorts were the first readers of this project and remain my most trusted colleagues. Thank you, Amber Day, Christina McMahon, Jesse Njus, Scott Proudfit, and Daniel Smith. While I am also indebted to Shelly Scott and Stefka Mihaylova for reviewing many drafts, I am most grateful to them for their good counsel and friendship.

Several friends and colleagues—Caroline Kiley, Michael Largey, Melvin Pena, Sam O'Connell, and Patti Rogers—offered valuable advice and critiques of this project at various stages. My colleagues Rob Roznowski and Chris Scales have served as important sounding boards and mentors. I am also incredibly grateful to Joanna Bosse for the open invitation to share ideas and for playing hooky with me. Many thanks to all.

To Tracy C. Davis, whose generous spirit, intellectual acuity, and practical advice have enriched my research, my teaching, and my life: thank you for telling me to wear a sweater in the archives.

The Folino and White families have sustained me, and so this project, in all the most important ways. They have taken great care to encourage me and to nurture and entertain my daughter June whenever this project required me to be away from her. To my mother and father, Anita and Dino Folino, thank you for teaching me the importance of perseverance and a well-timed joke. You have been my most important teachers and are the reason I became one. To my June, who requires the tooth fairy to sign for pick up, thank you for your impatience with and interest in me. My husband Marc ensured that I had everything I needed to complete this book. He is the kindest person I know and my truest friend. I am grateful that we share our lives.

PLOWED UNDER

Introduction

FAMED ATTORNEY AND LEADER OF THE AMERICAN CIVIL
Liberties Union Clarence Darrow, like so many others, thought the 1933
Agricultural Adjustment Act (AAA) to be immoral: How could the government pay farmers to leave fields fallow while children rummaged
in trash for food and thousands of Americans stood in breadlines day
after day? How could President Franklin D. Roosevelt actively throw
away food in the face of so much want? Darrow surely knew the currency of his rhetoric and likely believed in it as well. The cultural code
of conduct regarding food and the nobility of farming were so deeply
engrained in the American consciousness that the AAA seemed to flout
basic American morality when hunger's call to obligation was most in-
sistent, when access to food was truly at stake for millions of Americans.
Secretary of Agriculture Henry Wallace anticipated that this New Deal
agricultural program would "face an unfavorable public reaction,"[1] but
he underestimated the fervor, ubiquity, and persistence of criticism lev-
eled at the AAA. Throughout the 1930s, citizens from across the social
spectrum denounced the program as immoral and unjust and did so in

ways that exceeded the realm of rhetoric. They engaged in what might be called a "theater of food" in their protests to challenge the AAA's morality. The federal government also turned to food's potency in performance to convince the public of the AAA's benefits.

This book tells the story of the moral issues raised by the Agricultural Adjustment Act from the distinct perspectives of farmers, consumers, agricultural laborers, the federal government, and theater artists. It analyzes five case studies that map out the emergent controversies surrounding the AAA from its passage in the spring of 1933 (and its subsequent versions in 1936 and 1938) to the general adoption of its policies by 1939. *Plowed Under* begins by examining the U.S. Department of Agriculture's (USDA) promotion of the humanitarian aspects of the AAA through public exhibits at the 1933–34 World's Fair in Chicago. The next three chapters examine challenges to the official narrative, through protests by three groups of citizens, whose experiences with and complaints against the act were defined by their economic relationships to agriculture and the cultural significance of particular foods. They include the Wisconsin Cooperative Milk Pool strike staged by property-owning, white dairymen in 1933; the Women's Committee for Action against the High Cost of Living meat boycott in Hamtramck, Michigan, staged by female, working-class, Polish American consumers in 1935; and the Missouri sharecroppers' demonstration staged by black and white landless/ homeless laborer families in 1939.

These competing narratives coalesce in the book's final chapter, where national struggles over food form the central conflict of the Federal Theatre Project's play *Triple-A Plowed Under* (1936). Sponsored, ironically enough, by the New Deal government via its Works Progress Administration, the play presents a panorama of the AAA's adverse impact, featuring scenes based on actual anti-AAA protests. By investigating both artistic events and protests, *Plowed Under* shows how the politics of representation influenced public policy and strategies for sociopolitical change. Along the way, cultural battles over whether the protests and the play staged the "truth" or were "pretense" elucidate the role American antitheatrical bias played in shaping public debate in the period, as well as its impact on the writing of history.

Although this book concentrates on federal legislation and the actions of both the state and ordinary people, it is not a conventional political or social history. Rather, it employs insights from theater history and performance studies to explore what historic changes to the American agricultural and food system meant to citizens living in the midst of national economic and human turmoil. Examining the 1930s agricultural crisis through the performances and protests that it sparked illustrates citizens' beliefs about their rights, as well as the terms on which citizens believed they needed to stake their claims to food. The ways in which values and beliefs played themselves out on popular stages and in public spaces show just how problematic treating food as a commodity was in 1930s America. Citizens and the federal government negotiated the moral tensions between food as a biological necessity and as a vital commercial product by linking the right to food to "good" citizenship.

Indeed, the protests and performances that I examine exhibited contradictory inclinations concerning the right to food. On the one hand, they participated in a humanist moral discourse regarding food that acknowledged access to food as a universal right. At the same time, however, both sides used the producer ethic, the idea that good citizenship and morality are based on a person's contributions to the nation, as a trope to assert or circumscribe rights. The federally sponsored Chicago World's Fair exhibits, the play *Triple-A Plowed Under,* and the anti-AAA protesters represented the good citizen as the figures of consumer and farmer and their contributions to the country.

In each case of resistance, protesters called on the New Deal government to ensure their rights as citizens with respect to food both as commodity and as sustenance. Immediately following passage of the AAA in 1933, Wisconsin dairy farmers dumped milk as part of their strike because the legislation did not guarantee prices equal to the costs of producing dairy products—it failed to protect the "rights" of food producers. Two years later, working-class housewives in Hamtramck, Michigan, picketed butcher shops and groceries because the AAA had increased the cost of meat to unaffordable levels—it failed to protect the "rights" of consumers. In 1939, when the agricultural adjustment programs were fully institutionalized, Missouri sharecropper families

occupied the sides of highways because the AAA, inadvertently, provided incentives to plantation owners to evict sharecroppers—it failed
to protect citizens' "right" to earn a living. In these cases and dozens
of others, protesters demonstrated to the New Deal government that,
as productive citizens, they had fulfilled their responsibilities to American society. Farmers wanted to receive a just price for their products,
consumers wanted to pay a just price for their food, and displaced agricultural laborers wanted a just return for their labor. Nationwide, producers, consumers, and agricultural laborers alike defined "just" as a
minimal standard of well-being.

In addition, *Plowed Under* analyzes the political importance of theatrical culture, whereas other histories of New Deal-era politics tend
to disregard performances and protests as merely "dramatic" displays
designed to attract attention. The archives of the protests and performances that I have uncovered reveal participants' sophisticated understanding of theatrical traditions. They show that theatrical elements
—from casting to dialogue to props to scenery—mattered to protesters and authorities just as they did to the producers of *Triple-A Plowed
Under* and the designers of World's Fair exhibits, all of whom made aesthetic choices about how best to represent the human costs (or benefits)
of agricultural policy. For instance, USDA officials working on exhibits
for the World's Fair emphasized that staging the projected outcomes
of the AAA would do political work: "By presenting [facts] in inspir-
ing form we move the public to take certain action. This is the true
function of an exhibit."[2] Similarly, protesters clearly understood the
importance to their cause of *performing* good citizenship, as shown by
the theatrical tactics they used to deal with biases of race, ethnicity,
gender, and class, all of which both underlay and are masked by the
discourse of producerism.

Theatrical strategies affected the responses of media, state and federal authorities, and spectators, while they shaped the terms on which
agricultural policies were debated. Ironically, AAA advocates and protesters, authorities, and audiences variously challenged and girded the
boundary between the "real world" and theatrical performance (or staged
protest), by paradoxically demonstrating performance's capacity to impact everyday life while at the same time disavowing performance's

power. The ongoing tension in these cases suggests that this anxiety was bound up with the conception of American citizenship as a performance (that is, anyone can be an American by acting a certain way, namely, by subscribing to the producer ethic), rather than as an identity based on race or ethnicity.

The aesthetic and demographic diversity of these case studies is crucial because the New Deal's agricultural policy was far-reaching and raised conflicting concerns for citizens nationwide. The cases differ on multiple levels: from place and time to artistic genre or type of protest to the social identity of groups to the rights at stake. To date, these historic events have been studied in isolation from one another because scholars in the various subfields of history—cultural history, agricultural history, labor history, women's history, African American history, or even theater history—are concerned with different populations of citizens, political leanings, or forms of expression. Instead, treating an array of cultural performances alongside protests staged by different socioeconomic identity groups, this book throws into relief the constellation of anxieties that made up the lived experiences of the 1930s agricultural crisis, a formative era for U.S. food politics, one that initiated federal policies and cultural scripts that continue into the twenty-first century.

A Controversial Program:
The Agricultural Adjustment Acts

Citizens and the federal government produced and interpreted the protests and performances considered in this study at a time when the economic and human crisis had no foreseeable end. They were deeply concerned about rapid and volatile changes to the food system under the AAA, which would have a sweeping impact across economic, environmental, technological, and political realms. During its formative period in the 1930s, the effects of the AAA were uncertain, emergent, and, of course, complex, arising from a number of a contingent factors. In the next few pages, I offer a brief overview of the act that represents its embattled, changeable state during this time, concentrating on the central complaints lodged by farmers, consumers, and landless laborers—the primary subjects of this study.

Food rationing and substitution were not new concepts to the American public. During World War I, these restrictions were considered difficult but necessary patriotic duties; however, as the 1930s dawned, the recurrence of such practices became a symbol of the failure of the Hoover administration to protect its citizens. When Herbert Hoover served as the U.S. food administrator during World War I, he urged the public to substitute "lesser" foods for staples in order to feed the troops abroad. This initial period of rationing was a matter of weighing limited supply against national security. The first years of the economic crisis under Hoover's presidency, however, returned "hooverizing" to American life. After the stock market crash in 1929, Americans transformed the term, and the then-president's name, to denote the degradation of the American standard of living. They called makeshift squatters' villages "Hoovervilles," renamed newspapers "Hoover blankets," and sang about the substitution of woefully inadequate foods for essential ones:

> We have Hooverized on butter,
> For milk we've only water,
> And I haven't seen a steak in many a day;
> As for pies, cakes, and jellies,
> We substitute sow-bellies
> For which we work the county road each day.
> [Refrain:] Oh, those beans, bacon, and gravy,
> They almost drive me crazy
> I eat them til I see them in my dreams.

The song, "Beans, Bacon, and Gravy," was written sometime around 1931, which, according to the lyrics, was the "worst" year that the songwriter had lived through.[3] The song highlights the power of certain foods to structure expectations about rights and justice. The lyric "for milk we've only water" communicates milk's importance to life and health and the degradation that marks its absence. As anthropologist Janet Fitchen explains, hunger cannot be understood outside its sociocultural context because food is "invested with meanings that may outweigh its metabolic or nutritional aspects."[4] Consuming inadequate foods day in and day out is maddening to the songwriter. Nor is monotony the sole cause of the lyricist's frustration; each miserable food reminds the singer of other, better foods. Drinking water does not satiate; rather, it marks the hunger felt in not drinking milk. Yet, ironically, the need to substitute foods or simply go without staples occurred during a time of agricultural abundance. Fruit rotted on trees, fields went unharvested, and farmers burned their products. High levels of unemployment meant that consumers lacked money to buy goods, including food; demand plummeted, and surplus commodities piled up. Agricultural markets were glutted, and prices were so low that farmers could not afford to harvest crops or bring them to market. From the coexistence of thousands of hungry Americans and an ample food supply was born the phrase "the paradox of want amid plenty."

The Depression's widespread effects and Hoover's perceived inaction belied traditional faith in laissez-faire capitalism and the value of ever-expanding production as the key to American abundance. Indeed, Franklin D. Roosevelt persuaded U.S. citizens to elect him president by characterizing capitalism as an economic system that required intervention: "while [Republicans] prate of economic laws, men and women are starving. We must lay hold of the fact that economic laws are not made by nature. They are made by human beings."[5] With these words, FDR put the onus for the nation's welfare on the federal government, vowed to take action, and blamed, at least in part, Herbert Hoover's faith in a self-correcting market for Americans' misery. Immediately upon taking his office, Roosevelt, along with the Congress, began tinkering with the industrial and agricultural markets in efforts to restore the economy, and together they set up programs to provide immediate relief to the unemployed and the poor.

One of these programs, the Agricultural Adjustment Act, passed in May 1933. The AAA's primary aim was to ease farmers' desperate circumstances by raising the prices of agricultural products to align them with the costs of their production. In essence, the federal government would pay farmers to produce less by removing acreage from cultivation, thus decreasing the amount of commodities on the market. A tax was levied against food processors to fund the federal subsidies to farmers. The USDA anticipated that a decrease in available commodities would increase demand, which would, in turn, increase both the market price of agricultural products and farmers' purchasing power. The agency es-

tablished consumer councils to protect against price hikes. Thus, the
AAA was designed to work in conjunction with programs boosting industry, urban employment, and consumers' purchasing power.

In spite of its intentions, the AAA encountered controversy from
the start. Unlike the manufacturing industry, agriculture supplied products that Americans could not do without. Consumers called the AAA a
"policy of scarcity" and claimed that it was causing "unnatural" inflation
of food prices. Many farmers could not reconcile the idea of decreasing
production at a time when there was widespread need for food. John
Simpson, head of the prominent Farmers Union, testified before the U.S.
Senate that "The farmers are not producing too much. We need all this.
What we have overproduction of is empty stomachs and bare backs."[6]

For the owners of small farms, like the Wisconsin dairymen examined in chapter 2, the AAA threatened their livelihoods and way of life
by spurring the consolidation of small farms into large corporate enterprises. This sizable minority of farmers immediately objected to the
legislation on the grounds that it did not guarantee market prices at least
equal to the costs of production. Many farmers faced foreclosure due
in part to severely depressed prices and believed that processors would
lower market prices for agricultural products even further to offset the
cost of the AAA processing tax, concerns that were borne out. Additionally, these farmers could not decrease production and continue to
compete with large farms, which were buying up foreclosed land and
equipment. Corporate farms had the capacity to produce more commodities more efficiently and stood to collect huge federal subsidies
under the AAA by removing large amounts of acreage from cultivation.
Farmers running small operations also feared that the voluntary basis
of the program worked to the advantage of those not participating, who
could continue to produce at unaltered rates. Meanwhile, agricultural
prices did not improve at a pace with the rising cost of industrial goods.

The timing of the AAA's passage complicated matters further. By
May of 1933, farmers had already planted crops and impregnated sows,
so the Agricultural Adjustment Administration undertook emergency
measures to eliminate the anticipated cotton and pork surpluses that
would supposedly further glut the market and stall the program at its
start. That June, the government paid farmers to plow under one-quarter

of cotton planted prior to the legislation's enactment. Then, in August, at the World's Fair in Chicago, the epicenter of the American livestock trade and processing industry, Secretary of Agriculture Henry Wallace announced the so-called Corn-Hog program. This program entailed the federal purchase of six million swine, federal funding of hog processing, and distribution of pork products to relief clients—that is, citizens who received government assistance. It also ordered the destruction of that proportion of the corn crop grown for hog feed. In addition, the Corn-Hog program would remove from market both shoats (not yet matured for market) and sows (set to produce new litters). From the purchase figures and price increases estimated by Wallace, the *Chicago Daily Tribune* "calculated that relief fed persons have had little meat to eat and that their consumption of this huge amount will not interfere with the normal consumption."[7] Officials claimed that this adjustment would benefit farmers and relief clients while not unduly burdening consumers. Unfortunately, the public did not experience the Corn-Hog program as beneficial. Rather, it seemed to exacerbate their hardships and violate their ideas of American morality.

Shortly after the emergency program was announced and put into action, the public condemned it as immoral. The mechanisms by which the program operated—mass pig slaughter and plowing under crops— alarmed consumers and farmers, rural and urban citizens, alike. Within two weeks of Wallace's announcement, the *Marion* [Indiana] *Chronicle* observed that citizens "lie paralyzed at the enormity of the latest offense against every law of God and man."[8] Then, there was a quick failure of its ends—many shoats were too small for processing machinery, and a sizable amount of livestock was made into inedible grease and tankage, much of which also turned out to be unusable. The New Deal seemingly sanctioned waste while its citizens suffered hunger. Piglets were buried and dumped in the Mississippi; just over 20 percent of the pigs were distributed as meat to impoverished citizens.[9] The radical National Farmers' Holiday Association condemned the USDA's "wholesale destruction of the necessities of life, as being criminal and sacriligious [*sic*]."[10] Critics of the AAA and its emergency measures evoked farmers' noble calling, anthropomorphized piglets and sows by framing them in rich tropes of innocence and motherhood, and pitted the weakest of Americans—

hungry children—against the mightiest—men of government. Such rhetoric is rife with the Judeo-Christian doctrine of stewardship, which ties God-given abundance on earth to mutual obligation; wasting the land or its provender spurns God's gift just as it causes another's hunger. In an attempt to counter popular condemnation of the pig slaughter, the Roosevelt administration announced the formation of the Federal Surplus Relief Corporation (FSRC) on October 4, 1933. The FSRC managed distribution of agricultural surpluses to relief clients, not consumers.[11]

When food prices, particularly pork and beef, escalated rapidly at the start of 1935, consumers pointed to the AAA as the cause. Across the nation, women, such as the boycotters detailed in chapter 3, led protests against the high cost of meat. When the Corn-Hog program was first announced, the *Chicago Tribune* doubted the program's economic efficacy because "The possibilities of substituting other cereals for corn, other meats for pork and other foods for meat if hog prices are pushed too far out of line are obvious."[12] This reporter wrongly believed that consumers would substitute ungrudgingly one kind of food for another. Consumer protests over meat suggest that, for many, no substitute for meat existed. The USDA attributed the rise in prices to the 1934 drought, which resulted in significantly fewer cattle and hogs on farms in 1935 than in the previous year. Consumers, however, blamed the 1933 pig slaughter and 1934 livestock slaughters. In the latter case, the Agricultural Adjustment Administration instituted an Emergency Cattle Agreement through which it purchased and slaughtered cattle dying due to drought conditions from ranchers who had agreed to participate in future AAA regulations. When, some government-slaughtered cattle were deemed unfit for consumption, consumers registered their deaths as another instance of federal waste in the face of want and asserted that meat-packaging corporations were passing the costs of AAA processing taxes on to consumers.[13]

While the public cried out against the AAA on moral grounds, businesses opposed its effect on profits. Food corporations worked to end the processing tax through the courts in more than seventeen hundred lawsuits filed against the government by the end of 1935.[14] They campaigned for public support by suggesting that the AAA not only unfairly taxed corporations but that it pitted struggling farmers against struggling consumers. Republican Senator Daniel O. Hastings (Del.) agreed: "the worst of all this is found in the processing tax upon the food we eat and the clothes we wear, thus imposing a tax upon one class of persons for the benefit of another."[15] In a speech defending the processing tax, Wallace tried to distance the USDA from the allegation by repeatedly prefacing his points with the phrase "so far"—for example, "So far are we from a policy of scarcity that there is more meat available for consumers today than would have been possible had there been no AAA." Wallace repositioned the program as "an adjustment policy providing for increases when such increases make for the welfare of the consumer, and for decreases when such decreases make for the welfare of the farmers."[16] Despite these rhetorical efforts, many citizens felt that the AAA's timing and the USDA's ability to balance the needs of struggling consumers and producers was off-kilter.

Food corporations won the first (legal) victory against the AAA. The Supreme Court's January 1936 decision in *United States v. Butler* declared the processing tax unconstitutional and ordered the return of tax monies to processors and manufacturers. Following the ruling, when consumer prices failed to drop, processors, who had alleged that the tax was responsible for the rise in costs, were now seen as culpable.[17] As Wallace began his long fight against repayment of the processing tax, officials in the Agricultural Adjustment Administration scrambled to replace the AAA.[18] In March 1936, Congress replaced the 1933 act with another agricultural curtailment program, the Soil Conservation and Domestic Allotment Act (SCDAA). Like the AAA, the SCDAA removed acreage from cultivation in order to reduce agricultural output; but it used general tax revenues to fund payments to farmers, and it emphasized conservation. Ecological disaster had compounded economic crisis, and, by 1936, the Great Plains had been transformed into the "Dustbowl." The SCDAA aimed to avert future catastrophes of both kinds by paying farmers to plant soil-regenerating crops on a portion of their land.

In 1938, a renewed AAA continued to fund conservation programs but tried to guard against commodity surpluses—increased fertility and good growing conditions had produced a bumper crop in 1937—and food scarcity due to natural disasters—droughts had occurred in 1934 and 1936—by establishing crop-storage programs. Despite ongoing criticism of the adjustment programs, by 1939, 78 percent of farms had contracts with the federal government. In fact, agricultural historian John Shover credits the decline of the National Farmers' Holiday Association, one of the largest and most radical agrarian fundamentalist groups, to farmers' overall satisfaction with the AAA.[19]

For its own part, the USDA embraced the AAA's part in helping speed mechanization and create more profitable farms. The administration downplayed the act's negative effects on landless laborers, such as the Missouri sharecroppers discussed in chapter 4, who, by 1939, had come to be (dis)regarded as "surplus." To the government, "surplus" connoted a threat to economic prosperity or plenty for all Americans. Agricultural laborers were easily associated with surplus as the historic condition of large sharecropper families was complicated by the declining need for laborers in an increasingly industrialized agricultural landscape. Expanded mechanization during the decade—more than a hundred thousand tractors were used for the first time in cotton farming during the 1930s—eliminated the need for 1.5 million to two million laborers.[20] The AAA expedited capital investment and the transition to large-scale farming, which increased farm laborers' need to migrate, shrank the employment season, and left many individuals without any work at all.

The USDA's drive to modernize agriculture had dire effects on migrant laborers and sharecroppers. Although the AAA tried to safeguard against the evictions of sharecroppers from farms that had contracts with the administration, because acreage was removed from cultivation, fewer laborers were needed to work the land. Compounding the problem, farm owners, or their managing landlords, oversaw AAA contracts at the local level, rendering federal protections for laborers largely ineffectual. Moreover, the administrative purge of the officials who were most avid about farm laborers' rights indicates that prejudices against sharecroppers were not just local but part of the larger philosophy of the program.[21] Secretary Wallace himself failed to acknowledge fully the program's part in displacing sharecroppers. When Eleanor Roosevelt sent a private letter to him about the Missouri sharecroppers' dire situation, Wallace couched their displacement in a manner similar to "surplus": "Few people are aware of or appreciate the importance of the basic population facts. . . . there were in 1938 1,650,000 more people on the farms than there were in 1930, in spite of the technological advance under which the farm population of 1930 would have been entirely adequate to produce for the whole population of 1938. . . . There are few facts so fundamental to our whole economic problem of today." Mrs. Roosevelt sardonically responded, "Your letter on the subject of farm population and conditions among the sharecroppers is most interesting. Thank you very much. Should we be developing more industries and services? Should we practice birth control or drown the surplus population?"[22] The First Lady's Swiftian solution pointedly critiques Wallace's articulation of a limit to the government's obligations to those not recognized as productive citizens. The theatrical strategies used by the Missouri sharecroppers that first spurred deep humanitarian concern and then moral outrage from Eleanor Roosevelt also point to the significance of the politics of representation to debates about the morality of the Agricultural Adjustment Act.

The Dramaturgy of Protest and Uncertainty: Methodological Considerations

Within its larger aim to elaborate the relationship of theatrical strategies to politics, Plowed Under contributes to the methods that performance scholars and U.S. historians (of all stripes) use to study cultural performance and protest. First, I approach the distinct foods used in these political actions as unique cultural objects, instilled with meanings that are central to understanding the performances and protests.[23] In all the cases, food was a trope and a prop to articulate the demands and political identities of the various groups. In protest conflicts, protesters held out particular foods as central symbols—literally fought over during the Hamtramck boycott and the Wisconsin strike—and, in the performances, specific foods were placed "center stage." Throughout this study, meat and milk appear as these seminal symbols and objects of contest.

National myths, food industries' product promotions, philanthropic organizations' campaigns, scientific developments in nutrition, and government programs all contributed to meat's and milk's paramount importance to Americans in the 1930s. Milk and meat were not only considered imperative to health but were considered as necessary to creating ideal American citizens. Anthropologist Daniel Miller employs the phrase "blindingly obvious" to describe how an object's seemingly self-evident meaning "can determine our expectations, by setting the scene and ensuring appropriate behaviour, without being open to challenge. They determine what takes place to the extent that we are unconscious of their capacity to do so."[24] The "obvious" cultural meanings of meat and milk, discussed in chapter 1, shaped the stakes of protests and performances.

It is crucial to stress that battles over the AAA were waged not just for farmers' rights or consumers' rights, but, for example, for the right *to meat* or for control *over milk.* The cultural significance of these foods informed how and why citizens opposed the AAA, how both citizens and the government conceived of rights and government obligations, and how the AAA itself was implemented. Meat and milk functioned in the performances and protests as powerful symbols and political tools because of the historic narratives in which they were entangled, the social relations that they signified, and commonsense acceptance of these foods as vital to good citizenship itself.

Just as the objects used in these protests and performances were inextricable from their food politics, dramaturgical considerations shaped the arguments of these public spectacles. As a performance analysis of collective political acts, *Plowed Under* examines the complex ideological operations of form, genre, discourse, plotting, conflict, symbols, characterization, and embodiment. My dramaturgical view of protest joins a long line of performance scholarship interested in the convergence of events as varied as protests, carnival, funerals, and legal trials, for example, with theater. Like staged drama, protest requires preparation, tends to be distinguished temporally and spatially from everyday activities, establishes a line between performers and spectators, and is consciously constructed to elicit audience response.[25] From a sociological perspective, James Jasper has argued for the centrality of dramaturgical considerations to protesters in his study of the poetics of protest and social movements. Jasper writes that protesters choose tactics based on "what works, by what protesters know how to do and by their moral vision" and that "tactics are selected not simply for their efficacy, but also for their symbolic and emotional implications."[26] Proven conventions, historic repertoires, resources, skills, and morals inform protesters' tactics, indicating not only a shared set of values and community but also the impact protesters' presume their actions will have on an imagined audience.

My approach to the structuring principles of protest draws on the work of performance scholar Baz Kershaw. In *The Radical in Performance: Between Brecht and Baudrillard,* Kershaw describes the relatively idiosyncratic nature of protest aesthetics and argues that all protests share a common dramaturgy consisting of multiple scripts and actions that variously surge and ebb as a protest unfolds. For Kershaw, a protest's efficacy, what he calls its "historical resonance," is achieved by placing traditional cultural scripts and theatrical forms within a scene of "unpredictability" and "disorder." My approach to the microlevel elements of protest is adapted from dance scholar Susan Leigh Foster, for whom the efficacy of protest depends primarily on how protesters use their bodies. In "The Choreographies of Protest," Foster argues that protesters' collective movements communicate alternate social and political orders. Through their physicality and responsive movements, protesters structure the movements/responses of spectators and authorities, compelling these parties to embody support of, or opposition to, a protest's claim. Throughout *Plowed Under,* these insights are applied by charting the peculiar progressions of protests and considering the implications of the protesters' actions.

While these analytical templates are invaluable tools for understanding protests' performance dynamics, the particular history of the AAA challenges Foster's and Kershaw's implication that protesters' invention, improvisation, and mobility give them an advantage over a lumbering, institutional juggernaut. Material found in archives demonstrates how protests are often, if inadvertently, collaborative. Protesters may begin by choosing culturally significant sites and forms, using particular props, and presenting themselves as certain "types," but then, as protests play out, their tactics may change, as the responses of authorities, and sometimes bystanders, reshape the action in its very progress. Indeed, not only protesters but authorities also measure their emotional and political appeals to an audience. Each party involved in a protest expresses and enacts its own moral vision, but the meanings emerge and shift through cycles of action and reaction, both in the immediate context and as messages circulate nationally via media. To that end, then, local and national contexts and the media's power to impact, not just represent, a protest's development must be considered. Further, the unintended effects of carefully scripted actions and historic contingency are shown as vital types of "unpredictability" that shape the meanings of protests. Attention to the unexpected, idiosyncratic, and coincidental qualities of the protests and performances as they unfolded is of particular importance to conveying both the uncertainty of the historical moment and the nature of the debates about the AAA.[27]

Like any live performance, protests are situated in their local contexts. However, the issues motivating a particular protest are not inevitably or solely local. The protesters considered here staged complaints against the federal government and aimed to appeal to national sentiments. Simultaneously, the protests transpired among protesters, area police forces, and spectators, all of whom encountered one another physically and ideologically. Attention to the simultaneous "here-and-there" quality of these protests lays bare the tensions among local cultures, state power, and federal plans. It also helps explain why the federal government took a backseat in public discourse and action during some of the protests and reveals distinctions between local meanings of participants' tactics and the national reaction to them. In addition, fissures within the national goals of social movements during the New Deal era reveal the different stakes for groups of protesters embedded in local circumstances.

Evidence of Agricultural Acts

Uncovering and understanding the theatrical strategies used by disparate social actors in protests and cultural performances about the AAA required reading collections housed at universities, historical societies, and state and national archives, as well as extensive review of newspapers, and popular, academic, and government materials published during the period. While a number of the collections included in this study have been used in institutional histories of the New Deal or in histories of the various populations considered here, this is the first study to consider them in relation to one another and in terms of aesthetics and food politics.

Newspapers and still images are the predominant available evidence of the protests I consider. Although media accounts of historic events must be viewed with a critical eye, Kershaw suggests that news coverage indicates issues that are significant to a society and that such coverage may benefit protesters.[28] Indeed, the information I found supports this assessment, suggesting that protesters, as well as authorities, played to the press and relied on media to create remote audiences. Some media outlets championed protesters' causes, while others sought to undo them; and, on numerous occasions, media accounts directly informed the actions taken by protesters and authorities, entering into the collaborative cycle of protest. Media accounts are also significant because most of the public encountered the protests through newspaper articles and accompanying photographs. Print media, of course, employed narrative and visual devices that supplant the fundamentally loose scripts/scenarios of protest, in Kershaw's characterization, with neat plot structures. News accounts likewise replace the immediate improvisatory moment-to-moment "reading" of bodies by bodies, as explained by Foster, with an orderly succession of incidents. Linguist Peter R. R. White describes "the news report as ideological, as a value-laden story-telling mode by which key social values and cultural motifs are reproduced and ultimately naturalized."[29] In this project, we see that newspapers not only reported what occurred; the interpretive frameworks and representations that national, regional, special interest, and local media outlets used to dramatize events offered competing perspectives both about what was happening and why it mattered.

Myriad individuals who participated in or observed the protests and performances also produced official and unofficial versions of the events. Ranging from artistic expressions to investigations to private correspondence, these include congressional records, FBI investigations, agency field notes, telegrams, letters, cartoons, personal testimonies, poetry, photographs, films, production notes, and press. These documents offer a glimpse of the contemporary dynamics, allowing a reconstruction of the events as they unfolded. The perspectives of both powerful and marginalized actors reveal webs of cooperation and antagonism at local, state, and national levels that go beyond a monolithic conflict between the powerful and the powerless.

Unsurprisingly, the wealth of archival material also reveals competing narratives about each event. Organizers, audiences, and media often obscured or emphasized cooperation among races, genders, and classes. Some social actors seem to assume that they must act in accord with racial and gender norms of the times to persuade audiences, while others appear to work from a different set of beliefs about the social order. A complicated picture of racial, ethnic, class, and gender politics at the local and national levels emerges. Significantly, protesters' representations have resulted in archives that occasionally disclose alternate narratives to accepted history. I offer such revisions where possible and point to the alternatives when they seem probable yet are not verifiable.

Performing Citizenship/Citizenship as Performance: Theoretical Considerations

The scripts that powerful, relatively disempowered, or utterly marginalized social actors enacted do not fit neatly under a single political label of Democrat, Republican, socialist, conservative, or progressive, excluding perhaps those of the USDA officials who designed the World's Fair exhibits. On the one hand, this period witnessed major political upheavals: the New Deal divided Democrats; Republicans ranged from economic and social conservatism to progressivism in terms of farm-labor coalitions; socialism and communism surged through industrial and agricultural unions and among artists. The fervor with which cultural and political critics sought to pigeonhole politically *Triple-A Plowed Under* attests to the divided politics of the day. The play itself demonstrates the social and economic inclusivity of the Popular Front movement. Yet commentators hotly contested which political agenda the script endorsed; the press was primarily concerned with whether it supported communist, New Deal, or conservative interests.

Protest leaders and their followers usually avoided political affiliations. Instead, protesters represented themselves through their social and economic relationships to food and agriculture, concentrating on the urgency and commonality of their cause in populist appeals. Some protest leaders of the groups I consider maintained affiliations with left-ist organizations and sought support from these groups; however, most of the protesters' identities and political leanings are unknown. The am-biguity of activist groups' political visions illustrates the unorthodox political alliances forged by food and agricultural issues—recognizable even today in food movements. In many instances, it suggests strategic resistance to precise political categories. More significantly, it shows the shared presumption among disparate groups that, to some extent, all political factions valued producerist ethics.

Throughout the history of the United States, that producerist ethic was an integral component of the discourse surrounding a performance-based conception of citizenship. According to this ethic, a good citizen is a productive citizen, a person who actively contributes to the welfare of the economy and the nation. Historian Michael Kazin emphasizes that, following the Revolution, producerism came to define "the people" and to suffuse American politics: *"Producerism was indeed an ethic, a moral conviction:* it held that only those who created wealth in tangible, material ways ... could be trusted to guard the nation's piety and liber-ties."[30] This ideology seems to be egalitarian, appearing to include any American who joins her or his labor to the well-being of the nation and, thus, to set performance as a moral means of limiting rights. However, as we will see throughout this study, citizens faced specific burdens or enjoyed particular advantages in demonstrating their good citizenship to audiences. The relative values of their socioeconomic identities as pro-ducers—farmer, consumer, and sharecropper—intersected with how they were situated through gender, race, and ethnicity.

Given historical narratives of national destiny and biblical configu-rations of stewardship, perhaps no other American type was believed to contribute so fundamentally to the moral basis of the nation than the "farmer." Providence decreed that God granted us the land and animals and from them we must provide for one another; men should labor to-ward the benefit of all. God promised abundance in return. Agricultural cultivation of the vast North American territory manifestly produced the land of plenty. A historian of rural radicalism, Catherine McNicol Stock, traces the strength of the producerist ethic in shaping ideas about an American way of life, as well as the elevation of the farmer, well into

the late-twentieth century: "the desire to own small property, to produce crops and foodstuffs, to control local affairs, to be served but never
coerced by a representative government, and to have traditional ways
of life and labor respected is the stuff of one of the oldest dreams in the
United States. It is one of the dreams that *became* the United States."[31]
Although the 1930s witnessed the continuing shift of the national economy from agriculture to manufacturing, in the national imagination,
farmers maintained a direct relationship with the land and harnessed
its power toward the basic needs of life, in its most natural form. Depictions of the yeoman's work ethic, individualism, and connection with
the land as the basis of morality and the pinnacle of citizenship were,
and remain, ubiquitous. Iconic farm figures decorated public buildings during the 1930s, in the work of the Federal Section of Fine Arts
(established in 1934) and the Works Progress Administration (WPA,
established in 1935), that "celebrat[ed] the land as a source of American
democracy."[32] Whiteness and masculinity were assumed in the images
of these most valuable citizens, as was the ownership of land. Farmers were transformed into icons of national history and ideology, especially amid the excess, adulteration, and obsolescence of mass-produced
goods in a mass market.

By the 1930s, "consumer" also had become a vital socioeconomic
identity. At the start of the twentieth century, manufacturers' increased
production reoriented the market from producer controlled toward consumer controlled. Consumers now created product value through taste,
rather than need. Manufacturers marketed their products as lifestyle
choices, using advertisements that associated possessions with gendered
and racialized American identities. As consumers gained economic
power, "consumer" was becoming a politically and socially powerful
category because it was an identity available to nearly all Americans.
Consumer movements emerged in response to deceptive packaging,
false advertising, and product adulteration. Women's historic control
over household consumption feminized the role of consumer, just as
women-led consumer movements helped politicize the domestic realm.
"Consumer" emerged as a socioeconomic role through which citizens
came to expect and demand a particular standard of living as a right.
Indeed, some New Deal programs focused on consumers' purchasing

power as a central element in economic recovery. Consumers occupied a vital place in the nation.[33]

Of course, in practice, women and non-white Americans were largely excluded from social and economic gains, despite their contributions as producers. Performance studies and theater scholar Emily Roxworthy, in her study of the internment of Japanese Americans during World War II, calls attention to the myth of the performance-based conception of American citizenship:

> The myth proclaims that American citizenship is officially and effectively conferred upon any individual, regardless or race or national origin, based simply upon the performance of a codified repertoire of speech acts and embodied acts, ranging from the recitation of the Oath of Citizenship to public participation in patriotic pageantry and even enlistment in the armed services. What this myth obscures is the extent to which citizenship has been officially denied to various racialized groups and when conferred, has lacked the efficacy in terms of the unequal enforcement of its privileges based on proximity to whiteness.[34]

In the 1930s, the discourse of producerism and the "myth of performative citizenship" fortified the marginalization and "othering" of the historically poor, such as agricultural laborers and ghettoized urban groups, who were distinguished from those newly vulnerable to poverty—the "Depression poor."[35] Agricultural laborers were farmers by occupation and food consumers by human necessity. However, their migratory practices, lack of land, and annual reliance on charitable organizations hindered recognition of their citizenship. Even more, social scientific research of the 1930s validated the exclusionary attitude toward both black and white sharecroppers by questioning "not whether but why and how the poor were culturally different from the middle and upper classes."[36] Even 1930s muckraking distinguished the white rural poor as "trash," a nomenclature that makes explicit the social disregard of these citizens.[37] Racism against African Americans also facilitated class-based exclusions of sharecroppers. The cause of the rural black population's poverty was identified as African Americans' "inherent" laziness, stupidity, and immorality. These farm laborers' periodic idleness and need for local support seemingly substantiated their "natural" differences from citizens who contributed to the nation.

Protesters embodied symbolic and discursive acts that pronounced their participation in the American ethic of producerism, as they creatively operated within the norms of race and gender that constrained them as social and political subjects; that is, they acted within the ongoing processes of identity constitution and social recognition that Judith Butler has termed "performativity."[38] Roxworthy's important account of the "myth of performative citizenship" resonates with the ways in which protesters' presented their collective identities as "good" citizens —whether as "farmers," "housewives," or "sharecroppers"—their roles intersected with social attitudes about race, ethnicity, class, and gender. And the performative dimensions of gender, ethnicity, class, and race shaped how the media, the authorities, and the public interpreted protesters' actions. For instance, the Hamtramck women were represented as "naturally" innocent, the impoverished black and white Missouri sharecroppers as "naturally" "shiftless," and the white dairymen as "naturally" heroic. In addition, the theatrical elements of the events sometimes encouraged interpretation of protest actions and participants through conventional dramatic genres, iconic character types, wellknown conflicts, and familiar storylines that operate through and reinforce hegemonic constructions of racialized, gendered, ethnicized, and class-based identities.

Those attempting to counter activists' claims used the "myth of performative citizenship" by alleging that protesters' acts were "un-American." Despite the disparate circumstances of individual protests, allegations against protesters or their tactics were largely formulaic: protesters were accused of being communists or of being tricked into protesting by "red agitators." These allegations were gendered, racialized, or ethnicized based on the social identity of protesters. Red-baiting also quite famously led to House Un-American Activities Committee hearings on the Federal Theatre Project and, ultimately, to the defunding of the program. This common strategy indicates not only how "performative citizenship" cuts both ways but the importance of persuasive performances to social and political gains.

Ultimately, *Plowed Under* aims to recount citizens' responses to a sea change in the food system and so in their ways of life. While the pages that follow detail only a handful of the many activist performances that occurred throughout the 1930s, these citizens' struggles for their "rights" encapsulate the cultural changes wrought by the AAA, even in its nascency. As these responses reveal the period's complex construc-tions of citizens' rights, they also demonstrate the central role protest and performance played in 1930s food politics. To that end, each chapter is prefaced with a scene from the manuscript of *Triple-A Plowed Under*. These contemporaneous "dramatic" depictions of "real world" events in-vite multiple readings of each case study and signal the messiness of the politics of representation in both history and in writing about history.

SCENE TEN (Farm and Worker's families)

Voice of Living Newspaper (over loudspeaker): As our economic system works, the greater the surplus of wheat on Nebraska farms, the larger are the breadlines in New York City.

(As curtains open on brilliant blue glass curtain, against it are seen silhouetted a farm and city family, the city family, center, and the farm family right, on ramp. The scene grows angry as the two groups oppose each other)

Worker: We starve and they told us you had food in your fields.
Farmer: Food is in our fields but they told us you would not pay the cost of its harvesting.
Worker's Wife: We had no money.
Farmer's First Son: We raised eggs and milk, and you wouldn't buy them.
Worker's First Son: We had not the 15¢ to pay.
Farmer's Family (aroused): 15¢ for milk?
Farmer: We got only three.
Worker's Family (shouting): Fifteen, fifteen!
Farmer's Family: Three, Three!
Worker's Daughter (wail): I'm hungry.....
Farmer's Daughter: I can't go to school.....
Farmer (quietly): Food rots in our fields.....
Farmer's Second Son: No money to ship.....
Farmer: No money to buy.....
Farmer's Wife: No money..... (slight pause)
Worker: There is no work.
Worker's Son: No jobs.
Worker's Daughter: No food.
Worker: We have been evicted from our homes.
Farmer's Wife: And we from our land.
Farmer: We plough our sweat into the earth.
Farmer's Wife: And bring forth ripe provender.
Worker: We starve.
Farmer: The wheat stands high in our fields.
Farmer's Wife: Our fields no longer.
Worker's Daughter: Feed us.
Farmer's First Son: Pay us.
Worker's Family: Feed us.
Farmer: The wheat is better destroyed. I say, burn it.
Farmer's Family: Burn it! Burn it!

(Flame lights up changing the sky from blue to red. Against the flames is silhouetted the figure of a farmer in shadow, holding a pitch-fork. Farm and City families hold this tableau, and all through speech of General Johnson over the loudspeaker)

Worker: Why?

Voice of General Johnson—over loudspeaker (Loudspeaker is located center of proscenium): Something is depriving one third of our population of the God-given right to earn their bread by the sweat of their labor. That single ugly fact is an indictment under which no form of government can long continue. For slighter causes than that we revolted against British rule, and suffered the bitterest civil war in history.

Farmer and Worker (together): Words!

(Both families turn in protest toward the loudspeaker)
CLOSE TRAVELERS.

Script Excerpt 1. Editorial Staff of the Living Newspaper Federal Theatre Project under the supervision of Arthur Arent, "Triple-A Plowed Under," 1936, Federal Theatre Project Collection, Special Collections and Archives, George Mason University Libraries.

The New Deal Vision for Agriculture

USDA Exhibits at the 1933–34 Chicago World's Fair

AT THE END OF THE FIRST SEASON OF THE 1933 CENTURY OF Progress International Exposition in Chicago, C. W. Warburton, director of extension work, sent a memorandum to Secretary of Agriculture Henry Wallace regarding the monetary costs and political benefits of the USDA's participation in a second fair season.[1] Warburton stated that altering a number of exhibits to display the AAA's positive effects, for an estimated $15,000, was of "transcendent importance" because "the vast potential audience . . . warrants utilization of the opportunity to put before those millions of visitors a visual explanation of the Administration's program of agricultural adjustment."[2] Many federal employees agreed with Warburton. Believing in the power of performance, they embedded culturally significant foods in theatrical scenes to cast fairgoers in a story that praised New Deal-style capitalism as the connection between farmers and consumers.

Public opinion about the AAA was by no means settled when the World's Fair opened on May 27, 1933. President Roosevelt had signed the AAA only two weeks prior; the Wisconsin Cooperative Milk Pool strike against the AAA had just occupied headlines; and, while other farmer organizations publicly endorsed the legislation, consumers had not yet felt its effects. The controversy about the emergency Corn-Hog program would emerge in the summer and be full blown by the end of the fair's first season in November. Given the AAA's emergent status, the USDA exhibits presented and modified throughout the course of the fair's two seasons (May 27–November 12, 1933; and May 26–October 31, 1934) appear variously as advertising, a preemptive strike, and a counternarrative, rather than an authoritative account of the AAA.

The USDA exhibits staged an experience of America restored to social and economic stability, and visitors responded: exhibits featuring food items were some of the most engaging to audiences. As a result of the public's interest, many installations used at the 1933–34 Century of Progress were converted into touring exhibits. Some served as the basis for display design at the 1939–40 New York World's Fair and 1940 San Francisco World's Fair and were even reused at these venues specifically to promote the AAA.

This chapter considers the Chicago World's Fair's relationship to the AAA: the fair's spectacular consumerist atmosphere, its focus on "progress," the racial and gender dynamics in its displays, and the promise of the New Deal that framed it. USDA exhibits at the fair, and those that the department cosponsored, used theatrical devices to persuade visitors of the AAA's morality. In particular, staging techniques elevated ordinary food to the status of cultural artifact to cue fairgoers to take an active role in exhibits and perform as "ideal" Americans enjoying their "right" to plenty.

In the USDA exhibits, as well as those of the dairy, and meat and livestock industries that the USDA cosponsored, the fair's theme of "progress" presented an improved quality of life for American consumers. At one level, the emphasis on consumer interests in these agricultural exhibits relates to the nation's transition to a consumer economy and the growing political power of consumers. At another, it speaks to exhibitors' hopes that food's power to engage spectators viscerally would garner support for the New Deal's experimental agricultural programs. Thus, these exhibits blurred the distinction between performances that "make belief" or "create the very social realities they enact" (that is, performances of everyday life) and performances that are "make-believe" where "the distinction between what's real and what's pretended is kept clear" (that is, theatrical performance).[3] The exhibits were performative in their presentation of "ideal" citizens as white farmers and consumers, and in their reinforcement of "appropriate" appetites, attitudes, and roles for these Americans. Their aim was to induce fairgoers to act in accordance with and, in some cases, act out the beliefs and the behaviors that the exhibits promoted. By staging a view of a positive future (an inherently imaginative and theatrical endeavor), the USDA also tried to generate belief in imminent plenty under the New Deal.

The World's Fair in the Context of Economic Depression and the New Deal

In *People of Plenty*, David M. Potter introduces the predominant concept of America as a bountiful nation, unparalleled in its richness of resources and opportunities, quipping that "quotations [exalting American abundance] could be multiplied almost to infinity." Potter credits widespread abundance with producing the expectation of a high standard of living for any American who avails himself of the "opportunity to make his own place in society."[4] "Plenty," in its related senses of quantity, choice, and access for all, connoted both entitlement to a particular lifestyle and the reward reaped by productive citizens. Indeed, in his inaugural address, on March 4, 1933, Roosevelt evoked the biblical proportions of America's "plenty": "We are stricken by no plague of locusts. Compared with the perils which our forefathers conquered because they believed and were not afraid, we have still much to be thankful for. Nature still offers her bounty and human efforts have multiplied it. Plenty is at our doorstep, but a generous use of it languishes in the very sight of the supply."[5]

The spectacle of the Chicago World's Fair, along with America's political and social situation during the year it opened, supported the New Deal as the government that would return America to its "natural" state of plenty. Burton Benedict's classic anthropological study of world's fairs documents the standard use of "gigantism" and "monumentality" by host nations to "impress rivals and the public." By design—displaying

the best of a nation's culture, technology, and products on an epic scale
—world's fairs breed nationalist sentiment in citizens and admiration
in foreigners. Chicago's three miles of massive, multicolored structures
fit the type, physically engulfing attendees in festivity. But spectacle im-
pacts spectators on multiple levels, as museum studies scholar Eilean
Hooper-Greenhill notes: "Embodied responses are influenced by the
scale of things. Cognitive and emotional responses to objects are affected
in subtle ways by their size in relation to our own body size." *Newsweek*
described this fair's architecture as the "Triumph of the Modernists,"
whose "sweep of naked lines, of daring planes" contributed to "a new
rhythm . . . deriving from the rhythm of the machine," signaling American achievements and innovations. Parents could leave their children
with "trained attendants" on the Enchanted Island, playing in the Magic
Maze, enjoying pony rides, slides, or the miniature railroad, while they
enjoyed entertainment on the Midway, visited various exhibits or took an
aerial tour 210 feet above the exposition on the Sky Ride. The fair offered
visitors both a visual and embodied experience of a world of plenty.[6]

Typical of world's fairs, food was everywhere at the Century of
Progress. Approximately eighty food and beverage booths, as well as
restaurants and food samples in commercial, educational, national, and
cultural exhibits, pervaded the exposition. Exhibits sponsored by individual states used food to emphasize the state's unique contributions
to the nation. Among the many exhibits in the Food and Agricultural
Building, a 1933 season-long "egg-laying derby" featured prize hens from
twenty-eight states, Canada, and four foreign nations. The National
Biscuit Company showed the making of shredded wheat; W. F. Straub
Laboratories demonstrated how Lake Shore Brand honey turns ordinary
cereal into desserts. From their on-site bottling plant, Coca Cola sold
six million drinks in 1933. The smells, sights, and availability of food
emphasized America as the land of plenty. Meanwhile, visitors exercised
the American imperialist prerogative as they smelled, tasted, heard, and
felt the "other" in the foreign villages and on the Midway. Belgium, England, Germany, Holland, Ireland, Italy, Mexico, Switzerland, and Spain
contributed villages. There was also an "Oriental village." Food enabled
visitors to taste the exotic; foreign villages offered native cuisines in
which the "gastronomic adventurer [found] himself in his glory."[7] Thus,

fairgoers actually experienced the American promise of opportunity and freedom of choice.

Not only did the fair's structure and opportunities promote optimism, the homogeneity of the audience—predominantly white Americans—may have also inspired a sense of collectivity. Because of the effects of the Great Depression on Europe, there were fewer than typical international exhibitors and negligible international attendance; indeed, of the 4 percent of registered foreign visitors, roughly 37 percent were from Canada. These factors resulted in an overtly American fair.

Americans came from across the country to take part in the spectacle. The Century of Progress Commission estimated that, while roughly 80 percent of the 1933 attendees came from outside Chicago, Chicagoans repeatedly visited the fair, constituting five million paid admissions during the first season. Admissions to both seasons of the fair totaled 48,441,927; of this number, only 20 percent (approximately 9.7 million people) were given free admissions. Still, not all Americans could partake of the bounty. The fifty-cent adult admission, about three times the price of a movie ticket, would have excluded most impoverished citizens.[8] In addition, racism limited attendance by African Americans, thus removing these citizens in large measure from the narrative of food and citizenship. The New Deal vision of the nation operated in this context, performing its promise of plenty to the citizens it included and believed were necessary to restoring plenty.[9]

Exhibits presented images of white men, women, and families as the inheritors of the last century of American progress, while other exhibits reinforced racial hierarchies among American citizens by deploying stereotypes. World's fair historian Robert Rydell describes the racialized and exploitative displays: "the expositions, and especially the midways, gave millions of Americans first-hand experience with treating nonwhites from around the world as commodities."[10] Thus, the exhibits—presentations of national and white superiority—and the absence of African Americans and the poor as visitors to the fair constituted white Americans as the body politic.

Despite the reality, fairgoers shared a collective sense of having endured extreme hardship, and this allowed the federal government to promote the New Deal as a benefit to all Americans, regardless of race or class. Visitors entered the fair as citizens of a nation in transition with a newly elected president and the promise of a better tomorrow. By the time the fair opened in mid-1933, legislative bustle during Roosevelt's "first hundred days' fury" had been producing quick results: the National Recovery Administration (NRA) was credited with increasing wages for urban workers, the Home Owners' Loan Act slowed the tide of foreclosures, and the Federal Emergency Relief Act infused the states with much-needed federal monies. Early in the first season of the Century of Progress, federal intervention seemed to promise a positive resolution of the "paradox of want amid plenty."

Perhaps it was only serendipity, but the fair's theme of "the services of science to humanity" during the past century provided an ideal venue for showcasing the new administration's plan for America.[11] Federal participation in the fair had been approved in February 1932, so Hoover administration officials had started exhibit design. However, the Roosevelt administration's dedication of "this triumph over the depression" during opening day events couched the Century of Progress's manifest grandeur, festivity, and modernity as belonging to the New Deal.[12] On opening day, the *Chicago Daily Tribune*'s front page featured a cartoon that typified the hope the Chicago World's Fair offered to U.S. citizens. Titled "A Perfect Setting for a Great National Jubilee," it shows towers of light illuminating the buildings that line Lake Michigan's shore. Hearing fairgoers' jubilations, Uncle Sam, afloat in a makeshift raft, waves his iconic top hat and exclaims, "They must be expectin' me!" The words "America's Comeback after Three Years of Depression," printed on the base of the raft, reiterated the new era of prosperity that the Century of Progress foretold.[13] Ironically, the economic crisis offered an advantage by lowering expectations among fairgoers. Rufus Dawes, president of the Century of Progress, wrote that "there was a freedom from extravagant expectations on the part of the public due to the Depression. . . . A result of this was that the Exposition, when opened, so far exceeded the expectations of the public, even in Chicago."[14] In its totality, the Century of Progress depicted the Great Depression as a blip in American history, which would be resolved shortly through the combined operations of mass consumption, technological innovation, corporate enterprise, and the New Deal.[15]

Corporations too were a vital presence at the fair; they exhibited advances in production efficiencies and safety as well as a throng of products—edible and otherwise—designed to improve Americans' lives. Through mass production, Americans had become accustomed to and expected choice as their right. As anthropologist Sidney Mintz argues, choice is a central component of identity in U.S. consumer culture: "Exercise of choice heightens the illusion of individuality. . . . But this individuality is conditioned by the postulation of a 'group,' membership which is attainable among other things by certain consumptions."[16] Throughout the fair, corporate exhibits replaced "hooverizing"—substituting a less desirable product for a better one—with consumer choice, reinforcing the New Deal's restoration of plenty.

Many of the technological exhibits theatricalized women's work in an attempt to get white America to buy labor-saving products. While Quaker Oats featured "Aunt Jemima" making pancakes and singing "traditional" plantation songs, other exhibits in the Food and Agriculture Building demonstrated "accomplishments in commercial cookery that have changed woman's old sunrise-to-sun-up lot to a far happier and richer one." Kraft presented its new mayonnaise as a liberation from home cooking, and Heinz showed how its canning methods alleviated tedious work. These exhibits stressed that mass production eased white women's household labor.[17] Black women, however, were still in the kitchen. Through the mammy stereotype of "Aunt Jemima," who performed in a rustic cabin scene, Quaker Oats implied that white women could provide the comfort of "home-cooking" for husbands and children by simply buying a ready-made product. On the other hand, the corporation represented African American women as domestic cooks, content to labor for white people in white kitchens from "sunrise-to-sun-up," completing the objectification and dehumanization of the black female subject in a curvaceous bottle of syrup.[18] Representations that minimized the physical labor involved in domesticity were appeals to both rural and urban white women, who spent between one-third and one-half of each day fulfilling meal-related tasks.[19] Rural women who had the means purchased processed food from mail-order catalogues; these foods were marketed to farm women as not only easing labor but as fashionable products used by urbanites.[20] In her editorial on the Ag-

riculture and Foods building, Mrs. Lois Johnson Hurley attested to the
appeal of the food exhibits: they are "the high spot of woman's interest
at the Fair." After all, "What [is] more interesting to a woman than food,
its production and preparation?"[21]

As a marketing tactic, the promise of a more leisurely life was
aimed at other consumers besides white women; exhibits at world's
fairs throughout the 1930s, and in the decade's advertising in general,
also showed the benefits for the men of the house. A housewife's emotional support of and attractiveness to her husband apparently mattered
more than how hard she worked to create a nurturing home. The come-
liness of women performers in corporate food exhibits tied the ease
of labor to feminine beauty and charm. A press release for the Wilson
& Co.'s "bacon pit" typifies how food corporations glamorized mass
food production:

> Stunning blondes and brunettes, to the number 42—equally divided—all busily
> engaged in wrapping and packing bacon for the consumer.... Federal inspec-
> tors supervise the work of the girls, which consists of preparing 5,000 pounds
> of certified sliced bacon daily, the task being directed by a superintendent and
> four skilled male aides. Striking uniforms adorn the girls in this department.
> They are resplendent in white linen frocks with French red plaid lapels and cuffs
> and berets are white, tipped with red.[22]

Wilson and Co.'s emphasis on safe and sanitary conditions through
its feminization of labor demonstrates a trend used by corporations in
1930s exhibitions.[23] This promotion and others, like Libby, McNeill &
Libby's "smartly uniformed girls packing Spanish Olives artistically in
glass jars," presume the draw of lovely girls to male fairgoers, highlight
masculine control, and emphasize women as sexualized objects, who do
not work so much as express their creativity and fashion.[24]

Corporate food exhibits at the 1933–34 fair presented myriad images of a stable U.S. socioeconomic order that displaced the realities
of economic upheaval. The Depression had rendered many men incapable of fulfilling their roles as providers and caused some married white
women to work outside the home.[25] These exhibits, however, sometimes
contradicted their primary message about women's roles. Throughout
the fair, women worked in exhibits playing the parts of "factory worker,"
"entertainer," "wife," "mother," and "family cook." Food exhibits framed

less work for housewives in terms of time and intensity as the goal of mass consumption and production. Housewives' responsibilities—shopping, preparing and serving meals—were depicted both as drudgery and as creative outlets. Women were shown enjoying work that was represented as not-really-work, told that they should want to enjoy food-related tasks as an expression of love for their families, but also want to do less of it. These contradictions would have an effect on the female consciousness. In chapter 3, we will see the Depression's unsettled gender relations come to a head as housewives attempted to negotiate these contradictory expectations.

The Agriculture Industry and USDA Exhibits

Similarly, the USDA exhibits, as well as those it cosponsored, displayed socioeconomic stability as both consumer choice and American individualism under the New Deal. These exhibits restored meat, milk, and plenty to the American table as a cultural right, not a luxury. Exhibits also credited farmers for the high quality of American life, while they concomitantly suggested that good citizenship depended on the selling, buying, and eating of certain foods. In doing so, the exhibitors implicitly reinforced the preexisting links between whiteness, good citizenship, and the consumption of milk and meat.

By transforming these edibles into artifacts, exhibitors capitalized on the belief that certain foods were intrinsically linked with being a "true" American. First, artifacts, in all of their seeming "obviousness" (after Daniel Miller), often stand for a culture that is distant in place or time from the culture of the spectator and exhibitor. Exhibitors use the strange material attributes of the artifact to mark the difference in values between "us" and "them."[26] The food artifacts of the World's Fair agricultural exhibits, however, represented U.S. culture and its mores to Americans, not to foreigners. Second, an artifact's materiality is vital to the interpretative process: "The material properties and the physical presence of the artifact demand embodied responses, which may be intuitive and immediate. Responses to objects are culturally shaped, according to previous knowledge and experience, but the initial reaction to an object may be tacit and sensory rather than an articulated verbal level."[27] What

makes ordinary food such a good artifact, so attention-getting, symbolically resonant, and potentially politically persuasive is its ability to trig-
ger physical desires and aversions in the same instant that it (re)produces
identities and social relations.[28] Exhibitors not only elevated foods to
significant cultural objects but tapped into spectators' sense memories
and the already accepted nutritional and cultural meanings of foods.

The Dairy Industry Exhibit: Citizenship and Milk Consumption

During each day of the Century of Progress's first season, fifteen-to-
twenty thousand members of the public experienced the "story of how
'Dairy Products Build Superior People.'"[29] Exhibits in the 15,000-square-
foot Dairy Building epitomized the formal elements of spectacle. The
dairy industry aggrandized milk's (and its products') capacity to build
superior citizens by using stunning visual imagery, elevated rhetoric,
and the master-narratives of national history to encourage visitors to
embrace their exceptional Americanness.[30] The exhibit bombarded
fairgoers with images of ideal Americans, images that tied milk consumption to physical perfection and happiness. At its best, by deliver-
ing ideology through technological extravaganza, spectacle addresses
audiences as a collective; performance studies scholar Margaret Drewal
asserts, "spectacle derives power from its potential to move its audience
en masse. . . . The aggrandizing ethos of spectacle strives to unite spectators into a collective and, furthermore, to unite the audience with the
performance through collective, but passive, spectatorship."[31] Exhibits that were monumental in scale, technically novel, and visually dy-
namic made remarkable claims; namely, milk and dairy made everyday
American life extraordinary. The dairy industry exhibit aimed to exceed
spectacle's potential to unify an audience: by eating dairy products in
the industry's restaurant, fairgoers could take on ideal identities and reproduce the exhibit's ideology through everyday culinary performance.

Milk's cultural significance justified its spectacular treatment. By
the Great Depression, milk had come to signify motherhood, superiority, and morality. In biblical associations, milk described the holy land
of Israel and connoted salvation, abundance, and spiritual purity.[32]
Milk's physical origins helped bind women to its symbolism, just as

it reinforced a woman's "natural" capacity to nurture her family, morally and literally. In the United States, milk had been a controversial product in the nineteenth century because of its capacity to transmit disease; however, late-nineteenth- and early-twentieth-century pasteurization campaigns resulted in its regulation and cultural image as a pure, wholesome food. Suffragists confirmed the historic connection between milk, women, and morality in their attacks on crooked (male) dealers who sold unsafe milk, in which the women portrayed themselves as the conscience of America (thus, deserving of the vote).[33] Seemingly everyone from social workers to the Ringling Brothers promoted the vital importance of milk to children.[34] In the Progressive Era, milk's healthful properties and virtuous associations made it an ideal vehicle of assimilation. Children of immigrants, who were not fully formed physically and viewed as not yet fully formed ideologically, were the targets of reformers' interventions. Well-meaning endeavors to reduce infant mortality rates in New York City led to the creation of the New York Milk Committee, a group that regulated the diets of immigrant families and characterized milk consumption as integral to the transformation of immigrant children into "good" American citizens. One of their leaflets touted, "the Nation that has the babies has the future."[35] If we accept Bridget Heneghan's point that an object's literal whiteness distinguishes it in cultural whiteness, the committee's racialized ideal of "good citizenship" is thrown into relief.[36]

In the early twentieth century, federal agencies also instilled milk with a singular capacity to mold, produce, and sustain "ideal" citizens, both physically and morally. The USDA Extension Service film on the nutritional value of milk, *Milk for You and Me* (n.d.), emphasized the product as both a necessity and a right for all Americans but for children in particular. In 1931, the U.S. Department of Labor's Children's Bureau reprinted its pamphlet "Why Drink Milk? Milk Is the Indispensible Food for Children." In it, milk is not only "the child's best food, no other food can take its place."[37] Milk's purportedly unique properties took on a mythic charge in the American narrative of democracy; as another USDA extension service pamphlet put it, milk had the particular purpose of maintaining, "the [U.S.] position as a world power to which we have arisen."[38]

In his post-Depression history of the American diet, Richard Osborn Cummings lauded educational initiatives that taught consumers how to cope with the economic crisis by showing them how to substitute cheaper items for less necessary ones in order to "cut expenses and to provide money which could be used for more milk."[39] Many citizens may have welcomed these lessons in home economics; indeed, low-income families identified their inability to obtain milk as their number-one problem.[40] Perhaps female consumers felt milk's absence most acutely because, in the 1930s, advertisers "were encouraging mothers to make comparisons between the perfect 'test children' in [milk] advertisements and their own."[41]

Visitors to Department of Agriculture installations in the Dairy Building also could compare themselves to the perfect physical specimens who showed how dairy products "preserve the characteristics of youth," "build sound teeth," contribute to "safe weight control," and "build delicious satisfying meals." By using the visual tropes of science, the dairy industry claimed the "vital importance, to the consumer, of an adequate consumption of milk, butter, cheese and ice cream."[42] The exhibit "Milk—The Best Growth Food" featured animals typically used in laboratories to evince the effects of milk on human beings; it placed a small rat next to a larger specimen and displayed photographs of two different-sized puppies, two pigs, and two chickens. The benefits of this "nutritional science" were also applied to human beings in exhibits that used ideal embodiments. The exhibit "Physical Perfection" offers a clear example. On one side, three abstract renderings of women depicted how "The Liberal Use of Dairy Products Contribute to Personal Charm and Beauty: A Slim, Lithe Body; Smooth Skin; Strong White Teeth; Beautiful Hair; Keenness of Spirit." On the other side, men's "Physical Perfection" was represented via the athletic figures of "Co-ordination," "Rhythm," and "Strength." These bodies connected spiritual well-being to health and beauty, as well as connecting a strong body to a strong nation. The exhibit's comparison of average citizens' consumption to U.S. Olympians' consumption drove home the benefits of eating and drinking more dairy products. By drawing on normative gender identities, such installations instructed visitors on how to achieve the excellent physique, exceptional mental facility, and a high-quality life displayed throughout the building.

A USDA Bureau of Home Economics installation, "Dairy Products Lead in the Well Balanced Diet," instructed visitors about using
their budget wisely to achieve health, which required prioritizing milk.
Teaching household management practices that would optimize budgets, time, and health to create "rational consumers," this exhibit also
advised consumers on nutrition and dietary standards.[43] On display in
the Dairy Building, the exhibit showed that a "liberal" and a "low-cost"
diet for a family of five (two adults and three children under age fifteen)
necessitated a foundation of dairy products. Recommended family use
ranged from 24.5 quarts (approximately six gallons) of milk per week
for the liberal diet to fourteen quarts (3.5 gallons) for the low-cost diet,
with additional dairy products supplementing both. Pictures of fruit,
vegetables, meats, and grains (without recommended quantities) made
these food groups appear as secondary to dairy in the matter of health.

The USDA's three-panel installation on cattle breeding exalted the
cow as the "foster mother of mankind," thus invoking the significance of
milk for robust American children.[44] The central panel featured a three-
dimensional mechanical cow, designed to show how "Nature's Greatest Food Factory Transforms Rough Feed into Man's Most Complete
Food." The automaton moved its head from side to side and switched its
tail; the interior of its midsection displayed its milk-making machinery/
organs. Set within the cow's musculature, animated industrial tubes,
cylinders, and stick-figure laborers replaced the cow's internal organs.[45]
This machine-mother stood for improved farming practices, the result
of government-funded scientific research, which enabled the modern
cow to support the nation. The third panel illustrated "The Improved
Dairy Cow Produces Enough Milk for . . . 4 Adults and 6 Children" with
images of rural and urban families at leisure and play.[46]

USDA cooperative exhibits also showed how dairy farming contributed to the national economy. Atop an installation showing annual
consumption of dairy foods, an iconic farm mural signified the 4.6 million farms that provided 104.6 billion pounds of milk products annually.
Below this, large, white dials showed the difference in total consumption
of ice cream, concentrated milk, cheese, butter, and, most importantly,
milk and cream. The chart "Milk Production Highest Peak in U.S. Agriculture" evidenced milk's importance as agriculture's biggest industry. It

featured a series of triangles; the figure labeled with a milk bottle stood at twice the height of the poultry, hogs, cattle, and corn triangles. The chart graphically depicted that income from the dairy industry more than doubled income generated from all other agricultural industries combined. A huge map also showed milk production and usage by state. Hundreds of tiny illuminated holes—each one symbolizing the annual production of 1.5 million gallons—dotted every state on the map. Midwest states were the most heavily dotted, but the map also showed significant production levels from North Dakota to Texas, throughout New England, and from the Mid-Atlantic states to Tennessee. While the map manifested the nation's economic reliance on the dairy industry, lantern slides showed states' milk-usage figures, certifying milk's enormous importance to consumers' nationwide.

The Dairy Building's main attraction was the "color organ," a 90-foot-by-40-foot cyclorama, which served as the projection screen for Thomas Wilfred's lumia scenes. Lumia, patented by Wilfred in 1930, used light to manipulate color and shapes.[47] The operatic music of Charles Gounod, John Ansell's *Plymouth Ho*, Charles Skilton's Indianist *Deer Dance*, and Georges Bizet's cantata *Le Retour* accompanied the massive moving images. The national narrative showed the importance of milk from the "Dawn of Civilization" to the present. Heifer, the story's protagonist, plays the central role in the development of American superiority. Her "heavenly Milk" inspires Man to name the stars the "Milky Way." Brought to Plymouth Colony in 1624, her "life sustaining foods... bring HEALTH and Thanksgiving." She faithfully follows the covered wagon westward. "A source of Life," she assists as "CIVILIZATION conquers the wild west." By 1933, "she is the foundation of a Great Industry." The picture show rises to its climax with magisterial musical flourishes:

GONG - - - - - - A CENTURY OF PROGRESS! (Fanfare)
GONG - - - - - - PROGRESS IN HEALTH! (Fanfare)
GONG - - - - - - PROGRESS TOWARD THE GOAL OF PHYSICAL PERFECTION!
(Music)

The final image is a classical familial tableau (see figure 1.1). In Grecian garb, a muscular husband and lithe wife stand at the center. They are surrounded by three children. Underneath these "ideal" Americans,

Figure 1.1. Final tableau of lumia show, "Dairy Products Build Superior People," in Dairy Industry Exhibit, 1933–34 Chicago World's Fair. Dairy Products Build Superior People, brochure, ca. 1933, Century of Progress Records, series XVI, box 17, folder 217, COP_16_0017_00217_001_p15, University of Illinois at Chicago Library, Special Collections.

the machinery of the modern dairy industry shines light upward onto the message "Dairy Products Build Superior People." The narrative's homage to the cow collapses "civilization" into America, whiteness, and physical and economic superiority. Encouraging zealous nationalism, this installation worked in concert with others "proving" dairy's centrality to American greatness. The whole environment inspired collectivity and awe. Set within a building filled with "evidence" of the vital contributions dairy products make to the lives of citizens, part of a massive event dedicated to American progress, it seamlessly confirmed the greatness of the United States.

Hoard's Dairyman, a dairy industry periodical with national circulation, was quite pleased with the dairy industry exhibit's potential: "[Visitors] have not only seen everything presented in the most readily comprehended and convincing manner, but have had *the opportunity to apply the lesson personally* in the model restaurant. It is the most nearly complete presentation ever made of a food product."[48] The Dairy Building's spectacle attempted to shape consumption practices and create "ideological *communitas*" through technical extravaganza, reverent and symbolic treatment of the cow, and "ideal" specimens of Americanness.[49] But visitors did not have to remain passive spectators; fairgoers could support American greatness and assert their personal superiority by eating at the Dairy Industry Restaurant.

The Meat and Livestock Industry Exhibit: Audiences as Meat Consumers

The meat and livestock industry exhibit involved fairgoers in the narrative of progress by placing them directly within realistic environments and prompting them to participate in the exhibit's scenes of consumption. This exhibit offered "behind-the-scenes" experiences of livestock from range and farm to table.[50] Visitors were routed through life-size sites of food production, processing, and distribution toward a final section where the visitors could make food choices. This "in-situ" style of exhibition, so-called for its re-creation of environments, usually includes actors who create the illusion of authenticity by performing ordinary activities appropriate to the scene.[51] In the meat and livestock exhibit, however, there were no hired actors. Instead, this exhibit placed fairgoers within the scenes and reserved for them the leading role, that of consumer. A spectator's feeling of "being there" in the mimetic, naturalistic environments that define in-situ exhibition can persuade through a sensation of experiencing the "real thing"; the meat and livestock industry exhibit gave audiences the opportunity to exercise their right to meat by acting out their consumption practices.

The exhibit's transformation of fairgoers from spectators to consumers—its production of "actors"—calls to mind modern museums that present arguments spatially and prompt audiences to perform its ideology, by routing visitors through a specified course.[52] Similarly, at the starting point of the meat and livestock exhibit, spectators acted as tourists of the meat industry. By the end of the exhibit, fairgoers completed the successful operations of agriculture under federal control, which moved delicious and healthful meats to consumers' tables. They entered a space in which they examined the best cuts of meats, so that the gratification offered through meat consumption was shown to be accessible to all. The absence of paid performers and immersive environments enhanced the exhibit's production of pleasurable, ordinary American life.

In the 1930s, "meat" referred primarily to pork and beef. Chicken was thought of as "poultry," and lamb was a specialty meat. Region, race, ethnicity, and income influenced the balance of pork or beef in diets, as well as the quality of cuts and their preparations. But the American diet pivoted on meat's consumption, and, by the 1930s, it was "by far Americans' favorite food."[53] Of course, not all meats were equally valued. As the song "Beans, Bacon, and Gravy" indicates (see "Introduction"), in the early twentieth century, pork products were considered a lower class of food compared to beef, which was more difficult to raise, more expensive to buy, and more closely associated with rugged cowboys and ranchers.[54]

Meat's distinct place in American history also made it a symbol of masculinity. Its association with the physical aggression required of hunting, historically a man's activity, linked its consumption with the animal's virility and the hunter's mastery of nature. In the American context, meat's distinct place in transforming the frontier into the range tied it to individualism and Manifest Destiny.[55] Meat was the central component of the late-1800s health trend among urban white men, whose labor was divorced from the land. This diet was perceived as an exercise of self-control and self-realization; it signified "healthy ambition." From the anti-immigration campaigns of the nineteenth century to the Great War to imperialist programs in Africa, America's national, racial, and cultural predominance was attributed to its citizens' meat consumption. Indeed, during this period, nutritionists characterized meat-eating societies as superior to vegetarian and fish-eating cultures: "the intellectual elite of a country should be fed the most nutritious, meat-based diet to be of the best service to the nation's advancement."[56]

Citizens were conditioned to go without meat or find substitutes for it in times of national crisis, making its consumption a barometer of the nation's socioeconomic health and security. During World War I, meat was considered necessary for battlefield strength; the federal government urged housewives to observe "meatless" days, wherein proteins such as eggs substituted for meats in short supply, so that troops abroad could eat the valuable protein.[57] This campaign helped codify gendered consumption practices that differentiated the biological "needs" and "abilities" of men and women by distinguishing meat from other sources of protein. Nutritionists in the 1930s endorsed a diet of nutritional variety derived from fruits, vegetables, carbohydrates, proteins, minerals, and fats, with minimum requirements adjusted relative to activity, age, and gender. Despite nutritional science, it was believed by most Americans that men needed to eat meat more than did women or children and that its lack resulted in men's inability to work. In households impacted by the Depression, meat tended to be reserved for the man of the house.[58] Thus, for Americans, meat satisfied men's "naturally" large appetites and produced masculinity. The meat and livestock industry exhibit, however, enabled all fairgoers to perform as secure consumers who did not have to sacrifice their right to eat meat.

Above the exhibit's entryway, the sign "Live Stock and Meat Exhibit Visitors Welcome" invited the public into the packinghouse cooler and refrigerated car, visible just beyond the entrance. It also positioned visitors as consumers on a tour. Once inside, spectators would be privy to the inner workings of the modern meat industry; they would experience how the industry enabled a high quality of life for the American consumer. The left wall framing the entryway featured plaques juxtaposing "natural" hogs and cattle of 1833 and scientifically "improved" beasts of 1933; it flanked a three-dimensional view of the modern farm in miniature. The *Official Guidebook of the Fair 1933* describes the diorama with images of rural idyll: "The sun shines and there are lush corn fields."[59] On the right wall, a nearly life-size, three-dimensional cowboy diorama was presented. A man on horseback sits in the foreground with his back to the spectator, overlooking the distant range, a romanticized version of the cattleman's perspective.[60] The image of the cultivated frontier frames the story of meat within the myth that the West "was the place where institutions no longer towered over the individual man . . . the place where democratic growth and change was repeatedly re-enacted as a process and reaffirmed as a principle."[61] Visitors look through the cattleman's eyes to see how meat and farming are tied to liberty and self-determination and how both are foundational to citizenship.

Inside the exhibit, replicas of dressed sides of beef and pork hung in the literally chilled spaces of the packinghouse and refrigerator car, transforming three-dimensional, life-size dioramas into a heightened sensory experience for spectators (see figure 1.2). Dioramas, a burgeoning technique at the time of the Century of Progress exhibition, offered a new experience for fairgoers. The realistic scenes and perhaps the novelty of viewing from within were described in the exhibit brochure as "enhanc[ing] the impression of actually being [there]." At the same time, historical murals showing old-fashioned distribution methods reinforced the message that progress was oriented toward consumers' needs. When spectators walked over the loading ramp into the refrigerator car, they actually felt freezer temperatures and saw pork bearing USDA purple stamps certifying quality. Exhibit official A. W. Bitting explained the installation's dual purpose: "to show how the cut should be made to get the maximum of the best edible parts and have it very attractive, and . . . to demonstrate the sanitary side of holding these perishable products." The installation's white-tile backgrounds emphasized cleanliness, and the omission of slaughtering from the process, "as that is repugnant to many persons," hid the meat industry's more controversial and less appetizing aspects.[62]

Thus, visitors could participate in the narrative of meat without feeling disgust or guilt. According to folklorist Michael Owen Jones, both guilt and disgust "[resemble] the negative aesthetic response," which inhibits positive reception. Conversely, a "positive aesthetic response" creates affinity: "The outcome of this positive experience is a sense of well-being, sometimes even a sense of 'oneness' or unity of self with the object of attention."[63] Bitting's report on the exhibit makes apparent exhibitors' stress on consumer appeal: "The exhibit was not large, but told the part of the story in which the consumer is most interested without injecting unnecessary details."[64] The exhibit offered an ideal experience of the industry's work; it showed high-quality specimens in hypersanitary environments. The positive feelings created in production and distribution installations set up the subsequent consumption narrative.

After the refrigerated truck, the exhibit led visitors to a meat counter. Behind the counter, a mechanical butcher explained the different cuts of beef, pork, and lamb by referring to a "United States Department of Agriculture Meat Chart." Visitors could step up to the meat cases to peruse roughly forty different cuts and preparations of meats, such as luncheon meats, sausages, and steaks, while the life-size robot spoke. This installation's layout prompted spectators to enter the scene and enact real behaviors used at butcher shops. They could "shop" for meat in a "make-believe" framework. Consumer behavior could be performed in an explicitly mimetic environment that contained mimetic objects.

A pristine kitchen followed the butcher shop installation. Prepared entirely by the USDA, the kitchen featured white, modern appliances; the refrigerator and oven each contained meat. In front of the kitchen, a showcase containing three twelve-pound roasts compared the quality and cost of various cooking methods.[65] Visitors could not walk through this kitchen, but they could participate imaginatively. Phenomenologist and theater scholar Stanton B. Garner Jr. has suggested that food onstage can "activate the spectators' appetites, call to attention their bodily sentience . . . and pierce illusionism as it forces the audience into involuntary empathy."[66] Like the generic theater audience Garner references, fairgoers most likely had already tasted the kinds of meat on display. However, this installation was not a fiction with which an audience could identify in a general way. Fairgoers shared a cultural investment

Figure 1.2. Packinghouse Cooler Installation in Meat and Livestock Industry Exhibit, 1933–34 Chicago World's Fair. Courtesy National Archives, Photo no. 16-Ex-52-29396-C.

in meat as both pleasure and necessity and were aware of current price fluctuation, which affected its availability. Therefore, the desired effect was probably more profound than just recalling hunger or the satisfaction of eating meat. Given the narrative's concern with visitors' active participation, the sensory stimulation worked toward fully involving visitors in the illusion and enactment of choice.

The final installation, "Meat Cookery," consisted of a showcase with three rows "of models of cooked meats, with vegetables and fruits ready for the table. It included 15 combination dishes in which meat was the principal ingredient. Back of this, colored stereopticon slides showed various meats in process of cooking by different methods."[67] The phrase "Meats at Varying Price Levels for Every Occasion" surrounded the screen. One slide featured a man's hands carving a roast above the words "Plump, brown, juicy, evenly cooked."[68] The show of "component parts of a satisfying meat meal chang[ed] suddenly into a healthy [male] child playing."[69] Illuminated signs—"United States Department of Agriculture" and "Bureau of Home Economics"—on both sides of the meat case emphasized federal concerns for consumers' welfare. Labels identified types of meat and vegetables in the case but did not offer cooking instruction or dietary information. Likewise, the slide show did not explain the nutritional science of succulent roasts that built strong male children. Instead, appetizing foods depicted the pleasures of eating. The slides sought to whet the appetite and relayed the message that the New Deal would put an end to "hooverization." This home economics installation showed that meals at "varying price levels" would be fulfilling; *all* meals were exhibited as desirable. Flavorful-looking food models showed myriad delights available to the American consumer. They embodied the New Deal as an America entailing choice.

Upon exiting the enclosed portion of the exhibit, in the common agricultural area, three additional installations completed the meat and livestock industry display. "Meat in Well Balanced Meals" featured a large shadowbox containing nutritional charts. "By Products of the Live Stock and Meat Industry" showcased the industry's morality by demonstrating that no part of the animal goes to waste; the case contained medicines, leather, baseball gloves, a tennis racket, and other objects made from cattle. According to D. S. Burch of the USDA Bureau of Animal Industry, the by-products showcase was a success; it held visitors' attention "even longer than food products" displays. The explicitly gendered mechanical display "Radiant Health Is Your Best Style" included rotating cutouts of "The Bride," "The Stroller," "The Tennis Girl," and other figures of ladies at women's work and play, figures who clearly benefitted from meat consumption. This installation failed to meet exhibitors' expectations: "the average time spent in examining this revolving display was 32 seconds, or approximately one half the time required for

one complete revolution." Burch decided that gender made little difference in preference for the exhibits. The contradiction between expectation and reception may point to the instability of gendered desires
and interests, to the dullness of the display's two-dimensional nature in
comparison to "real" artifacts, or both. Burch concluded that the level
of "human interest," which he suggests mundane objects possess, determined visitor attention.[70]

Burch's report, "The Effectiveness of Various Types of Agricultural
Exhibits," conducted during the first year of the Chicago World's Fair,
demonstrates the significance of objects derived from food to these displays. Based on observations of visitors' behaviors and the length of time
they spent at exhibits, Burch comments that theories that "mechanical
movement," "artistic effects," and "general attractiveness" determine interest in an exhibit do not hold because "Among the six characteristics
studied the item of human interest had the predominant effect." He
concludes from the example of the meat and livestock exhibit that "The
display of realistic models of cooked meat held attention considerably
longer than similar models of raw meat and sausage. Actual by-products,
including medicinal preparations . . . and the like held the attention even
longer than food products. The revolving display of manikins . . . failed
to compete successfully with the very personal appeal of medicine and
food." Burch's study shows that both self-interest and an installation's
concreteness gained and sustained visitor attention. From his observations of this exhibit, specifically the "many favorable comments which
the exhibit of cooked meat models received," he suggested a "permanent
[USDA] exhibit on culinary art" and that "models displayed in the livestock and meat exhibit would serve as an excellent nucleus for such a
permanent exhibit."[71]

In his general comments, Burch notes that exhibits have the capacity
to give "general impressions" rather than impart detailed information.
The meat and livestock industry installations were designed to impress
upon fairgoers that the industry, with the help of the federal government, could produce an American lifestyle that fulfilled more than daily
nutritional requirements: it could also produce pleasure and agency.
The exhibit presented narratives of progress and of consumption. On
the one hand, it affirmed meat's "inherent" qualities and its historic as-

sociation with national fortitude, ingenuity, and individualism, while, on the other, it reinforced the trope of plenty and the access to food and opportunity that trope suggested.

The USDA Exhibits: Educating Citizens about Their Rights and Obligations

In 1933, the Federal Building and its Hall of States had more visitors than any other building at the fair, with a total of 15,500,000 patrons.[72] The building's monumentality allowed for an impressive expanse of exhibits that stressed progress over the past century. The exhibits were also oriented toward federal service to citizens and aimed to stimulate faith in the new administration's ability to restore prosperity. Rydell surmises that "the building's exhibits recited a narrative of national progress designed to emphasize the temporary nature of the depression."[73] The *Official Guidebook of the Fair 1933* made explicit the building's symbolism: "The Federal Building stands on Northerly Island. Above its gold dome three pylons, fluted towers 150 feet high, typify the three branches of United States Government—legislative, executive and judicial. . . . At its back, and in V-shape seeming to embrace it, is the States Building, with its Court of States, thus typifying the increased feeling of loyalty of the citizens to the Union."[74] The architecture stressed a shared belief in capitalist democracy; it actualized the interdependence of the federal and state governments, while the three towers embodied the federal government's power. The Federal Building's awesome stature was intensified by the adjacent relatively low-lying Dairy Building and Food and Agriculture Building, which housed the meat and livestock industry exhibit.

In the Hall of States and outside the Federal Building, state government exhibits showcased the nation's natural abundance. Florida transplanted lemon, orange, grapefruit, and other tropical fruit trees outside the agricultural group buildings.[75] Georgia's exhibit included various agricultural products; the National Pecan Growers Exchange of Albany showcase featured a succulent ham topped with pineapple and pecans.[76] Washington depicted its wildlife, landscape, housing, and rail and ocean transportation on a six-foot, seven-hundred-pound cake.[77]

James O'Donnell Bennett's tour of exhibits in the Federal Building at the 1933 Chicago World's Fair inspired in him a joyful sense of responsibility to America: "The exhibition is a great patriotic service. It makes better Americans. I don't mean blatant 'hundred per-centers,' but Americans who will be humbler, I should think, when here they view in epitome their mighty inheritance and come, please God, into the reverent consciousness that a people's possession of great riches carries with it a great obligation. Consider thine inheritance and be thankful that thy lot is cast in such a land." Bennett's column is a clear pronouncement of the moral obligations of citizens to respect and contribute to the nation's abundance. Throughout this June 6, 1933, *Chicago Daily Tribune* article, "Reporter Sees the Glories of Our Own Land," Bennett makes evident the potential of federal exhibits to stir nationalistic gratitude through grand depictions of abiding myths. In these exhibits, the sum of ordinary objects produced the sense of monumentality. Bennett lauds exhibits that cast him and millions of other citizens as "exceptional Americans" through white, middle-class embodiments of men and women, destined to thrive in the land of plenty.

Housed in the Federal Building, the USDA's 6,500-square-foot display represented its nineteen divisions using primarily in-context technique. This display used the conventional technique of natural and cultural history museums, in which "objects are set in context by means of long labels, charts, diagrams, [etc. . . . and] by means of other objects, often in relation to a classification or schematic arrangement of some kind, based on typologies of form or proposed historical relationship."[78] In-context display traffics in objectivity; the artifacts' materiality creates the illusion of a singular context and confirms it. The connotations of this orderly aesthetic as both educational and objective contextualized the foods and other ordinary objects the USDA displayed as American artifacts and products of the department's effort.

The USDA's typical exhibition techniques may have maximized visitors' comparative perspectives; displays of ripe fruit, prime cuts of beef, filled plates, and harvested fields yielding a healthy bounty supplanted while they also evoked the present reality that was visually and rhetorically defined by the "paradox of want amid plenty." The *World's Fair Weekly* article "Your Uncle Sam Thinks of Everything" opened its lau-

datory description of the USDA exhibit by stating, "You wonder how so
many farmers can be so up against it when you pace through the tremen-
dous show that the Department of Agriculture has staged here." This
comment suggests the potential prevalence of the agricultural crisis in
fairgoers' minds, but the writer's assurance that "You will never imagine
that nobody cares what becomes of you after you visit the U.S. government building" points to the display's success in presenting the message
of a new and better deal for citizens.[79]

USDA installations positioned agricultural adjustment as a method
of sustaining farmers' revered place in the union. By featuring such items
as popular cosmetics, common plants, and staples of the American diet,
showcases compelled citizens to consider the USDA's contributions to
their daily lives. The department's exhibit "simply" displayed products
developed over the course of a century: common objects "proved" that
the government helped its citizens achieve a better life by connecting
farmer to consumer.

In addition to various other methods, USDA exhibits "educated" the
fairgoer through the use of taxonomic object descriptions and causal nar-
rations. Descriptive labels of ordinary household goods tied high-quality, healthful, and safe objects to the governmental efforts. For instance,
a display case devoted to "Standards for Farm Products" contained
specimens such as dressed poultry, canned fruit, butter, and cream to
illustrate quality criteria for commodities. Superficial descriptions of
strange and modern scientific apparatuses, pictures of men scribbling
on clipboards, and food objects and robust bodies positioned as results
took the place of in-depth explanation of the science of agriculture itself.
Metallic mechanisms, test tubes, and tubes linking one object to another
depicted the improvement of such things as fertilizer in the Chemistry
and Soils section and Roquefort cheese in the Dairying exhibit. Through
such installations, the USDA glorified farmers as the nation's providers
yet still took some credit by championing its efforts to enable prosperous agriculture and strengthen its citizens. The overall message was that
USDA experts—white men in white lab coats—used potent technology to enhance American life. Indeed, the Dairying section's central
placard emphasized agriculture as the basis of the nation's superiority:
"A SOUND AND PROSPEROUS DAIRY INDUSTRY is essential to the

economic welfare of our Nation and to the physical well-being of our people."

The central feature of the Home Economics section highlighted the attention the bureau gave to helping consumers make smart dietary choices throughout the economic crisis.[80] Peering through windows, visitors could see a "typical" American family (white, middle-class family of four, the father's suit denoting white-collar employment). Behind the first window, the family sits at the kitchen table, working out a budget. A pie graph behind the family shows the proper portion of the budget for particular food groups. Behind the next window, the family sits at dinner enjoying a well-balanced meal of milk, bread, butter, vegetables, and meat. The final window offers an ergonomic kitchen design.[81] These scenes offer a stable and well-fed family as the outcome of acting on the advice of USDA home economists.

According to Milton Danziger, a collaborator in the U.S. Office of Exhibits, "The department exhibits gave a feeling of 'museum' displays. They were annoyingly neat and orderly." His appraisal presumably arose from the recurring horseshoe pattern for each section's exhibit, the symmetry of individual installations, and the glass encasement of nearly all displayed items. Perhaps Danziger felt the exhibit lacked the entertainment value of the Midway or the immersive dioramas and giganticism of other exhibits. He emphasized that the USDA's conventional techniques destroyed the exhibit's dramatic potential: "The Department of Agriculture exhibits as a rule are too reflective. 'Don't reason with an audience,' advises a psychologist. 'Give them images! Stir up their emotions! The more emotional a crowd is, the more suggestible it is.'"[82] But perhaps Danziger missed the point: the Department of Agriculture relied on the public's acceptance of a museum as an educational venue and presented an orderly collection of mundane foods to symbolize a nation restored. It wasn't exciting, but it was effective.

Food as Cultural Artifact and Political Tool

The USDA exhibit may not have had a dramatic, dazzling design, but its choice of artifacts and conventional presentation technique manifested stability. The profusion of food in pictures and dioramas—a mise-en-scène of plenty—intimated that New Deal agricultural programs would restore both stable access to food and economic prosperity. The rows upon rows of ideal food specimens validated the USDA's right to control food production and suggested the possibility of plenty through adjustment. In-context technique, particularly the use of glass showcases, creates an immediate, physical, and seemingly unmediated spectator experience with objects. Artifacts' power in museum display derives from a learning protocol that poses "an opposition between the use of primary and secondary sources, with the objects being understood as pieces of unmediated 'reality.'"[83] Explanatory labels, glass showcases, and the repetitive arrangements encouraged visitors to contemplate again and again how the USDA was vital to their well-being.

Use of vitrines to display food also bolstered the USDA display as an educational apparatus, while reinforcing its authority. Museum studies scholar Michael Belcher writes, "To many visitors showcases are an irritant, creating a physical and psychological barrier between viewer and object, and filling a gallery with monotonous rectilinear forms."[84] While Belcher states that the glass case inhibits connection, his observation also implies the way in which a vitrine transforms a displayed object. Belcher intimates spectator desire to have physical contact with the "real thing"; thus, protecting the object within glass denotes authenticity and significance. The bulk of the objects displayed in the USDA exhibit, excluding scientific instruments, were not valuable—neither costly nor delicate nor rare. Yet putting them behind glass suggested that these ordinary items are precious because they epitomize American values and customs. A brief inventory illuminates the utter ordinariness of some artifacts: newspaper clippings and advertisements, fruits and vegetables, plants, meat, noodles, bugs, and seeds, among other mundane items. A press release by the Century of Progress commission on the USDA's plant industry exhibit demonstrates their multitude:

> In a glass case are wax reproductions of scores of the nation's best known apples. Labels inform that the Rome Beauty originated in Ohio in 1848; the Jonathan in New York in 1826 . . . and that the Golden Delicious, among the youngest, was born in 1916. Anyone interested can find brief pedigrees of other favorites. . . . Adjoining are samples of the finest hybrid corn in white and yellow varieties, sweet corn and popcorn. The skilled American farmer, guided by government experts, has developed a big eared corn, rich in food values,

uniform in shape and color and a heavy producer. No one needs any further
argument than these two cases of typical corn to be convinced of the profits
that lie in scientific breeding of a grain.[85]

The plant industry display offered the most concentrated encounter with
foodstuffs; each showcase was dedicated to one type of fruit, vegetable,
or grain, including wheat, corn, apples, cotton, peaches, berries, and
sugarcane. Specimens (both real and reproductions) were arranged scientifically in neat rows with labels indicating variety, origin, and other
qualities. Baskets of peaches, oranges, and berries were similarly set in
angled eye-level displays. Wall displays and waist-high, free-standing
cases contained specimens. The exhibit also featured photographs and
sketches of grain and fruit varieties. It was one of the most popular installations; officials noted that the cases containing corn and apples were
continuously surrounded by fairgoers.[86]

The aesthetic predicament of the in-context exhibition and the physical experience that it shaped for fairgoers transformed the foods in the
displays from the prosaic to the remarkable. By offering privileged views
of food, concentrating attention on them as scientific evidence and as
objects for consumption, the exhibits enhanced the USDA's paternalis-
tic argument. The act of display elevated the ordinary "because it [the
displayed object] has been offered for inspection, [the spectator] takes it
that the object has been considered worthy of inspection."[87] Vitrines also
transformed edible items into prized ethnographic objects. Because the
foods were ordinary, they evoked the pleasures of everyday American
life. Thus, food artifacts were staged in such a way as to prompt responses
based on personal, commonsense cultural knowledge and to substantiate the government's authority to determine the food system.

As performance scholar Barbara Kirshenblatt-Gimblett theorizes,
these staged foods potentially "activate the sense memories of taste and
smell. Even a feast for the eyes only will engage the other senses imaginatively, for to see is not only to taste, but also to eat."[88] By offering food for
visual consumption, the USDA exhibits capitalized on citizens' physical
responses to food, perhaps causing fairgoers' to "feel" or "taste" the promise of plenty. Coining the term "foodie gaze," performance scholar Helen
Iball writes, "in the 'moment just before' contact with or absorption into
the [actor's] body, it might be suggested that the actor is upstaged by the

food. Rather than an acute awareness of the performer's embodiment, the spectator's own corporeality is likely to be foregrounded, because [the spectator's] gaze has been claimed (seduced) by food."[89] In the USDA exhibit (and the meat and livestock industry exhibit), there were no actors to vie for the gaze; no actor enjoyed privileged access to consumption. Instead, the showcases and dioramas repeatedly engaged spectators in the "moment just before" consumption through the direct relationship established between spectator and food object. Foods' placement within vitrines may have stimulated reflexive bodily reactions as spectators moved from installation to installation examining familiar foods. (Of course, the restaurant at the end of the dairy industry exhibit allowed visitors to realize fully the promises stimulated by the gaze.)

Agricultural Adjustment Exhibits: Displaying Federal Service to the Nation

By including agricultural adjustment in an exhibit celebrating science's contribution to farming and American posterity, the AAA was positioned as a humanitarian program. Proximity worked in favor of this; other USDA-related exhibits situated adjustment within the story of modern progress and federal service to the "People." Though ideal America was not yet functioning outside the fair's gates, the AAA installations demonstrated the manner in which the act, with the support of Americans, would shortly restore stable access to food and economic prosperity. Significantly, the AAA was depicted as a policy that strengthened the relationship between farmer and consumer.

Upon entering the exhibit, fairgoers encountered a "semicircular alcove" that served as an informal meeting place where they could speak with docents about the USDA's work and peruse USDA pamphlets.[90] In 1933, this installation consisted of a curved wall with a center pillar showing the words "United States Department of Agriculture." Both the left and right sides of the wall featured pictures of USDA activities. The words "Serves Agriculture" and "Serves the Public," which framed the photos, linked the improvement of citizens' daily lives to a thriving agricultural industry. Placed high on the center pillar, a plaque, "handwritten" and "signed" by Secretary of Agriculture Henry Wallace, stated

"Science has conquered the fear of famine and has created abundance, and now we must learn to live with abundance."[91] The handwriting and signature personalize Wallace's authority; the plaque manifests paternalism. At the same time, Wallace's words intimate an ominous underside to the bounty. The statement splits the meaning of "abundance." It denotes the United States as the land of plenty but then alludes to "surplus"—the current glut of agricultural markets that inhibited national prosperity. Wallace implies the need to attend to agricultural economics to assure food security. Positioned near the top of the wall, the secretary's words oversee the photographs attesting to the USDA's past successes and the potential of the AAA.

One exhibit was removed during the fair's first season, deemed a failure for not being forward looking. Near this main entrance, the Agricultural Economics and Agricultural Adjustment Section originally featured an installation titled "The Shadow of Surplus." It was designed to grant "visitors an interpretation of how the vast surpluses of farm crops for which no markets were available had cast their shadows of depressed prices over the whole United States and brought uncalculable [sic] distress to American agriculture."[92] The gloom suggested worrisome instability rather than future promise. Dark drapes, hung from the ceiling to the floor, framed a concave niche containing a platform U.S. map.[93] Illuminated sacks of "Surplus Cotton" and "Surplus Wheat," placed on the map's west side, cast a shadow over the bulk of the map. The signage "The Shadow of the Surplus Covers the United States" emphasized the problems depicted in seven drawings underneath the map. According to Colonel Causey, assistant administrator of the Century of Progress, the installation had two major problems: rhetorical emphasis and mood. The depiction did not sufficiently separate "surplus" from known need or demonstrate how decreasing production would result in plenty for all Americans. The notion of "no markets" conflicted with visible hunger and its economic equivalent: demand. Causey disliked the exhibit and wrote that "this is not the time or place to show anything as casting a shadow over the United States."[94] The early removal of this installation, sometime around July 1933, demonstrates the desire to depict the AAA as part of the New Deal's promise, with emphasis on a bright forthcoming future, not the depressed present.

The replacement for the dreary installation used frontier-style rhetoric to envision progress and shifted the emphasis from problem to
solution and from surplus to plenty. "The NEW TRAIL in Agriculture"
showed the adjustment program's benefits for farmers and consumers
alike. Above the central tableau, a banner stated that this new trail "Leads
to Greater Purchasing Power for Farmer." Five life-size cutouts demonstrated the manner in which prosperity would circulate from farmer
to urban consumer. At the left, County Agent and Mrs. Wheat Farmer
discuss farm production and cost records. In the center, Mr. Wheat
Farmer receives a check from Uncle Sam. Farmer states, "Thanks, Uncle
Sam for helping me and my neighbors get organized for production
control. I'll carry out my contract with the Secretary of Agriculture."
Mrs. City Housewife, just to the right of Uncle Sam, is "glad to pay a
little more for food" because she knows that the money benefits producers and that the farmers could then purchase her husband's industrial
products. As a consumer, she too could help maintain farm families by
maintaining her own. These eponymous figures modeled the behavior
that the USDA deemed patriotic—teaching consumers and farmers how
to act as "good" citizens—and the installation transformed an economic
program into an embodiment of the American way of life. Narrative
emphasis on the farmer and the iconic image of his sturdy body clad
in coveralls also offered assurance that the AAA would save the family
farm. The exhibit stimulated positive, iconic associations of the rural,
including "connection," "closeness," "family farming, community and
'quality,'"[95] thus suggesting that the AAA would preserve the fundamental source of American morality.

Thirty-three thousand visitors to the USDA exhibit in the Federal
Building picked up the free forty-five-page souvenir booklet "Science
Serving Agriculture." It offered further explanation of the USDA's role
in citizens' lives. "The United States Department of Agriculture Touches
Your Life in Scores of Ways" headed the opening chapter to this guide
of the department's services. The narrative positions the USDA as the
paternal protector of American life and the reader as a consumer:

> Every day the United States Department of Agriculture does for you a multitude
> of necessary things that you could not possibly do for yourself. It guards your
> food supply from adulteration and dangers to health and improves its quality

through plant science and animal husbandry. It keeps watch on production at home and abroad, so that the supply may be adjusted to demand and prices kept in line with values. . . . At breakfast you eat a slice from a ham bearing a little purple stamp. . . . The cream on your cereal came from a dairy using practices standardized by the Department. . . . Your fruit, no matter what its kind or variety, shows the results of the Department's scientific labors.[96]

The individuals' vulnerability is emphasized in each of the pamphlet's subsequent examples to set up the USDA as a humanitarian agency. This opening paragraph also highlights the significance of the relationship between farmers and the USDA. It suggests that the Department of Agriculture protects the farmer's way of life and, through this relationship, the entire nation benefits. The narrative stressed an agrarian ideal that is also consumer oriented.

The brochure culminates in the section "Farm Relief Act Is a Great New Responsibility." The previous chapters establish the moral contract between the government, the farmer, and the consumer, so this final section obliges citizens to do their part and contribute to prosperity. The narrative intensifies the duty of the American public through the metaphor of the farmer in "bondage." The implication is that the AAA will set the country free: "Farmers surrender to nonfarmers, for no equivalent return, what they have produced by applying their labor, skill, and capital to the land. It is not in the interest even of consumers that this should continue. . . . City dwellers, if they think about the matter, . . . will agree that economic justice for agriculture promotes economic progress for the Nation."[97] By allowing the farmer to stay enslaved, the American public starves itself—it perpetuates want. Yet by accepting responsibility as consumers, supporting the act, and paying reasonable prices for agricultural commodities, the public can provide for the nation; led by the USDA, the "People"—farmer and consumer together—ensure plenty.

Adjusting AAA Exhibits to Counter Controversy

Farm week at the 1933 Century of Progress occurred in mid-August. The *World's Fair Weekly* summarized the celebrations in honor of the nation's providers: "It will be a week packed with events, from the impressive Candle Lighting Company on Sunday, Farm Youth Day, through the

parades, bands, barn dancing, and pageants, to the lively contests ranging from sheep shearing to husband calling on Farms Sports Day, which
will conclude the week's ceremonies." The week's special programming
increased daily attendance; figures ranged from around 170,000 to more
than 190,000 visitors each day throughout this week. Daily programming included speeches by prominent members of the Roosevelt administration, as well as farm organization leaders. A pageant, "Evolution
of the Farm Woman," honored rural women's contributions to the nation. A mile-long parade down Michigan Avenue and into the World's
Fair celebrated the great achievements of farm men, women, and industry. Large crowds of farmers witnessed the pageantry and pomp of the
nation's debt to them.[98]

These glorifications of farmers occurred amid intense debate about
the AAA's benefits for small farmers and its disproportionate attention
to various agricultural commodities. Although, throughout the summer,
prices had risen for some agricultural commodities, the cost of manufactured goods rose more rapidly, driving up the costs of agricultural
production and resulting in little gain for small farmers. While powerful
American Farm Bureau and National Grange leaders made speeches at
the World's Fair praising the AAA before thousands of farmers, the National Cooperative Milk Producers' conferees (360,000 dairy farmers)
in Chicago denounced Wallace and AAA administrator George Peek.
They stated that the AAA crop reduction program had only shifted agricultural production by allowing crop farmers (corn, wheat, and such)
to turn fields to pasture, thus inducing some farmers to turn to dairying.
Dairymen feared that this would increase competition and worsen current overproduction, driving down already depressed prices.[99]

At the close of Farm Week, Secretary Wallace took the opportunity to allay such concerns by announcing new AAA measures. Wallace
received a nineteen-gun salute (an honor bestowed on one individual
each year) upon his arrival at the Hall of States, where he was to speak
to an estimated fifteen thousand farmers. The audience also included
thousands more who heard the broadcast across the fairgrounds and via
radio.[100] In his introduction of the Corn-Hog program, Wallace stressed
the administration's support of the farmer. The day before this speech,
he had announced that the federal government would purchase $30 mil-

lion of dairy products and enforce Chicago cooperative milk marketing agreements.[101] A *New York Times* editorial on September 23, 1933, "Plenty and Want," focused on the plan's moral end and its American character:

> This grant is putting the nation as a whole under a share of the burden. What is thus given will come back and much of it immediately—all of it in time "as bread cast upon the waters"—in the saving of a multitude of lives from hunger and utter want, in the purchase of the wheat, cotton and meat from those who have been unable to find a market for their products, and in providing revenues for those engaged in processing.... It is a triple good that should come from this single act. And even if it had but a single good, it were necessary on the ground of humanity. It is all for each. It should, incidentally, stir the devotion of each to all under such a benign purpose as has prompted this provision.

The plan did not stir devotion; many citizens felt that the USDA was attempting to erase the "paradox of want amid plenty" by throwing away the plenty rather than providing for the nation. The *Chicago Daily Tribune* criticized the Corn-Hog program from the start and offered revelations about federal "waste," as the stench of tankage from West Side processing plants pervaded parts of the city.

In May 1934, President Roosevelt inaugurated the second year of the Century of Progress with a grand flourish. The president pressed a telegraph key on his desk in Washington, DC, sending an electric signal to illuminate the fair in Chicago. While his celebratory address alluded to some errors in the administration's attempt to restore national greatness, it also stressed his resolve to continue the New Deal experiment.[102] Roosevelt did not specify the problems with his initiatives, but USDA correspondence from October 1933 makes clear that this department was actively attempting to repair the AAA's reputation and resurrect its promise of plenty at the 1934 World's Fair. At Warburton's request, the USDA revised the entry installation and the "New Frontier" installation "to present . . . new information which was not available at the time the original exhibit was prepared [for the 1933 season]."[103] The changes made the economic benefits of AAA explicit and used strong agrarian rhetoric to promote a vision of plenty. The USDA also printed the pamphlet "Agriculture and the Consumer" for the 1934 season, which explained how "The Agricultural Adjustment Act has from the first recognized the necessity of protecting consumers."[104] The revised framing of the AAA countered the morally problematic aspects of crop and livestock

destruction, its wastefulness, and scarcity tactics by focusing on economic outcomes, consumer needs, and high-quality products. The USDA
exhibited the act's ability to create stable access to food by displaying
food objects as agricultural economics applied in the interest of consumers' daily lives.

For 1934, in order to bring the display more "in line with the new
agricultural program," a pair of enormous scale pans became the central
feature of the USDA's introductory installation (see figure 1.3).[105] The bar
weighing the loads of "Supply" and "Demand" was labeled "Prosperity
Requires Balanced Agriculture." On the left side, a sign under the words
"The Goal" elaborated on the AAA's purpose: "Adjustment of agriculture
to the quantity that the nation and the world will buy at a fair price so the
farmer may obtain an equitable share of the nation's income." The right
side's sign explained the economic "Progress Made" and employment
created due to the AAA: "Prices of farm products improved. Purchasing
power of farmers increased by 20 per cent. Business revival accelerated,
factory employment gaining. More than 185 million dollars distributed
to growers restricting production of cotton, corn, hogs, wheat, and tobacco, under self-financing programs. Producers of the other commodities aided by marketing agreements and licenses. Progress continuing
through 1934."[106] These results refuted the public's doubts about the
AAA's effectiveness. The sign also emphasized the public as a major ben-
eficiary of agricultural adjustment, opposing arguments that farmers
benefited to consumers' detriment. The scale manifested plenty as balance, the result of adjustment. Adjustment was framed as part of modern progress, another innovation like those exhibited in the dioramas,
maps, charts, and installations dedicated to consumer protections. It
transformed agrarian fundamentalism into modern adjustment—federal regulation of agricultural production or economically informed production. In the new world, capitalist-savvy farmers cooperating with the
government would save the country.

For the 1934 season, the USDA also changed the title of the "New
Trail in Agriculture" installation to "Adjusting Agriculture to Fit Today's Conditions." Though it employed the same basic structure of the
original, this new exhibit retained only the life-size cutouts of Uncle Sam
and Farmer. Mrs. City Housewife no longer stood next to Uncle Sam.

Figure 1.3. Revised entry to United States Department of Agriculture Exhibit for the 1934 Chicago World's Fair season. Courtesy National Archives, Photo no. 16-EX-51-29510-C.

The archive does not disclose why this figure was removed. However, its absence, interestingly, reflects the unwillingness of actual American housewives, unlike the cardboard replica, to "pay a little more" for food. In place of this government-consumer-farmer cooperation, Uncle Sam's and Farmer's dialogue intimates farmers' sacrifices for consumers' benefit. They discuss the agricultural situation in a manner indicating continued improvement and showing the government's gratitude for the farmers' patience.[107] This portrayal of farmers' trust in the USDA appears highly prescriptive when viewed in the context of the numerous agrarian protests occurring since the establishment of the AAA, one of which is examined in the next chapter. Even more, through the embodiment of "Farmer," the display invoked family-owned farms, and by extension traditional values, thus displacing the corporate interests of the AAA and the ongoing consolidation of small farms—a central complaint of farmer-activists. The iconic embodiment of the farmer not only suggested preservation of an American moral democracy but also that federal intervention would assure profitable family farms.

Throughout the New Deal era, officials utilized exhibits that had debuted at the 1933–34 fair to promote the morality of the adjustment program. Following the close of the Chicago World's Fair, C. W. War-burton requested another seven thousand dollars to revise certain USDA exhibits for use at state fairs "in the light of present agricultural situations." Wallace agreed with Warburton and sent a proposal to the secretary of state and to the U.S. Commission to a Century of Progress.[108] Four of the ten proposed exhibits—modifications of existing exhibits and new exhibits created through assemblage of various installations— dealt directly with agricultural adjustment. It was estimated that a mere $1,620 would enable production of "Adjusting Agriculture to Fit Today's Conditions," "Cotton Farming to Fit Today's Conditions," "Livestock Farming to Fit Today's Conditions," and "The Dairy Industry of the United States."[109] Destined to circulate throughout the nation, these installations would continue to promote the AAA's promise of plenty. By 1939, the mechanical heifer from the dairy industry exhibit had become a standard at state fairs and inspired similar displays. It ranked as the USDA's "Number 1 exhibit" at the 1939 New York World's Fair. At this same exhibition, the USDA featured "America's Table," which contained almost nothing but food, and was the "second high scoring exhibit" in the federal building. These confirmed for officials that "power" is in the "method of presentation." "Extremely well made," "lifelike" food is referred to as the potent technique, the mechanism that drew visitors to displays, held their attention, and enabled immediate and visceral reinforcement of plenty, helped along by the federal government, as a right of citizenship.[110]

The USDA, as the agency devoted to farmers and food, had to navigate the economic shift toward manufacturing and the AAA's part in the changing agriculture and food industry. One the one hand, the department welcomed the greater efficiency, profitability, and safety afforded by technological innovations. On the other, it was charged with ensuring the welfare of farmers and consumers. In its exhibits, the USDA negotiated these competing interests by affirming the importance of consumer choice and minimizing the role of corporations in its displays of agricultural progress. By using idyllic images of farming, the USDA countered allegations that the AAA operated to corporations' benefit. By highlighting consumer choice, exhibits countered the idea that the AAA violated consumers' rights to indispensible foods. These installations enacted a partnership between the American farmer and federal government, which emphasized preservation of farmers' way of life to ensure plenty for all. Exhibits, as well as pageantry such as Farm Week, condensed the relationship between farmer and consumer by excluding processors and distributors, essential actors in the program. These abridged versions of the food system under AAA played upon "the broader sense of the local, [which] might be associated with an ethical relation of trust between consumer and producer."[111]

Nevertheless, the exhibits of the USDA and the dairy and meat and livestock industries slip between scenes that emphasize the farmer-consumer relationship as foundational to renewed prosperity and those that hail the wonders of technology for improving on nature and giving consumers access to higher quality and convenient foods. The uneven cultural positioning of an industrializing food system indicates public wariness of corporate investment in consumers' welfare and entrenched utopian ideas about the "natural." On the one hand, the public believed that industrialization distanced farmer from consumer, while, on the other, it sensed the freedom and opportunity provided by mass markets and technology.

The next chapter explores one of the first protests to question the federal government's claim that the AAA safeguarded traditional American values. The 1933 strike by dairy farmers in Wisconsin showcases milk as a political tool, used to impress upon spectators the moral implications of corporatizing agriculture.

SCENE and DISCOVERED

As overture ends, voice over the loudspeaker speaks
Voice of the Living Newspaper: Triple A Plowed Under

SCENE 1 (War and inflation)

Voice of Living Newspaper (Continuing): 1917—Inflation.
(At rise spotlight (red) is on soldiers marching in continuous columns up ramp placed
upstage left. After a brief interval there is an increasing volume of marching feet.
The entire scene is played behind scrim.

  Spotlight up on three speakers and crowd of farmers behind scrim in 2. Speakers
stand on highest level on set, stage right. Some of the farmers stand on lowest level
stage right, and some at stage level, right.)

First Speaker: Your Country is at war.
Second Speaker: Your country needs you.
First & Second Speakers, together: If you can't fight—Farm.
First Speaker: The fate of our country rests upon the farmer.
First Speaker: Do you want our land invaded?
Second Speaker: Do you want your daughters ravaged by Huns?
Woman: Farmer, save the Nation!
 (Trumpet)
First Speaker: The boys in the trenches need the men in the fields.
Woman: Farmer, save our boys.
 (Trumpet)
Second Speaker: Every bushel of barley is a barrel of bullets.
Woman: Farmer, save democracy.
 (Trumpet)
First Speaker: Every hand with a spade is a hand-grenade.
Woman: Farmer, save our honor.
 (Trumpet)
Second Speaker: Every man behind a plow is a man behind a gun.
Woman: Farmer, save civilization.
 (Trumpet)
First Speaker: Every head of cattle can win a battle.
Woman: Farmer, save our flag.
 (Trumpet)
First Speaker: Plant more wheat.
Second Speaker: Plant more potatoes.
First Speaker: More corn.
Second Speaker: More cotton.
First Speaker: More food, more seed, more acres.
First and Second Speaker (Together): More! More! More!
Woman: FARMER, SAVE THE WORLD.

CLOSE PORTALS.

Script Excerpt 2. Editorial Staff of the Living Newspaper Federal Theatre Project under the supervision of Arthur Arent, "Triple-A Plowed Under," 1936, Federal Theatre Project Collection, Special Collections and Archives, George Mason University Libraries.

2

Milk Dumping across America's Dairyland

The May 1933 Wisconsin Dairymen's Strike

THE MAY 27, 1933, ISSUE OF *NEWSWEEK*, PUBLISHED ON THE SAME day that the Chicago World's Fair opened, told a very different story about the Agricultural Adjustment Act's impact on the American way of life. It featured a panoramic image of men, with bayonets fixed, running across an open field; they charge forth in profile, virtually silhouetted. The photo captures motion from right to left, along receding horizontal planes; the figures seem to run into and out of frame, in focus in the foreground and blips in the background. This perspective creates the impression of a continuous stream of men entering the field of battle. The photo's caption states "National Guardsmen Charge into Milk Strike Pickets at Durham Hill, Wis., before the Armistice." The drama unfolding before the reader is war.

During six days of protest, from May 13–18, 1933, the Wisconsin Cooperative Milk Pool strike took over the eastern half of Wisconsin along Lake Michigan, from the Illinois border to the far north and west toward the middle of the state. Throughout the roughly thirty counties included in this area (of Wisconsin's seventy-one counties

total), Milk Pool strikers cruised highways and flagged trucks to stop
for inspection. If a truck refused to stop, the strikers would throw out
harrows, chains, and other obstructions to block the road. The only
trucks allowed through picket lines were those bearing a white cross
on the windshield: these trucks carried "public welfare" milk. All other
trucks were subject to attack, an act that entailed strikers jumping onto
trucks, yanking out milk cans, pouring milk onto the road, and smash-
ing the cans. Armed county deputies and national guardsmen rode in the
trucks to ensure that the milk would arrive at dairy corporations. They
carried gas bombs, rifles, clubs, and bayonets. They stood guard over
arrested strikers with machine guns. Due to the occupation of towns
by deployed men, hundreds of guard patrols, and protesters, some Wisconsinites encountered strike participants during daily activities. The
gas-permeated atmosphere also impacted bystanders caught in the fray.
Meanwhile, many Wisconsin citizens sought out milk dumping. They
drove down rural roads, gathered and waited near hot spots such as
dairy processing and distribution plants in anticipation of milk dumping, and visited sites where milk dumping had occurred.[1] It was a display that mattered to them and that they had been anticipating because
of months of news headlines. When cultural studies scholar Jon Robert
Adams critiques the "United States's time-honored link between its
sense of national self and the performance of American men at war," he
considers wars that pit an American "us" against a foreign "them."[2] In
the May 1933 Milk Pool strike, the dairymen (us?) and the state of Wisconsin (them?) staged the very real challenges to an imagined national
self in the context of the AAA.

By examining the relationship between audience expectations set
for the May 1933 strike and the strike's enactment, this chapter explains
how the theatrical—as a narrative, symbolic, sensate, and material form
of expression—contributed to the moral arguments of protest. The May
Milk Pool strike stands apart from many protests because it cultivated
an audience. Though protesters and authorities often work with the media to publicize protests and curry favor, they also tend to operate from
scripts to which only they are privy. Audience ignorance in this respect
can be a vital tactic for protesters interested in interrupting people's daily
routines and the status quo. Surprise can be just as vital to authorities'

efforts to contain a protest. The May Milk Pool strikers and Wisconsin state authorities, in contrast, flooded the public with information about planned actions months prior to the protest. Indeed, the May strike is different in this regard from other Milk Pool protests in 1933. The Milk Pool staged three strikes in 1933, in February, May, and October.[3] The duration, intensity, and amount of information about the planned strike for May created a countdown atmosphere in Wisconsin, generated excitement, and set up expectations for this event. The strike scenarios that circulated publicly also cast consumers as political actors in the conflict, by compelling them to involve themselves in acting out scripts and instilling these actions with ethical significance.

For more than two months, from the end of February to the beginning of May, Wisconsin state authorities and Milk Pool officials gave interviews and documents to reporters that elaborated on their causes. The state of Wisconsin, actively working to avert a strike, used agrarian discourse in its negotiations with the Milk Pool and in its appeals to the federal government on behalf of all Wisconsin dairymen. The Wisconsin Cooperative Milk Pool, likewise, rooted its demands against the federal government in agrarian discourse about the farmer as the nation's providers and men as the nation's protectors. This rhetorical move appeals to the symbol of "[independent] agricultural production [as] the source and preserve of equality, freedom, democracy and strong family" used in U.S. farmers' movements since the colonial period.[4] In 1933, the discourse of agrarianism was shaped by both the immediate context of the Depression in terms of farmers' anxieties about federal and corporate takeover of agriculture and the recent history of the Great War, which dairymen (and others) claimed had morally indebted the government to farmers and caused farmers' crushing financial debt.

Both the state and the Milk Pool rendered milk the material stakes of the May protest in their prestrike declarations and appeals for federal aid. Both highlighted the strike's seminal gesture of milk dumping and its associated promise of violence. Both employed milk's historic connection with Americanism. And both used agrarian discourse, which was affected by World War I, setting up a conflict between the state's (masculine) duty to protect and the farmers' (masculine) duty to provide, and echoing the logic used to justify violence in the form of war.

The Roosevelt administration, largely, fell out of the frame, and stayed out, of this contest. And while the Milk Pool initially pitted itself against dairy corporations, the state of Wisconsin came to represent corporate power. Prior to the strike in May, the two sides had agreed to protect a limited quantity of milk—"public welfare" milk—conveyed in trucks marked with a white cross. This designation and the accompanying signs contrasted "essential" milk to "non-essential" milk sold by non-striking dairymen. The Milk Pool stated that it was striking against corporations; these dairymen would withhold their milk from processing plants, not from consumers. The state of Wisconsin had a trickier problem; it promised to protect consumers' milk supply, respect farmers' rights as producers to strike and withhold their milk, yet also ensure nonstriking dairymen's rights to sell their products to processors. The restrictions placed on milk by both the Milk Pool and the state transformed consumption into an ethical practice, as it required consumers to weigh their needs and rights against those of (striking and nonstriking) producers.

When the May strike finally came, its staging resonated with reminders of the Great War. Perhaps recent memory of this war's unprecedented trauma and the rhetoric used in strike publicity and plans converged to constitute war as the "obvious" frame through which to interpret the strike. Like epics of war, the masculinity of the opposing leaders—signified by their performance skill and physicality—influenced the perception of their actions and those carried out by their troops. Yet some of the Milk Pool and the state's political and tactical decisions had effects that the participants did not foresee. Milk Pool president Walter Singler's extraordinary oratorical talents matched his large physique. Singler's heroic proportions were further inflated due to an eleventh-hour decision to strike despite almost certain defeat. In contrast, Governor Albert Schmedeman's authority was diminished by comparison to Singler. The elderly governor, imagining a scenario of violence between striking and nonstriking dairymen, took the position of peacekeeper. Yet Schmedeman deployed the National Guard; this was both an expected act and an unprecedented one. He ordered the guard into service equipped with gas bombs and other weapons but in plain clothes as "civilian deputies" to protect both white-cross trucks carrying "public welfare" milk and unmarked trucks carrying commodity milk. The incongruity of guardsmen dressed as civilians yet carrying an arsenal of weapons was not lost on the public nor was the irony of a state claiming to embody neutrality while deploying armed guards to secure the rights of only one side.

Publication of strike plans attuned the audience to deciphering events and granted them performance options. Because of this, spectators' critical engagement with the AAA's effects on farmers derived from the difference between the strike actions as scripted (that is, imagined possibilities) and its performance (that is, an embodied reality). The distance between anticipated violence over milk dumping and the reality of violence raised the question of whether independent farming mattered to the moral standing of the nation. But the situation also confirmed that milk could never be seen as just a commodity and so questioned both producers' and consumers' right to milk. The May 1933 Milk Pool strike brought historic justifications for engaging in war— justifications such as freedom, security, and honor—to bear upon economic arguments in favor of or against the corporate takeover of U.S. agriculture via the Agricultural Adjustment Act.

American Farmers and the Nation's Debt

Wisconsin Cooperative Milk Pool dairymen were some of the poorest farmers in the state. In 1932, they had organized around the mission of receiving prices that covered at least the cost of milk's production and wanted to establish a single state-wide dairy cooperative to pressure processors for higher prices. Like other milk pools, the Wisconsin dairymen created a democratic organization that used farmer collectivity to compete with corporations' market power. Milk pools had capitalist, business-minded missions. Frederick Bergelin, vice president of the Wisconsin Milk Pool, rallied dairymen during the strike by emphasizing the power cooperation could exercise over corporations: "you are not going to make these octopuses [large corporate food companies] surrender with 960 different cooperatives, I do not care what you are calling it, but let us get together and see if with a large organization we cannot meet these octopuses."[5] Milk Pool farmers were landowners; many stood to lose property that was once very valuable. These farmers did not base strike demands on the value of their labor or the right to control the commodities that they produced. They did not cast themselves as laborers or capitalists in public or in private. Some historians have pointed to the "ambiguous class position" of U.S. farmers because they have both capital and labor interests.[6] Yet these dairymen were clear in their own minds as to who they were; they identified as "owner-tillers." The Milk Pool extended the rights of representation and leadership in their organization only to men who owned (or held the mortgage on) *and* operated a farm. It also explicitly excluded agricultural laborers (that is, unpropertied classes) and absentee landlords (that is, capitalists and corporate interests) from the category of "farmer." These exclusions secured the image of dairymen/farmers as a unique, morally superior class of producer. Milk Pool chairman Harry Jack's speech during the May strike compared the pool's fight to that of America's forefathers: "Farmers in the strike have shown the same spirit as those farmers in '75 and '76 that followed Washington from Valley Forge to Yorktown under the banner designed by Betsy Ross. This is the same spirit of Americanism and protection—interest in the home. This is what we are fighting for and proves what a man can do if he gives himself to the service of his community."[7] The Milk Pool framed its organization and protest actions in terms of foundational freedoms and duty created by those who worked their own land, notions that were socially and economically conservative and deeply entwined with ideas of masculinity. The Milk Pool represented the importance of owner-tillers, not corporations, holding private property to the moral core of the nation.

According to these owner-tillers, the May strike was to restore to American farmers the liberty that they had preserved for others in both war and peace. Milk Pool dairymen had engaged in wars before to serve the nation and sought to remind the government of its debt to farmers. A Milk Pool strike poem, composed sometime between February and May 1933, distills the perceived masculine implications of the historic transition from family-owned farms to corporate-run agriculture not only for farmers but for the nation:

> We've all been patiently waiting
>   for the government to act

> But they didn't reconize [*sic*] us
>   that you all know is a fact
> . . .
> Now if we all stick with Singler
>   that good stern jolly fellow
> We then will show United States
>   that Wisconsin isn't yellow
> When the war was on with Germany
>   the farmer sent his son
> He was told that he must fight
>   until the war was won
> The farmer and his children
>   stayed home upon their land
> They worked from sunrise to sunset
>   with blisters on their hands
> All the money that we earned
>   we gave to Uncle Sam
> We were glad to let him use it
>   if he'd return it like a man
> The farmer ate the outside
>   of barley wheat and rye
> And the inside went to Wall [S]treet
>   to make the rich men cake and pies
> . . .
> Now this farmer has a mortgage
>   which he cannot meet
> And some millionaire is waiting
>   to put him on the street
> After all these years of labor
>   the farmer lost all hopes
> Because this man Borden [Milk Products LP]
>   had him tied with two inch ropes.
> . . .
> Now when the strike is over
>   and the battle we have won
> Hurrah for old Wisconsin
>   and Singler and his son.[8]

The poem indicts the government's failed masculinity and champions the farmers' abiding American manhood; it does not question either as such. According to the poem, farmers gave their sons to the Western front, while they mortgaged their land, forwent the food they produced, and enlisted their noncombatant children in grueling agricultural labor to feed the soldiers abroad.

The poem (or my synopsis of its content) may appear hyperbolic, but its rhetoric was accepted because recent history substantiated it. During World War I, men from the countryside not only fought in Europe, but the Wilson administration militarized farmers' agricultural labor at home through propagandistic slogans—"The man behind the plow is the same as the man behind the gun"—that entreated farmers to increase production.[9] To do so and to build the infrastructure of rural America, farmers incurred new taxes and debt to increase land holdings, improve herds, and invest in capital equipment. True, they profited substantially from high demand during World War I and also became accustomed to high prices and high levels of production. Following the Great War, however, less and less food was shipped overseas, surpluses piled up, and, as Europe restored its lands, foreign agricultural markets virtually closed. In this economic atmosphere, dairy corporations' power to determine milk prices became a problem for dairy farmers. At the same time that food corporations like Borden operated at a profit, the prices paid to farmers fell to levels well below immediate operating expenses and prohibited Wisconsin dairymen (and farmers throughout the United States with very similar stories) from meeting their heavy tax burdens and paying down their sizable debt. When the national economy crashed in 1929, farmers witnessed rampant foreclosures and the forced removal of families from their land. They believed in the sacrifices they had made but did not recognize what they gained during the war as profit. Although farmers made these sacrifices at the Wilson administration's request and Hoover purportedly dismissed them, the poem obliges the Roosevelt administration to make things right: wrest control of agriculture from corporations and place it back in farmers' hands.

In November 1932, the Milk Pool petitioned Wisconsin governor-elect (and Madison mayor) Albert G. Schmedeman, outgoing President Hoover, and the incoming Congress for cooperative marketing agreements with corporations "based in and on individually controlled ownership." The declaration and petition linked the Milk Pool's cause to master narratives of nation building. The Milk Pool exalted fallen Union soldiers and President Lincoln for sacrificing their lives in defense of the Homestead Act, so that "this Nation and these people should be forever free." According to the Milk Pool, the ruinously depressed agricultural market threatened to undo the practices on which the nation's bounty, so "unstintingly" given by God, and republicanism relied: "We declare it to be our firm and unalterable conviction that, as land owners and occupants,—i.e. owner-tillers of the soil—we constitute the foundation upon which the whole modern structure of private ownership of property rests in this country and, moreover, that as our Constitutional system of government is based in the private and the individual ownership of property that it, too, rests in the same foundation."[10] Indeed, dairymen's cultivation of their private property constituted much of Wisconsin's economy, inscribed its geography and its people, and so its identity. Wisconsin ranked first in the nation in dairy production.[11] In 1930, 47 percent of the population lived in rural areas, and more than one-quarter of residents were employed in agriculture or agriculture-related industries.[12] Throughout the 1930s, dairy products and agricultural implements ranked as the fifth, the sixth, and the seventh most valuable manufactured products for the state, and dairy farms dominated the landscape: "about 200,000 farms [occupied] three-fifths of all the land in the State . . . crowned by the richest dairy development in the world." The cow population was equal to 70 percent of Wisconsin's human population.[13] When the state slogan first appeared on Wisconsin automobile license plates in 1940, it proclaimed the state as "America's Dairyland."[14] In response to the Milk Pool's petition, Governor-elect Schmedeman pledged to back dairymen: "you may rest assured that it, and the other suggestions in your letter will have my earnest support."[15]

Regarding the extinction of the American farmer through his loss of property, the Milk Pool's 1932 resolution states, "[W]e are inexorably pressing thirty million of farm people back into serfage, which, relatively [sic] to them, is worse than slavery." The assessment of serfdom may seem disproportionate relative to the horrors of slavery. But the rights of white men are discussed in this statement, as racism was entrenched in the conception of "farmer." Take, for instance, Governor Schmedeman's address of May 25, 1933 (given six days after the May strike ended and two days before the World's Fair opened in Chicago) commemorating the eighty-fifth anniversary of Wisconsin's statehood: "This year, too, marks as the 300th anniversary of the coming of the first white man to Wisconsin. . . . the men and women who followed this man sought to make this land their home and its transformation into that which we now see about us leaves indelibly recorded on the pages of history a story of toil, privation and fortitude."[16] The governor's history does not mention the removal of Indians from lands and onto policed reservations, supplanting that reality with a Jeffersonian narrative of farmers' cultivation of the nation. As we will see, the state and the Milk Pool iterated this racist imagination, which configures "farmers" through white masculinity and erases Indians from the hegemonic conception of "American," by failing to acknowledge the participation of Oneida men as strikers and Menominee men as deputies during the protest.

The particular history of dairymen in Wisconsin amplified for them the effects of the loss of self-rule that accompanied ceding control over agriculture. William Rubin, attorney for the Milk Pool, voiced concern to A. R. Sanna of the Federal Surplus Relief Corporation: "Washington does not understand the complexion of the Wisconsin people. Its farmers are mainly German and Scandinavian, who evaluate property and private property rights to the tantamount degree."[17] The ancestors of Wisconsin farmers had fled feudal structures to realize the autonomy and greater equality tied directly to farming land in the United States. A number of these German descendants had families who had escaped from a failed democratic revolution in the mid-nineteenth century; for them, a straight line ran from European feudalism to contemporary fascism. Like many farmers throughout the United States, under the Homestead Act, the immigrant parents and grandparents of Wisconsin farmers had earned ownership of lands through their labor, lands initially exempted from seizure against debt. When President Lincoln spoke of the proposed act, he stated that "the wild lands of the country should be distributed so that every man should have the means and opportunity of benefitting his condition."[18] While the 1933 rural landscape of Wisconsin seemed to embody American ideals, farm foreclosures and the resultant transformation of farms from family owned to corporate businesses also suggested that the corporations were invading the preserve of American democracy.

By 1933, farmers needed, and demanded, intervention by federal and state governments, but they were also wary of government paternalism. The New Deal's proposed AAA threatened farmers' basic autonomy. An April 10, 1933, editorial in the national publication *Hoard's Dairyman* summed up these farmers' problem with the act: "The bill, in reality, makes the Secretary of Agriculture a dictator in the field of farming.... We may well ask, can any group of men formulate a plan that will meet the approval of millions of farmers who, in many instances, are farmers because they have been permitted to carry on their industry in their own way and to express their own individuality?" According to *Hoard's Dairyman*, the proposed farm bill did not merely benefit large farming enterprises to the detriment of small farms: it risked farmers' control over their daily labor practices. The AAA threatened how men realized the discourse of producerism through their bodies. These rural men likened their labor and land with self-determination, which is the measure of the democratic subject and so a central tenet of American masculinity.

The discourse of the farm as the basis for American meritocracy and of the farmer as a nature-bred ideal citizen adhered to the Milk Pool. Milk Pool members were not alone in believing in the superior morality or masculinity of dairymen. Nor were these dairymen simply paranoid about their self-determination slipping as they became increasingly marginalized in the national economy. However, the transition from a producer to a consumer economy, from an agricultural nation to a manufacturing one, and from rural to urban majorities was ongoing and ideologically vexed. Agribusiness as we know it—dairies consisting of thousands of cows—was embryonic in 1930s Wisconsin. It existed in manufacturing, processing, and distribution, but not in production. Even well-off dairymen tended to maintain only a few dozen cows.[19] In the midst of the Depression, food producers throughout the country faced a "growing conviction on the part of many influential citizens, politicians, and scholars that there were too many farmers on the land . . . that the best interests of society would be served if those far down the economic ladder were persuaded or forced to abandon the land and migrate to the cities."[20] Concurrent with this emergent desire (from nonfarmers) for the efficiencies of factory-style agriculture was the fitting of urban men to a model of masculinity based in agricultural practice.[21] Farmers were considered to be the real deal: the noble capitalist who earned capital and land through his own labor in the interest of providing for the nation.

In fact, it is rare to find a public or private statement against the May Milk Pool strike (voiced both before and after) that does not express gratitude to the farmers. The *Milwaukee Sentinel,* in an April 18, 1933, article, "Peace Parley on Milk Starts," included the following "statistics": "Look here. Here is the milk receipt for Ole Ellefson, Cameron, for two weeks. He worked more than 60 years carving a home out of the wilderness. His return for 3,118 pounds of milk was $14.51 in cash and a credit of $1.17 for butter, a total of $16.22 for two weeks' work." On May 12, the *Marshfield Herald* article "Preparing for the Holiday" declared, "No one can deny that the farmers [*sic*] cause is just. They produce the food for the nation. Theirs is a noble calling and they produce a basic commodity." Urban citizens and public officials also wrote to members of the Roosevelt administration urging the federal government to improve dairymen's income. Earl Young's letter to Secretary Wallace expressed the consensus regarding the negative economic and political consequences of a strike: "I believe a strike at this time would be injurious to both the Administration and the Farmers, and we all know that the Farmers cant [*sic*] afford to take this chance."[22] Though city residents, such as Young, expressed the thought that dairymen needed to exercise patience and give the new administration time to effect changes, they also express deep concern for farmers' livelihood. When well-respected labor mediator Harry Bragarnick agreed to facilitate talks between the state and the Milk Pool in the interest of preventing the May strike, he wrote Milwaukee's mayor Daniel Hoan: "The farmers are the people on whom we in the cities really depend upon for our living. . . . While factories have been cloased [*sic*] and men lost the right to earn a living the farmers continued to produce food for us so that we might have a plentiful supply at all time."[23] From the end of the nineteenth century, the number of U.S. farmers decreased as the nation shifted toward a manufacturing economy. The Great Depression and the AAA threatened those remaining farmers, who had *chosen* the noble vocation of agriculture. For Bragarnick and others, the loss of these men as farmers threatened to weaken the moral backbone of the nation, just as the failure to acknowledge indebtedness to the farmer was symptomatic of moral vulnerability.

Setting Expectations for the May Strike

The First Milk Pool Strike

The Milk Pool had recently been incorporated in April 1932, and Albert G. Schmedeman assumed the office of governor on January 2, 1933, so they were somewhat unknown factors to the public at the time of the May strike. The major incident that informed these parties' emergent reputations was a February 1933 strike staged by the Milk Pool.

The Milk Pool had delayed a proposed December 1932 strike to see what help the new Congress might offer. When none came, Milk Pool president Walter Singler ordered a February "withholding" action, which he declined to call a "strike." Instead, he decided to do what, he claimed, the state and federal governments failed to: he set milk prices at $1.40 per hundredweight (the cost of its production) and declared that, beginning on February 15, 1933, dairymen would not sell below that price.[24] For one week, February 15–22, Milk Pool members attempted to take control of farm prices by mimicking tactics that the Farmers' Holiday Association had used in Iowa in August 1932; that strike had resulted in an 80 percent price increase to Sioux City-area dairymen.[25]

This strike, however, proved ineffectual at raising prices. The action was localized due to what William Rubin, attorney for the Milk Pool, privately referred to as the Milk Pool's "sudden, over-night attempt to organize and strike."[26] A number of the Milk Pool's local units did not have sufficient time to organize participation in the February action because they had not received adequate notice of a county planning meeting.[27] Finally, despite the pool's ambushing of trucks, milk continued to move to factories throughout the state; the withholding mostly affected smaller processing plants in the Fox River Valley where the Milk Pool had a large membership.

In February, physical encounters between county deputies and strikers had displayed a certain civility. Milk Pool members had set up blockades on roads and highways to stop trucks, took milk cans off the trucks, poured out the milk, and then replaced the cans onto the trucks. A number of dairy plants opted to close to avoid confrontation, and county deputies enforced order. The strike in May was a different story. One journalist contrasted the violence of the May strike to the neighborly tenor of the February action: "To those who were on the firing line in the February battle, it is apparent that law enforcement agencies do not intend to be lenient with the pickets [now]. There is no longer the good-natured bantering between deputies and strikers and no mingling of the forces."[28] After one week of strike activity, Governor Schmedeman called a conference with leaders of Wisconsin farm organizations to set truce terms. On February 22, twenty-one leaders, including Walter Singler; Arnold Gilberts, president of the Farmers' Holiday Association Wisconsin branch; and prominent citizens like publisher Harry Hoard signed a resolution that acknowledged "their full appreciation of the Wisconsin Milk Pool in its active and effective withholding of farm commodities." The governor shook hands with Singler and publicly pledged to advocate on farmers' behalf to the incoming Roosevelt administration. The performances at the close of the February strike cast Milk Pool men as heroes and placed the governor in the service of these producers.

But the February strike truce came with a caveat: the Milk Pool promised a greater show of strength if the federal government did not meet farmers' demands. The Milk Pool consented to halt all strike activity during the transition from the Hoover administration to the incoming Roosevelt administration and as long as the new government included cost of production guarantees in its proposed AAA legislation. At the same time, the February Milk Pool strike steeled the conviction of Milo Reno, president of the National Farmers' Holiday Association, that a national action was the only means to secure federal support of agriculture.[29] The Milk Pool determined to strike with the Holiday Association, which was orchestrating a national withholding of all agricultural commodities in some forty states, "in the event that the incoming National Administration fails to fulfill its pledges to agriculture, [if it fails to give] to agriculture that which it grants to all other industries, the cost of production."[30]

From February 22, 1933, to what would be the start of the Milk Pool protest on May 13, print publications, intentionally or not, hyped the Wisconsin Cooperative Milk Pool strike scheduled for May 1, 1933. The set date and time for the strike's resumption inspired endgame sce-

narios in state and city newspapers and agriculture periodicals. They
juxtaposed the May deadline against questions about whether state-
facilitated price agreements between milk producers and dealers could
avert a strike, regardless of what Washington might do. Almost every
piece of correspondence to and from Washington, discussions between
Milk Pool and state officials (of those retained in the archives), and the
groups' preparations for action appeared in newspapers. State officials
worked to fulfill the governor's February pledge to Milk Pool members,
and the press reported these efforts. Within a week of the strike truce,
Harry Bragarnick began negotiating terms to avoid a strike in May.
Bragarnick immediately invited Milwaukee dairies and producer cooperatives to a conference to work out pricing agreements. On March 6,
1933, Governor Schmedeman outlined the problems in Wisconsin before
the just-inaugurated President Roosevelt and U.S. governors. Governor
Schmedeman also formed a state dairy committee, on which Singler
served; at their March 21 meeting, they unanimously voted to grant Schmedeman "extraordinary powers" to fix dairy prices.[31] At the beginning
of April, Schmedeman sent his chief advisor Leo Crowley to Washington with materials that proposed national solutions to the economic
emergency in dairying for Secretary of Agriculture Wallace's benefit.

By mid-April, columns updating the strike situation ran daily
throughout Wisconsin. And from one day to the next, the ground seemed
to shift. Headlines represented the National Farmers' Holiday Association's and the Milk Pool's growing power and determination as time
moved toward the association's national convention scheduled to take
place in Des Moines on May 3, at which time delegates from throughout
the country would vote on a national strike action.

Milk as the Stakes of the Conflict

During these weeks, the Milk Pool and the state capitalized on milk's
unmatched moral force as "indispensible to the human race and the
keystone of the food arch."[32] Yet the strike was not exactly over milk. In
actuality, Wisconsin did and did not provide the nation with milk; most
of the milk produced in Wisconsin, roughly 75 percent, was used for
the manufacture of cheese, butter, and other processed products. More

significantly, the Milk Pool dairymen's merchandise was and was not milk. Most Milk Pool dairymen did not produce milk for the fluid (that is, drinking) milk market; they sold their milk for processed dairy goods. The cultural significance of milk, however, rendered it the ideal symbol for the dairymen's fight, as well as for the state government's requests for federal aid. When Governor Schmedeman appealed to President Roosevelt on behalf of Wisconsin's dairymen at the March 6 Conference of Governors of the United States, he stated, "The milk that flows to the great centers of population from the dairy farms of Wisconsin is the very life blood of rural Wisconsin and the mother lode of our agricultural prosperity. . . . [I]t is upon the solvency of the farmer that industry and the urban population must depend, both for profit and the fundamental necessities of life itself."[33] Schmedeman emphasized milk as the source of agricultural prosperity with words such as "flows," "mother," and "life," while leaving unmentioned other dairy products. Similarly, the Milk Pool appealed for consumer support by publicizing that, during the upcoming May withholding action, "Our merchandise—MILK—will continue to be available to you and for your use without interruption."[34]

In their public appeals to economic logic, the Milk Pool asserted producers' rights to a "reasonable profit" because the commodity they produced was essential to well-being. In a *Wisconsin State Journal* interview, Ingvald Quam rhetorically asked, "Is a storekeeper considered a traitor to his country because he decides to let an article stay on his shelf rather than sell it to you below cost?"[35] Quam inverts accusations against Milk Pool dairymen for being un-American because of the moral implications involved in withholding milk by affirming the Americanness of capitalist exchange. The implied answer to Quam's question is "no," thus compelling readers to consider the moral contradictions of commodifying a necessity. The Milk Pool and the state treated milk as if it were a public good, recognizing the impossibility of regarding milk as the same type of commodity as nylons, automobiles, or chocolate. The Milk Pool's demand for "cost of production," not even or always "plus a reasonable profit," iterated dairymen's moral vocation to produce. On the one hand, dairymen's association with fluid milk elevated the Milk Pool members' status as ideal citizens. On the other hand, Milk Pool dairymen leveraged their widely acknowledged rights to a just price on milk's status and were complicit in (even as they fought against) the disparate pricing system that valued milk relative to its use by consumers; manufacturers purchased raw milk to bottle for distribution as drinking milk at a significantly higher price than they purchased raw milk for processing into cheese, butter, and condensed milk.

Belief in fluid milk as essential to building superior Americans was unequivocal, and it affected state and federal agricultural policies. The Wisconsin legislature treated fluid milk "virtually as a public utility" by enacting a minimum price law on the product to ensure its continued production during the Depression.[36] At the federal level, the USDA also treated fluid milk in this manner by making pricing agreements an immediate priority. From 1933 to 1939, this pricing system became codified through the work of the USDA, which began regulating fluid milk prices, while leaving the pricing of manufactured dairy products to supply and demand. In 1933 and at the request of the powerful Pure Milk Association cooperative, Agricultural Adjustment Administration officials brokered the first milk pricing agreements between producers and distributors in the Chicago milkshed. In his speech at the Chicago World's Fair, Wallace heralded these pricing agreements as a major achievement of the new administration. The success of these agreements, however, varied for different producers due to the local politics of cooperatives; competition between Illinois, Wisconsin, and other out-of-state producers; and cut-rate dealers operating outside city limits. Not until 1934 would Wallace announce that, once the fluid milk market had stabilized, the AAA would expand the agenda of pricing agreements to include manufactured dairy products. This goal, however, was never realized. In 1937, the USDA took control of dairy markets nationally via AAA legislation that gave the federal government authority to set minimum prices for fluid milk. In 1939, the two-price system was fully institutionalized in new milk marketing orders; federal milk marketing orders continue to determine milk prices today.[37] Just as the Milk Pool and the state used the rhetoric of milk to set it above other foods, they also affirmed the legitimacy of the two-price system in milk markets by positioning fluid milk as a prize worth protecting.

During prestrike negotiations, both the state and the Milk Pool accorded milk the status of a right for children and the infirm. A conference between Arnold Gilberts, Leo Crowley, and Milwaukee health commissioner Dr. John Koehler resulted in assurances that milk would be delivered safely to hospitals and children: "Each child 8 years of age or under is entitled to one quart of milk per day during the holiday."[38] Similar agreements were generated in towns and cities throughout Wisconsin. The state's plan permitted the white-cross trucks to distribute milk. Not only did the Farmers' Holiday Association and the Milk Pool agree to let these "public welfare" relief trucks pass through picket lines, but they also offered to supply free milk to these vulnerable populations and the poor. Walter Singler also announced that the Milk Pool would offer milk for purchase on farms. Given this offer, Singler argued that "There is no excuse for any Milwaukee consumer to buy milk from any dairy company during the farm holiday."[39] Availability of milk on farms restructured the dairy processing and distribution system, if only temporarily, by reestablishing the traditional agrarian relationship between producer and consumer.

State regulation of milk during the strike required extraordinary measures by citizens to ensure their supply. Consumers either had to stock up or register with the state Board of Health. Although Health Commissioner Koehler was working with federal health officials to develop a milkless diet, reports of prestrike hoarding quickly followed the governor's proclamation that, during the strike, all plants would be closed. Consumers' responses to the threat of an immediate shortage suggested that a viable substitute for milk seemed implausible.[40] On May 13, the *Milwaukee Sentinel* featured a picture of grocer Gust Blatz "dispensing several days' supply of farm products to Miss Dorothy Hendricks." (Another photograph depicted farmers' rushed attempts to deliver milk to the Luick Dairy plant before the suspension of deliveries began at midnight on May 13, 1933.) That same day, the *Marshfield News-Herald* ran the report "Housewives Are Hoarding Milk, Butter and Eggs." In the article, store supplies of fresh and condensed milk in Milwaukee were said to have been exhausted quickly the day before the strike. One grocer stated that a year's supply had been bought up in one day. In the same edition, anecdotes of the first "Echoes of the Strike" reiterated consumers' rush on groceries and featured the tale of a local woman who unthinkingly "placed a bottle of buttermilk in the lunch box of her milk-loving husband, upon whom the full significance of the agrarian revolt did not dawn until he placed the bottle to his lips at lunch-time."

Singler's call for ethical consumerism and the governor's requirement that citizens register for welfare milk infused consumers' actions during the protest with moral implications. By motivating spectators to make consumption choices, the Milk Pool strike extends Susan Leigh Foster's choreographic paradigm of protest, in which protesters' collective movements induce ideological performances.[41] Foster argues that protesters' bodies compel authorities and spectators to make physical choices in response. The spectators' and authorities' responses reveal the systemic meanings of their everyday actions. This model requires close proximity. The sprawling nature of Milk Pool protest activity created varied proximities of spectator to protester and to the state. Milk's indispensability, however, contained its own compelling force for consumers, and agreements between the state and the Milk Pool that ensured access to milk as a fundamental right transformed the buying and selling at farms, roadside stands, dairy plants, and grocery stores into ethical acts. Consumers had to choose how, and from whom, they would purchase dairy products. In doing so, they physically acted out complicity with or dissent from the status quo (even if consumers' choices were based on a complex set of factors that exceeded the immediate conflict).

Prospects of and Plans to Prevent Civic Violence

State authorities issued plans to prevent civic violence between strikers and nonstriking farmers while also protecting consumer entitlements to milk. The state's preemptive actions simultaneously produced the need for armed guards and suggested that welfare milk and citizens were vulnerable to strikers. The bulk of the executive orders issued by Governor Schmedeman centered on safe milk delivery to vulnerable populations: families with children, hospitals, and elderly and disabled persons. All such persons were to preregister with the state Board of Health. The governor "charge[d] sheriffs and district attorneys of the various counties to facilitate without molestation or interference, the transportation of milk for such purposes."[42] On May 12, the day before the strike, Adjutant General Ralph Immell, the commander of the Wisconsin National Guard, estimated for the *Daily Northwestern* that, in some counties, "a minimum of 200 deputies are necessary to start this plan and that these patrols would have to be augmented in proportion to the activities of belligerents."[43] Meanwhile, Wisconsin Attorney General J. E. Finnegan defined legal "peaceable picketing" for the public: "Peaceable picketing is the mere act of inviting attention to the existence of a strike as by signs or banners and the seizure or destruction of property or the use of force or the use of threats and the calling of vile names is not peaceable picketing." The attorney general elaborated that "the blocking of roads so as to prohibit the transportation of persons and merchandise" constituted a "violation of peaceable picketing."[44] Strike instructions given to sheriffs by Adjutant General Immell included a reminder that strikers and deputies were neighbors: "You are dealing with people in your community who will be with you during your lifetime."[45] Singler publicly ordered strikers to follow the rule of law: "All farmers in every territory are to withhold all farm produce peaceably on the farm. Any picketing that may be done must be done in conformance with constitutional rights, in peaceful form. While farmers may assemble and ask trucks to stop, they cannot use any obstruction. The highways must be kept clear."[46] While such statements assured continued civility on the part of the state and the strikers, along with milk regulations, they also distinguished some milk as a commodity, not a necessity.

The prospect of civic violence between Wisconsin farmers over milk dumping in May arose from economic competition among dairymen in Wisconsin and was fostered through the use of media by Schmedeman's office and the Milk Pool. On April 17 and 18, Wisconsin papers widely reprinted an Associated Press report in which Bragarnick warned that a strike would result in "bloodshed" and his faith that "somewhere there is a solution without farmer fighting farmer." The two-price dairy market system created two classes of dairymen. Dairymen living near major cities—Madison, Milwaukee, and Chicago—cornered the fluid milk market. On the other hand, the milk of more rural dairymen, such as those in the Milk Pool, commanded less than half the price received for fluid milk. One fluid milk dairyman described the resentment that existed: "The inner-ring farmers who belonged to the Milwaukee Milk Producers and the Pure Milk Association tended to be larger, relatively prosperous farmers who 'despised' farmers who were '[Milk] Pool-minded.'"[47] If a strike were to occur, major interstate markets for both processed dairy products and fluid milk, such as Chicago, might respond by sourcing from elsewhere. Those who sold to fluid milk markets had relatively secure positions that they did not want to see endangered by a strike. Just as Bragarnick called on Gilberts and Singler to join him in a second "peace conference," Gilberts ordered 130,000 Wisconsin Farmers' Holiday Association members to back the Milk Pool and withhold their products. Meanwhile, the Milk Pool organized "'flying squadrons' whose aim will be to tie up completely all movements of [nonstriking farmers'] dairy products from the farm to markets." On April 19, Singler declared before five thousand farmers that "the strike will proceed as planned unless adequate legislative relief is obtained before May 13." A United Press report followed two days later; papers throughout the state led the report with headlines such as "Probable Need for National Guard in Farm Strike Seen" and "National Guard May Be Called for Milk Strike."[48]

Following the reported failure of Bragarnick's second peace conference, it was becoming clear that only federal action—particularly, cost of production provisions in the AAA—would stop the national strike. Bragarnick wired President Roosevelt "[urging] that the federal administration give full consideration to dairy products in its farm relief program and that this program be speeded. Serious trouble was averted in the strike on milk in Wisconsin in February by a truce founded on the pledge of legislative aid." In Milwaukee, Mayor Hoan's radio address to farmers on April 28 resulted in a total breakdown of state mediation. Hoan stated that a strike would ruin Wisconsin farmers. He based his comments on a report prepared by Bragarnick. Singler then publicly refused to negotiate any longer with Bragarnick, stating that the mayor's speech showed that Bragarnick could not be trusted as a neutral party and that the state was protecting the interests of milk corporations.[49]

By April 30, everything in Wisconsin depended on how Holiday Association delegates would vote at their May 3, 1933, convention. There, Milo Reno delivered a mixed message. He demanded that the federal government pass two laws, which he deemed more important than all others:

First, that society recognize, by legislative enactment, that the production of human food is a public service and is basically so, and this being true, the farmer is entitled to production costs estimated by the same methods used by the interstate commerce commission in adjusting railroad rates and tariffs, public utilities and so forth.

Second, that no nation or civilization can continue a prosperous and happy existence with the economic life blood of that nation controlled by a bunch of usurers and it should be the uncompromising demand of this organization that the congress of the United States take back its constitutional right.[50]

Yet Reno also advised farmers to allow time for the new government to act. Despite his urging, Holiday Association delegates voted to call a national embargo on farm commodities to begin at 12:01 AM on Saturday, May 13, 1933. Papers ran articles about the probable rejection by the U.S. House of Representatives of a cost of production amendment to the farm bill. In his May 9 radio address, Bragarnick reminded listeners of the "broken faith of friends and neighbors" as a result of the February strike; he asked them to see reason and follow Reno, not Singler: "Last week at Des Moines, Milo Reno, National President of the Farmers' Holiday Association, pleaded with the farmer to give the United States Government, through the Dept. of Agriculture, a reasonable chance to act. . . . But Walter Singler was not willing to wait or cooperate. He urged the farmer to strike and when a vote was taken the poor farmers who were *inspired by Singler's oratory* and promises, followed this leader and voted to strike."[51] According to Braganick, neither Reno's prominence nor his rational argument for patience could match Singler's oratory. Singler's performance was apparently powerful enough to persuade Farmers' Holiday Association delegates from the Midwest and from as far away as Maryland and New Mexico to vote to strike.

On May 11, two days before the strike was scheduled, Governor Schmedeman justified the state's (potential) use of force in a preface to his executive order by stating that "methods of intimidation" were being used by strike organizers against "unsympathetic" dairymen and businessmen.[52] His strategy entailed six measures, all of which regarded milk transported during the strike. First, he ordered state-wide closure of all cheese factories, condensaries, milk distribution plants, and creameries. This constituted a preemptive removal of the trucks carrying nonstriking farmers' milk from the roads, apparently to avert milk dumping and physical conflict between farmers. However, dairymen did not necessarily haul their own milk; corporate drivers would transport milk from farm to plant. Four orders, mentioned in the previous section, pertained to regulation and safe transport of welfare milk. The governor's sixth order stated that dairymen could, "by petition or any other convenient means" that demonstrated their majority, call for the reopening of the plants of which they were patrons and receive police protection during delivery. Ostensibly, the governor deferred to farmers' self-determination. He would act as they wished and support the dairymen by keeping plants closed if they agreed with the Milk Pool. Conversely, if farmers wanted to sell their dairy products to distributors and processors, he would use his power to protect their right to do so. Through these measures, Schmedeman created the opportunity for farmers' not to support strikers, but he also muddied the terms of what and who the state was protecting. The strike contest shifted from a civil conflict between equal forces (that is, Milk Pool dairymen and nonstriking dairymen) to an unequal conflict, the armed, powerful state against striking farmers. Together, these orders meant that, when the strike began, all dairy plants would be closed, unless dairymen petitioned the state to reopen them. However, his announcement of the upcoming closure of all plants gave dairymen an incentive to sign petitions because of the likelihood of spoilage. Unlike other agricultural products, which could be stored for months, milk is produced and goes to market twice a day. Most farmers lacked the capacity to store their milk. A closed plant meant that farmers would experience immediate losses.[53]

Articles about petition signing by noncooperating farmers filled the presses in the days immediately preceding the strike. Associated Press reports stated that farmers in Kenosha, Burlington, Appleton, La-Crosse, and Sheboygan were circulating petitions seeking the reopening of plants in their areas.[54] Likewise, the *Wisconsin State Journal* reported that the Madison Milk Producers' Association had signed petitions to reopen plants. Meanwhile, numerous dairy plants were reported to have ignored the governor's decree and were determined to remain open despite mandated state-wide closure. The governor's office received reports stating that the Dairy Distributors, Inc., of Milwaukee refused to stop distributing milk to its regular customers.[55] Milk Pool leaders

questioned the authenticity of the petitions and called upon the state
to enforce the governor's strike mandates. The governor's office refused
Milk Pool officials' request to review the documents.[56] By the time the
evening edition of the *Daily Northwestern* was issued on the first full day
of strike activity, May 13, the governor had "reopened" plants for milk
deliveries in all but nineteen of Wisconsin's seventy-one counties, and
Adjutant General Immell predicted that ten more counties would be
reopened by Monday, May 15.[57] The counties that the governor initially
kept closed were Milk Pool strongholds. Within hours of the strike's
start, trucks were (again) hauling milk.

Leaders of the Opposing Factions:
Singler vs. Schmedeman

The public personae of Walter Singler and Albert Schmedeman informed how the public, state officials, and the press interpreted the encounters between the state and the dairymen throughout the May strike.
Heroes of war, at least how they tend to be conceived of in canonical
tragedies, epics, and histories, exceed the qualities of common men.
Public representations of Singler, and by contrast Schmedeman, faithfully reproduce this long-standing convention.

Walter Singler embodied the American farmer as autonomous,
moral, and masculine. By numerous accounts, Singler exuded "It": that
seemingly innate and incomparable charisma and allure. Performance
scholar Joseph Roach describes this unique quality as "emerging from
an apparently singular nexus of personal quirks, irreducible to type, yet,
paradoxically, the epitome of a type or prototype that almost everyone
eventually wants to see or be like."[58] And just as persons with "It" are
apt to do, according to Roach, Singler attracted both disciples and media attention. Singler embodied, or was represented as embodying, ideals of American manliness such as self-control, ambition, self-reliance,
athleticism, valor, and a strong work ethic. And he was not only the
exemplar of the American man in this respect; he also distinguished
himself through his manner and dress.[59] From accessories to hair to
clothes, Roach argues that appearance is vital to producing the contradictory qualities necessary for "It," so elusive to the rest of us. Descrip-

tions of Singler's magnetism and skill as an orator were fixtures in the press. These commentaries on his character are also remarkable for the attention given to his physical appearance.

Physically, Singler exhibited the athleticism much admired in film stars, football players, and pugilists of the era. When the Milk Pool elected him as president, he was thirty-seven years old. His age set him apart from Albert Schmedeman and Milo Reno, both of whom were Singler's senior by a full generation. Singler stood at over six-feet tall and weighed more than two hundred pounds. He had thick black hair and a trimmed toothbrush mustache and goatee.

Young men copied Singler: "In many communities of this region [Sheboygan and northeastern Wisconsin] Walter M. Singler is fast assuming the proportions of a hero. So he is being emulated. Numerous youths are doing their best to grow goatees, like the one the strike chief wears." Singler's size—noted in regional and national media—highlighted his unconventional sartorial style. His clothing signified not merely the self-made man but also the man-made nation. He dressed in a waistcoat, spats, and cowboy hat among men commonly attired in flat caps, denim, and boots. The hat nodded to his time in Texas outside his home state of Wisconsin. Nearly twenty years after the strikes, one reporter recalled that Singler's "costume and appearance were those of a circus barker rather than a farmer, and by rights the farmers should have hooted him out of town. Instead, they practically worshipped him."[60]

Implications that Singler was a communist may have been a media ploy designed to heighten tension or just plain red-baiting, but they also gave Milk Pool supporters cause to profess Singler's patriotism. In various estimates, his performances were taken as his very nature and given as evidence of his Americanness. At the beginning of March 1933, Milk Pool attorney William B. Rubin responded to a query from Harry A. Jung regarding Singler's politics; the national media had characterized Singler's speech to the Wisconsin legislature after the February 1933 strike as "militant," causing Jung (founder of the anticommunist American Vigilant Intelligence Federation) some concern. Rubin reassured Jung that Singler was an American by detailing Singler's manliness: "Mr. Singler, [sic] is destined to become one of the great leaders in this country. Nature has endowed him with a physique, with a brain and

power of espression [*sic*], which make for leadership. He is unspoiled by
non-opportunity for over-schooling."[61] Singler's intelligence, perceived
through his oratorical and rhetorical capacity, matched his imposing
physical stature. His "common-man" history—one lacking the femi-
nizing privilege associated with college-educated men—reinforced the
sense that he possessed uncommon ability. In an editorial titled "Support of Every Loyal American Citizen," Clarence R. Hathaway, editor
of the *Hartford* [Wisconsin] *Times,* disputed negative depictions of Singler: "We believe that those that have pictured Mr. Singler as a Red, an
agitator, a communist, do the gentleman a great wrong and surely they
do not understand the man. He is perhaps justified in becoming hot under the collar once in a while. . . . Mr. Singler carries a happy, reassuring
smile as he speaks. He has a twitching dimple in either cheek that flashes
as he talks, and disarms any dangerous statements that might have been
made against the man."[62] Hathaway's excitement appears to be based on
the fact that Singler's "contradictory" qualities seem "suspended at the
tipping point," similar to the allures of other celebrities.[63] Singler's performances hung between radicalism and patriotism and balanced world-
liness with folksiness. In a puff piece published after the end of the May
strike, a description of Singler's appearance characterizes him as a native
son returned: "A former automobile salesman and oil well promoter, he
returned to run the farm of his elderly parents on the outskirts of this
village of a thousand people three years ago." The article continues with a
description of Singler's wife, Nell, that shows Singler to be a family man,
but not uncomplicatedly so: "Singler met his wife—his second—while
visiting in Paducah, KY., three years ago. She was a slim and attractive
widow with a six-year-old son. Shicton considers her its best-dressed
woman."[64] The handsome couple, both exceptional specimens of their
genders, is presented as both admirable and potentially scandalous.

Singler, like many who have "It," produced the sense that he was
"unbiddable" because his performances were as militant as his rhetoric.[65] While he subscribed to the same politics as many of his fellow
farm movement leaders, he possessed an explosive style that generated
power. In a *Milwaukee Sentinel* article describing the major players scheduled to attend the April "peace conference" held to avert the May strike,
Wisconsin Farmers' Holiday Association president Arnold Gilberts is

described with relative affability as "a youthful, fervent farm leader, who has something of the evangelist in his farm relief pleas." In distinction, Singler is reputed to be "firebrand of the farmers favoring revolt."[66] Singler's rhetoric was, indeed, militant in the sense that he continually employed violent metaphors to insist that empty political promises and doomsday economic scenarios could not deter the Milk Pool. In nearly the same breath, Singler showed compassion, reason, and militancy: he "request[ed] milk pool members to refrain from violence" during the strike, offered free milk to consumers, and declared "Milk is the club we will use to achieve our aims."[67] During the strike, Adjutant General Immell ordered Arthur M. Evans to keep Singler "under surveillance and report any of his private or public utterances which might be construed as inciting to riot, as un-American, etc." Evans, working undercover, reported that Singler and other Milk Pool officials continually warned strikers against violence.[68] After allegations that communists were attempting to participate in the May strike in Oshkosh, Singler stated that the Milk Pool would not allow "red agitators" into their ranks.[69] Milk Pool farmers' picked up and enacted Singler's performative utterances by charging into the climatic May battle waving the American flag.

In January 1934, *Fortune Magazine* chronicled the contemporary Midwest farm revolt. The article devoted considerable space to describing agrarian leaders, as well as state and federal officials. John Bosch (vice president of the Farmers' Holiday Association), John Simpson (president of the Farmers' Union), and Milo Reno were considered together. Walter Singler, however, through individual attention and a picture that took up one-quarter of the printed page, ranked in importance with Secretary of Agriculture Wallace, AAA head George Peek, and *Minneapolis Tribune* publisher Frederick Murphy. This is particularly noteworthy given that Singler led a relatively small organization in comparison to the other farm leaders and lacked the institutional power enjoyed by state and federal executives. The article's richly detailed description of Singler aligns him with great American men of the past. We learn that he is a "small town bad boy grown to six feet and several hundred pounds of adult flesh who sports his gaudily checked shirts and his Texas hats through the milk belt [and] is as native to America as the buffalo he curiously resembles."[70] The writer mocks modern comparisons of the United States to Europe and refutes associations of Singler with Fascist political leanings. His portrayal of Singler as rough, wild, and instinctual collapses the manliness of the agricultural Midwest into that of the American range, symbolized by the buffalo and the Platte River Valley, the gateway to the American frontier. He puts Singler in the company of Henry Clay, who coined the "self-made" American man and titles the article "Bryan! Bryan!! Bryan!!! Bryan!!!!" after Vachel Lindsay's 1919 poem about William Jennings Bryan.[71] Like Bryan, Singler embodied what theater historian Charlotte Canning describes as the democratizing function of oratory and populist politics that elevated agrarianism: "Public speaking had not been simply an expression of opinion. For most nineteenth-century Americans, it was the means through which patriotism's agenda could be articulated."[72] The *Fortune Magazine* article's comparison between Byran and Singler contains both deep admiration of Singler's masculine prowess—details such as Singler's "forceful personality," "magnificent bass voice," and "his thick easy shoulders" pervade the entire article—and a sense of the certain failure of Singler's and his followers' hopes for agriculture. The writer's misgiving about Singler's acceptance of contemporary economics has the quality of lament, not mockery; he is drawn in by the man, while he admits that owner-tillers are destined to become men of the past.[73]

Governor Schmedeman, *when* portrayed, was depicted as inconsequential. In tellingly indirect contrast, *Fortune Magazine* introduces Schmedeman as "[u]nhappy little Governor Schmedeman of Wisconsin." Albert Schmedeman had been a popular mayor in Madison, elected to four consecutive terms. He was a college-educated businessman who ran a successful men's clothier store. Schmedeman took over the governor's office at the age of sixty-nine, the first Democrat elected—and the first to contend legitimately against a Republican candidate—since the 1890s in Wisconsin. Republicans historically had controlled Wisconsin's state politics and its national interests because of the party's associations with individualism and Lincoln. In 1932, Wisconsin voters' values did not change so much as they followed the national trend. Likewise, they did not vote for Schmedeman so much as Democrats swept Wisconsin state elections by riding the wave of Roosevelt's promised New Deal, replacing Republican incumbents who were guilty by party affiliation with Hoover.[74]

Initially, Schmedeman seemed right for the job of governor, but this impression was short lived. He pointed with pride to his father who had been a "forty-eighter," a man who had revolted for democratic freedoms in Germany. During his 1932 campaign, Schmedeman aligned himself with Roosevelt's call for experimentalism and rhetorically reoriented Wisconsin Democrats' conservative, business-minded platform toward a more "progressive" one, using the label that belonged to La Follette Republicans, who were invested in farmers' and laborers' rights. (Despite their politics, these Republicans lost out in 1932.) As governor-elect, Schmedeman publicly pronounced as part of his gubernatorial agenda the importance of improving the incomes of farmers "forced to wage an almost superhuman battle for mere subsistence."[75] Once in office, he offered farmers relief consonant with his fiscally conservative agenda to cut state expenditures and balance Wisconsin's budget.[76] While both political opponents and associates stated that Schmedeman was fair and easy to work with, in terms of gender politics, these were backhanded compliments: "Descriptions of Governor Schmedeman by contemporary leaders and articles of the day, [sic] refer to Schmedeman as physically frail, not forceful and a weak leader not suited by temperament to dominate the affairs of men."[77]

Governor Schmedeman's time in power was short. He accounted for his loss of the 1934 election by suggesting that the amputation of his leg that year limited his ability to campaign. However, numerous historians count his loss as due to his "timidity" or his being a "reactionary": "Schmedeman's defeat was personal, to the extent that the Democratic lieutenant governor, state treasurer, and attorney-general were all returned to office in 1934."[78] Indeed, Schmedeman's conservatism amid New Deal experimentalism and his mishandling of the three 1933 Milk Pool strikes and then the 1934 Koehler strikes are reasons numerous historians give for his defeat. The public's impressions about Schmedeman as a man are also counted as reasons for his fall. From his "failed" body to his actions against farmers and laborers, Schmedeman seemed to lack the masculinity requisite of a worthy antagonist or leader.

Further, the governor's unprecedented use of the National Guard against farmers in May 1933 breached codes of masculine honor. Paradoxically, the lack of self-control associated with excessive violence also opened up Schmedeman to charges of being a puppet. After the May strike, Singler dismissed Schmedeman by stating that Leo Crowley, the governor's chief advisor, controlled Schmedeman and so governed Wisconsin. In his Milk Pool convention speech following the May strike, Singler stressed the governor's unmanly character, as he praised the integrity of dairymen. He cited use of the National Guard and claimed that the governor deputized "prisoners," who "insult[ed] women in the fields." He then declared, "We lived up to every rule in the book of etiquette . . . but every rule in the book was violated by our dictator, Mr. Crowley . . . I don't say our governor, because I don't believe he [Schmedeman] is governor."[79] Sixty years later, from the same unquestioning perspective through which several historians detail Singler's physicality and performance skill to add color to their histories, Leo Crowley's biographer Stuart Weiss noted that Crowley "managed Schmedeman as a parent might his children."[80]

The Milk Pool's rapid growth, which arguably contributed to the state's shift toward progressive leadership in 1934 was credited to Singler. By August 1934, the Milk Pool established its own processing plant and distribution system, the Milk Pool Products Cooperative, to manufacture and market proprietary dairy products. In the summer of 1932, when the Wisconsin Cooperative Milk Pool was incorporated, the pool counted 3,381 members. By the pool's second annual convention, held on June 1–2, 1933, it recorded 9,892 paid memberships. Other estimates, published around the time of the convention, put the membership total at 11,283 and 24,000.[81] Singler's followers "cheered vociferously" when he took the stage at this convention in Beaver Dam, Wisconsin. In describing Singler's speech to delegates, United Press staff correspondent William F. McIlrath wrote, "The spectacular young farmer with the black goatee and the broad brimmed hat repeatedly refused to act as chairman of the convention. Singler said he did not want it to appear that the officers were trying to steer the convention." Singler insisted that his ambition was for the men he represented. Expressing deep humility, he told the men that he would serve as they wished: "I feel that a better man, a man who is fresh, should take my place [as Milk Pool president]—and there are better men in the pool. I will be glad to help out." Singler was reelected, and his wife was elected president of the women's auxiliary.[82]

Theater of War: The May 1933 Strike

In the final days leading up to the May 1933 strike, Singler would express his implacable will when he refused to back down and follow Milo Reno's order to postpone the national strike. Reno had officially suspended the national withholding action the day before the scheduled strike to "give the Roosevelt administration an 'opportunity to fulfill pre-election pledges to the farmer.'"[83] Reno's action and Singler's response transformed the impending May strike from a national withholding of all agricultural products to one by a minority of producers, hailing from one state, and involving one type of agricultural product. These changes to the strike's conditions flattened its potential to radicalize the agriculture industry because it severely limited the protesters' advantages in the economic realm. A nationwide strike had the capacity to restructure the U.S. food system. The withdrawal of the Farmers' Holiday Association replaced the coercive possibilities of nationwide deprivation with localized inaccessibility to dairy products. Combined with the overall economic failure of the Milk Pool's February protest, the situation changed the imminent strike from a significant disruption of the food system to a symbolic act.

It is uncanny how Reno's withdrawal elevated Singler's persona to that of the tragic hero and helped instill the violence enacted against dairymen during the May strike with tragic proportions. As if following Aristotle's *Poetics*, the Wisconsin drama unfolded with a hero, who was considered "better than in actual life," a "reversal of situation," and a final "scene of suffering."[84] The abrupt disempowerment of the Milk Pool, along with Singler's warning of what would befall the Wisconsin dairymen if they carried on with their protest, was realized in scenes in which pool members were outmatched by the state's artillery. According to the Milk Pool, Milo Reno had "left the farmers with no protection or hope of retaining their markets."[85] Singler justified the Milk Pool's determination to continue without the support of Farmers' Holiday Association farmers by evoking valor in the face of overwhelming odds: "We're going to have everything or nothing," and "It's too late to stop now ... Somebody has brought pressure to bear on the National Holiday. They've brought lots of pressure to bear on us, too, but it won't bring them anything."[86] Singler romanticized the righteousness of the Milk Pool's cause by attaching it to men's heroism in the face of violence, regardless of anticipated defeat. When Milk Pool farmers proceeded alone expecting to face combat-grade weapons, the strike became not only about producers' rights but about honor. Victory no longer hinged on economic or legislative gains.

By the evening of May 13, 1933, all bets were off, but, paradoxically, many expectations were fulfilled. Singler pointed to the governor's dubious closure/reopening of dairy plants as the reason for dumping milk. Singler, reportedly, announced, "Our men in the closed counties are not going to sit still. ... The closed county men will picket the open counties and they'll picket them thoroughly. Men can travel fast and far during a strike. Milk will not go through."[87] This was a veritable declaration of war against Governor Schmedeman for his purported violation of the agreed terms under which the Milk Pool strike would be conducted. Singler promised the Milk Pool would dump milk being transported to (now open) processing plants. Former reporter Herbert Jacobs recalled what he witnessed during the protest:

> The pickets took to cars instead of camping at crossroads. They swooped down on trucks [en route to processing plants] when no guardsmen were present, dumped the loads, and vanished. Near Mukwonago I saw a new wrinkle, when pickets tossed an old harrow in front of a line of trucks to stop them by puncturing the tires. But the authorities were even more forehanded. The lead truck had a snowplow, which brushed the harrow off the road. The deputies wore gas masks when they exploded their triple-action bombs. And the pickets wore leather gloves to toss the bombs right back before they exploded.[88]

Once the governor opened some counties, trucks hauled both kinds of milk—public welfare and commodity milk—through closed counties to open ones. The state now extended its protection to nonstriking dairymen's milk. Milk Pool dairymen responded by setting up barricades and attacking trucks just beyond the limits of county deputies' authority, at county lines.

The State's Actions

On Monday, May 15, after opening the majority of counties, Governor Schmedeman ordered the National Guard into service: "The members of all units will be in civilian dress and will be prepared to serve as civil deputies to assist the sheriffs in the affected counties in maintaining law and order."[89] From the start, these men were equipped and prepared by order to use force. Adjutant General Immell and his unit commanders were extremely attentive to minimizing the guard's visibility as "the Guard." The state initially deployed guardsmen without uniforms as "civilian deputies."

Nevertheless, perception of military rule developed because of guardsmen's occupation of towns and cities throughout Wisconsin. Deployed men needed to be housed and fed in the counties where they were stationed and to run training exercises. Guard commanders sent reports to Immell's office about civilian displeasure with troop behavior: "Col. Williams called the sheriff of Juneau Co. in regard to the resentment of people at Mayville that deputies were quartered in Turner Hall. Sheriff said the fact of the matter is that they are in sympathy with the strike and are trying to squeeze the deputies out of the city." At Shiocton, where Singler resided, "a few individuals ... spoke very bitterly over the fact that the National Guard had been called out for service in the strike area." At Tess Corners, Fred J. Mattingly, troop commander in Waukesha County, ordered Captain Baumgarde to move his men to the Gridly Dairy and "not make a display of the men and weapons." Following this, he found that businessmen and community members "were very much pleased and [they] seemed to have a different feeling towards the whole situation after the men were made less conspicuous." On May 17, Captain Mattingly assured Colonel Williams that he would "see that [troops] acted in a more dignified manner." The guard's visible presence belied the governor's insistence that these men were police, not military forces.[90]

The state not only tried to make the guard look like armed civilians, but it also attempted to control media coverage. Immell asked Col. Holden, who was deployed to Shawano, to court journalists: "be careful how you handle the newspaper men up there. You might give them a little information once in a while."[91] The absence of uniforms, however, failed to inhibit media representations of military force, despite the fact that, in photographs, one is unable to tell a guardsman from an ordinary citizen. A report in the *Sheboygan Press* about a May 16 incident in Shawano stated, "Shawano resembled an armed camp although none of the deputies is in uniform. The sight of guns on the hips of guardsmen, however, seems to have taken effect."[92]

Regardless of Immell's desire for inconspicuousness, his men, or county deputies, aided in creating an image of Wisconsin as a militarized state by posing for portraits. These pictures were often published alongside photographs taken during the conflict. Four subjects dominated protest photography that circulated throughout the state and the nation: portraits, milk dumping, battle landscapes, and physical combat. Photographs exhibit a consistent style in which images tended to be either set against a landscape of milk running down the countryside or close-ups of men fighting. Portraits, field photography, and graphics in effect configured Wisconsin as not only a military occupied state but as the "Front." The *Milwaukee Sentinel* published a close-up of Sheriff Oscar C. Dettman at his desk marking troop positions and planned maneuvers with tacks and flags on a county map. The same paper also printed a map of the state showing counties numbered to designate strike activity; it referred to the territory as the "Milk Strike Front."[93] The *Milwaukee Sentinel* featured a portrait of three men in civilian clothing and gasmasks (see figure 2.1). They all hold gas bombs in their right hands, which are raised in "the throwing position." The image is jarringly dissonant. The leather masks cover the entire face; imbedded oversize goggles and a flexible tube protruding from the middle of the mask obscures the men's human features. In addition, captions for in-situ portraits—often men on top of trucks or marching in formation, looking toward the camera—grant special attention to clubs and sidearms and almost invariably mention gas.

Formal elements of strike photographs mimicked those circulated during and about the Great War, which used destroyed landscapes, the dead, and combat scenes to represent how war makes and decivilizes men. As Susan Sontag has argued, such images are not necessarily designed for pacifist purposes; they do not reveal the futility of violence so much as they offer corroborating arguments for "us" against "them"

Figure 2.1. Armed special deputies pose for newspaper photographer. "Ready for Showdown at Shawano," *Milwaukee Journal*, May 17, 1933, reproduced with permission from Journal Sentinel, Inc.

by showing glorious or ignoble ways of waging war.[94] Published images and articles represented the glory and brutality of the strike. Indeed, the lack of adjacent articles or headlines to contextualize the cartoon "Two Pictures," published on September 18, 1933, on the front-page of the *Chicago Daily Tribune*, indicates that photographs of the milk dumping in May helped define the moral implications of various dairy groups' subsequent actions (see figure 2.2). The sketch is a split scene. The bottom illustration of the innocent children and vulnerable mother suggests the horror of the protesters' actions depicted in the top panel. "Pickets seize and dump milk after battling deputies"; the words "sketched from photography" printed at the base of this image serve to verify that the depiction does not exaggerate the scene. In fact, the drawing virtually replicates a photograph published in the *Milwaukee Sentinel* on May 15, 1933. Beneath the milk dumping scene, a gaunt woman looks upward at puddles of milk on the ground; she cradles an infant and bottle. In front of her, her son looks on with confused expression. Her crying daughter clings to the back of her skirt, complaining, "I'm hungry." Chicago's reliance on Wisconsin for a sizable percentage of its fluid milk, along with the *Chicago Tribune*'s conservative editorship, might explain the focus on the costs of the strike for consumers rather than the stakes for farmers. Of course, the cartoon also captures the profound moral implications of dumping milk and the inability to recognize it as a good to be bought and sold like any other.[95]

Other photographs bore out war-style correspondences; these progress in a steady rise of complications toward a climax that ends in decisive victory or defeat. At the same time, papers frequently implied the inadequacy of farmers' artillery: "While several hundred special deputies, many of them deputized national guardsmen, patrolled highways, striker pickets . . . armed themselves with rocks and clubs in desperate efforts to block roads." More poignantly, the caption to a photograph showing picket Arthur Dreblow's arrest read, "Former soldiers and their friends are digging out the old tin hats of wartime days as protection against the clubs of deputy sheriffs in Milwaukee county."[96] On May 18, the *New York Times* recounted the last day of strike battles:

> The encounter at Appleton was apparently invited as a test of strength by the strikers, who came into town in a mile-long procession of motor cars and, as they passed the armory, taunted the guardsmen. Trucks of the guardsmen followed to the western city limits. . . . Guardsmen and deputies leaped from the trucks with sticks swinging. Dozens of gas bombs popped in the crowd, the gray vapors soon veiling the action. Strikers were soon fleeing in confusion, coughing and shielding their eyes. Guardsmen rounded up a truck full of prisoners.

Figure 2.2. Effects of milk dumping from Chicago consumer perspective. Carey Orr, "Two Pictures," *Chicago Tribune*, September 18, 1933, Carey Orr Cartoons, Special Collections Research Center, Syracuse University Libraries. Reproduced with permission from Chicago Tribune. All rights reserved. Used by permission and protected by the Copyright Laws of the United States. The printing, copying, redistribution, or retransmission of this content without express written permission is prohibited.

Strike Weapons

The Milk Pool chose milk as its primary weapon; the state chose gas. The physical properties of both, along with their historic associations, were integral to the interpretations of the strike as war in the media and by the public. As a rule, the Milk Pool did not surreptitiously destroy milk. Milk was dumped in open spaces at all times of the day on local roadways and outside dairy plants.[97] The Milk Pool's style of milk dumping in May differed from that of February. Now, pool members smashed cans and left the wreckage, marking sites of conflict. They destroyed milk in such a purposefully public, highly visible, and consistent manner to suggest conscious attention to the action's visual, auditory, olfactory, and kinesthetic dimensions. Indeed, Adjutant General Immell attributed the uniformity of protesters' manner of milk dumping to careful coordination.[98]

Milk Pool protesters tended to stand on running boards and climb into truck beds to pour milk onto roads. The milk pouring from a height created a cascade effect. The white waterfall emphasized volume and fluidity, as if a person could pass through and displace it. Our sense of fluidity mimics consumption: "When you eat you are taking an object, some other 'thing' in the world, and adding it to your being. The great distinctions between me and the so-called object world fall away."[99] As this most perfect food poured from trucks, the dumping was perceived by some as violent and destructive, not only a crime against health but violation of the moral code. Within hazy, gas-permeated scenes featuring upturned cans and rifles, milk puddles on the ground also signified bloodshed.

On the other side of the conflict, the state chose gas as deputies' and guards' primary weapons. Tear gas is designed to disperse crowds and, consequently, avoid immediate physical encounters between authorities and belligerents. The *Wisconsin State Journal* ran an article on May 15, 1933, that detailed the effects of both CN gas (chloroacetophenone or "tear gas") and CN-DM gas (diphenylaminochloroarsine or "K.O. gas") under the headline "Immell Commands State's 'War' Machine, Plenty of 'Bombs' Ready." "DM gas reduces respiration about 50 percent, acts on the stomach and intestinal tract and produces hysteria. Neither gas is fatal and neither has any lasting effects." It is not clear how or when this newspaper received information that the state had a supply of CN-DM gas. However, the state's tactic for averting greater violence resonated visually and emotionally with the merciless suffering of soldiers during World War I, maiming that breached the rules of war. Gases used in the Great War varied in potency—tear, chlorine, phosgene, and mustard gases were all used. While such gases actually caused fewer casualties than machine technologies like tanks and rapid-fire guns and both the Entente and the Triple Alliance used gas, in the United States, the haze connoted interior damage and disfigurement to the human body by the most caustic gases. These were seminal symbols of the atrocities of modern warfare committed by German soldiers. The spectacle of men wielding rocks against men wielding nightsticks, bayonets, guns, and gas bombs contradicted the visual trappings of a civil war, despite the common attire of all combatants. The apparent differences between makeshift and manufactured weapons spectacularized the repressive power of the state exacted against its own people.

Martial weapons used against dairymen armed with found objects seemed to some like an unfair fight on the most basic level. The idea of the mighty against the powerless stood in opposition to how and why Americans believed they waged wars. The Milk Pool called the state's use of the guard "Prussianized and un-American" and refused to call off the strike until the state discharged these special deputies.[100] The Milwaukee Federated Trades Council adopted resolutions that denounced Schmedeman's protection of the "milk trusts" and his deployment of the National Guard "merely disguised as special deputies."[101] On May 16, the Wisconsin Senate debated its official position on the strike. Senator Bolens (Democrat) vociferously opposed Senator Polakowski's (Socialist) resolution to sanction the Milk Pool's distribution of free milk to Milwaukee's needy based on reports that the Milk Pool had dumped white-cross milk. Senator Hunt (Progressive Republican) voiced his support of Governor Schmedeman but questioned Schmedeman's use of force: "When you put your army in the field and the truck drivers of the big milk companies, armed with guns, go on the highways to shoot down our farmers it is about time we wake up." When pushed by fellow senators on what he meant by "army," Hunt pointed to the deputation of the National Guard.[102]

Deputies and guardsmen armed with gas bombs also, even if un-wittingly, divested bystanders of their freedom to carry on with their ordinary lives. One school cancelled classes because gas used during a fight between strikers and authorities at Durham Hill seeped into the building. The *Wisconsin State Journal* reported that several women and children who had to be driven through the same protest site complained to county officials about suffering the effects of tear gas.[103] Likewise, the *Milwaukee Sentinel* reported "Residents of the community were wrought up over the fight. They were especially irate because the children were not given an opportunity to clear out of the danger zone before the gas was hurled."[104] Communities' outrage focused on the danger the guard posed to civilians. Mobile pickets, deputies, and guardsmen all defined citizens' movements throughout the state. Milk Pool strikers' actions compelled bystanders and consumers to make choices, while the state's actions inhibited choice. For instance, in Menasha, against warnings of pickets, a Mrs. Strohmeyer walked through barricades to attend church.[105] Unlike Mrs. Strohmeyer's active refutation of protest-ers' demands—while they compelled her to act, they did not determine her choice—the uncontrollable effects of gas victimized bystanders, and the press reported on its effects on women and children, in particular.

Bringing the Strike to a Climax and an End

Over the first two days of the strike, deputies seemed outnumbered by the Milk Pool pickets. The *Milwaukee Sentinel* featured a picture of roughly thirty men standing in milk. The paper emphasized the protest-ers' determination: "Disregarding gas, clubs, and fists, several hundred pickets succeeded in dumping 20,000 pounds of milk [more than 2,300 gallons] at the Walworth-Waukesha county line." To the left of this photo, a member of Waukesha County's bomb squad was shown, ac-coutered in a gas mask and protective clothing, hurling a bomb onto a highway between East Troy and Mukwonago. Below this, another pic-ture showed pickets' successful road barricade of railroad ties, harrows, and ice picks.[106] On May 15, the *Wisconsin State Journal* reported that the Milk Pool shut down Shawano County after the governor had re-opened it when a thousand strikers overtook deputies and dumped two thousand pounds (approximately 233 gallons) of milk.[107] That same day, Colonel Holden of the 128th National Guard Infantry forced Shawano County sheriff Otto Druckery to resign his post. Druckery had refused to deputize additional men, was unwilling to use gas to disperse fifteen hundred strikers gathered at the Badger Cooperative Dairy, and would not call in the National Guard as reinforcements.[108] That same day, Lou French, a guardsman (rank unknown), telephoned Leo Crowley to discuss different tactics for breaking the strike:

> CROWLEY: Do you know anything about this new sheriff?
>
> FRENCH: They say he's OK. What are you figuring on doing?
>
> CROWLEY: Open them all up.
>
> FRENCH: Open the Badger?
>
> CROWLEY: Yes sir; we might as well have a showdown there instead of Milwaukee, don't you think so?[109]

By opening the Badger plant despite a mass performance that called for its closure, which was supported by the former sheriff, Crowley exercised the power of the state to suppress the will of the people. Crowley's conversation with French was not public knowledge. However, the state would make a spectacle of its power at Shawano within days.

National Guard troops were deployed to Shawano County. On the morning of May 16, authorities took twenty-nine prisoners and closed Shawano County plants following another struggle in which strikers used clubs and stones against deputies.[110] Immell telephoned sheriffs of surrounding counties requesting that they prevent strikers from entering Shawano.[111] Based on rumors heard on May 16 that the Milk Pool would concentrate its forces in Shawano, on May 17, Colonel Schantz requested three additional National Guard units, and Sheriff Dettman deputized Native Americans from the Menominee Reservation. Though they were not in police uniforms, these new deputies pinned red-plaid cloth on their shoulders to signify they were Dettman's men.[112]

The *Wisconsin State Journal* reported the movement of troops and additional tear gas into the area under a May 16, 1933, headline threatening a massive battle: "Call for More Deputies at Shawano: State's Army of 600 Fears New Threat of 10,000 Invaders." On May 17, the *Milwaukee Sentinel* set the scene of imminent battle in Shawano with a photo of seventeen strikers gathering rocks. Calling protesters a "motley but determined crew," the sight was compared with the "barbed wire entanglements of France" and said to have the "aura of war." That same day, the *Wisconsin State Journal* ran the headline "State Moves to Bring Strike to Crisis; Fears Reds Seeking Control of Farmers." In the article, Immell pinned state suppression of protesters on Communist infiltration: "cars from Indiana and Illinois filled with *strangers*" were entering strike areas: "There will be no dickering with the strikers from now on, officials revealed, the strike will be broken and counties open for delivery of milk will remain open."[113] Meanwhile, the adjutant general telephoned the secretary of war to ask for an army plane to send additional supplies of five hundred fast-burning CN tear gas candles and two hundred CN-DM gas candles. General Drum of the War Department agreed to send the CN gas but cautioned Immell against the use of CN-DM gas because of its capacity for bodily harm.[114] General Immell insisted on the need of CN-DM gas because of the severity of the threat in Shawano; Drum sent CN-DM gas to Wisconsin. Immell also insisted that he "did not want any publicity in regard to this."[115]

The next day—May 18, the day of the predicted battle—Governor Schmedeman ordered all guards into uniform. The *Marshfield News-Herald* reported that uniformed guardsmen "fully equipped for military duty," were still acting as sheriffs' deputies because, according to Immell, "martial law does not exist anywhere in the state."[116] Edgar Barnes wrote Immell from Chicago that he "was greatly pleased to see" the guards in uniform because deployment in civilian clothing "invited resistance and a loss of prestige."[117] In their reports to the adjutant general on mobilization during the strike, a number of the commanding officers also noted the positive change in guardsmen's morale once they donned uniforms and so warned against subsequent deployment in civilian dress. The uniform conferred legitimacy on the men's service through state sponsorship. It also materialized state-sanctioned violence against farmers.

Visibly militarized authorities in conjunction with Crowley's, or Schmedeman's, order to open all the counties brought the strike to its violent climax. Violence reached its peak with the battles of Cemetery Hill (Shawano County) and Durham Hill (Waukesha County) on May 18, 1933. The *Milwaukee Sentinel* described the movements of the Shawano

County battle in great detail. Converging on Cemetery Hill, a twenty-mile area located between two cemeteries, strikers, joined by Native Americans from the Oneida Reservation, lined the highway.[118] When guardsmen and deputies arrived in gas masks, strikers reportedly fled the gas bombs' effects. However, barbed wire trapped many pickets, and authorities clubbed strikers prior to their arrests. In all, the guard captured roughly 250 men.[119] At Durham Hill, according to details reported by Second Lieutenant Wood, the guard arrived via truck at 9:00 AM. Strikers "marched thru [the guard's] rank with U.S. colors flying." Milk Pool leaders then made speeches. During an attempt to arrest one of the leaders, fighting ensued. The pickets armed themselves with rocks. By 3:15 PM, the guards received support from three additional units. They dispersed the group of approximately 300 strikers with gas, bayonets, and side arms. Following this, the guard escorted seven milk trucks to the county line.[120] Authorities played out two spectacular shows of force, and the build up to these climatic battles allowed the *Milwaukee Sentinel* to capture them in a May 18, 1933 photo exposé, titled "Milk Strike War Told in Pictures." That night, an arbitration committee met at the Governor's office to write a peace accord.

On the morning of May 19, 1933 the Milk Pool and Governor Schmedeman issued a joint statement that blamed violence on outsiders:

> The undersigned members ... asserting the right of the farmer to withhold his products in order to gain his just demands in an orderly and peaceful way, deplores the fact that, in his making said demands, outside and undesirable elements have entered upon unlawful activities of intimidation and violence, and the said Milk Pool emphatically repudiates such elements as undesirable and uninvited allies. As good citizens of the state of Wisconsin the Milk Pool members join with the governor in condemnation of such unlawful activities.[121]

From the steps of the capital building to the five thousand gathered farmers, Governor Schmedeman proclaimed his admiration for the pickets: "Boys, I'm glad to see all of you. I wish I had the chance to shake hands with you."[122] The speech contradicted what citizens witnessed during the strike. The conviviality between the parties failed to be complete or long-lasting. Attendees at the Governor's public address booed General Immell.[123] When William Rubin spoke, he defended the governor's efforts to secure peace, but held Immell culpable for the strike's bloodshed:

"Some one was anxious to put on the adjutant general's uniform . . . It hadn't been worn for a long time."[124] The same day, farmers signed affidavits claiming that deputies attacked pickets without provocation; this led to two opposing opinions regarding sherriffs' authority to enlist city police in their ranks. After three hours of debate, the Wisconsin State Senate rejected a resolution acknowledging the Senate's "alarm at the unwarranted use of military power to suppress the milk strike and to subdue the farmers into unconditional surrender." The Senate rejected all proposals commending or condemning the governor's use of the guard.[125] On June 13, 1933, Governor Schmedeman issued a special statement to the Wisconsin legislature addressing official criticism of the National Guard's use. Under the title "Governor Defends Use of Troops in Milk Strike," the *Capital Times* published Schmedeman's address in full. The governor's message closed by rebuking a motion introduced in the State Senate that asked Adjutant General Immel to identify "who called the National guard into service during the recent milk strike." Governor Schmedeman's effort to legitimize his use of the guard was also an effort to legitimize his own authority: "There is no mystery about this. Under the constitution the governor alone can call out the National Guard."

While Singler's power grew following the May strike and Schmedeman was voted out of office for, in part, this unprecedented use of the National Guard, the 1933 conflicts between the state and farmers also affected the political careers of numerous men involved in them. Milk Pool attorney William Rubin lost his bid for Supreme Court justice in 1933 and bitterly parted ways with former political allies. When State Representative Alex McDonald (Democrat) refused to support Rubin's 1934 campaign for governor, Rubin responded, "I am frank to state to you that I am proud of my association with Singler, and feel chagrined that I took part in helping elect you to the legislature. I would rather go down with a man like Singler, than stay up with a man like you after scanning your record, and, Mr. McDonald, when I am in your counties I shall tell the constituencies of your work in the legislature and will do my bit to defeat your return."[126] In 1934, Crowley abandoned Schmedeman to facilitate a coalition between third-party Wisconsin progressives and the Roosevelt administration. He then left state politics and rose to national political prominence, moving through the ranks of Roosevelt's administration to become a cabinet member. In 1938, when Immell came under fire for misallocation of WPA monies, an anonymous Madison businessman sent William T. Evjue, editor of the *Capital Times,* a postcard enumerating the general's misdeeds: "Clubbing farmers in milk strike" topped his list. Thirteen years after the protests, real estate and insurance agent M. J. Donovan asked that Evjue publish his letter in which he doubted the sincerity of Immell's gubernatorial campaign remarks in support of farmers because "farmers were clubbed and otherwise mistreated."[127] Immell did not win the election.

In May 1933, Wisconsinites' knowledge that this strike would be potentially unlike any other, generated from a combination of prestrike declarations and the strike's antecedents, allowed them to decide in advance whether to watch it. Coverage by the press told them where to find the action. Throughout the six days of strike activity, Wisconsin citizens could witness for themselves heroism, glory, and brutality acted out on the streets. The *Milwaukee Sentinel's* "Crowds Clutter Up Roads Seeking Strike Excitement" noted the thousands of citizens attracted to sites where strike action was anticipated or had occurred. The report renders the final site of strike performance a memorial, depicting ruined milk as the trace of violence: "Evidence of the clash, in which tear bombs and 'K.O.' bombs were used by the officers was clearly visible. The pavement was white with milk for a considerable distance, and puddles of water at the side of the road and even over the fence in the fields in some places were white."[128] The frame of war did not deter audiences; neither did warnings against attending the protest, nor even a May 17 incident involving the shooting of a teenaged spectator by a deputy.[129] Commenting on the incident, the district attorney emphasized the danger of being a bystander: "I believe it necessary to warn all persons to remain away from these so-called battle fronts. . . . No one knows just what will happen. Stay away, because peace officers can not [sic] distinguish between rioters and spectators when a riot breaks out."[130] Despite escalating violence, spectatorship remained so popular that, on May 18, the *Milwaukee Sentinel* issued its own warning: "WARNING! The Sentinel suggests that citizens stay away from picketed areas of the milk strike. There is grave danger of serious injury to sightseers and innocent bystanders." Citizens in cars racing to protest sites and those crowding around plant entrances went to experience something of the sensuousness of war. News media offered extensive, vivid coverage of the strike, but still images and articles distanced Wisconsin audiences through their narrative and compositional closure. In the midst of a local and national crisis, the complexity of the stakes of this protest performance defied cogent storytelling. Citizens went to see theater in the streets, linking the sensate experience of violence to discerning the truth. In the act of watching, they gained embodied knowledge of the impact of gas, the enormity of ruined milk, the physical effects on men's bodies, and the power of the state's corporate interests.

SCENE TWENTY

Voice of Living Newspaper (over loudspeaker): Detroit, July 17, 1936. [*sic*]
Housewives rebel against high meat prices.

(Butcher shop window and door. Meat prices displayed in window as follows:)
ROUND STEAK.................35¢ lb.
BEEF POT ROAST............21¢ lb.
VEAL ROAST...................27¢ lb.
LEG OF LAMB.................27¢ lb.
LOIN................................29¢ lb.
HAM................................31¢ lb.

(Then lights come on two women carrying the following banners;)
(""WOMAN'S ACTION COMMITTEE—AGAINST HIGH COST OF LIVING
AND ALL OUT TO PICKET FRIDAY AND SATURDAY.
STRIKE FOR A 20% CUT IN MEAT PRICES."")

(Cross stage right to left. A man and woman start crossing from stage left. As they
come to entrance of store, they start to enter. Woman notices the picketing, and pulls
man away from doorway.)

Woman: Don't go in there! There's a strike. We'll go some other place to buy!

(They start walking to stage right, suddenly a man comes through the door with a package.
A number of women come from stage left. They see the man, and start for him.)

Group of Women (Ad lib.): Don't let him pass! Get him! Strike breaker. The package!
Get the package. Show him we mean business. Get him!

(As the man emerges from the mob, his package is seized by a woman who rips it apart
and throws it offstage. He is then surrounded by a furious mob intent upon tearing
him to pieces. The female leader of the strike mounts a box.)

Leader: Wait! We've got a bigger fight than this on our hands. We're not going to be satisfied
with boycotting only butcher shops. Once organized we'll look into milk prices, and gas and
electricity rates. In the present strike we don't want the small butchers to suffer. We want
to get results from the big packing houses!
Male Voice: Why don't you go to Washington? They started this.
Leader: Maybe they started it by killing the little pigs and cattle. We don't know and we don't
care. But we're not going to pay such high prices for meat and that's all there is to it!
Voices: We won't buy meat. Prices must come down. We won't buy meat! Prices must come down.

(The roar of a truck coming to a stop is heard offstage.)

Leader: A meat truck! A packing house truck. Soak the meat in kerosene!
Voices (ad lib.): Kerosene on the meat. Soak the meat. Down with the meat packer millionaires.
Prices must come down. We won't buy. We won't buy. We won't buy, we won't buy.

(Mob rushes off to truck)
(They all exit down left)

BLACKOUT

Script Excerpt 3. Editorial Staff of the Living Newspaper Federal Theatre Project under
the supervision of Arthur Arent, "Triple-A Plowed Under," 1936, Federal Theatre Project
Collection, Special Collections and Archives, George Mason University Libraries.

Playing "Housewife" in Polonia

The 1935 Hamtramck (Michigan) Women's Meat Boycott

IN 1935, WHEN WOMEN FACED AN IMPOSSIBLE SITUATION AS wives and consumers, the costs of the Agricultural Adjustment Act to men, and so to the American moral order, occupied public discourse once again. On June 10, 1935, as a consumers' movement showed its strength in protests across the nation, *Time* magazine narrated the march toward women's activism as inevitable: "Slowly through the winter, while the meat supply was dwindling, the price to the consumer was creeping up. By February, housewives everywhere began to complain."[1] The costs of vegetables, fruits, and other foods advanced during January and February. The price of meat was predicted to "soar." In March, Secretary of Agriculture Henry Wallace tried to quell consumers' concerns by offering that the prices of foods *other than meats* should not continue to climb.[2] The *Detroit Free Press* estimated the price escalation of meat at 24 percent from the previous year and 62 percent over the past three years; *Newsweek* assessed the rise from June 1933 to June 1935 at 54 percent.[3] That year, unemployment levels hovered around 20 percent nationally.

Five years of low-income levels due to pervasive unemployment compounded the incredible and incredibly rapid rise of meat prices.

Throughout the spring and summer of 1935, women in Los Angeles, New York City, Seattle, Cleveland, Detroit, and other urban areas protested the cost of meat. Women's groups, adopting versions of the name "Action Committee against the High Cost of Living," coordinated these protests. The United Conference against the High Cost of Living, an organization that coordinated multiple groups with common consumer interests, helped organize efforts nationwide. In May, the Communist Party also sent directives to its section organizers in a number of cities with instructions on how to agitate for lower food prices, "especially meat" at the neighborhood level, while rallying women via its serial publication the *Working Woman* to stage a nationwide, one-day meat strike on June 8, 1935.[4]

The Hamtramck (Michigan) Women's Action Committee against the High Cost of Living began organizing in mid-July following the Los Angeles meat boycott in March and the New York City meat boycott in May. Members elected Mrs. Mary Zuk as their chair. As these women organized, they met with neighborhood grocers and butchers. According to the women, these local shop owners agreed to support the boycott. At the Hamtramck City Council meeting on July 24, 1935, the women announced their intention to protest because "meat has become a luxury for many of our homes."[5] At this meeting, the group presented a resolution to Mayor Joseph Lewandowski and asked that he send it to both President Roosevelt and Secretary Wallace; the resolution called for a federal investigation of meat prices to discover if corporations were passing the cost of the AAA processing tax onto consumers.

On Saturday, July 27, 1935, the Hamtramck Women's Committee carried signs that demanded a 20 percent price cut on meat and urged a meat boycott, as they paraded through the city's shopping district, down Joseph Campau Avenue (see Figure 3.1). They blocked butchers' shops and delicatessens. Early on, many of the meat markets closed up shop. The pickets also stationed themselves at entrances of groceries to inspect shoppers' parcels upon exiting. They took any meat that they found and destroyed it. In doing so, the pickets fought with male and female shoppers. This first day of picketing resulted in businesses shutting

Figure 3.1. Members of the Women's Action Committee against the High Cost of Living picket Hamtramck's shopping district on the first day of the meat boycott, July 27, 1935. Walter P. Reuther Library, Wayne State University, Detroit News Collection #29813_6.

down and an estimated loss of $65,000 in sales on Hamtramck's busiest shopping day of the week. A week into their campaign, the Hamtramck housewives vowed to extend their battle to include milk, butter, and other staples vital to their families as soon as they won price reductions on meat.

In the days and weeks that followed the first violent day of protest, weekend picketing in front of Hamtramck shops and at metropolitan Detroit meat packaging plants continued and spread rapidly through neighboring towns and into other Midwestern cities. Within days of the first Hamtramck picket, Detroit-area women's activist groups chose programs of activism in direct response to the Hamtramck housewives' actions. Some women's groups threatened to use "Hamtramck tactics," while others sought to distance themselves from the Hamtramck women by signing a pledge as their form of activism. Their initial performance also adhered to the Hamtramck women, specifically Mary Zuk, in the housewives' rise to national renown and onto the political stages of Washington, DC.

Although much has been written about the accomplishments of the national housewives' movement, no attention has been given to how the cultural significance of meat and the protest tactics of the Hamtramck housewives shaped public discourse about the AAA during this phase of consumers' rise in economic and political importance. Many historians argue that, on a national scale, women's economic power as consumers and their moral authority as mothers inclined the federal government to regard the women as legitimate political actors.[6] In these analyses, "mother" and "housewife" are treated as synonymous social categories in a manner that implies that the role of "mother" eclipsed activists' overt representation of themselves as "housewives." As I will argue, taking into account the local elements of the Hamtramck protest, the centrality of meat to it, and "housewife" as a specific theatrical, cultural, social, and political role, women articulated their claims to consumers' rights through the connection between (paid) labor and citizenship. By deciding to prioritize the goal of lower meat prices, these women positioned themselves and their cause in direct relation to their husbands' needs. In theatrical and rhetorical ways, the Hamtramck protesters framed the absence of meat on their tables, blamed on AAA programs, as a threat to the ability of their (mostly unemployed) husbands to (find) work.

In giving critical attention to meat as the contested object and its connection to the cultural figure of "housewife," the moral arguments lodged by the Hamtramck Women's Committee against the AAA did not only, or principally, rely on the humanitarian discourse evoked through the vulnerability of the child via the "mother" figure; rather it turned to the producerist ethic as a viable and popular appeal. This is not to suggest that the women's own needs or those of their children did not motivate them, but that these activists recognized the currency of producerism, the idea that the best citizen produces a commodity that benefits the nation's economy—men were workers, and they needed meat to perform at optimal capacity. Further, while these women may have desired meat for themselves, they could not make a rights claim to it because meat was considered indispensible to men only. By focusing on the role of "housewife" as performed by the Hamtramck women activists, this chapter investigates nuances of the performative constraints within which the Hamtramck housewives operated and through which local authorities, media, and other women's activist groups engaged with the Hamtramck activists' progressive ideas about gender and race.

Gender norms dictated that women's activism should exist in service of the domestic and public patriarchy and, in numerous historical periods, compelled it. Not only did gender expectations produce and circumscribe the forms of activism deemed appropriate to women, but the federal government had helped codify a repertoire of appropriate acts of activism for women through wartime and Depression-era programs. These programs, which politicized consumption practices, reflected and shaped cultural notions about how women should perform "good" citizenship. In her influential account of the national patterns of the 1935 housewives' movement, historian Annelise Orleck identifies the "ambivalence" with which the media treated housewives' activism, noting that media simultaneously mocked and took notice of the activists' power: "Writers never tired of suggesting that, by its very existence, the housewives' movement emasculated male adversaries."[7] Orleck here refers to national media depictions of Secretary Wallace's encounter with Mary Zuk, an incident discussed later in this chapter. The ambivalence expressed by media, as well as by other witnesses to and participants in the Hamtramck boycott, reveals the contradictory expectations that demanded that housewives act on behalf of laborers but did not trust them when they did so. The economic crisis unsettled gender roles. The focus on emasculation as an effect of the women's actions registers contemporaneous concerns about restoring men's socioeconomic and citizenship status as laborers and women's growing power in the economic and political realm as consumers. The social and cultural dynamics of Hamtramck tend to amplify gender relations (and ethnic relations) that operated nationally, as well as to highlight the connections between meat, labor, and citizenship. This suggests that, for the Hamtramck community, the experience of the consumer crisis was qualitatively distinct yet, paradoxically, exemplary.

An important aspect of this chapter is how media and audiences portrayed the boycott, the activists, and the Hamtramck women's critique of gendered notions of performance-based citizenship. Very little evidence gives account of the moment-to-moment performance dynamics of the Hamtramck boycotts throughout the summer of 1935. Orleck, in fact, states that the scantiness of evidence concerning the Hamtramck protest led her to focus primarily on the activities of the New York women for which a deeper archive exists. In their accessibility, number, and consistency (thanks to the Associated Press and the United Press), articles published by national media, major Michigan news organizations, and the local Hamtramck papers overwhelm the (almost literal) handful of partially identified correspondence, writings, and speeches that appear in both Polish and English in the papers of Mary Zuk. Indeed, despite evidence that shows the participation of some men and children in the Hamtramck boycotts, the protesters self-representation as "housewives" largely confused their participation in media accounts. Likewise, the failure of local and national media to report on African American women's and children's participation in the Hamtramck protest stemmed from the designation of Hamtramck as a "Polish American" city. The extent and nature of interracial cooperation and activity during the weeks of protest cannot be found, for the most part, from archival sources, and confusion on this point has occurred in the historical analysis because the Hamtramck boycott tends to be folded into the larger Detroit and national housewives' movements.

The elusiveness of the Hamtramck women's perspectives on their actions, as well as the persistence of the documents created by male-dominated national and local institutions, stands as a larger implication of the women's public performances as "housewives." Theater historian Odai Johnson has written, "evidence also has a peculiar and sometimes pernicious way of surviving largely on its ability to conform to and endorse certain existing hegemonies and narratives."[8] The available evidence about the Hamtramck housewives' protest largely consists of documents that, consciously or unconsciously, diminish the efficacy of the women's actions, organizational capacity, and agency. The writers of these documents employ melodramatic conventions that insist on the societal importance of watching and controlling the wife.

What is particularly compelling and disquieting about the surviving evidence and uncritical melodramatic historicization of Mary Zuk is that she was typical of her fellow activists. When Zuk was elected to chair the Hamtramck Women's Committee against the High Cost of Living, she was thirty years old, a native-born Polish American woman, and the mother of two children. Her husband, Stanley, had immigrated from Poland as an adolescent. In 1935, Stanley was unemployed, and the Zuk family was on welfare relief rolls. Although the historical record does not illuminate Zuk's perspective on her experience, it draws attention to its absence and obliges an answer to gender historian Mary Elizabeth Perry's call to "[look] beneath surface meanings for subtexts and silences that they can tell us" when trying to discover women's experiences in the archive.[9]

Meat and Laborers' Needs as Women's Motivation to Boycott

Members of the Hamtramck Women's Committee share characteristics common to the various 1930s women's consumer groups that organized throughout the nation: motivations, demographic circumstances, and protest tactics. The activists involved in this national movement most often appear in scholars' analyses as diverse groups of women collectivized as "consumers" through "female consciousness": "a sense of rights and obligations that provides motive force for actions."[10] Historian Meg Jacobs cogently distills the nature of "female consciousness" during the 1930s as an emergent "consuming public," a conception of citizenry that held the New Deal government responsible for the maintenance of consumers' living standard.[11] Women activists tended to be working-class African Americans or immigrants; the Hamtramck women were indeed working class and regarded as "immigrants," regardless of whether they were born in the United States. They were Catholic Polish Americans. Similar to many of their activist counterparts, the Hamtramck women used violent tactics during pickets in shopping areas and at packaging plants. They likewise shared the rhetoric of the other women's groups, stating that they supported local butchers and farmers, were fighting meat corporations that passed the cost of the AAA processing tax on to consumers, and blamed AAA "scarcity" policies for creating meat short-ages. On the boycott's first day, Zuk informed reporters, "One of the packers told us 'Why don't you go see President Roosevelt? He started this,'... Maybe Roosevelt started it by killing the little pigs and the cattle. We don't know and we don't care. We aren't going to pay such high prices for meat and that's all there is to it."[12] Though Zuk ostensibly diminishes her concern with discovering the causes of the meat prices in compari-son to her demand for just prices, she handily implicates both the federal government and the meat packing industry.

From many Americans' perspectives, exorbitant meat prices com-pounded the problem of restoring economic and social stability. Re-lief personnel, dieticians, social workers, and housewives were con-cerned with the Depression's detriment to health, particularly in relation to men's ability to work. Studies and comments about the crisis of access to vital foods exhibit the feedback loop of gender performativity in which the "needs" of heads of households must be met first—and men head the household. Edward Corsi, the director of the Home Relief Bureau in New York City, deemed relief payments allotted by the government inad-equate to sustain men: "The average allowance for the home relief family or adult in the family is predicated upon a condition of inactivity. If that man moves about the city looking for a job, and does any amount of work in looking for a job, then he has not enough to feed him."[13] Beginning in 1933, Dorothy G. Wiehl studied the consumption habits of native-born and immigrant families on relief; some families were newly poor because of the Depression, but others had suffered poverty for more than five years. Based on her findings, Wiehl urged low-income families to redistribute their budgets. Her data showed that families spent less on milk when their income levels dropped, thus risking a "diet 'safe' for children."[14] Wiehl, however, doubted the ability of nutritional educa-tion to change consumers' habits because their purchases showed the "desire of practically all families for more meat than is allowed in the minimum cost adequate diet."[15] Consumers' spending "too much" on meat or spending on meat first was inextricable from gendered distribu-tion of food in families. In all probability, among the low-income families Wiehl surveyed, the meat that was bought was purchased for the head of household. Grace Hutchins, writing for the *Working Woman*, tied Corsi's remarks about insufficient relief allowances directly to the recommendations of dietitians like Wiehl, who suggested that families on relief substitute legumes for meat. Hutchins "reveals" these recommendations to be the sinister machinations of capitalists against the working class: "the diet of dried beans and lentils really means—a weakened condition of the jobless worker, of the children and of the other members of his family."[16] While Hutchins's suspicions about why experts encouraged substitutions for meat show her politics, her view that there was no adequate nutritional alternatives to meat was the opinion of most people at the time.

Hutchins used men's meat deprivation to motivate women across the nation to protest:

> Do you know that thousands of unemployed are told by Welfare "dietitians" to do without meat while one billion pounds of meat are stored away in the meat storage plants? For what? 1) To keep prices high. 2) For war purposes. This meat is intended to feed future military armies. At the same time our boys in the c.c.c. [Civilian Conservation Corps] camps receive inadequate food. We, wives and mothers of the unemployed, of the underpaid, sped-up workers, demand that these one billion pounds of meat be turned over for free distribution (by trade unions and workers' organizations) to feed the huge army of the unemployed.[17]

Hutchins appropriates the historic link between women's patriotism and their consumption practices. In this instance, the history of foregoing meat for national security is turned toward a present class battle on home soil. It argues that women must intervene in the government's exploitation of the male worker, whether he is a soldier in the army of unemployed or a young man working in Roosevelt's Works Progress Administration.

In Polish American households, meat was extremely important. Under stable economic circumstances, it was eaten at every meal because it was believed to be "the most essential food. A child raised without a sufficient quantity of it would be frail and a man could not do a proper day's work if he did not have enough meat."[18] Meat's centrality to the definition of a complete meal for men and the reservation of meat for men during economic hardship "educates male bodies in the knowledge of their freedoms and privileges."[19] In addition to the gendered power relations that support the cultural inextricability of meat from masculinity, in Hamtramck, meat consumption also expressed the success of immigration on a domestic and community level. The regular diet of peasant classes in Central Europe was meatless due to their poverty; they characterized meat as a celebratory food consumed only on special occasions such as weddings or religious holidays. During the boycott, an elderly man drew a comparison between the contemporary situation and his life in Poland: "This is just like the old country. . . . Why in Poland meat was a luxury."[20] Polish immigrants and the first generations of Polish Americans living in Hamtramck transformed the practically meatless diet of their Polish ancestry into an Americanized standard of living that also accorded the right of meat consumption first to the male laborer.

Meat's necessity to workingmen was not merely articulated as the motivation for the Hamtramck boycott: it determined the picketing schedule. The Hamtramck Women's Committee chose to begin their picketing on a Saturday, stop picketing and boycotting during the week, and resume picketing each Friday and Saturday because, according to one of the protesters, "the men do not have to go to work the next day and can get along without meat."[21] Women's conscious structuring and staging of the boycott around men's needs staged what we might call the "housewife's dilemma" because the term denotes both the difficulty in choosing an action given the sacrifice involved in all options and the need to choose due to the compelling force of the circumstance. The Hamtramck women faced a true dilemma: they had to buy meat because their husbands' abilities to (find) work depended on it, yet they asserted that buying meat was impossible, or at least unsustainable, given its cost and men's unemployment. The tension between the women's boycott as a choice that deprived men of meat and one necessary to gain men's access to this essential food was expressed in a *Detroit Free Press* report about the aftermath of the boycott's first day. It focused on the housewives' search for recipes for Sunday supper that "would satisfy the appetites of their already meat-starved husbands," while husbands were left to "[wonder] whether the stuff from the gardens would keep their ribs apart long enough to get them to work."[22] A husband, as the head of the household and the family's provider, had a right to a meal that satiated his appetite and tastes. Not buying meat/boycotting was an action compelled by circumstance—men were "already meat-starved"—but one that further risked a husband's (restored) position as a producer.

Ensuring a man's right to meat was a housewife's concern. Regardless of how individual women felt about the role of housewife, meat prices imperiled their ability to succeed in enacting a principal behavior that culturally defined them as good wives. As historian Tracey Deutsch observes, "Beginning at least in the antebellum period . . . cooking and serving were celebrated as the stage on which women could best enact the work of efficiency and generosity—work that would maintain familial coherence. Meals were the vehicle for love, nutrition, the reinforcement of communal norms, the education of children, and displays of skill—for all the ways that women might convey their affection, nurturance, and fitness."[23]

Because women were in charge of feeding their families, and cooking was considered a means by which women expressed their love and citizenship, women were held responsible to help restore the socioeconomic order and the dignity of the workingman. Although there were national economic causes for meat's absence on a table, the missing food could also signal a wife's "insolence" toward her husband and cause conflict. One extreme case in Hamtramck crystallizes how meals as emotionally meaningful performances in the context of the 1930s economic crisis caught women in a double bind. A woman named Eva pressed charges of assault and battery against her husband, Mike. In his statements to police, Mike recounted how his long-term unemployment had serious implications for his wife's behavior toward him. In addition to "nagging" him about keeping up with house payments for fear of foreclosure, "After Mike had been out of work for a long time, he came home at 4 PM and asked his wife to prepare his meal. She warmed some things over for him but she refused to prepare a regular supper when he was not working."[24] Eva may have resented Mike's idleness and perceived it as his failure as a husband. While Eva may have sought to punish Mike by exercising her bodily and culinary control over him at mealtimes, she probably had good economic reason and very likely believed Mike did not need a "regular supper" because he was not working. Mike justified beating Eva by linking her refusal to prepare such a meal to his unemployment, yet he simultaneously held the contradictory view that her actions were an attempt to emasculate him, not a result of the economic constraint on their family's diet.

Extremely high levels of unemployment combined with rising food costs exhausted consumers' purchasing power and strained marriages throughout the United States. The subjects interviewed by Laetitia M. Conrad in her 1935 study of sixty-six families in Grinnell, Iowa, seemed uninterested in talking about life on relief, "hoping to get away from relief in the near future."[25] Yet roughly one-quarter of Conrad's interviewees discussed marital problems. Wives described their husbands as irritable and acknowledged that they too had been unpleasant to their husbands out of frustration with having "nothing to [make] do with." All those interviewed expressed that they wanted more and better foods. When asked, "What do you miss most?" 80 percent of the interviewees (fifty-two adults) identified "meat." Meat signified economic stability, happiness, and dignity for both the wife and the husband. The shame that men suffered because of their lost status as breadwinner and, even more, by going on the relief rolls was recognized as a national problem. A political scientist weighing the moral dangers of New Deal unemployment insurance against the exceptional economic moment stated plainly, "It is an indignity for a man thrown out of work to be dependent on public charity."[26] Relief—government payments to the unemployed—was not only a largely unrecognized indignity for a wife, but it also placed her in an untenable situation.

The "Housewife" in American Culture

Playing "mother" has proven to be a potent tactic for women in a variety of historic moments, across the globe, and for various ends; state institutions and political regimes have politicized this revered figure to strong effect as well.[27] While the roles of mother and wife were certainly linked in the lives of 1930s women, "mother" and "housewife" signify distinct, even if related and simultaneously embodied, femininities. These categories have distinct cultural statuses and place specific performative demands on women. These demands governed the consumption practices of women, stratified a woman's household labor, and placed contradictory and competing expectations on women through the disparate needs of husbands and children.

Historically in the United States, the role "housewife" does not enjoy the deference reserved for the figure of "mother." "Housewife" was, and continues to be, culturally constructed as a role, while "mother" was, and continues to be, perceived as a state of being. Women do not experience a physical transformation when they become wives as they do when they become mothers. Pervasive ideology "did not think of motherhood as a job that women performed or a role that they assumed, but rather as a sacred estate that they entered" when they gave birth. From this, mothers were believed to experience and express an unwavering emotional state of "Mother Love" for their children.[28]

In multiple modes of cultural expression, "housewife" is a source of conflict because she is liable to the lesser aspects of feminine "nature." American proverbs show a shared sentiment with the Polish saying "Woe to the home where the woman rules the husband." Lois Kershen concludes that, on the whole, popular adages deem that "a wife exists to be of service to her husband as hostess, cook, and lover. Anything else and she is a troublesome shrew who only brings a man misery."[29] Women's primary duties as a wife consist in assuring the husband's comfort (hostess) and satiating his physical and sexual appetites (cook and lover). Thus, she also has the means to exert a worrisome level of control over her husband because the emotional "truth" behind a wife's performance is uncertain. Paradoxically, the manner in which a wife performs her duties as hostess, lover, and cook signals that "truth." That is to say, "wife" is discursively constituted as an actor, and "she" is liable to raise similar social misgivings. Theater scholars Paul Allain and Jen Harvie define acting as "intentional, social, and mimetic": to act is to "be self-reflexive about [one's] craft, its practice, and its aesthetic and social functions."[30] For the role of "housewife," as for that of the actor, intentionality connotes dissembling. However, the wife's performance is more dangerous than the actor's for its insistence that it is sincere and for its appearance outside the theatrical frame.

The character type of the housewife endures in various dramatic genres from tragedy to melodrama to realism. It also persists in the cultural imagination through canonical housewives such as Lady Mac-

beth, a character made even more problematic for her adversarial relationship to motherhood (magnified via her foil: the martyr mother
Lady Macduff). In artistic and cultural constructions, the housewife is
prone to deception, has sexual knowledge at her disposal, and is capable
of violence. She is also susceptible to her whims and desires, even when
motivated by the best intentions—those oriented toward her husband's
success. The untrustworthy housewife was a fixture of early twentieth-
century American comedies, domestic realist dramas, and cinema. For
example, film historian Kathleen Anne McHugh argues that melodramatic films of the 1930s depicted a wife's principal and most important
role as loving her husband. She needed to show this love by keeping herself and "his home" pleasing in appearance and by tending to his physical
and emotional needs. At the same time, cinematic narratives presented
ambitious or even well-meaning wives who manipulate their husbands,
jeopardize his respectability, and cause ruin. This character type affirms
the morality and necessity of the patriarchal hierarchy of social and political power. Depending on the genre, the drama may end tragically or
happily, but the risk taken by the wife is always the husband's.[31]

During the economic crisis, preoccupation with the housewife's
troublesome potentials was exhibited in social, legal, and political realms.
To raise families' living standards, and often to avoid relief rolls, some
women brought work into their homes. Other women, who had previously left the paid workforce once married because of employment
regulations and cultural traditions, sought outside employment. Despite
the gendering of labor, as historian Lois Scharf writes, the Great Depression heightened long-held antagonism toward women's employment.
Throughout the decade, "marriage clauses" were introduced in state
and federal legislation, and the National Recovery Act banned home
work in numerous industries. Other New Deal programs, such as Social
Security and the Works Progress Administration, codified the segregation of labor by sex and diminished women's occupations and earning
potential, just as these policies shored up men's economic security and
social status.[32] However, these policies did not solely or simply suppress
married women's desires to work or to express an identity outside the domestic realm. Married women's work struck many women and men as an
undesirable necessity, symptomatic of economic dysfunction: "If there

was any increased recognition of women's economic role in the family, it did not represent a gain in status, for no one was comfortable with the new state of affairs, and the reversal of roles was resented by everyone involved."[33] Feminists and New Dealers, women and men, many involved with writing policies, advocating for fair labor practices, and fighting for women's rights, expressed concern for the welfare of children, husbands, and households when married women worked and men did not. Laetitia Conrad's interviewees offer a sense of the endemic animosity toward women for exceeding the domestic realm. Conrad noted that interviewees scapegoated women as one of the three reasons for the Great Depression and men's unemployment. These individuals also blamed machines for their replacement and the Great War, and it was true that technological efficiencies diminished the need for human labor in a number of fields and the markets created during World War I no longer existed. Yet women's employment increased; of course, the jobs they performed were deemed inappropriate for men. Aligning women with technological innovations and global conflict expresses the level of resentment toward women, as well as men's sense of entitlement and their concerns that the economic situation whetted women's appetites for public and domestic power.

The Hamtramck Women's Violence

Recognition of housewives' obligations and the extraordinary economic circumstances of the moment went a long way toward allowing women's activism, but these factors did not give women license to ignore gendered norms of conduct. Even the *Working Woman* took pains to convince its presumably radicalized female readers of their place in politics: "Is woman's place, as we have be told for centuries, still in the home? Is it still not woman's place to mess around in politics or debates about the N.R.A., or bother with things like strikes and picket lines?"[34] Although the answers to these rhetorical questions by Hamtramck women was a resounding "No!," both fellow activists and opponents criticized and scoffed at them. Why? Because the Hamtramck women's physically uncompromising picketing unsettled gendered ideas of performance-based citizenship.

National media sensationalized the violence that broke out during the first day of picketing when protesters wrestled meat products away from the shoppers who breached their picket lines. Associated Press (AP) reports, published in the *Los Angeles Times* and the *New York Times,* framed the violence as the "universal" battle of the sexes by suggesting that the protesters targeted men.

Baz Kershaw theorizes that, in protest, a spectacle's powers of persuasion operate not only by depicting master-narratives in an astonishing manner but by staging fundamental social conflicts: "spectacle seems always aimed to produce excessive reactions—the WOW! factor—and at its most effective it touches highly sensitive spots in the changing nature of the human psyche by dealing directly with the extremities of power."[35] In the historical moment of the 1930s, the Hamtramck women's violence jabbed at the "highly sensitive spot" of shifting power relations between housewife and husband, women and men. Media anxiously sought to contain women's power.

The *New York Times* ran AP coverage of the protest under the shocking headline "Buyers Trampled by Meat Strikers: Women Picket Butcher Shops in Detroit Suburb, Slap, Scratch, Pull Hair—Men Are Chief Victims." Such reports titillate with rich description of the distinctly feminine violence unleashed on men. The vicious, but reportedly inadequate, actions of slapping, scratching, and hair pulling are physical metaphors that attempt to render the women ineffectual relative to men. In interviews, male victims, Hamtramck officials, and policemen also stressed their fundamental control over the women. The *Los Angeles Times* report included a quote attributed to "one of the victims" that encapsulates the men's diminishment of the women's radical acts: "I wouldn't let Joe Louis muss me up the way some of these women did . . . but what can you do to a woman when she starts in on you?" This man characterizes his experience of the assault not as being victimized but as his exercise of self-control. Collectively, these comments and articles' sensational tone condescend to the day's violence: the men afforded the women a certain latitude to act out because the women were understandably upset; the men promise that, had it been necessary, which it never would be because of the feminine nature of the violence, they could and would enforce order.

Spectator-Participants and the Hamtramck Pickets

While exactly what happened on the first day of picketing in Hamtramck is unclear from the archive, from published reports it seems certain that both male and female consumers crossed picket lines to buy meat and that the boycotters attacked them. By committing themselves to embodied action, and specifically to what Susan Leigh Foster calls "a recalcitrant physicality that refuses to comply with the bodies of those in positions of authority," the Hamtramck women politicized consumption.[36] Significantly, they also critiqued the limitations on women's performances of citizenship and the masculine authority of these norms, and disclosed the gendered politics of consumption through their encounters with fellow consumers. In the first place, their picketing literally and instantly disrupted the economic and political operations of the food system under the AAA. As the boycotters' bodies blocked fellow consumers' access to shops or regulated their purchases, they symbolically reenacted consumers' loss of choice under the AAA. They also more directly engaged fellow consumers of both genders in the dilemma of the housewife. Meat, like milk in the previous chapter, contained its own compelling force for consumers. The consumer-spectators too needed meat, but the pickets required them physically to defend their choice to buy it during the boycott.

The most violent episode involved the women beating a man upon his exit from a shop. AP coverage published in the *New York Times* reported that a number of female spectators goaded their husbands to cross picket lines to buy meat by taunting, "You aren't afraid of a few women, are you?" The men apparently breached the housewives' picket lines. Some of the men managed to enter shops; others failed under the women's attacks. When the men exited the shops, the protesters grabbed the men's parcels and tore them apart. Against the protesters' disregard of female passivity in the face of masculine power, the counterperformances of spectators enacted socially sanctioned gender behaviors. By asking husbands to cross the strike lines for them, the female spectators positioned themselves as defenseless bodies—naturally vulnerable—in need of masculine protection. They recognized their husbands' superiority and the legitimacy of enforcing that superiority physically. They also created the opportunity for men to act gallantly on their wives' behalf and honorably in encounters with the female protesters. At the same time, these husbands acted out something akin to the housewives' dilemma, though they chose an oppositional means of confronting it: if they were unwilling to enter the fray, the men risked cowardice; if the men breached the picket, they risked serious injury; if the men fought back, they risked recrimination.

Police and the Hamtramck Pickets

The Hamtramck housewives' violence not only transgressed gender norms, but their assaults broke laws. The response of police and community supporters exhibits how gender norms constrained women's full citizenship. Hamtramck police chief Joseph Rustoni's statements bordered on the permissive: "We aren't going to interfere with the women as long as they are reasonably peaceful." He asserted that police presence was in the interest of preventing "communists" from causing trouble, a comment that dissociates these agitators in character and behavior from the women pickets. Rustoni followed up these comments by stating, "However, I'd like to catch my wife out there." Rustoni's colloquialism presumes that his wife is absent and that the female protesters have subverted their husbands' authority—sneaking out into public as it were. He indicts such disobedience in other men's households, while offering that he maintains order in his own home. Rustoni's choice of phrase also raises the specter of misogynistic desire by indicating that he would take pleasure in punishing his wife. The tension between "she would never" and "she better not" constitutes the figure of "housewife," who is no less problematic for acting in her husband's interest. As a representative of the law, the police chief affirms the women's rights as citizens, although he simultaneously belittles their efficacy. As a husband, he exercises his entitlement to condemn the audacity of the women's public behavior as an affront to masculine honor.

The recognition of women as wives first and foremost was borne out the following Saturday, August 3, 1935, during a second round of picketing. Police detained women and men who tried to accost shoppers and arrested four protesters at a meat packaging facility for attempting to pour kerosene on meat that was being unloaded. Police released the women later that evening when hundreds of people arrived at the station and demanded that the women be allowed to "spend Sunday at their homes," before their scheduled court appearance on Monday.[37] No one advocated for the men's release, and they remained in custody. Though both the male and female activists committed the same crimes for the same reason, the public called for and the police mitigated the women's legal punishment in order that the women's service to their homes could remain undisturbed. The public's and the police's disparate treatment of the jailed protesters based on their genders shows the trouble women had in being perceived as political actors and autonomous citizens.

The Acts of Other Women Activists

Within four days of the Hamtramck action, Mrs. Mrytle Hoogland, president of the newly formed Lincoln Park (Mich.) Downriver Housewives' League, assured a *Detroit Free Press* reporter that, during this group's upcoming weekend boycott, "We contemplate no violence. If women tell us that their husbands are doing hard manual labor and must have meat, we will allow them to sign our pledges and become members of the league." To become a member, a woman with a working husband had to promise to buy only enough meat for him. Hoogland's goals were virtually identical to those of the neighboring Hamtramck Women's Committee for Action against the High Cost of Living. The Downriver group planned to set up tables on the sidewalks of Lincoln Park's shopping district, at which women could sign pledge cards promising to (mostly) boycott meat. They would not picket. Orleck gestures to this decision as possible evidence of friction between activist groups of different ethnicities throughout the nation, noting that the Downriver group was predominantly Protestant and Anglo citizens.[38] Hamtramck's reputation, xenophobia, and anti-Catholic sentiment may very well have influenced Hoogland's protest performance. Hoogland's only published statement about the Hamtramck women was that picketing is "bad psychology."[39]

Hoogland and fellow organizers displayed themselves soliciting pledges. Hoogland requested permission to do so from her City Council, and she envisioned order: "We intend to set up desks on the sidewalks in the Lincoln Park business section where women may sign cards pledging themselves not to buy meat." Seated at desks, the Lincoln Park women neither approached nor accosted individuals; they invited female pass-ersby to sign the cards. Hoogland embodied the patience and physical reserve that exemplified the appropriate comportment of women in pub-lic. She coupled the display of modesty with sympathy for and measured expectations of women, who managed the difficult task of their family's consumption. Hoogland welcomed into her league even those women who could not boycott meat entirely on weekends.

Hoogland's group invoked historic precedents for performing wom-en's citizenship when they chose to pledge and not to picket. Pledging is a discursive performance of citizenship, predicated on predictable be-havior scripted as an acceptance of a set of principles.[40] When Myrtle Hoogland decided to set up desks for women to sign pledge cards, she cited a long history of pledging and its recent incarnations as the ap-propriate and efficacious political action for American women—even or specifically in times of crisis. The National Recovery Administra-tion (NRA) offered the opportunity to both industry and consumers to pledge their support of the New Deal's recovery programs. Blue Eagle signs with the slogan "We Do Our Part" politicized consumption prac-tices as citizens volunteered to patronize only businesses cooperating with the NRA. During the First World War, the U.S. Food Adminis-tration ran an aggressive campaign to persuade citizens of the impor-tance of food conservation to national security. It issued pledge cards targeted at housewives, encouraging them to vow to "join [the Food Administration] in the service of food conservation for our nation."[41] To support their sacrifice, the U.S. Food Administration sent member-ship signs for display in house windows, published recipes, and sug-gested substitutions. Literary scholar Celia M. Kingsbury equates the pledges and membership signage with surveillance and social control: "Only those middle-class women who perhaps need to gain status from their patriotism must make a show of [food] conservation. These are the women at whom, as we have seen, much propaganda was aimed, and one of the places where propaganda was most effective."[42] This act of national "service" was enforced and rewarded with the opportunity to display membership. The signs replaced a need to show the embodied domestic labor of food conservation. Absence of a sign was conspicuous, regardless of whether a household actually conserved food. Displaying the sign became the performance.

By signing a pledge, women became activists and politicized the domestic realm while reinforcing the priority of being a wife over being a citizen. In the context of the Hamtramck housewives' picketing, Hoogland's pledge negated a woman's body as a vital site of power and critique. The signatures on the cards signal not only ongoing actions that occur out of public view, but they assert the superfluity of bodily engagement to women's activism. The pledge reinforced behavioral norms for American women and the gendered parameters of performance-based citizenship. The pledge also set apart Hamtramck activists from other women.

The City of Hamtramck and the Hamtramck Pickets

Hamtramck had a lot at stake economically and culturally when the housewives occupied the city's shopping district on a Saturday. To salvage the city's reputation, media, legal authorities, and influential community members rehearsed a common arc of melodramatic dramaturgy: "moral reform melodramas . . . trace their victim's temptation and downfall from modest position and public esteem to the depths of ruin and shame, sometimes, however, ending with their reformation and success."[43]

Hamtramck is an independent city that at certain geographic points falls within Detroit. During the 1930s, it was an industrial, working-class enclave of Polish culture, dominated by first-generation Polish American families (about 90 percent of the population). The African American population of Hamtramck was small (7.2 percent in 1940) and geographically and socially segregated from the city's Polish American majority. Almost 36 percent of Hamtramck's adult population was foreign born, though many of these immigrants had lived in the United States for decades and had migrated from eastern states to Michigan in the early 1900s, drawn to employment opportunities in the automobile industry. Prior to the economic crisis, most of the men worked at Ham-

tramck's massive Dodge factory (called "Dodge Main") and in related
car parts manufacturing plants. Women worked in Hamtramck's cigar
factories. In 1936, 50 percent of Hamtramck families registered on welfare relief rolls.[44]

In the 1930s, this tiny city was also locally reputed for vice, crime,
and government corruption. Mismanagement of the city contributed
to Hamtramck's bad reputation, but classism, xenophobia, and anti-
Catholic sentiment also played major roles in scapegoating Hamtramck
for crime in and around Detroit: "Some personal prejudices appeared on
the pages of newspapers, which contributed to Hamtramck's reputation
as a free and easy city. . . . Detroit's previously settled immigrants took
pleasure in the seemingly endless series of stories revolving around the
community's difficult adjustment to American life."[45] In his 1955 study
of Hamtramck's reputation as a "cultural island" within metropolitan
Detroit, sociologist Arthur Evans Wood defends Hamtramck as comparable to any other city, while he inadvertently repeats the discourse
of Americanness as middle class, Protestant, and Anglo. Wood desig-
nates the neighboring city of Highland Park as his "control," thus con-
structing it as a socially and economically normative site and, in doing
so, "othering" Hamtramck in terms of class and ethnicity. In the 1930s,
Highland Park was a middle-class city in which men were employed
predominantly in professional, clerical, and merchant/proprietor occupations. Unlike Hamtramck, Highland Park experienced one of the
lowest rates of Depression-era unemployment. While Highland Park
had a comparable rate of foreign-born residents to Hamtramck, roughly
60 percent of its residents came from the English-speaking United King-
dom and Canada.[46] Conversely, Hamtramck was visibly, audibly, tangi-
bly "foreign." Print materials, such as newspapers, advertisements, shop
signage, and campaign materials were published in Polish, or Polish
and English, and many Hamtramck community members spoke Polish to one another, while they called people that did not speak Polish
"Americans."

Despite its reputation, during the daytime, especially on weekends,
Hamtramck's business district enjoyed the second highest rate of sales
in the metropolitan area, just behind downtown Detroit. The Federal
Writers' Project book *Michigan: A Guide to the Wolverine State* described

the many shops on Joseph Campau Avenue, Hamtramck's main thoroughfare, as the draw to this distinctly Polish community: "The windows of the white and gleaming *sklad wedlin* (delicatessens) are neatly packed with Polish foods that attract shoppers from all parts of the Detroit district. These stores, as well as the meat shops, display an amazing variety of sausages—big, small, round, loaf-shaped, red, brown, black, ringed and curled—for which Hamtramck is locally famed."[47] Attention to the aesthetic categories of line, color, composition, and scale in this description suggests the value placed upon these businesses as markers of the best facets of Polish heritage brought to America. The positive ideas consumers associated with the commodities available in Hamtramck gained the city and Polish ethnicity some cultural capital within an otherwise assimilationist America. The practice of culinary tourism offers the consumer an exploration of the others' tastes; through appeal to the senses, culturally foreign foods serve as a (misdirected) vehicle for judgments about another culture. From the perspective of "native" metro-Detroiters, if nothing else could be said for Hamtramck or Polish culture, Polish butchers had the ability to prepare delicious cuts and varieties of meat. Picketing and blocking shop entrances on Saturdays interrupted the busiest shopping day of the week, and some residents of Hamtramck feared that these actions would confirm outsiders' negative view of the city.

"Town Fathers" and the Hamtramck Pickets

As members of an ethnic community and as women, the Women's Committee bore the burden of representing Polish Americans to those outside the community. In 1930s Hamtramck, "[s]o sensitive are the leaders of public opinion to the reputation of their town that any one of their own group who gives publicity to some unfavorable incident, be it criminal or otherwise, is socially ostracized as a traitor."[48] The *Polish Daily News,* a local, conservative Polish-language newspaper, initially supported the Hamtramck housewives by advertising the Women's Committee meetings on July 19 and July 26, 1935, to which "Polish housekeepers" were invited. Throughout the boycott's planning stage, this newspaper showed sympathy with the housewives' cause. For example, the article "Organizing against High Prices" (July 19, 1935) led with, "Food prices are rising steadily, with people making no earnings at all, or getting only slightly better. Housewives in different cities of the U.S. are protesting against such a thing."[49] Women's public involvement in a domestic cause was praiseworthy; it also had the virtue of being an American movement conducted by women throughout the nation. After the first day of picketing, however, the Hamtramck City Council—the "town fathers"—denied the request of the Women's Committee to use the stadium to hold a meeting. Mayor Lewandowski also chastised them for the violence and for ruining Hamtramck business.[50]

The *Polish Daily News* shifted its characterization of the women in an effort to mitigate the damage it perceived the female pickets caused to the city's reputation. On Monday, July 29, 1935, the paper reported on the previous Saturday's events under the headline "The Communists Provoked a Scandal with the Meat Strike." It bears out the sexualized allusions of its title, in which a communist villain bamboozles the women. Much like conventional melodramatic dramaturgy, the action is sensational, the characters personify good and evil, and the conflict appeals to salient values by imperiling women's virtue. Reportedly, communists, unconcerned with the "honor of Hamtramck" led "honest housewives into error." On the police's arrival, the communists "hid," "leaving behind their friends and honest women led into error." The latter phrase is repeated throughout the article. Why the "communists" seduced the women is not explained because, like most villains in a melodrama, they are driven by an innate desire to corrupt women. The article portrays the housewives as heroines in this performance in an attempt to excuse their behavior; they are as inherently good as they are vulnerable. The women's "natural" naiveté is no match for the unexplained but presumably ingenious trickery of the communists. The dénouement of this melodrama is atypical in that the evil evade punishment, while the women are left to repent: "honest and respectable housewives allowed themselves to be led out in the Communists' fields and today, definitely, more than one regrets it." The unseen happenings in picturesque "fields" are rife with sexual connotations. The women's fall from grace and respectability to shame is conflated with a political fall from "American" to "Communist." The women's reported regret and realization of their error function to warn other women against such a course of action, at the same time that the article offers the repentant a reintroduction into society.

The next day's headline, "The Case of the Meat Strike in Hamtramck in Light of the Facts," promised revelations. Violence was framed as the "fact" that "confirmed beyond a doubt that in this justified action of the Hamtramck women, elements of communism were mixed in, desiring to take advantage of their subversive goals for this movement of law-abiding, respected and well-known citizens of Hamtramck." When read in light of the paper's promotion of the boycotters' planning meetings prior to the protest, violence committed by "well-known" women presented a major problem for Hamtramck's image. The paper expresses the concern that violent women would confirm the "natural" differences between the ethnic population and "Americans" and reinforce biases against Polish American citizens. The *Polish Daily News* could not avail itself of the common explanation that violent women are aberrant and unnatural, given the women who participated in the picketing.[51] Historian Denise Lynn argues that the accusations of "Communist influence" in news reports on the housewives' boycott "stripped women of any agency in the strike and painted Communists as antagonists."[52] The *Polish Daily News* portrayed women as passive to dissociate them from their behavior. The use of "Communist" by the *Polish Daily News* was also gendered in that it was evoked specifically to regulate women's behavior by sexualizing their activism. Mayor Lewandowski similarly rebutted accusations that the women were communists by stating that "The big majority are good honest citizens with a legitimate complaint."[53]

The women in Hamtramck, including leader Mary Zuk, emphatically denied that their actions stemmed from party directives, claiming that the need for meat was apolitical; it was a universal concern. The fact that Communist Party section leaders took credit for the Hamtramck women's work following the women's rise to prominence did not help the women's cause. The party's narrative "How the Meat Strike Started in Hamtramck" not only suggests that it had organized the protest but credits itself with liberating women from the private sphere and empowering them: "Women who never spoke in public and did not think they were capable, became not only fine speakers but leaders of the strike."[54]

In doing so, it inadvertently substantiated the claim that the Hamtramck women's forms of activism were un-American performances.

Racial Politics and the Hamtramck Women's Actions

Many Polish American residents perceived the systemic racial discrimination in Hamtramck as groups separated by distinct cultural practices, rather than racial prejudice per se.[55] Their provisional acceptance and simultaneous marginalization of African American residents is typified in a 1938 article on festivities celebrating the city's twenty-fifth anniversary. The "surprising" fact contained in the title "Negroes Have Lived in City for 50 Years" reveals the social boundaries operating within the city. At the same time, the article embraces African Americans as community members by noting that, in the anniversary parade, "a generous sprinkling of [African American] children . . . [marched] to the ringing applause of spectators" and by enumerating the civic contributions of African Americans through their work as council members, city trustees, policemen, and physicians (the extremely small number of African Americans holding such positions suggests the list is a gesture of tokenism). In praising the athletic accomplishments of several African American students from Hamtramck High School, the article treats Hamtramck's racially integrated public schools in a matter-of-fact manner.[56] Most Polish American children attended Catholic schools that taught them written and spoken Polish, as well as Polish history and culture. While, for the time period, the city was remarkably integrated, segregation was enforced at some businesses along Joseph Campau Avenue into the 1960s, a period during which the City Council also illegally undertook a program of "Negro removal" under the guise of a federal Housing and Urban Development urban renewal project.[57]

Opponents and supporters of the housewives' movement did not recognize the Hamtramck women's potentially progressive views on race. While a photograph dated Friday, August 2, 1935, shows African American children among white children, women, and men (see figure 3.2), the interracial cooperation of boycotters in Hamtramck went largely unacknowledged or misperceived by those outside the movement. Pro- and anti-Women's Committee camps engaged in racist and

Figure 3.2. Children pose with boycott signs in front of a restaurant in Hamtramck, Michigan, August 2, 1935. Walter P. Reuther Library, Wayne State University, Detroit News Collection #29813_1.

theatrical discourse in efforts to discredit the other. The *Worker's Tribune*, a communist Polish-language paper, reported on "enemy propaganda" against the ongoing pickets. Allegedly, in an effort to "start a racial fight" and disperse two young pickets from outside his store, a Mr. Zawadzki hired an African American man to hold a sign reading "I will help my sweetheart to picket." According to the article, the radicalized women were undeterred by the ploy and took it as an opportunity to raise the consciousness of the unwittingly complicit man: "the picketers explained to the black man that he should not let Mr. Zawadzki use him in such a disgraceful manner. The black worker was persuaded. He went back to Mr. Zawadzki's store and threw the [illegible word] sign at his feet."[58] This brief narrative exhibits contradictory racial politics. Paradoxically, it paints a condescending portrait of the African American man as unenlightened to affirm the radical Left's pursuit of racial equality. It also refutes the stereotype of the hypersexualized, aggressive black man, while it denies the possibility of romantic interracial relations. The article aims to spark outrage against antiboycotters by positioning Mr. Zawadzki as the sponsor of a theatrical performance that breaches the social boundaries of even the most progressive racial politics.

Hamtramck's socially conservative constituency alleged that Mary Zuk exploited sacred celebrations of Polish heritage to stage a political stunt. The *Polish Daily News* reported on the anger Zuk created among members of the Polish Women's Alliance. Mrs. Jozefa Marasowicz, chair of Group 561 of the national Polish women's fraternal organization, went before the Hamtramck City Council to recount Zuk's affront during the blessing of the flags of the Circle of Polish Women, a ceremony designed to preserve and honor Hamtramck's common culture. According to Marasowicz, as Women's Alliance members processed in a march of devotion to St. Florian's Church—the symbolic cornerstone of Hamtramck's Polish cultural identity—two African American women joined in: "When [the members of the Polish Women's Alliance] pointed out to them that it was a march, in which only people who have been invited could participate, the women stated that they were sent by Zuk, that they were marching in her name and that after the march they would speak. As proof that they were telling the truth, the black women showed authorization from Mary Zuk." The allegation suggested Zuk's outrageousness and her utter disrespect for the community's dearest, and defining, values. Zuk claimed the whole thing was a "frame up." The City Council ruled that the Polish Women's Alliance should condemn Zuk's behavior.[59] The incident speaks to the belief among conservative community members that Zuk actively worked to cause discord within a community that was purportedly in solidarity in matters pertaining to race relations. Mary Zuk's public cooperation with African American women as part of the Detroit housewives' movement (if not also as part of the Hamtramck boycotts) rendered her susceptible to such accusations, but Zuk's 1936 election to the Hamtramck City Council may also indicate that many Hamtramck residents held opposing ideas about racial and gender equality.

Hamtramck Housewives on the National Stage

The national momentum of the housewives' movement pressured corporations and the federal government into defending their policies to the women. By the second week of August 1935, the Hamtramck Women's Committee had collected enough donations to send women to march on the stockyards with Chicago activists and to send a delegation to Washington, DC to meet with Agricultural Adjustment Administration officials. The delegation included Mary Zuk, Elizabeth Moss, Pearl Alterman, Katherine Mudra (all white women), and Irene Thompson (an African American woman). Zuk is identified as the "leader" of the activists; the other women are not further identified in photographs of the delegation's ceremonial presentation of their resolution for an investigation into meat prices to their representative, Congressman John Dingell (Democrat-Mich.).[60] Newspapers reported that this Detroit housewives' delegation was in Washington to advocate for the abolition of the AAA processing tax.

Mary Zuk Confronts a Congressional Opponent

The constitutionality of the AAA processing tax was already under fire in the Hoosac Mills lawsuit against the federal government, and the number of lawsuits was growing. Packers took advantage of the housewives' complaints about high prices to campaign against the tax. Corporations argued that they had been losing money while paying the federal government through the processing tax to create shortages and to pay the farmer not to raise livestock. On July 29, 1935, seventeen Chicago packaging companies filed a writ to stop the collection of these taxes, adding to the number of suits against it. The "big four"—Armour & Co., Swift & Co., Oscar Mayer & Co., and P. Brennan & Co.—led the charge. In Detroit, Thomas W. Taliaferro, president of the Hammond Standish Co., took the housewives' boycott as an opportunity to substantiate the packagers' stance that the federal government's duplicity was simply found out by natural disaster: "They began with the scarcity economics which led to the slaughter of little pigs at the instance of the Federal Department of Agriculture and were augmented by the drought conditions

which resulted in the slaughter of 7,000,000 head of starving cattle a year
ago. . . . While scarcity may have been artificially started it is none the
less real and inescapable."[61]

In defense of the processing tax, Congressman Clarence Cannon
(Democrat-Mo.) called for an investigation into the Hamtramck housewives' actions from the House floor on the weekend before the women's
scheduled arrival in Washington, DC. He alleged that the Hamtramck
protest was theater, specifically a "fake food strike," sponsored by the
meat packaging industry. Cannon laid out evidence of theatricality to
substantiate his allegations. The congressman contrasted the behavior
of protest participants and their "angry babble of foreign tongues" with
the appearances and behaviors of Missouri farmwomen "of the finest
type of American womanhood." He placed into the record a photograph
of the protesters, which "shows women clad in the latest fashions. Their
marcelled coiffures indicate that they have recently visited beauty par-
lors, and there is not a hat in the picture that is not of the latest model . . .
Evidently many of them have just returned from their bridge clubs or are
on their way to the movies.[62] Cannon reduces the Hamtramck women to
insincere "actors," engaging in protest with the same pleasure-seeking,
carefree attitude that they enjoy during other divertissements typical
of middle-class women.

The congressman's attempt to discredit the Hamtramck women's
claims to economic hardship by using their appearances against them
was not original. Throughout the 1910s, 1920s, and 1930s, labor opponents
and media scrutinized the legitimacy of women workers' strikes based
on how they dressed, interpreting the women's fashionableness as not
only an economic signal that belied their claims to needing higher wages
but also as a sign of their "natural" inability to be serious politic actors.
In turn, "Labor leaders understood the threat of women's fashion to the
public images of the strikers, and responded by strategically shaping a
view of the strikers to match public expectations."[63] While Cannon recognized the women as housewives rather than workers, he too banked
on the public expectation of protesters' threadbare dress, and he put
an explicitly xenophobic spin on this tactic. Following his description
of the Hamtramck women, Cannon read into the record a letter from
a woman from "one of the greatest agricultural counties in the nation"

about her inability to afford either proper clothing or a proper diet for her family. By overtly contrasting these two feminine types, Cannon sought to raise nativist indignation at the notion that "foreigners" were attempting to bilk the government for rights they were not entitled to, while "real" American women suffered desperately and properly—that is, out of public view.

Based on visual evidence, it seems that the Hamtramck housewives dressed for their public appearances. All wore high heels and dresses; most wore hats and carried purses; some had on pearls; and everyone's hair was done. They looked like American wives were expected to look in public, which proved problematic for their representation of need. The Hamtramck women's appearance was so utterly ordinary that it seems to have been an unconscious performance of self-respect on their parts. At the same time, like other working-class and ethnicized women, their dress may also have "spoke[n] clearly to the goals and aspirations of the immigrant woman" to be recognized as culturally American.[64] (Many of these women were born in the United States, after all.) Dressing the part of "housewife" signaled a collective identity, common cause, and made a performance-based, somatic claim to citizenship.

Cannon categorized the women's coordination as an attempt to create an illusion; he aimed to dismantle it by theatricalizing its elements and transforming the activists into actresses: "When we come to examine this so-called 'strike' in Detroit we find every evidence of an artificial demonstration staged to serve the interests of a carefully concealed promoter. The women had been drilled. The Associated Press reports that they moved 'with the precision of a military force.' Their forces were composed entirely of women and no men participated."[65] Using the language of theater to turn collectivity into casting, dress into costume, coordination into rehearsal, and organizational support into the dealings of an impresario, Cannon cynically marvels at the miraculous appearance of news reporters and filmmakers at the picketing, the "unknown source" of the banners and signs provided to the women, and the curious timing of the protest, which coincided with packers' litigation against the AAA. He ultimately calls for a counterinvestigation to discover who sponsored, scripted, and directed the protest.

Zuk confronted Cannon in his Washington office. She demanded that he retract his statements alleging that the protest was "a pure fake" and that Hamtramck women were foreigners. Zuk asserted, "We're American citizens" (in English, of course) and called Cannon's accusation that the women were in cahoots with packers "absurd." She answered this allegation with the fact that the women chose meat, specifically pork, because its price had escalated the most.[66] Zuk not only defended the legitimacy of the Hamtramck women's claims but argued for their right as citizens to make demands against federal government. By going to the congressman's office solely to tell him "what we think of you," Zuk asserted her equality to Cannon as a citizen and publicly laid bare the ethnic and gender biases on which he based his exclusion of the Hamtramck women from citizenship.

Mary Zuk Confronts Secretary Wallace

Media reports of the meeting between Mary Zuk and Henry Wallace expressed, what Orleck calls, an "ambiguous" perspective. They seemed to agree with Zuk's emotional condemnation of the AAA, yet they dissociate from this apparently feminine perspective by ridiculing Wallace's "cowardice" when he was confronted with it. Wallace arrived at the meeting, which was already underway in the office of AAA consumer council Calvin Hoover and taking place in front of reporters. Wallace wanted the press to leave in order to have a "frank discussion" with the women. However, Zuk insisted on an "open" conversation. News reports plotted a conversation escalating toward climax: Zuk raises question after question; each of Wallace's responses fail to appease her; Zuk will not relent; so Wallace abruptly leaves the meeting. Headlines captured the drama of the confrontation and the dénouement, rather than the substance of Wallace's or Zuk's remarks. On August 20, 1935, the *Washington Post* ran the story as "Wallace Flees Food Strikers' Plea for Slash: Feminine Logic Too Much for Secretary as Group Cites High Prices." Wallace's unmanliness allowed "feminine logic," a sociocultural oxymoron, to trump economic rationalism. In its recap of the week's news, the *Washington Post* recounted how Wallace's "retreat was considered the most disorganized since the French straggled back from Moscow last century." The *Los Angeles Times* mocked the assertion that the secretary left to take a phone call. The news was Wallace's cowardice.[67]

The coincidence of Secretary Wallace's authorization of the emergency pig slaughter, the Hamtramck Women's Committee's goals, and Disney's Silly Symphonies' "The Three Little Pigs" (1933) and "The Big Bad Wolf" (1934) facilitated parody of Wallace's and Zuk's abbreviated meeting during the visit of the women's delegation to Washington, DC. Visually and narratively, *Newsweek* caricatured Wallace as the Big Bad Wolf. Titled "MEAT: Women Want the Big Bad AAA to Let the Little Pigs Alone," the August 31, 1935, article covers how the "5-foot housewife" Mary Zuk bested Wallace in their debate. An image of Wallace laughing frames the article; it is recoded to connect him physically to Disney's version of the wolf. Like the cartoon predator, Wallace's broad grin becomes bared teeth at the mouth-watering sight of the women, featured in an adjacent picture in which they look modest and cheerful. Wallace's mussed hair is resignified as standing on end. The contrast in bodies of the wolf/Wallace and Little Red/Zuk, as well as her little pigs, signals the "natural" dispositions of man and woman.

The cartoon genre, which can punish incorrect behavior and reinforce gender distinctions through laughter, exaggerates "natural" gender difference and the excesses of desire that those differences produce. Much like the prescriptive functions of melodramatic heroines and their contradictory constructions of femininity, the fairytale genre produces Little Red "as rowdy spectacle, as punished perpetrator, and finally as rehabilitated good girl . . . to contain and regulate the feminine body."[68] In the Disney version just as in the *Newsweek* article, masculinity is also explicitly regulated. Film historian Jane Gaines, in her study of Tex Avery's WWII-era cartoons modeled on Disney characters, describes how visual focus on the wolf's response, rather than the object of his desire—Little Red, a showgirl—presents the spectator with a formula for "looking, arousal, then aggression" that both affirms heterosexual aggression as a sign of masculinity and polices intemperance.[69]

The pattern that Gaines delineates forms the core of Disney's Silly Symphony, "The Big Bad Wolf," which was the sequel to the animated short "Three Little Pigs." It begins with Little Red Riding Hood and the two carefree pigs ignoring their responsible brother's warning to avoid the temptation of a short-cut to grandmother's house. The two silly pigs tell Little Red that the wolf is full of hot air, causing fear and maintaining control only by bluster: "All he does is huff and puff. . . . We'll call his bluff." The wolf's masculinity—something unquestionably authoritative—is all pretense. The two pigs and Little Red are easy and attractive targets for a hungry wolf; all three are as plump as they are naïve. They narrowly escape the wolf's various attempts to devour them. Each attempt "coincidently" lands the wolf in an emasculating predicament, for example, dressed in women's clothing. But the third industrious pig comes to the rescue. In the end, he scares the wolf away by putting hot coals and a little popping corn in the wolf's pants. The wolf yelps and scurries in retreat. The cartoon ends with Red, her grandmother, and the three little pigs reprising the well-known song "Who's Afraid of the Big Bad Wolf." The two carefree pigs delight in new lyrics, "Who's afraid of the Big Bad Wolf? He's a great big sissy." The cherubic, girlish boy pigs have gelded the wolf entirely.

Importantly, the *Newsweek* article meshes the parodic with the conventions of news narrative. Parody is a process of "transcontexualization" in which a performance is repeated in a new frame, "so that the two texts or performances exist side by side," placing a critical lens on an event. Humor and critique arise from the ironic fit of the original in a disparate context.[70] Wallace's performance is transcontextualized to cartoon, yet the authoritative journalistic frame is unbroken. As a publication, *Newsweek* sets the expectation of objectivity in accounts of real world events, and the encounter between Zuk and Wallace employs the conventions of news narrative. The article situates Wallace's statements and actions as absurd in reality. He is depicted as naturally out of proportion: a wolf in Washington. Indeed, *Newsweek* uses a photograph of Wallace to evidence that the article is not caricature, but that it captures Wallace's unwitting betrayal of his "real" nature. By extension, it casts Wallace's AAA programs as an excessive response to economic crisis.

Zuk and Wallace are depicted in the realist mode: their physicality is used to signify the "truth" of their moral character. The article emphasizes Mary Zuk's petite stature in comparison to Wallace's imposing height. Their bodies externalize their social and political power and "prove" their gendered natures, as well as the nature of gender difference. Zuk's actions are representations of archetypical, unwavering femininity. Though remarkably persistent, she does not emasculate Wallace so much as Wallace reveals his effeminacy. This very powerful man's fear of a woman—and feminine logic—is what registers as cartoonish. In both the *Washington Post* and *Newsweek,* Zuk's retorts to Wallace's sound economic explanations are not represented as sophisticated theory; hers are emotional pleas:

> The lanky Iowan looked down into Mrs. Zuk's deep-sunken brown eyes and gulped his Adam's apple.
>
> MRS. ZUK: Is the government going to reduce prices 20 per cent?
>
> MR. WALLACE: Under drought conditions it is impossible to guarantee future prices.
>
> MRS. ZUK: Why does the government pay farmers not to grow little pigs?
>
> MR. WALLACE: The government is only concerned with not raising pigs for European consumption, a market that no longer exists.
>
> MRS. ZUK: Doesn't the government want us to live? Everything in Detroit's gone up except wages.
>
> Finally Mr. Wallace gave up and fled.[71]

Here, as in other coverage of the incident, Zuk's questions do not cause Wallace to show the illogic of his agricultural policies, as is the conventional function of political parody. Instead, Wallace reveals his nerves at the outset and is scared away by the rhetorical equivalent of popcorn in his pants. This gender parody centers on Wallace's failed masculinity as an indication of his knowledge of the immorality of his agricultural program.

From their work in Washington, DC, the women won congressional approval for an investigation. However, the Federal Trade Commission sent word to Zuk on September 5, 1935, that the appropriations bill to provide money for the investigation did not pass.[72] In the days following, the Women's Committee for Action against the High Cost Living called on people to boycott meat twice a week, while it turned its attention to establishing a permanent women's league to fight all high prices. Due to six weeks of "much sacrifice," however, the Hamtramck Women's Committee cancelled picketing "until further notice."[73]

Mrs. Mary Zuk and Historiographic Melodrama

Neither Mary Zuk nor her opponents were finished, however. The Hamtramck Butchers' and Grocers' Association, representing roughly 150 shops, had openly broken with the women during the third week of the boycott, vowing to keep their businesses going.[74] They filed an injunction against Mary Zuk specifically and other housewives generally to keep them from obstructing shops' entryways or blocking the sidewalks. By the time Zuk returned from Washington, with the joint resolution authorizing the investigation, the injunction was signed and in force. In mid-September, after Zuk had publicly called off picketing, storeowners took out another injunction against her, banning any campaigning for lower meat prices in order to silence the Women's Committee. Zuk addressed the Polish community via radio, in Polish, to invite them to join in the establishment of a permanent Women's League to fight all high prices; the milk trusts were its next target. In this address, Zuk aligned the league's mission with the work of Maria Konopnicka, a famed nineteenth-century Polish children's author and advocate, and with Thaddeus Kosciusko and Casimir Pulaski, "who were declared heroes because they fought for the freedom of this country," that is, they were "true" Polish Americans.[75]

When Mary Zuk emerged as the women's leader, she became the target of personal attacks. Her story, as created by Hamtramck community media over the course of five years and sustained by extant documents in the archive, progresses toward a rather predictable dénouement. While narratives that celebrate Zuk laud her as a woman who achieved greatness at much personal cost, those that disdain her show how she fell victim to her own misguided ambitions and the lesser inclinations of women. Both sides imagine Zuk as facing the dilemma of the housewife in which she must sacrifice the private for the public, or vice versa. While I am not denying that Zuk may very well have experienced her situation as a painful dilemma, I am cautious about the archive's conformity to conventional melodramatic dramaturgy and its prescriptive functions against women's embodied activism.

As soon as she became a public figure, Zuk was accused of being a communist. In this case, the charge came not only from the *Polish Daily Tribune* but from Chicago packers, Detroit packers, and local butchers, who had been essentially shut down by the housewives' movement during the first two weeks of the boycott. They persuaded Police Commissioner Heinrich Pickert to investigate Communist influence on the Hamtramck women.[76] The *Polish Daily News* also alleged that Zuk conspired to bring disgrace upon entire community: "we ask why Mary Zuk is exposing Polish immigrants to persecution by the Americans? In the name of exactly what does she want the Polish people to be ensnarled with? The local Polish society has to live the life of the American society."[77]

Despite persistent allegations about Zuk's communist agenda during her campaign for City Council in the spring of 1936, she won the office. Her election indicates that voters shared her progressive agenda and that they viewed a woman's perspective as appropriate to politics. Running as a "housewife," she beat out two men—one ran as a "housepainter" and the other as a "journalist"—for the new People's League party nomination. Zuk received double the votes of the other candidates; her two male opponents for the nomination received more votes than the "old time politicians of Hamtramck."[78] The People's League advocated for a farm-labor coalition, antidiscrimination policies, unionization of labor, no police interference in labor disputes, and welfare reforms. Another final point in the platform was to get the Dodge Corporation to pay its Hamtramck city taxes. Zuk was the first woman elected to City Council in Hamtramck. Her election made national news, and media invented her as a character whose biography begins in the moment of fame: "The 31-year-old mother of two children will serve two years at a salary of $3,500 a year. From the obscurity of welfare rolls, she assumed the leadership last August of a housewives' committee which conducted a strike so intensive that more than a score of meat dealers closed their doors under the force of feminine picket lines."[79] Such articles stage the protest as the inciting incident for the drama of an ordinary housewife turned public figure.

Mary Zuk was sincere in her progressive politics. She publicly advocated for equal rights for African Americans. She helped form the Wayne County Farmer-Labor Party, celebrated the creation of the Polish local of the United Auto Workers (UAW; October 1936); participated in the 1937 women's seated strikes in cigar factories, and helped the UAW negotiate with General Motors during the same time.[80] In August 1936, following a heated City Council debate about Spain's civil war and in response to reporters' questions about her party affiliations, Zuk stated that "what you call Communists are simply the majority of the working people of the country. . . . I belong with the majority." The *Hamtramck Citizen* reported this as Zuk's "open admission" to being a communist.[81] Local papers published "proof" of Zuk's communism through to her failed reelection campaign in 1938.

Upon her election in 1936, Zuk stated that her election showed that "a mother can organize and still take care of her family."[82] Yet the *New Deal*, a Hamtramck publication, suggested otherwise: "Her husband . . . shows signs of uneasiness. He will have general housework and the care of two children on his hands now, neighbors explain."[83] By spring 1937, Mary Zuk entered into divorce proceedings. During the alimony hearings, she charged Stanley Zuk with "beating her, excessive drinking, nonsupport, and falsely accusing her of flirting." In his counterclaim, Stanley Zuk alleged that Mary was a Communist Party member, neglected her children, stayed out all night, and wrote love letters to another man: "Mary thought she was a big shot and I was only a laboring man."[84] Mary Zuk refused to comment to newspapers on Stanley Zuk's allegations.[85]

Conservative papers, by their accounts, were vindicated. Writing just after her divorce, Leo J. Kirchner represented Zuk's divorce as recompense for exceeding her place as a wife: "She achieved a certain form of fame—notoriety. But she lost her husband. She became a public official, but she lost the home life that is woman's chief career when her husband divorced her."[86] Following the failure of Zuk's 1938 bid for reelection, *Detroit News* reporter Lou Tendler wrote that, according to men in Hamtramck, Zuk's defeat was the inevitable outcome of her bad behavior. Purportedly, she had behaved like a housewife given too much power and control over consumption: she had frittered money away on a house, a fur coat, and a car; she had dispensed with "'a good man' who had stuck by his family through adversity." She had transgressed gender norms not only through her employment but in its kind as well as its remuneration, making a supposedly exorbitant salary many times greater than her husband's wage when he was working. Mary Zuk stated that she lost the election because her progressive politics did not prove radical enough for the communists, so they withdrew their support.[87]

Mayor Rudolph G. Tenerowicz appointed her as the Water Department commissioner, and then she worked briefly in the U.S. Immigration Department before her second marriage.

Don Binkowski, a retired Michigan judge and independent scholar who writes on the history of Detroit and Polish America, donated his papers to the Walter P. Reuther Library at Wayne State University, which is known for its collections on U.S. working-class and labor organizations. Within the Binkowski Papers are a handful of files on Mrs. Mary Varto, née Mrs. Mary Zuk. Binkowski searched for first-hand accounts of the protest, gathered newspaper clippings and police reports, and retrieved Zuk's papers from her only surviving son. Zuk's papers are amazingly sparse for a person who held elected office and who was intensely active in city politics and union organizing from 1935–38. Though her silence in the archive seems appropriate to a woman who left public life upon her second marriage in 1940 because, according to her son, "her husband, Joseph Varto, made her promise not to get involved in politics and she honored that promise, participating in Christian church activities."[88]

Binkowski collected information on Zuk and the meat strike as part of his ongoing effort to gain recognition of Zuk by the Michigan Women's Historical Center and Hall of Fame, a goal unrealized to date. The "Timeline of Michigan Women's History" available on this organization's website showcases women's "firsts" as historically significant but does not include the events of 1935 or Mary Zuk.[89] Binkowski concluded his nomination of Zuk for the Hall of Fame as follows: "Ahead of the feminist movement Mary Zuk proved to be a female pioneer in both the labor movement and the social movement. Like any pathfinder, she paid a price for her individualism and her feminism." When Binkowski shared this narrative with me, he implied concern that allegations about Zuk's "un-American" politics might play a pivotal role in her not being recognized by the organization, writing, "I redacted any references to communism or progressive organizations" in the nomination narrative for Zuk.[90] Binkowski's move is an understandable appeal to hegemonic expectations of acceptable performances of women's citizenship. The documents that remain support a conventional structuring of Zuk's history that pertains to the melodrama of "housewife," in which she rises, falls, or sacrifices, and then quietly disappears.

SCENE NINETEEN

Voice of Living Newspaper (over loudspeaker): It is estimated, three hundred and seventy-five thousand share-croppers lose their places in acreage reduction.

(The scene is played against the eye, in frame of 1st travelers. It is possible that a scene column might be used to indicate the veranda of a southern plantation. Five share-croppers enter, all very shabbily dressed.)

Farmer (Drawling): I guess I can't use you croppers no more. Ain't raisin' no more cotton.
First Cropper: I heard tell you got money for not raisin' cotton.
Second Cropper: We figgured some of that was ours.
Farmer: Since when you croppers started figgerin'? You git you stuff together and git. The Guv'ment ain't wantin' me to plant the land you been workin'.
Third Cropper: Wait a minute. The guv'ment's payin' you not to plant, and it says here . . . (waves a paper) . . . that you're supposed to pay us.
Farmer: Every durn one of you owes me money, and I ain't a sayin' nothin' if you git.
Third Cropper: C'mon croppers. I want to talk to you alone.

(He draws them away from the farmer who stands watching them suspiciously)
Listen.

(The others crowd around him)

The way I figger it, this Guv'ment stuff may be ahelpin' us, Them Congressment said we wouldn't lose our homes, but by God, We ARE losin' our homes. I ain't been waitin' to join the Union 'cause I was a'feared. But, by God, I ain't a'feared no more! The Union is demandin' 10¢ an hour for cotton pickers. It's demandin' Constitutional rights. I don't know how it's a goin' to get 'em. But, by God, I'm a'goin' to help 'em. Are you with me? Then, come on!

(They follow him toward the farmer as the scene blackens.)

BLACKOUT

Script Excerpt 4. Editorial Staff of the Living Newspaper Federal Theatre Project under the supervision of Arthur Arent, "Triple-A Plowed Under," 1936, Federal Theatre Project Collection, Special Collections and Archives, George Mason University Libraries.

Hunger on the Highway in the Cotton South

The 1939 Missouri Sharecroppers' Demonstration

ON JANUARY 19, 1939, THE *SIKESTON HERALD* OFFERED ITS readers the silver lining to the recent damage to their reputation: "The wave of patriotism and cooperation aroused by the unjust condemnation of Southeast Missouri last week is one of the most interesting and worthwhile results of the demonstration. The people of this section are 'riled up' over the untrue stories that have been reported and the unjust criticism that has been made of the people of Southeast Missouri." The hyperbolic language, invoking an image of the populace standing against a grave injustice, signals the depth of these Missourians' concern for their public image following the sharecroppers' demonstration.[1]

For five days through January snow and rain, in thirteen camps along thirty-eight miles of Missouri highway U.S. 60 and seventy miles of Missouri's U.S. 61, thirteen hundred women, men, and children squatted in protest of their unlawful evictions from the cotton plantations on which they farmed. These sharecropper families, the majority of whom were African Americans, were surrounded by what appeared to be all their worldly possessions. The few makeshift shelters that they had assembled

protected some belongings and individuals. However, most sharecroppers, along with their domestic objects—dolls, furniture, pans—incon-
gruously occupied the same open space as trucks, chickens, and camp-
fires. The scene constituted both their meager households and their dire
poverty. From January 10–15, 1939, the sharecroppers simply lived on the
roadsides, engaging in the activities of daily life. They cooked the little
food they had and shared it; they prayed together; the adults tended to
the children; they entertained themselves by singing and talking. While
this protest bore little resemblance to other radical activity of the era,
its very public display of what everyday life was like for sharecroppers
was an audacious performance in the midst of a Missouri society that
believed propertied white men had the cultural right to control the lives
of their white and African American workers and, even more, knew
"what was necessary in 'handling niggers.'"[2]

Sharecroppers had moved to the highways because they believed
that visibility of their dire living conditions was vital to attaining their
goals: secure sharecropping agreements and the enforcement of federal
protections for farm tenants under the Agricultural Adjustment Act.
Protest leader Reverend Owen Whitfield's speech to fellow croppers in
the days before the demonstration illustrates the affective power of staging hunger: "If we are going to starve, let's starve out there where people
can see us!"[3] Missouri landowners, officials, and local media shared the
idea that the protesters' display of their dire living circumstances was
powerful enough to force changes in cotton culture. And so, authorities
in Missouri worked to get the croppers out of sight by designating the
roadside protest a health menace. On January 13, highway patrolmen
and deputized men began removing croppers; by January 15, the highways were clear. Authorities dumped the families in remote locations.
They discarded croppers in an abandoned church and in barns. They
also removed croppers to spillways referred to as "concentration camps,"
which were guarded "to keep visitors out and campers in."[4] Meanwhile,
Missouri landowners and local presses sought to undermine the display
by claiming that it was a charade. The *Sikeston Herald* maintained that
croppers were "pretending to the world at large that they had been cruelly driven from their homes."[5] Detractors alleged that protesters were
not really sharecroppers but transients, that they had not been evicted,
and that the croppers were not actually hungry.

Just as Missouri plantation owners and local presses associated share-croppers with theatrical pretense to deny the profound moral obligations raised by public starvation, national and regional media characterized the protest as human drama to express the depth of the injustice. The *Cleveland Call and Post,* an African American press, asked readers to "visualize ... night, a cold drizzling rain pelting down unmercifully on homeless hundreds.... these hundreds of homeless tenant farmers tragi-cally dramatized a mass protest against the cruel attempt of planters [*sic*] eviction of their tenants."[6] In the former case, the implication is that the protesters were acting; in the latter, they are depicted as living an in-situ performance. The notions of faking or authenticity, respectively, were attendant and crucial.

Sharecroppers needed to present a seamless illusion as well as a tidy narrative because their character was subject to doubt. Writing for the *Christian Advocate,* W. F. Baxter criticized the common sentiment that croppers were "lazy, shiftless families, seeking to evade the responsibili-ties of society and good citizenship."[7] For unlike the other Depression-era cases considered here, in which economic dysfunction was accepted as the cause of protesters' struggles, in the case of Missouri Bootheel sharecroppers, the onus was on them not only to prove their hunger but to demonstrate its socioeconomic roots.

Sharecroppers staged landowners' violations of the AAA and argued for federal enforcement of AAA protections. By affirming producerist no-tions of citizenship as a valid measure to determine rights, even the right to food, their demonstration critiqued the image of the shiftless share-cropper, incapable of acting as a productive citizen. Staging their protest along national highways to signal their displacement, the croppers' col-lective bodies as families, carrying on their everyday activities, signified their desire to belong. By "simply living" on roadsides (or staging a protest that lacked the common behavioral and spectacular elements of such radical activity), sharecroppers deployed the genre of in-situ exhibition. This theatrical convention produced the illusion that the demonstration was unmediated: an authentic performance of daily life in public view.

At the same time, the racial markers, as well as the class and re-gional markers, that defined the sharecroppers privileged a racialized mode of interpreting their actions on the highways. Mainstream white audiences understood the poor, rural, black (and white) families' performances of community and mutual support through the popular theatrical entertainment of minstrelsy. Like in-situ exhibition, minstrelsy's power lies in its cultural claims to authentic depictions of rural blackness and plantation life. In sympathetically constituting the sharecroppers through minstrel types and narratives, national and regional media argued that croppers shared the fundamental conservative American values of hard work, family, community, and Christianity, while simultaneously reiterating established race- and class-based hierarchies. The scene of croppers' living conditions, as well as the actions of powerful Missourians during the demonstration, effectively disclosed and challenged the operations of cotton culture, and disputed the racist and classist discourse of shiftlessness upon which it relied.

While the sharecroppers' performance in January 1939 could not change the economic realities that left these men, women, and children without a viable place in agriculture, it did unsettle social givens, triggering national disgust and deep shame in elite Missourians. The sharecroppers' organization of the demonstration typifies Michel de Certeau's notion of the "tactic," "the clandestine forms taken by the dispersed, tactical, and makeshift creativity of groups."[8] Jarod Roll's superb social history of sharecropping in Missouri catalogues the croppers' use of "tactics" throughout the fall of 1938 in planning their mass demonstration. For historic, economic, and social reasons, the sharecroppers had to use furtive means to organize against their oppression. This chapter's attention to the theatrical dynamics of the protest reveals how, in performance, the "tactic" was exceeded to render visible the "net of 'discipline'" in which croppers operated.[9]

Sopping It Up: The AAA's Exacerbation of Farm Laborers' Ills

Missouri Cotton Culture

Rufus Lark sent a letter to the Southern Tenant Farmers' Union (STFU), an interracial socialist organization established in Arkansas to advocate for farm laborers' rights, about one month after the Bootheel sharecroppers' demonstration. Lark asks for any kind of aid the organization might provide to him and his family of thirteen:

> Dear Sir, Just a few lines to you—to let you no my condition. I want to no is it
> anyway you can help me git sitawated. I ant in the Road side camp But I had to
> move Because the man told me to move he say we didn't due the 3¢ money an
> said if any gravy was in the Boal he was going to sop it his self this year."[10]

The "man" to whom Lark referred was his landlord, who was evicting
Lark and his family in order to keep the entire AAA payment. Though
Lark did not camp on highways U.S. 60 and U.S. 61, his situation epitomizes the inhumanity suffered by sharecroppers at the hands of plantation owners in the Missouri Bootheel.

Plantation owners, indeed, sopped up the land's profit through
management practices that kept croppers not only in poverty but in
peonage. Three types of laborers worked cotton plantations: renters,
sharecroppers, and day laborers. Renters supplied their own equipment
and paid for leased land with either cash or crops. Sharecroppers provided their labor in return for a share of the crop they produced. Day
laborers worked for a wage. Croppers and renters lived on the farm and
landlords provided them with credit to sustain them throughout the
year. This credit, called "furnish," as well as the housing that plantation owners provided, was wholly inadequate. The owners' disregard
for sharecroppers' dignity and well-being was not merely greed. As one
federal report remarked, it was also due to "a feeling in general [in southern culture] that the Negro does not 'need' so much as the white. This is
a direct outgrowth of the widely accepted belief in racial superiority."[11]
For instance, J. V. Conran, a Missouri landowner and district attorney
for New Madrid County, derisively marveled at social workers who advocated for a more balanced diet for sharecroppers: "Can you imagine
wanting to give a negro lettuce and mayonnaise."[12] That Conran spoke
these words to an FBI agent, who was investigating whether landowners had violated their AAA cotton contracts as part of the larger investigation into the sharecroppers' demonstration, speaks to the explicit
and widely accepted expressions and treatment of African Americans
as fundamentally inferior to whites. Many white Missouri landowners believed that "natural" differences between African Americans and
privileged whites not only explained sharecroppers' living conditions
but indicated that sharecroppers did not experience their poverty as
deprivation or degradation.

Food shortage among sharecroppers was a persistent problem not only because they lacked money to buy food but also because landowners discouraged tenants from maintaining home gardens. Cotton often surrounded tenants' homes, leaving little or no available space for subsistence gardens. Moreover, cropper families had little time to tend to anything but cotton since they depended on their own fields' productivity. Even when home gardens existed, the Missouri heat and the lack of space for food storage made effective preservation improbable. Sharecroppers' large families—favored among landlords because more hands promised greater productivity for crop yield—compounded the difficulty of securing enough food. "Rich Land—Poor People," a 1938 study of Missouri sharecropping by the Farm Security Administration (FSA, formerly the Resettlement Administration) showed that hunger, malnutrition, and resultant disease and high infant mortality rates among sharecroppers were caused by inadequate access to food. In response to an FSA interviewer's question regarding the colitis endemic on farms, one woman stated, "Yes, there is an awful lot of colitis around here, but no wonder —we can't change our food, can't afford it. It means greens, when it is season, but otherwise potatoes and beans or nothing. We would eat differently if we could get it." The dilapidated shacks on plantations—often two-room structures with dirt floors, no insulation, no windows, and failing roofs—according to FSA agents, "fail in every respect to meet the barest standards of comfort, health and decency." Housing worsened croppers' susceptibility to disease.[13]

At the end of any given cotton season, landowners deducted croppers' and renters' furnish plus interest from their portion of crop income. Calculations invariably came out in the landlord's favor because "the landlord keeps the books, and the tenant is often too ignorant, or, particularly in the case of the Negro, afraid to question the accounts."[14] Sharecroppers' poor literacy skills, a result of numerous factors that hindered access to formal education, also meant that many could not read the lease agreements that virtually indentured them. The three cents Lark did not receive for his family's labor was not exceptional. Such unabashed exploitation of sharecroppers kept them beholden to plantation owners, perpetually reliant on furnish, and in need of annual government relief to sustain them through the winter months following the cotton harvest.

Shifting and Shiftlessness

By common practice, landowner-sharecropper agreements lasted only one year, and both parties often sought out new arrangements in the hope of securing more profitable deals. Many sharecroppers avoided furnish debt at the end of a season by clandestinely "shifting" to a new farm. In 1935, approximately 34.2 percent of the nearly 2.9 million tenant farmers nationwide had lived on their current farm for only one year.[15] While it was improbable for a sharecropping family to escape cotton culture, by shifting, they could leave behind a plantation and furnish debt for the possibility of a better situation on another farm.

Though shifting offered a small reprieve to sharecropping families, plantation owners also used the practice to substantiate the notion that croppers were shiftless. "In the minds of southern planters, [and many other Americans] shifting was intimately related to croppers' 'shiftlessness,' an all-purpose term used to refer to indolence and moral laxity."[16] The FBI report on the demonstration showed that many Missourians blamed croppers for immoral behavior in their communities. An otherwise unidentified "some" reported to investigators that "the emergence of the so-called night club, with its bar, gambling devices, dance floor and other diversions, is also related to the impermanence of residents." These ostensibly disreputable venues, along with the fact that croppers' mobility supposedly "discourage[d] membership in the church," was thought to indicate a lack of moral fortitude borne of shifting, or vice versa.[17] While FSA officials recognized that the constant movement of farm families was detrimental to croppers' well-being, they also described shifting as a kind of "mental insecurity" that resulted in "bad citizenship, because no family can educate its children properly, or find a solid place for itself in the community, when it is continually on the move."[18] Roll's research contradicts this assessment, showing that croppers' community and cultural ties to Missouri were long held, beginning generations prior to the 1930s. Croppers were simply and systemically excluded from recognized institutions of citizenship.

The historical condition of large cropper families was also used as evidence of their shiftlessness. The response of J. R. Butler, president of the Southern Tenant Farmers' Union, to a concerned citizen who had

written to him during the protest demonstrates the unconscious reitera-
tion of shiftlessness even among cropper advocates. In her letter, which
contained a donation for the Bootheel sharecroppers' relief, Anna M.
Emerson of Sioux Falls, South Dakota, suggested to Butler that "the best
help [the STFU] could give would be to get Margaret Sanger . . . to teach
them birth control." Butler gratefully responded to Emerson's letter, stating that "Poor people as a rule are more prolific than the well to do for
several reasons—lack of knowledge—no outside interests—failure to
understand the results of carelessness both to themselves and their off-
spring."[19] Despite his cultural knowledge of economic imperatives and
moral values as an important factor in sharecroppers' fertility and his
knowledge of the changing agricultural industry, Butler fails to cite them.
Moreover, the excess of laborers was seasonal; cotton-picking season ab-
sorbed unemployed laborers each year. Blaming croppers' poverty on
their fertility rendered these individuals human surplus, a tactic that
vividly resonates with the explanation Secretary of Agriculture Henry
Wallace gave to Eleanor Roosevelt for the sharecroppers' poverty (see
"Introduction"). Landowners cited croppers' supposed shiftlessness to
justify their exercise of paternal authority over these workers, their poor
treatment of croppers, and as an example of the "natural" differences
between propertied whites and poor white and African American agricultural laborers.

AAA Cotton Contracts

Rufus Lark's recounting of how the landlord evicted him and his family—"the man told me to move"—also discloses the AAA's exacerbation
of the cotton industry's problematic power dynamics. The 1933 AAA,
the 1936 Soil Conservation and Domestic Allotment Act, and the 1938
Agricultural Adjustment Act did provide some economic and legal protections for sharecroppers, by including benefit payments for them and
tenant farmers in the cotton contracts between landowners and the federal government. Like subsidies in other AAA contracts, those included
in cotton contracts were designed to ease the loss of crop income for all
farmers (owners and laborers) with a stake in the crop yield. Croppers
and tenants both worked for a share of the crops and, so, were included

in the provision. Day laborers worked for a wage and, thus, were not entitled to a portion of the subsidy. However, local governance of AAA programs by county committees that generally consisted of powerful landowners facilitated abuse of the AAA to sharecroppers' detriment and landowners' profit. Sharecroppers blamed the AAA for their evictions because, while the act included legal protections for croppers, in practice, it kowtowed to landowners and incentivized them to evict sharecroppers.

Plantation owners skirted federal provisions for croppers by making croppers give up benefit payments as part of their lease or by using furnish debt plus interest to reduce croppers' share of the subsidy check. Farm labor organizations such as the communist Southern Croppers' Union (SCU) in Alabama and the STFU sought to protect croppers' rights under the law. The SCU instructed its members "not to sign the joint parity checks unless the landlords paid their portion in cash rather than use the funds to settle debts."[20] Likewise, the STFU distributed pamphlets such as "Government Programs Lesson One: The Agricultural Adjustment Act," that explained the Soil Conservation and Domestic Allotment Act, the 1938 AAA, and the benefit payments under each. It stressed the croppers' legal right to these payments: "This check is your own money and you should be careful not to sign it over to the landlord."[21] Landowners also avoided paying out AAA benefits by evicting croppers—claiming they had evicted the workers for incompetence—and hiring day laborers to work the land.[22] Often, these croppers remained economically compelled to work on plantations as "day laborers," losing their federal subsidy share as well as their crop share and housing.

Before the 1933 program had been in operation for even one year, the Agricultural Adjustment Administration was receiving complaints from tenants and croppers regarding evictions and unfair distribution of AAA benefit payments. Yet because "most of the members of the county committees are landlords," their oversight of local AAA operations and adjudication of the merit of croppers' complaints made proof hard to come by and rendered federal legal protections against evictions largely ineffectual.[23] A minority report by W. L. Blackstone, representing the STFU, was included in the findings of a 1937 federal Special Committee on Farm Tenancy. Blackstone "recall[ed] vividly our inability in the days of the [1933] A.A.A. to get adequate redress of our grievances as to the disposition of benefit payments and as to dispossessing us from our slight foothold on the land in violation of the cotton contract."[24] However, in the federal offices of the Agricultural Adjustment Administration, disagreement existed as to whether landowners' cotton contracts obliged them to keep the same number of croppers and share payments with them or if the AAA contract was exclusive to the landowner and federal government, thus giving the landowner prerogative to keep or reduce his sharecroppers. AAA general counsel Jerome Frank interpreted the 1934–35 cotton contracts in favor of the croppers, stating that landowners not only had to keep the same number of tenants on the farms but had to keep the same tenants, unless just cause for their eviction existed. Frank's action led to the dismissal of the "liberal" men, those most avid about tenants' rights, from the Agricultural Adjustment Administration.[25]

Changes to how AAA payments were allocated from 1937 to 1938 effectively increased croppers' portion of federal subsidies for their crop share. In 1937, one-half of the payment was divided between landlord and tenant at a flat rate, and the other half was divided based on crop share. In 1938, the entire payment was divided based on crop share —if the crop share was on a fifty-fifty basis, croppers' would receive 50 percent of the payment. In a confidential memorandum to Secretary Wallace, Assistant Director of Information S. B. Bledsoe stated that the AAA "provides direct inducement" for landowners to dismiss croppers and employ day laborers.[26] Missouri landowner Thad Snow, who was a friend of the Reverend Whitfield's and exceptional for his advocacy on behalf of sharecroppers, wrote an editorial published in the *St. Louis Post-Dispatch* that claimed the 1938 USDA cotton contracts "doubled planters' incentive to turn to day labor in 1939."[27]

The La Forge Experiment: An Eden Inciting Rebellion

While the AAA left many sharecroppers without a viable place in agriculture, the FSA undertook programs to aid landless farmers. Among these was an extensive photography project to document rural poverty, a series of cooperative farming projects, and the administration of migrant labor

camps in California for those fleeing the Dustbowl. The FSA's cooperative farming programs came under fire from large-scale farm operators
for being socialistic and for poaching laborers from plantations. In Missouri, landowners disdained the FSA's La Forge project for these reasons
and for its interracial arrangement. According to Missouri landowners
and powerful figures in Missouri's rural cotton counties, the federal government's 1937 socioagricultural experiment in La Forge, Missouri, laid
the foundation for disorder and rebellion in 1939.

In 1937, the FSA bought a 6,700-acre plantation near La Forge, Missouri, in New Madrid County. This cooperative farming experiment
was designed to improve the land's fertility and create better economic
and social conditions for farm laborers. The land was divided into individual farms (on which cotton, corn, and soil-regenerating crops were
planted), and the FSA gave each family a $1,300 loan. Families rented
homes and land from the federal government. Tenants and croppers living on the land at the time of purchase became the project's residents, including about sixty white families and forty African American families.
The FSA's report on the project intimated the social program within La
Forge's economic interests: "It wanted to find out whether these run-of-
the-mill share-croppers could make a decent, secure living if they had a
chance under different conditions." La Forge tested the capabilities of a
social group that was largely perceived as culpable for its own plight.
Fully operational in spring 1938, La Forge consisted of new homes, "an
efficient barn, a sealed well, fences, food storage vaults and a sanitary
privy." La Forge residents cooperatively purchased major equipment
and ran the gin on the plantation. Additionally, the FSA provided educational programs on such things as home gardens and raising livestock.
Schools were built for the white and African American children, and a
health program was established. By December 1939, each family's worth
had increased from $28 to $1,474.71, and the government had already
recouped nearly $100,000 on an approximately $800,000 investment. La
Forge was an indisputable success according to the federal government
and the residents.[28]

Opposition from powerful Missourians squelched federal plans to
aid additional landless farmers through programs modeled on La Forge.
The same year La Forge was established, the federal government in-

tended to purchase five thousand acres in nearby Mississippi County on which to resettle African American sharecropper families. Congressman Orville Zimmerman (Democrat-Mo.) urged Dr. Will Alexander of the FSA to halt plans. In his letter, Zimmerman enclosed petitions signed by county court judges, county officers, and citizens from the Dogwood, Armer, and Belmont school districts. He expressed sincere concern that such a settlement would cause an outrage: "I am convinced that a serious racial situation would be created in that county if this proposal is carried through. This section of Missouri is essentially Southern, being populated by Southern people and maintaining many of the traditions of the South." U.S. Senator Bennett Champ Clark (Democrat-Mo.) and Secretary Wallace received letters from the Urban League urging the government to withstand this pressure. However, the monies designated for the project were withdrawn.[29] Objections to this aborted project magnify the social context in which the La Forge Project operated and in which the protesters would stage their demonstration. By providing housing, space for gardening, predetermined rental costs, a long-term arrangement, and greater self-determination for black and white sharecroppers, the federal government modeled a desirable form of patronage—one that entailed the possibility of independence and recognized the equivalency of needs and abilities between propertied whites and African Americans. For many Missourians, however, La Forge unsettled the established social order in Southeast Missouri.

When Orville Zimmerman defended Missouri "farmers'" (read: plantation owners) in the U.S. House of Representatives during the protest, he claimed that the sharecropping tradition fostered a peaceable coexistence founded on landlords' concern for their tenants' welfare. Zimmerman then introduced the Missouri landowners' resolution, a complaint that linked the sharecroppers' demonstration to La Forge. Landowners alleged that "this movement to the highways of this [Mississippi] county is the result of unscrupulous and scheming agitators who have been deceiving the Negro tenants and sharecroppers by making them believe that they were going to be given property and money by the Government and that they will not have to work."[30] Similarly, in a January 16, 1939 article, titled "Squatters Quit Camps on Highways," the *Southeast Missourian* described landowners' theory that "the squatters, particularly the Negroes, have been impressed by the 'luxury' of those living . . . at La Forge" and stated that the demonstrators believed the federal government was going to give them "'40 acres' and an easy life." The *St. Louis Globe-Democrat*, too, suggested that "promises of extravagant largess from the government" caused the protest.[31] Recurrent references to croppers' naïve belief that postemancipation promises would be fulfilled aimed to "expose" their desire for "handouts" and made federal officials appear ignorant of the sharecroppers' "shiftlessness." According to landowners, federal officials misunderstood the "needs" of cotton culture; worse, federal meddling disrupted the society's tranquility.

La Forge did demonstrate to sharecroppers the possibility for a better life *as a farmer* with a little assistance to break the cycle of agricultural peonage. In a December 1939 interview, Owen Whitfield referred to his good fortune to secure a home at La Forge as connected to his drive to advocate on behalf of other sharecroppers: "If'n I were in the Garden of Eden an I heard a lil baby cryin on the other side o that door, I couldn't be happy less'n I got that baby in too."[32] Urban advocates for the rural poor shared Whitfield's vision of La Forge as an Eden. Just days before the demonstration, an article in the *St. Louis Post-Dispatch's Everyday Magazine* featured pictures of La Forge with the tagline "They Call It a Miracle." The report referred to the project as the "promised land." It described the transformation of female sharecroppers from field hands into "proper" women: "They have homes now, and . . . assurance for the future because now they are farmers' wives."[33] For this reporter and the women who praised La Forge, the transformation of women's labor from agricultural to domestic was a culturally desirable outcome that represented how the federal project granted dignity to croppers' lives.

For sharecroppers living from year to year without any security and experiencing worsening conditions, La Forge may have motivated them to show themselves on the highways. At the time of the protest, croppers, however, primarily articulated the desire to earn their living by continuing to farm and, even more, to do so through secure tenure agreements with landowners. One federal investigator summarized interviews conducted with 102 participants in the demonstration: "some spoke of their hope that the government would set them up in cotton growing. The movement as yet has formulated no definite demand for a resettlement project, however."[34] Out of the eighty-six cases available in the archives, only seven demonstrators explicitly mention the desire to work on a government project: Dave Coffey stated that he wanted to live on "Government land"; Isaac Haynes expressed his hope to "work for the Government because 'we get fair dealings than from these land owners'"; Robert Haynes, who was beaten and pistol-whipped during the sharecroppers' removal from the highways, also said that he wished to "'work on farm for the Government if possible,'" because landlords are "unfair." In a letter to the STFU, protester and sharecropper Elijah More expressed the potential farm laborers saw in themselves if given a chance: "We wont a project like the one at le forge homes and land. Give me a hand and i will make my living like other men." Farm laborers' hope for a situation like La Forge is apparent. However, many demonstrators express foremost a desire to continue farming, not to change their patrons or their status. Further, when interviewed by FBI agents, Whitfield insisted that he told the sharecroppers, "Don't get the idea that this is a social equality movement. . . . No social mixture—we don't desire that. You are satisfied, I am sure, with your white women and I am tickled to death with my tea kettle brown. You and I must unite for a higher standard of living."[35] Whether these statements are earnest expressions of producerist ideology and Southern beliefs about racial boundaries or conscious performances of these social orders, the croppers countered accusations of their shiftlessness by stating their desire to work. These utterances were part of sharecroppers' larger embodied performances of rootedness, faith, and community, which challenged the discourse of shiftlessness that depicted croppers as undisciplined.

Putting Croppers' Condition before the World: The Roadside Demonstration

Nobody Will Believe It: The Protest's Organization

The protest was an intricately orchestrated event designed, in Rev. Owen Whitfield's words, to "put [the sharecroppers'] condition before the entire world."[36] Yet the sharecroppers' surreptitious gathering of resources and coordination of individuals, the secret nature of which was necessary for their safety, disguised months of organizing. The clandestine nature of the undertaking capitalized on landowners' sense of imperviousness to croppers and the government and led to the impression that the protest was a last-ditch effort. One month before the protest began, on December 1, 1938, Whitfield sent a letter to H. L. Mitchell, secretary of the STFU, informing him that landowners planned to evict nine hundred families. Whitfield told Mitchell of the croppers' intention to "pile their household goods on sides of the hightway [sic] and see what happens."[37] Whitfield, a member of the STFU, enlisted local STFU-CIO union leaders to support the protest. According to Snow, Whitfield also confided in his friend and in Hans Baasch, manager of the FSA's La Forge project, about protest plans. Snow recounts that Whitfield asked Baasch to keep the demonstration a secret but also went to Congressman Zimmerman days before the protest in the hope of securing tents for shelter on the highways. Snow also remembers Whitfield inviting St. Louis Post-Dispatch reporter Sam Armstrong to attend a final planning meeting held a few days before the demonstration. Whitfield, however, apparently debated whether to allow Armstrong to publish the story before the protest started. Snow quotes Whitfield as finally saying, "'Mr. Sam, I've been thinkin'. You go ahead and print what you wants in tomorrow's paper. Nobody won't believe it, so it won't make no difference.'"[38] Whitfield was correct; numerous accounts demonstrate that powerful landowners and state officials believed croppers would not dare rebel.

Despite the appearance of Sam Armstrong's article on January 8, 1939, two days before the protest, and its detailed description of sharecroppers' plans, farm owners reportedly doubted that the demonstration would actually occur. At the protest's start, the St. Louis Post-Dispatch reported that C. L. Blanton, publisher of the local Sikeston Standard, "shared the doubt of planters that any organized demonstration would be held."[39] Likewise, the FBI report on the demonstration concluded, "the majority of those [landowners] who did learn of the contemplated demonstration prior to its occurrence took the view that such a demonstration could not take place in their district."[40] The sharecroppers turned landowners' hubris and power against them. Easy and violent suppression of earlier sharecropper movements, landowners' manipulation of federal AAA programs since 1933, and race- and class-based bias allowed the Bootheel croppers to catch landowners off guard.[41]

Taking Advantage of Ten Days Grace: The Protest Date

Plantation owners were vulnerable the moment the evictions took effect. As was typical, croppers were given notice of eviction after the harvest, at the beginning of winter, and were expected to vacate a plantation by the tenth of January. Evictions officially began on the first of January each year, but, by tradition, croppers were given ten days grace. Moving en masse under the cover of darkness from shacks on cotton plantations to roadside camps, croppers used the dawn on January 10, 1939, to reveal a scene of hundreds of people suffering hunger, degradation, and exploitation. Jarod Roll writes, "Whitfield latched onto the idea [of moving to the roadside from one of his followers], realizing that the landless could use their greatest trouble—eviction—as a weapon against the planters."[42] By occupying the roadsides along U.S. highways 60 and 61 on the date that marked the end of the grace period, sharecroppers demonstrated landowners' exploitation of federal legislation to sharecroppers' harm (see figure 4.1). This was significant, as croppers had to establish not only the fact of evictions but also the evictions' illegality. They could not do so through established channels, so they used this theatrical one. Showing the scale of evictions, all at once and in continuous waves of croppers moving to the highways, exposed the systemic opportunism of the landowners; sheer numbers belied landowners' claims that an individual cropper's transience, incompetence, and general shiftlessness justified each and every eviction from farms.

Premised on eviction, sharecroppers framed the demonstration as paradoxically both forced and chosen: a last resort. The decision to move to the highways was represented to the public as occurring on January 7, 1939—a mere two days before the protest—at a clandestine meeting in an African American church. Accounts of the meeting are dramatic, entailing elements of Whitfield's sermon in which he compared the sharecroppers' move to the Israelites' flight under Moses' leadership.[43] Ben Morris Ridpath's article for the *Christian Century* describes the decision to move to the highways as inspired:

Figure 4.1. Sharecroppers gather for demonstration at Missouri U.S. 60. Photograph by Arthur Rothstein, Evicted Sharecroppers along Highway 60, New Madrid County, Missouri, January 1939, LC-DIG-fsa-8a10628, Farm Security Administration/Office of War Information, courtesy Library of Congress.

> Mr. Whitfield called a meeting. . . . One of the sharecroppers rose to speak and shouted: "Rather than stay in my shack and starve to death with my family, I'll take them out on the highway and walk until we drop in our tracks." The idea was spontaneous. "Let's go out on the highway," suggested Mr. Whitfield. "If we are going to starve, let's starve out there where people can see us!" A chorus of 'ayes' and 'amens' resounded through the room and the exodus to the highway encampment followed.[44]

A sense of spontaneity masked the diligent grassroots organizing that enabled the protest to take place. Representation of the protest as unplanned, rather than carefully scripted, suggested that the display was a truthful reflection of reality, a sincere depiction of the sharecroppers as products of their social and environmental circumstance. It was a naturalistic illusion.

Missouri's Most Traveled Roads: The Protest Site

Protesters took advantage of Missouri's two major highways' potential for easy and broad access. Journalists, federal officials, and union agents quickly descended on the camps, and travelers and tourists reportedly caused traffic hazards when they stopped along the highways to offer money and supplies.[45] A *Sikeston Herald* report on January 12 bemoaned the highways' access: "a sorrowful sight . . . attracts the attention of motorists on Highway 61—one of the most traveled roads of the Middle-West. Many motorists having cameras stop and take pictures of the odd sight—and will doubtless remember Sikeston as the place where the sharecroppers were 'driven out' and had to camp along the roadside."[46] Articles on and images of croppers' wretched state circulated swiftly and nationwide in film, radio, and print media.

While the site facilitated publicity, the staged camps also played on the practical and symbolic associations of the roadside in relation to croppers' historic transience. In gathering at a particular place, sociologist John Lofland contends, "protesters lay an ownership claim to the exact territory they have elected to seize."[47] Typically, symbolic protest actions (for example, marches, rallies, and sit-ins, as opposed to strikes) overtake otherwise-employed public space as a means of suspending ordinary activity to compel examination of the place's operations or to stop daily life so that all bear witness to a sociopolitical issue. Roadsides, however, lack function; at most, they enable brief periods of rest for travelers on the way to elsewhere. So, in one sense, the choice of roadsides became about sharecroppers staying put. Ike Tripp, like his fellow protesters, told federal officials that he wanted to "make an honest support for my family and won't have to be moving so much."[48] Sharecroppers claimed the Bootheel as their home when they reconstituted their households on the highways. These customarily mobile people parked their trucks, if they had one, and used them as sleeping quarters and shelter, rather than loading up and moving east into Kentucky on highway U.S. 60, south to Arkansas on highway U.S. 61, or even north into the urban center of St. Louis. By remaining in the counties where they had labored, croppers challenged the notion that, because they moved around, they were from nowhere and belonged to no place. Ernest Lindley, writing for the *Des Moines Register,* identified this as a central issue: "a great many sharecroppers move from place to place, anyway, so that no one in particular has a moral responsibility for seeing that they are cared for."[49] They embodied their marginalization in society by standing on the side of the road in their local community. On January 12, the *St. Louis Post-Dispatch* named the protesters "Missouri's refugees," who were, "Dispossessed by A.A.A." In doing so, this newspaper recognized the croppers as Missourians and held this state and the federal government culpable for the croppers' situation.

From Hidden to Exposed: Transforming Clandestine Tactics into Performance

Croppers' secrecy in organizing the protest and even getting to the highways was necessary to ensure that the protest would not be suppressed. The protest's organization is a straightforward example of what Michel de Certeau calls "tactics": momentary, creative and undetectable forms of resistance used by disempowered people to gain reprieve from oppressive sociopolitical and discursive systems. Tactics rely on "opportunity"; in a sense, they are performed in the moments when no one is looking or in the instances when the powerful show vulnerability.[50] Throughout the course of the protest, croppers and their supporters would continue to turn to tactical means to protect themselves and sustain the demonstration.

The public was not aware that sharecroppers received assistance from friends and family. Some families left children in others' care while they camped on the roadsides; some left equipment or animals with friends. While on the highways, various individuals (like union members or croppers still living on farms) would drop off supplies in the night. Juke joint and dance hall owners provided overnight shelter and helped pilfer and distribute goods. Roll writes, "Invisible to onlookers these local institutions sustained the campers."[51] Labor historian Bonnie Stepenoff, in her biography of Thad Snow, intimates that the invisibility of this support may have been intentional: "Each night for nearly a week, a caravan of vehicles appeared and vanished, leaving supplies at the campsites. Croppers who had not been evicted brought provisions to their friends and relatives. For every family in public view, there was someone behind the scenes, supporting them physically and in spirit." The STFU, however, asserted that they took supplies to croppers "under cover of darkness" because of threats and intimidation made by landowners against supporters.[52] Regardless of the reason, the clandestine support functioned in a manner analogous to masterful stage management. It was vital to sustaining a performance of gross exploitation, persistent hunger, dire poverty, and mass evictions.

The demonstration exposed why croppers "shifted," as well as this tactic's socioeconomic and political limitations. Lacking a suitable place of their own, they were forced to rely on the places of others, who, in turn, could define them. De Certeau argues that "A tactic insinuates itself into the other's place, fragmentarily, without taking it over in its entirety, without being able to keep it at a distance. It has at its disposal no base where it can capitalize on its advantages, prepare it expansions, and secure independence with respect to circumstances." In brief, "whatever it wins, it does not keep."[53] In Missouri, and elsewhere, sharecroppers literally maneuvered within the other's place. Without an economic, social, or physical base, they could not capitalize on shifting. A cropper family might gain advantage over an individual landlord, but they would remain subject to the power of property holders, while landowners turned shifting toward their power by using it to perpetuate the discourse of shiftlessness. In choosing to start the protest on January 10, 1939, in staging it on roadsides in the cotton counties where they farmed, and by performing their everyday lives, croppers capitalized on their literal and social placelessness. From site to performance mode to embodied action and rhetoric, the protesters exceeded the clandestine tactic's typical capacity to grant disempowered people some relief. They transformed it from a covert improvisation into a public critique of cotton culture under the AAA.

In-situ Exhibition: An Atypical Form of Protest

The demonstration's "uneventful" nature—its lack of typical theatrical elements associated with protest—instilled the display with a sense of authenticity. There were no constructed signs or symbols, no parades or costumes emblematic of the croppers' grievances. Nevertheless, croppers' homelessness—their sleeping, eating, and praying in public—became a cultural exhibition, an event to behold and interpret. The actions performed by sharecroppers offered a "drama of the quotidian" to the public.[54] Performance scholar Barbara Kirschenblatt-Gimblett explicates this term and the act of going about everyday life while on display by drawing on John MacAloon's idea of generic confusion, in which one person's life becomes entertainment for another person.

The performers' mundane activities "creates the effect of authenticity, or realness. The impression is one of unmediated encounter."[55] In theater historian Roger Hall's words, this theatrical genre—better known by historical examples like "Indian villages" at Wild West shows and foreign villages at world's fairs—traffics in the idea that spectators "vicariously experience another culture."[56] Similarly, the theatrical entertainment of minstrelsy, whether presented on a stage or under the guise of the educational style as it was in the "Old Plantation" exhibit at the 1901 Pan-American Exposition, was perceived by white mainstream America as an authentic portrayal of blackness and antebellum plantation life.[57] Due to the fact that the majority of Bootheel protesters were African Americans and that the protest was a decidedly southern and rural event, the performativity of minstrelsy shaped much of the national (northern and urban) media's interpretation of croppers' in-situ performance. In national reports, croppers were portrayed sympathetically through minstrel paradigms. These articles unconsciously repeated theatrical conventions of minstrelsy as if factual, objective accounting. The repetition of these hegemonic representations had the ironic effect of relaying a sense of the scene's authenticity while also critiquing contemporary cotton culture.

By positioning the protest as paradoxically both a necessity compelled by eviction and a choice by croppers to expose their situation to the world, sharecroppers maintained the sense of "real" as they showed the power dynamics of in-situ exhibition. When untroubled, in-situ display defines difference; it affirms a hierarchical relationship between "us" (read: spectator) and "them" (read: displayed/other): "'We,' those who look through the eyes of the explorer, are (like the explorer) positioned safely outside the frame, free to define, theorize, and debate their (never 'our') societies. The 'encounters with the native create 'us' as audience just as much as the violence of definition creates 'them'—the primitives."[58] Self-imposed display, alternatively, implicates spectators in the process of objectification; spectators are forced to question racist notions about the cultural superiority of "civilized" nations/peoples when they witness the spectacle of a person exposing his plight to public view.[59] In choosing the degradation of self-display, sharecroppers fractured the frame that distinguishes "us" from "them." They situated the Cotton South as a "primitive" culture hiding within "our"/spectators' own society and called on viewers to bear witness: "A person who bears witness to an injustice takes responsibility for that awareness. That person may then choose to do something or stand by, but he may not turn away in ignorance."[60] Sharecroppers' roadside living made public the dehumanization they suffered due to the landowners' violation of croppers' private space and degradation of their bodies. Exemplified by the rhetoric "let's starve out there where people can see," protesters' deprivation of the biological necessity of food and the cultural necessity of privacy—two fundamental markers of subjecthood in the United States—laid bare the socioeconomic processes that transformed the individuals on roadsides from private subjects into exhibited public objects.

Croppers' Social Degradation: The Private in Public View

In the United States, private and banal activities, such as sleeping or washing, are deemed unfit for public consumption; as performance scholar Diana Taylor notes, performing these behaviors in public view affirm the "supremacy and authority of the viewing subject."[61] Cultural valuation of privacy and the presumed passivity of the persons on display work together to this effect. Kirschenblatt-Gimblett's summary of the operations of in-situ human display regards control over privacy as a vital humanizing mechanism: "The issue is the power to open up to sight differentially, to show with respect to others what one would not reveal about oneself—one's body, person, and life. . . . To make people going about their ordinary business objects of visual interest and available to total scrutiny is dehumanizing."[62] To show the injustice of their lives, demonstrators offered up their "ordinary business" for scrutiny.

Figure 4.2. Sharecroppers and their households line the shoulder of the highway. Photograph by Arthur Rothstein, Evicted Sharecroppers along Highway 60, New Madrid County, Missouri, January 1939, LC-DIG-fsa-8a10410, Farm Security Administration/Office of War Information, courtesy Library of Congress.

Croppers capitalized on the technologies of photography and publishing that had historically driven Samuel Warren and Louis Brandeis's argument about the need to recognize in law the belief that "the individual is entitled to decide whether that which is his shall be given to the public." Family units on roadsides were only distinguishable when distance existed between huddles or mounds of belongings (see figure 4.2); photographs portray the sense that not even makeshift shelters or tents could provide security from the public site croppers occupied. And media, as is its predilection, focused on domestic activity—a "form of possession intangible," hallowed in its seclusion from the world but spectacular as a public occurrence—as compelling evidence against landowners.[63]

In the American context, privacy is marked by "the sacred precincts of private and domestic life."[64] Women's domestic behaviors on the highways obscured their participation in a radical political activity by stressing their roles as mothers and wives and their victimization by landowners via the exploitation of their husbands, who were considered the farm laborers. One indication of the significance of seeing women and children together with men is the media's masculine gendering of "croppers."[65] For instance, a *St. Louis Post-Dispatch* front-page report on January 10 reads, "Crowds of evicted sharecroppers with their wives and children, carrying their only possessions, converged on highways of the Southeast Missouri cotton country today." Though female sharecroppers and their children worked the fields beside their male family members, women cooking and tending to children on open roadsides easily obfuscated their (unseen and unperformed) agricultural labor. In fact, cultural images of women as domestic caretakers in combination with their actions suggest that it would otherwise have been difficult to represent these women convincingly. Indeed, even government-sponsored farmer education programs worked to end the socially undesirable field labor of female sharecroppers. An FSA chart created by a home management supervisor for the La Forge project praises the many roles of the farm woman. Of the seventeen roles listed (including wife, mother, nurse, interior decorator, and canner), only "farm hand" receives the parenthetical qualifier "Not encouraged."[66] Media's failure to recognize these women as farmers per se, though historically significant, was not at issue during the protest. Further, unlike the Hamtramck housewives, female sharecroppers lacked the socioeconomic capital to access the discourse of consumer-citizen. The Bootheel women's show of domestic labor and their very presence, along with their children, at the protest site, seem to have made it difficult for the public to imagine the protest as staged (when "staging" connotes insincerity or dissembling). Their presence also framed the male croppers in familial, private compositions.

The depiction of black and white men in a domestic framework emphasized the protest as their struggle to fulfill their role as men (see figure 4.3). A white man sitting next to a teenage girl and a small girl, in a filmed news interview, stated, "We can't make an honest decent living at it and that's the reason we out here on Highway 61 right today." In another newsreel, an African American man, surrounded by a woman and three small children, maintained, "142 families on this highway,

Figure 4.3. Sharecropper men and girls at a roadside camp. Photograph by Arthur Rothstein, Evicted Sharecroppers along Highway 60, New Madrid County, Missouri, January 1939, LC-DIG-fsa-8a10508, Farm Security Administration/Office of War Information, courtesy Library of Congress.

homeless people, and the only thing they want is shelter and food and a decent place to live."[67] These croppers situated their display as a plea for fundamental masculine dignity: the ability to provide for their families. Positioned in this way, the interracial unity exhibited by African American and white croppers transgressed cultural norms but aligned with common national demands against the Roosevelt administration.

Croppers' Physical Degradation: Eating as a Sign of Hunger

Sharecroppers represented their hunger as authentic—as suffered and outside their control—through two primary actions: by living on the side of the road and by eating. First, the site of the protest elevated the sense of in-situ display as a "panopticon": the belief that every moment is totally exposed and available to view. Theater scholar Nick Kaye defines "site-specificity" as interplay between a site's established denotations and the actions that occur there: a "palimpsest [troubling] the oppositions between the site and the work."[68] In distinction from the sociological relationship between protest and place mentioned above, Kaye points out that performance also actively sets in motion "place" (in de Certeau's sense) as ideology. The Bootheel demonstration occurring over time in open space gave the impression of persistent and total exposure. The roadside location invokes, what Kirschenblatt-Gimblett terms, in situ's "panoptic approach [that] offers [spectators] the chance . . . to penetrate the interior recesses, to violate intimacy."[69] Just as the roadside bore the traces of its meaning as a place "in between," its public openness also suggested croppers' inability to conceal anything (such as food) from public view.

While croppers situated hunger as the protest's impetus, many of them cooked and ate during the protest. That the croppers were seen eating, together with the kinds of food they consumed, established the authenticity of their hunger. On the one hand, hunger seems to defy representation. As noted by Elisabeth Angel-Perez and Alexandra Poulain, editors of *Hunger on the Stage*, "the original vocation of theatre (*thea:* eyesight) [is] strangely subverted, as a mere lack [hunger] is offered to the spectator's gaze."[70] In short, what constitutes a proper performance of the hungry body is uncertain. Some performance theorists suggest that this leaves representations of hunger vulnerable to doubt since the experience of hunger is difficult to communicate, in a manner similar to aesthetics theorist Elaine Scarry's views on pain.[71] The Bootheel protest shows that hunger is not always and not merely a generalized absence, which reveals mimesis's failure. Rather, hunger may be staged and, more significantly, may be perceived as authentic, through foods that, by their very presence, signal deprivation.

Some foods can be signs of hunger. Cultures prize certain foods as nutritious and others as decadent; this cultural assessment, as well as racializing, gendering, or classing foods, determines how individuals perceive consumption of and (in)access to specific foods.[72] (As we know from contemporary concerns regarding malnutrition and childhood obesity, a McDonald's Happy Meal signifies hunger on a nutritional level, while it signifies gluttony in terms of taste; class connotations are also readily apparent.) Croppers' roadside eating actually emphasized their bodies as hungry, as the food items seen and consumed on the roadsides reminded viewers of the absence of a healthy meal. Hunger, in this instance, did not mean being without food, but indicated physical and social degradation or insufficient consumption, as well as the consumption of "low" foods.

Specificity generates authenticity, not the sensational tone associated with hyperbole, drama, or acting. By consuming not enough and not the right food, croppers performed the slow starvation of daily, historic deficiency. An Associated Press report featured in the *New York Times* on January 12, detailed the diet of croppers on roadsides: "Some of the more provident brought cooking chickens with them, but fat pork, bread, and coffee was the fare for the majority of refugees." On that same day, the *Chicago Daily Tribune* expressed alarm over the lack of available milk for infants and children. The *St. Louis Post-Dispatch* questioned when promised supplies from state Social Security and AAA offices would arrive by reiterating the lack of milk for infants and the waning supply of bread, fat pork, and coffee in two consecutive days of reporting. Sharecroppers staged this hunger as ordinary to their lives. Though sharecroppers generally subsisted on very little, and vegetables, meats, and milk were rarely accessible, when mediated through a middle-class perspective, roadside meals were humiliating and alarming experiences. Images of people eating in the open and narratives that emphasized "infants," "children," and "women" raised the urgency by iterating gendered notions of vulnerability.[73]

Scenes of Suffering in National and Urban Media

According to sharecropper and demonstrator Alex Cooper, onlookers "were completely baffled by the sheer number and how orderly it was done and the effect it had was just quite confusing, just like an owl in the chicken house."[74] Befuddlement at croppers' behavior was born not only of the violent exchanges of other farm laborer movements but of the specific brand of Depression-era racism and classism that naturalized poor rural whites and blacks as "shiftless." As Cooper's recollection indicates, daily roadside activities confounded interpretation of these black and white families as unruly or degenerate. Yet African American dignity was nearly unintelligible in white imagination. National media outlets and the major regional newspaper *St. Louis Post-Dispatch*—distributed throughout Midwestern states—appear unable to comprehend the uncanny nature of this interracial gathering except through the lens of minstrelsy, as we have seen, a predominant paradigm for representing plantation life and rural southern blackness. Performance scholar Amma Y. Ghartey-Tagoe Kootin remarks that "That type of 'darkey' [an acceptable idea of blackness within white hegemony] was a white creation from the minstrel stage, a caricature of black culture that not only came to be known as an accurate representation of black people but also defined and constructed blackness itself."[75] While local media attempted to incite fears associated with racial anxieties of the time, major newspapers with wide circulation outside the Missouri Bootheel were sympathetic to the sharecroppers but showed sympathy by attaching nostalgic minstrel allusions to croppers' behavior.

Mainstream media commented on the peacefulness and organization of the protest and picked up Whitfield's comparison of sharecroppers' struggles to well-known Christian narratives, littering articles with this rhetoric. Sam Armstrong, in his January 8, 1939, preprotest exclusive for the *St. Louis Post-Dispatch*, quoted Reverend Whitfield as calling the pharaoh's men "ridin' bosses" and telling croppers that they too must make an "exodus."[76] Jarod Roll's study details the centrality of Christianity to Whitfield's organization of croppers and their collective vision of the future. While sharecroppers expressed their faith by aligning their plight with God's chosen people, the docile presentational mode of human exhibition, the presumed meekness of bodies-in-pain, and the exposure of private domestic life also facilitated representation of croppers as "not only exemplars of virtue, but natural Christians." In other words, the media's treatment of the Bootheel croppers resonates with what social and cultural historian Eric Lott describes as nineteenth-century "sentimentalist strategies for representing white women and blacks [that] were often identical, each image lending the other emotional and political force."[77] Abolitionists had used plantation fiction's positive, albeit patronizing, stereotypes of African Americans as emotional and natural, rather than rational and civilized, to demonstrate the evils of slavery. In the case of the Bootheel, the rural, agricultural context readily affirmed an antebellum plantation narrative, while croppers' enactments and the juxtaposition of black and white familial compositions lent to sentimentalist interpretations.

The visual construction of the protest in national media brought out the vulnerability of suffering to render the protesters' docility. Photography archivist Nicholas Natanson notes that, while an estimated 90 to 95 percent of the Bootheel protesters were African Americans, AP photographs of white women, children, and families were featured as frequently as those of African Americans and that AP photographers tended to take close-ups of whites and long-shots of African Americans. Natanson concludes from the disproportionate and disparate photographic treatment of demonstrators that press photos "made extremely unconventional sharecropper activity more palatable, at the expense of the all-important black angle."[78] However, he neglects the context of these photographs by analyzing only the photos themselves and ignoring their captions and the articles they accompanied. Even more, given that legal and de facto racial segregation concerned proximity, the presence of white bodies would not diminish the concomitant presence of black bodies. What Natanson construes as a more "white" and less "black" interpretation of the protest actually proves to be part of the operations of the sympathetic minstrel paradigm that Lott describes. The St. Louis Post-Dispatch made much of protesters' display of faith and admirable nature while displaying the interracial nature of the protest. Arthur Whitman's photographic exposé devoted entirely to the croppers showed black and white families gathered in prayer. The narrative accompanying the pictures of the supplicant families read, "Patient, devout, and inured to poverty and hardship. The homeless croppers carried out their demonstration without making trouble. Their leaders, mostly preachers, exhorted them to obey the law and compared their plight with the exodus of the Children of Israel from Egypt to the Land of Canaan."[79] Through its theatrical representations of the protest, the media presented the protesters as inured to suffering and brought to bear the whole history of the plantation system on the protest in the process.

A *Chicago Daily Tribune* special report on January 11, titled "Denied Farms, Sharecroppers Sleep on Roads," features only a map of the Bootheel, no images of protesters. It encapsulates how news reports remarked on protesters' actual suffering but presented the croppers' diversions from their suffering through minstrel scenarios:

> They huddled around camp fires or makeshift stoves, sharing the contents of huge steaming kettles. Men feeble with age, one woman so ill she had to be carried on a cot, and babies crying from fright and hunger added to the distressing picture. But all was not tragic, for at supper time some camps presented scenes reminiscent of plantation days. Strummed guitars furnished an accompaniment for singing.

On the one hand, the report depicts the sharecroppers as calling forth the better days of past plantation life to gain some small comfort in the present. On the other, the suggestion that the scene on the highways recalled an image of the Old South that was, in fact, a historical and theatrical fiction reflects how deeply minstrelsy's representations pervaded American consciousness.

Like the *Chicago Daily Tribune*, the *St. Louis Post-Dispatch* described with vivid detail an "authentic" experience of cotton culture:

> White sharecroppers, a minority among the Negroes, joined in the service and knelt with the rest.... "On Jordan's Stormy Banks I Stand. [*sic*]" was a favored hymn of this group long after the preacher had left. Hymns and old songs of the South were to be heard about the campfires far into the night with accompaniments of guitars, banjoes and, occasionally, a violin. At a camp of several hundred ... a snowy-haired Negro with a harmonica varied such melodies as "Swanee River" with gay dance tunes that set young bucks to jigging.[80]

In its extensiveness, duration, and depictions, coverage of the protest by the *St. Louis Post-Dispatch* boarded on advocacy. Yet the above article used racist language such as "buck"—Black Buck is a stock minstrel character who is young and virile—and identified only Stephen Foster's popular minstrel song "Swanee River" (1851) in the repertoire of tunes played that evening. It is entirely possible that the protester played the song, as it was a tune as familiar to most Americans as any nursery rhyme. Whether he did matters less than how the song's mention in the article would signal both the protester as a harmless figure and the level of sharecroppers' despair to white audiences; the chorus with the scene of the protest nostalgically summoned croppers' misfortune: "All de world am sad and dreary, / Eb-rywhere I roam; / Oh, darkeys, how my heart grows weary, / Far from de old folks at home!" Under the headline "Evicted Campers on Roads Await Food from State," this account indicates how media representations of the protest made croppers' suffering inextricable from the theatrical and cultural stereotype of the African American. One of the foremost stereotypes was that blacks possessed a natural propensity for song and dance. Minstrelsy, thus, became the vehicle through which media perceived and conveyed the protest's authenticity; that "old songs" could be heard into the night mattered.

The media rendered croppers minstrels, specifically Uncle Toms: "toms are chased, harassed, hounded, flogged, enslaved, and insulted, they keep the faith, n'er turn against their white massas, and remain hearty, submissive, stoic, generous, selfless, and oh-so-very kind. Thus they endear themselves to white audiences and emerge as heroes of sorts."[81] Whitfield smartly deferred to landowners in his public statement on January 12, 1939, to the Enterprise Courier: "We must obey the law, get out when the notices say, and make no trouble." His utterance of obedience placed culpability for the display on landowners. Croppers' actions exemplified docility, vulnerability, and natural goodness, not the shiftlessness of the minstrel "coon" figure. As "misguided" as the media's "positive assessments" of sharecroppers were, to use Eric Lott's words, the nostalgic model of minstrelsy worked in croppers' favor. Croppers' performance recontextualized familiar theatrical scenes of plantation life, transforming them from idyllic to brutal.

Pulitzer prize-winning novelist Josephine Johnson's report on "conversations" she overheard while visiting the protesters' roadside camps theatricalized the protest as a quotidian scene from the contemporary Cotton South:

> The Planter stood above them on the edge of the ditch and looked down at their faces. "Now what worries me," he said, "is some of you folks get sick and die out here in the cold. Why, suppose you all got sick—then what're we gonna do in cotton plantin' time when we need you again? You got no right to do this!"
>
> "Ain't no place to go. Can't go back."
>
> "Well, I guess no planter'd want some of you on his place! . . . Shiftless—moving out just to get a nickel more somewhere else!" . . .

"I ask my boss, and he said, 'I can't use you no mo,' he said—"
"Lissen, nigger," the Planter said, "this is a white man talkin'. And don't you forget it."
"Yes suh."[82]

Johnson's staging of the planter elevated above the croppers symbolizes the brutal power of the discourse of shiftlessness to silence and constrain. The landowner is represented as viewing the croppers as existing only for the benefit of the cotton industry, degrading them as being without rights, and ultimately silencing them through assertion of white supremacy. The article mimics in-situ display and naturalistic dialogue to show croppers' powerlessness and paradoxically position their visibility as the edge of their agency.

Acts in Opposition to the Demonstration

Powerful Missourians responded to the scene on the highways with two strategies. They actively worked to end the protest and to discredit its claims. These strategies were interdependent, and the discourse of shiftlessness suffused the detractors' insistence that the protest was hoax. The *Enterprise-Courier* ran an article on its front page titled "Evicted Sharecroppers ????" designed to refute the "great volume of publicity [in which] it was taken for granted that the roadside campers were each and all evicted; that they were without shelter, without food, without almost all of the necessities of life."[83] The various accusations against the authenticity of the display lacked a definitive causal order; it could begin with the protesters' fabrication of evictions, with protesters' misrepresentation of their status, with their foreignness, with agitators, or with croppers' desire for handouts. On one level, discrediting the display appeared vital to maintaining AAA contracts. Within the first day of the protest, Secretary Wallace stated in a press conference that the administration would withhold AAA payments from any landlords found to have violated the cotton contracts. According to the *New York Times*, however, Wallace stressed "that he did not mean the landlords there had violated the act, saying he had no official information and would have to await action by the county committees."[84] At another level, landlords discredited croppers in the interest of salvaging their own public reputations. While powerful Missourians had the influence to break the demonstration, it was not enough. They felt compelled to counter the moral imperatives that the croppers' display called forth.

Denying Evictions, Asserting Transience

Detractors asserted that the protesters misrepresented themselves as "sharecroppers." The *New York Times* quoted Colonel B. M. Casteel, state highway patrol superintendent, as stating that the protesters were migrant workers from surrounding states, "who were out of a job 'as usual at the close of the picking season.'"[85] The genius of the strategy of denying protesters' status as "croppers" is that accusations were superficially true. Some protesters were currently day laborers or transients, but this was due to landlords' proclivity to evict croppers and hire them back as day laborers. Additionally, as of the early 1930s, the southeast counties affected by the protest had grown between 20 and 50 percent in population, which verified that many of farm laborers were not native Missourians.[86] Evictions rarely left a paper trail, and the frequent changeover of laborers often was used to rebut croppers' reports of bona fide illegal evictions to AAA county committees. During the demonstration, the *Southeast Missourian* reported Mississippi County AAA committeeman L. B. McPheeters's finding that only one family out of the ninety-nine he interviewed actually had an eviction notice.[87] The *Enterprise-Courier* cited two highway troopers who found only one family out of sixty-five to seventy had an eviction notice.

In an article featuring the subheading "Some Are Newcomers," the *Southeast Missourian's* negative coverage of the demonstration utilized scare quotes around "evicted" to cast doubt on the validity of protesters' claims.[88] Outsider status was readily conflated with "agitator." In a *St. Louis Globe-Democrat* editorial titled "Sharecropper Eviction Hoax," the reporter moves swiftly from suggesting sharecroppers publicly misrepresented themselves as "homeless casuals, bereft of shelter and livelihood because the government's crop control program had influenced landowners to kick them out" to "the sorry parade of farm laborers seems unquestionably to have been planned and carried out by a group of ambitious union promoters who mustered their following by

promises of extravagant largess from the government."[89] Here, croppers' purported laziness meant they desired government "handouts"
like La Forge. La Forge's experiment with cooperative farming and racial integration was construed as essentially communistic. Accusations
of communism could easily incite fear of manipulative agitators leading
croppers to the highways, especially because racism's and classism's
performativity constituted croppers as vulnerable to persuasion and
intellectually incapable of organization. Various permutations could
exist because allegations interchangeably served as evidence. The STFU
countered these claims, distributing a press release that acknowledged
that perhaps some croppers could have stayed on the land, but by "threat
of eviction [landowners could] further intimidate those who stayed into
greater docility."[90]

Claiming that the protesters were not native Missourians allowed
landowners to deny abuse of the AAA, rendered evictions impossible,
and freed the state government from responsibility for these individuals.
As noncitizens, the protesters had no rights. Here, croppers' miserable
conditions are not denied. Rather their *character* becomes the subject
of doubt and justification for their poverty.

Man-made Disaster: Local Agencies Sustain the Demonstration

Detractors also tried to undermine the scene on the highways by attacking the authenticity of croppers' suffering. They worked to dispel the
notion that landowners starved sharecroppers by alleging that the croppers' hunger and suffering was self-inflicted, temporary, solvable, and,
therefore, acted. While no party referred to the roadside demonstration
as a "hunger strike," opponents pinned croppers' hunger on the protest
itself, as a show designed to manipulate the public. Literary theorist
Maud Ellmann asserts that a hunger striker's "secret is to overpower the
oppressor with the spectacle of disempowerment, a hunger strike is an
ingenious way of playing hierarchical relations rather than abnegating
their authority."[91] State relief agencies and local presses insisted that they
would not be played.

The Missouri Red Cross took the official position that, because the
protest constituted a "man-made disaster," "the situation [is not] in our

field."[92] This official statement varied from St. Louis Red Cross Director Baxter's statements in a War Department memo. Colonel Franklin reported Baxter as stating, "It is not in any sense a Red Cross responsibility. Adequate shelter can and will be provided by the local communities or farm owners to any of these people who are willing to accept this. I do not feel that any useful purpose would be served by providing tentage to enable these people to remain on the highway."[93] According to Baxter, ending the disturbance outweighed meeting sharecroppers' immediate needs. Arthur Rothstein, the FSA photographer assigned to document the protest, wrote to his superior Roy Stryker about the lack of local aid: "while they were along the road people brought them food and clothing, altho [sic] the Red Cross refused to do anything under threats of no contributions from the planters."[94] Perhaps it was against Red Cross policy to provide shelter in "man-made" circumstances, but Rothstein's concerns reveal that the problem with relieving the crisis was not that it was "man-made" per se. Instead, it was a matter of which men were in crisis. The Red Cross's performative utterance deemed the demonstration to be a "show" put on by the shiftless, while simultaneously disavowing the social and economic conditions that caused the display.

The Red Cross, the Missouri National Guard, and the War Department also denied requests for tents and shelter for protesters. On January 10, 1939, the St. Louis Post-Dispatch reported that National Guard Adjutant General Lewis M. Means had received two such requests but was unable to provide tents "without orders from the Secretary of War."[95] STFU President J. R. Butler appealed directly to Secretary of War Harry H. Woodring and Missouri Governor Lloyd C. Stark. The governor replied by stating that the state did not own any tents.[96] In a January 13, 1939, telephoned report, War Department Chief of Staff General Craig suggested that the department take the position that "intervention . . . would be illegal" and stated, "they [the demonstrators] have been offered relief in the form of shelter and clothing and food and everything else by three different sources but apparently they do not want to take it."[97] Attached to this document is a confidential memorandum containing a transcription of a telephone conversation in which General Means requested that the War Department assume a "'hands off policy'"; he asked that this request remain both confidential and off the record.[98]

While the Agricultural Adjustment Administration authorized the distribution of surplus commodities, the Missouri state Social Security Administration running the operation insisted that it could not distribute food at the protest site. Eight surplus commodity warehouses were set up at different locations in the affected areas. However, to receive foodstuffs, sharecroppers had to travel to the warehouses and fill out applications in person. Some did use their trucks to travel to warehouses; others asserted that they lacked any means of transportation. The *St. Louis Post-Dispatch* featured a photograph of eight croppers huddled around O. E. Wright's desk, applying for surplus commodities. When representatives for the croppers complained that many could not travel to fill out applications, Wright stated that he had to follow regulations.[99] The local social security officials running the eight surplus commodity warehouses told reporters that "[croppers] can have it if they come to the food depots and apply for it . . . but food will not be taken to them."[100] Roadside distribution of food by the government surely could have facilitated continuation of the protest, but refusal to engage in such distribution failed to dismantle it. It is not known whether some croppers simply stayed put because, by leaving the highway, their absence would diminish the protest, but bureaucratic demands and disdain for croppers sustained the highway occupation as a display of hunger and suffering.

Restrictions on surplus depots and describing croppers' hunger as "man-made" attempted to present their suffering as artificial. Local presses and authorities set out to expose croppers' deceit. Highway troopers reported to the press that they observed families with many weeks of food supplies. *The Sikeston Herald* reported that a nearby grocery sold fifty dollars in food to croppers and that "One man alone bought $17 worth of groceries—and paid in cash."[101] The *Southeast Missourian* repurposed a picture taken by a *St. Louis Post-Dispatch* photographer of sharecropper children laughing to suggest that croppers feigned hunger: "The group above seems to be having a picnic or an outing and other pictures of this kind have been featured in the metropolitan press which is making a sensational event of the sharecroppers' demonstration."[102]

This caption posits that croppers were well fed through use of the term "picnic" and suggests that the children's joy is incongruous with the pain of hunger. Arguments by local presses and authorities waged against the authenticity of croppers' hunger were countered by national and regional press coverage because, in part, sharecroppers performed disempowerment by displaying their hungry, weather-beaten bodies as the limit of their agency. Croppers portrayed their hunger as ordinary to their lives, thus creating a space for the possibility that children's laughter might coexist with, not contradict, their pain. Instead of making a metaphor of the body to perform a call for justice that surpasses an individual human life (that is, a hunger strike), the croppers claimed that their lives depended on compassion.

Ironically, the Red Cross's desire to dissuade croppers from continuing their protest by refusing assistance, the National Guard's and the War Department's failure to step in, and the use of bureaucratic restrictions as an excuse to break the protest worked in the demonstrators' favor. They affirmed the authenticity of the croppers' display of powerless and vulnerability. The lack of tents enabled national headlines like those in the *New York Times* and *Philadelphia Inquirer,* which implied croppers' determination and righteousness: "Rain, Snow Defied by Sharecroppers" and "Ragged Sharecroppers Keep Protest Vigil in Raging Snowstorm."[103] Croppers' literal exposure to the elements made images of vulnerability easy to interpret. A photo of white toddler Verna Lee Daniels was titled "Out in Cold"; she stands with a spoon in her mouth, dirty, and without mittens, coat, or hat for warmth. Underneath her picture, the title "Sharecroppers Face Weather" encapsulated two photographs, one of an African American family "huddled beside their tin stove in a makeshift tent for protection" and the other of a white family fortunate enough to have the shelter of an actual tent.[104] Images like these were featured in cinema newsreels and the national presses, circulating as metonyms of the Cotton South to national audiences. It caused citizens from as (geographically and culturally) far away as Philadelphia to send letters to the Roosevelt administration asking questions such as "What has been done for evicted sharecroppers in Missouri?"[105]

Within the conditions of in-situ exhibition, "man-made" might be said to have signified that croppers lived at the leisure of farm owners, entirely dependent on them for a meager existence. That is to say, the sharecroppers' display and its mediation positioned them as the literal embodiments of exploitation. Philosopher Elizabeth Telfer states that witnessing hunger causes "a strong sense that there is something morally wrong. It involves the thought that something could have been or still can be done about the situation, and that this action is not a discretionary one but an obligation which some person or persons have failed or are failing to meet."[106] The lowest of the low shamed landowners through a performance which, in both form and content, embodied docility. The individuals on the highways performed themselves as being at the mercy of the (good or ill) will of others, not as activists. They proffered a performance of what humanity looks like when it has no place to go and no one claims responsibility. In the context of widespread vulnerability and a call for government obligations to citizens' welfare, croppers' public act of private living was uncanny: they revealed the power dynamics at work within public display as evidence against the crimes of landowners.

Removal of Croppers from the Roadsides

On January 13, State Health Commissioner Dr. Harry F. Park declared the demonstrators a "menace to public health" and issued an order to have them removed from the highways.[107] Over two days, Missouri authorities loaded the croppers into trucks and dumped the families out of sight. After spending the morning of January 15 on the highways, National Youth Administration representative Herbert Little telephoned his boss Aubrey Williams. The matter-of-fact tone of the conversation belies the alarm implicit in the questions that Williams asks, as well as in Little's answers:

> MR. LITTLE: We went up about 20–25 miles of highway and there were four camps along the road. One camp had 250, another 60 or 70.
>
> MR. WILLIAMS: Are they going to break up those camps?
>
> MR. LITTLE: Yes, they have already done it today. They moved them away starting about 10 o'clock on trucks to an isolated place down the country.
>
> MR. WILLIAMS: What have they there?
>
> MR. LITTLE: Forty acres and no provision for keeping them, according to what the Sheriff told me.
>
> MR. WILLIAMS: They are just going to dump them on the ground?
>
> MR. LITTLE: That is the impression the Sheriff gave me.

MR. WILLIAMS: Is that in Missouri or Arkansas.

MR. LITTLE: Missouri, about 50 or 60 miles from Arkansas.

MR. WILLIAMS: What do they think they will do down there?

MR. LITTLE: I don't know. My impression is they will probably starve or go back to day laboring jobs mostly.[108]

The following week, Aubrey Williams reported to the president that the grave condition of these camps represented one of numerous violations of croppers' civil liberties: "Their living conditions in the two concentration camps to which they were moved are as conducive to serious epidemic sickness, if not more so, than in their highway camps. . . . In addition, there is an apparent guard, or at least a consciousness of compulsion for the demonstrators to remain at the two concentration camps, away from the highways."[109]

Although croppers were removed from public view, the battle in the press continued. The *St. Louis Post-Dispatch* reported that deputies patrolled the spillway camp, called "Homeless Junction" by the croppers, under the false pretense that "Negro sharecroppers had virtually taken charge of a white school and had frightened the teacher and her pupils away."[110] Meanwhile, the *Sikeston Herald* characterized croppers as brilliant charlatans, "pretending to the world at large that they had been cruelly driven from their homes" and that, by naming this floodway to which authorities removed them "Homeless Junction," croppers were "keeping with the genius they have shown . . . in bidding for the sympathy of those not conversant with the facts."[111] Missourians also asserted that the FSA's declaration of an emergency situation in the Bootheel brought (more) undesirables into the area. In an interview that Bancroft Wells conducted for the *Enterprise-Courier* with Bootheel attorneys and landowners, J. M. Haw stated that croppers would rather receive relief than work, and O. W. Joslyn asserted that recipients would misuse FSA funds to buy "trinkets."[112] County businessmen and landowners cited the federal government's "'paternal' attitude toward sharecroppers" as creating a state of dependency, driving down land values, killing private farming, and "destroying the morale of sharecropper, day laborer, and landowner."[113] These men positioned federal aid stimulated by croppers' performance of suffering as threatening a total decline of cotton culture.

Missourians Aim to Restore their Reputations

It seems more than anything else, including interference in "local matters" by the federal government, that Missouri's public officials and landowners fixated on their disparagement in the press and scrambled to
restore their images on the national scene as upright citizens. On January 12, Harry S. Truman, at the time a U.S. senator (Democrat-Mo.),
read into the Senate Record resolutions adopted by landowners from
New Madrid that denounced depictions of Missourians circulated by
the press. On January 16, after protesters had been removed from the
roadsides, Governor Stark wrote to Secretary Wallace that reports given
to him by Robert K. Ryland, state director for the National Emergency
Council, and Colonel B. M. Casteel, State Highway Patrol superintendent, verified that the protesters were not sharecroppers. Stark asserts
that the roadside spectacle "was an organized demonstration of cotton
pickers, transients, day-laborers—a large portion (probably 60%) from
other states, and a considerable number of town negroes. I am reliably informed that most of them had been promised federal aid and an individual farm of their own."[114] The governor wanted an investigation to prove
this and to identify the communists within the FSA that encouraged the
protest. On January 18, Congressman Orville Zimmerman submitted a
resolution adopted by Mississippi County landowners, which invited an
investigation to determine the truth behind the protest. Zimmerman
stated for the Congressional Record, "we all know that a community and
its people can be libeled by overzealous reporters who are looking for
good stories for their papers."[115] The "people" to whom Zimmerman refers were, significantly, white property owners; these Missourians feared
the intangible repercussions of public dishonor. Of the fifteen allegations made by landowners, two concerned defamation. These allegations
include "that an erroneous impression had been given and grossly exag-
gerated and unfavorable publicity received by the residents of Southeastern Missouri to the effect that the demonstrators had been evicted,
which was untrue" and "that the press was biased and printed grossly ex-
aggerated and unfavorable articles concerning the demonstration." The
slander itself regarded croppers' hunger and homelessness; landowners
claimed "those moving to the highway were not without shelter and food

and that some, in fact, were well supplied with provisions."[116] As sociologist Gary Fine notes, "Negative reputations emerge when [individuals or groups] are perceived to have violated canonical values of society"; "that person [or group] serves as a synecdoche; [standing] for a historical period or set of events."[117] Landowners violated a tacit code of paternalism by fundamentally starving the croppers. The Bootheel sharecroppers' 1939 performance reiterated the mode and ideologies of theatrical in-situ exhibition to prove the lie of landowners' honor, not only damaging the reputations of Missouri's property-owning farmers and government officials but indicting the practices of cotton culture as immoral.

These Missourians defensive strategies and their demands for a federal investigation into the protest had the ironic effect of substantiating the repressive forces operating within cotton culture. The FSA and FBI investigations of the demonstration exposed the advantage landlords took of sharecroppers. The FSA found that the bulk of the protesters had been living in Missouri "in recent years" and were sharecroppers, at one point. While noting that it was "not literally true" that eviction notices had been served, "In substance, however, the charge is true." Though only one eviction notice was actually filed, FSA investigators found several other written notices "couched in legal language" and discovered that many croppers were told that owners were going to use day labor, that the house was wanted for a bigger family, or simply that the owner did not want the cropper next year—all constituting oral notice to vacate the land.[118] The FBI reported similar findings. The protest was not a hoax staged by union agitators; sharecroppers convinced federal investigators that they had not heard of the Southern Tenant Farmers' Union.[119] Investigators also disproved the allegation put forth by Governor Stark and the landowners that "fully 50% of the demonstrators had not lived in Missouri longer than five or six months and were, therefore, not entitled to the status of citizen, for which the people of Missouri were responsible under the ruling of the Social Security Commission."[120]

The socioeconomic truths within the display appeared obvious to President Roosevelt, even before the investigations were complete. He wrote an urgent memo to Secretary Wallace stating, "This situation, serious as it is for the individual families and the communities in which they are located, is even more serious as a symptom of the widespread situation throughout the South." Roosevelt further instructed Wallace to have the Federal Surplus Commodities Corporation (FSCC) send supplies to the concentration camps, "especially milk, eggs, butter, citrus fruits, meats and cereals."[121]

Throughout 1939, powerful Missourians continued to hinder federal attempts at both emergency and long-term interventions for sharecroppers, although federal support was also incremental and too slow given the croppers' dire circumstance. Rev. Whitfield continued the work of organizing croppers and advocating for their relief. The FSA could not support cooperative farming projects, hampered as it was by conservative southern democrats in Congress, but it did combine efforts with citizens to give croppers greater autonomy. By April 1939, the St. Louis Sharecropper Committee, also called Committee for the Rehabilitation of Sharecroppers—a relief organization founded by Whitfield, writer Fannie Cook, and former communist Al Murphy—raised sufficient funds to purchase ninety acres of land in Harviell for the protesters. With the support of this committee, a group of students from Lincoln University, and FSA grants, nearly one hundred families were settled on the land, which became known as "Cropperville." In December 1939, the FSA announced a five-point program for southeast Missouri that included leased land for laborers' homes and subsistence gardens, sanitation improvement, and a farm laborer rehabilitation program that provided loans for housing and land. In the spring of 1940, the FSA also created the Group Workers' Homes Project, in which the FSA secured land and built homes for roughly 502 farm laborer families (including 175 African American families).[122]

Perhaps more significantly, in the months following the 1939 demonstration, Governor Lloyd Stark created a Landlord-Tenant Committee and appointed Whitfield as a sharecropper representative to the state committee. Whitfield knew this was a triumph: "I licked the doggone Governor until he had to appoint me to his landlord tenant committee—for the first time in the history of this state a Negro has been appointed on a level with landlords."[123] Likewise, county committees were established throughout the state and included both a white and an African American sharecropper representative in all counties except Pemiscot. When evictions loomed again in January 1940, signs along the highways reading "Lest You Forget, One Year Ago Today, sat on this roadside, 1,500 croppers shelterless for days in snow and freezing cold," promised another protest would follow. So warned, Governor Stark called on landlords to postpone evictions.[124] In the face of the declining need for laborers in an increasingly mechanized agricultural industry and with the knowledge that the federal government enacted little more than emergency relief for sharecroppers following the 1939 protest, the threat of a repeat performance was still potent enough to garner such a concession from the governor.

Bootheel sharecroppers accomplished astonishing gains when viewed in light of the economic conditions, racism, classism, and the primacy of property rights as a determiner of citizenry. Historian Louis Cantor credits the 1939 demonstration as a primer for the nonviolent protests of the Civil Rights era.[125] More recently, Jarod Roll argued that this protest was an exemplar of grassroots organization that garnered unprecedented national attention, support for croppers, and compromise from the Missouri and federal governments. Attention to the dynamics of the Bootheel demonstration helps answer the question of why the public believed it to be real and not artifice and why they cared. Roadside living and its mediations cautioned a public vulnerable to economic instability that "to condemn migrants as 'lazy, shiftless families, seeking to evade the responsibilities of society and good citizenship' is to overlook mighty factors operating in rural America."[126] The spectacle on Missouri's highways perhaps could not achieve transformation of the agricultural economy, but recognition constituted a radical reinterpretation of a social group regarded as (inherently) culpable for their poverty.

Three years before the Bootheel demonstration, *Triple-A Plowed Under* had staged the federal government's culpability for the suffering of sharecroppers, farmers, workers, and consumers under the AAA. Yet these Federal Theatre artists also struggled to envision rights to food based on inclusivity rather than productivity, as we will see in the next chapter.

SCENE ELEVEN

Voice of Living Newspaper (over loudspeaker): Washington, May 12th, 1933—the A.A.A. becomes the law of the land. It is hereby declared to be the policy of Congress . . .

(Spot up on Secretary Wallace)

Secretary Wallace (picking up sentence): . . . to increase the purchasing of power of farmers. It is, by that token, farm relief, but also, by the same token, National Relief, for it is a well known fact that millions of urban unemployed will have a better chance of going to work when farm purchasing power rises enough to buy the products of city factories. Let's help the farmer . . . It is trying to subdue the habitual anarchy of a major American industry, and to establish organized control in the interest of not only the farmer but everybody else. The bill gives the Secretary of Agriculture the power to . . .

(Lights fade on Wallace. The projection of a map of the U. S. showing acreage reduction comes up on the scrim.)

Voice over Loudspeaker (staccato): . . . Reduce acreage. The visible supply of wheat diminished from 212 million bushels in 1932 to 124 million bushels in 1934.

(The projection changes to a number of little pigs in front of a number of large pigs, labeled "1933 production", the smaller pigs labeled "1934 production".)

Voice over Loudspeaker (Continuing): To curtail production. Hog production was cut from 60 million in 1933 to 37 million in 1935.

(Projection changes to a slide depicting two loaves of bread. One is labeled "1933—10¢" the other "1934—11¢".)

Voice over Loudspeaker (Continuing): To levy a tax on processing of basic farm commodities. Wheat advanced in price from 32 cents a bushel in 1933 to 74 cents a bushel in 1934.

BLACKOUT

Script Excerpt 5. Editorial Staff of the Living Newspaper Federal Theatre Project under the Supervision of Arthur Arent, "Triple-A Plowed Under," 1936, Federal Theatre Project Collection, Special Collections and Archives, George Mason University Libraries.

Staging the Agricultural Adjustment Act

The Federal Theatre Project's Triple-A Plowed Under (1936)

TRIPLE-A PLOWED UNDER PREMIERED AT MANHATTAN'S BILTMORE
Theatre on March 14, 1936 and was produced four more times between
April and August 1936 by regional Federal Theatre Project (FTP) units
in Chicago, Cleveland, Los Angeles, and Milwaukee. At the time of the
writing, rehearsals, and productions of *Triple-A Plowed Under,* public
debate about the political, moral, and economic wisdom the Agricultural
Adjustment Act had reached a fever pitch. Debate was also heating up
about the practicality and morality of the Works Progress Administration, and the Federal Theatre Project in particular. The play debuted
within two months of the Supreme Court's ruling against the federal government on January 6, 1936, and within two weeks of President Roosevelt's signing on March 1, 1936, of the Soil Conservation and Domestic
Allotment Act (SCDAA) to replace the AAA.

Triple-A Plowed Under was also the first "living newspaper" play
performed before the public, premiering just five weeks after the State
Department shut down the first FTP living newspaper, *Ethiopia,* on January 24, 1936. Concerned that this play's depiction of Italy's occupation

of the east African nation would offend Mussolini, the State Department issued an order: "no issue of the living newspaper shall contain any representation of the head or one of the ministers or the cabinet of a foreign state unless such representation shall have been approved in advance by the Department of State."[1] *Ethiopia* not only compounded the varied concerns about government-sponsored theater voiced by unions, cultural critics, commercial theater producers, and New Deal opponents, it established the living newspaper genre as an inherently antagonistic political form. As a sociocultural event, *Triple-A Plowed Under* captured tensions present in each of the protests examined in this book. It was a perfect storm of circumstance and aesthetics for using antitheatrical prejudice as a tactic to circumscribe citizenship. While the opening of *Triple-A Plowed Under* on heels of all this political jockeying may have overdetermined much of its reception, the play—its narrative arc, its representations of American politicians and controversial public figures, and its revelations of the intimate effects of political decisions on Americans' lives—called attention to itself as (a product of) the contemporary situation.

Triple-A Plowed Under was theater, but it would not be neatly contained as such. Like the protests and the Chicago World's Fair exhibits discussed in previous chapters, the play refused to uphold the binary opposition between real and illusion, authenticity and dissembling necessary to the belief that theater or protest (when accused of being "theater") does not have direct material effects on everyday life and, therefore, is superfluous. It made apparent the capacity for theatrical performance to impact quotidian matters. The peculiar irony of *Triple-A Plowed Under* is that, unlike any other Federal Theatre Project production, food was at stake in the drama and for the artists portraying it.

Like the Wisconsin dairy farmers, the Hamtramck housewives, and the federal government, the play argued that the solution to hunger in capitalist America was farmer-consumer connectedness facilitated by the federal government. Depictions of men, women, and children suffering from hunger, federally sanctioned food destruction, and those gaining from the AAA placed New Deal food policies under moral scrutiny. *Triple-A Plowed Under* demanded government regulation of an amoral economy and immoral "middlemen" in the interest of restoring each citizen's "opportunity to make his own place in society."[2] This idea was represented as the universal entitlement to food. Yet while *Triple-A Plowed Under* advocated for a "state that permits no man to go hungry," it presented men and women who had "earned" their livings. These characters—all white, excluding "sharecroppers" and "Sam, a Negro farmer"— speak to the racialized and gendered constructions of "producer" and "consumer" that mitigated full recognition of citizenship. The play called on the government to create opportunities for employment. Everyman figures decry handouts—"No charity!"—and call for jobs. In performance, this demand played out in a complex and contradictory manner. The actors onstage on a WPA job were, to many minds, receiving a form of charity: the government had created jobs, but these existed outside or in competition with the free market. The finale, intentionally or not, commented on the conditions of theatrical production.

Federal Theatre Artists and Producerist Discourse

Beginning in 1935, the Works Progress Administration (WPA), of which the FTP was a part, offered a temporary, partial, and problematic solution to the social problem of relief—perceived as degrading to the enterprising American spirit—by putting citizens to work in their fields of expertise on projects benefitting society. The FTP, with regional operations in twenty-two states, was arranged into "units" that produced a vast array of theater (including vaudeville, foreign-language, children's, marionette, operetta, and living newspaper theater), employed roughly 12,700 people at its peak and provided low-cost or free entertainment to more than twenty-five million Americans before its funding was terminated in 1939.[3] In *Arena,* written by FTP head Hallie Flanagan and published within eighteen months of the project's defunding, Flanagan quotes a letter of apology from an unnamed senator: "It really seemed that if the Senate refused to yield in its efforts to protect the eight thousand employees on the theater projects, that we would have the entire two and a half million WPA relief workers thrown out of employment."[4] Many scholars have addressed the question of how a rather small program within the WPA, allocated less than seven million dollars of a five billion dollar project, could jeopardize the welfare of millions of citizens.[5]

In discussing the ways in which *Triple-A Plowed Under* as an event and a play calls into question the belief that theater and performance are separable from "real" life, I will highlight the two aspects of the FTP that were considered most problematic.

First, FTP theater artists were not considered independent agents. Though these artists did not necessarily share a predominating political perspective from which they made claims about the AAA, they did occupy the clearly defined social position of government employees on a work relief program. Government funding of artists raised questions tied to freedom of expression. FTP personnel in the New York City unit tried to correct the perception that this theater was the mouthpiece of its patron. On April 6, 1936, Arthur Garfield Hays, general counsel of the American Civil Liberties Union, gave a talk titled "The Federal Theatre and a Free Stage" prior to the performance of *Triple-A Plowed Under.*[6] Nevertheless, WPA projects interested in building American infrastructures appeared apolitical, while theater artists were paid out of general tax revenues to produce ideas. William F. McDermott, drama critic for the *Cleveland Plain Dealer,* wrote, "Perhaps unconsciously, its plays will reflect the political views of the administration from which it draws its money and to which it looks for orders."[7] For as gently as McDermott stated his concerns, other critics vehemently opposed the FTP based on Fascist and Communist states' similar arrangement with their national theaters. In the days after *Triple-Plowed Under* premiered, Congressman Robert L. Bacon (Republican-N.Y.) sent a telegram to WPA director Harry Hopkins, which was widely reprinted in the press. In it, Bacon noted the Russian government's subsidization of theater for propagandistic purposes, and he quoted the People's Commissar for Education's championing of the stage as vital to the revolution.[8] Bacon further contended that the FTP was a central apparatus in Roosevelt's campaign machine.[9] For Bacon and other WPA opponents, the FTP offered a strong example of the New Deal's socialist impulses. Linked to this, commercial theaters deemed the FTP to be unfair competition from the government because it offered the same product, though purportedly a degraded version, at a reduced price.

Both supporters of the FTP and those opposed to it appropriated the content of *Triple-A Plowed Under* as ammunition for debate over the value of theater, largely neglecting to consider the value of the AAA or the play itself. Whether for or against the FTP, these critics interpreted *Triple-A Plowed Under* through "the red, white, and blue official emblem, [of the] W.P.A. on the doors of the Biltmore Theatre," regarding the living newspaper as pure propaganda. No unanimity existed as to whether *Triple-A Plowed Under* was pro-WPA, anti-New Deal, or communist. Did *Triple-A Plowed Under* close with an appeal for a third party as suggested by the *Survey Graphic*? Was *this* Farm-Labor party in line with a communist agenda as stated by the *Times*? Was the *Pennsylvanian* right? Was the play's "clos[ing] with a poignant plea for a strong Farmer-Labor Party . . . vicious satire on the Administration's farm program"? The *Topeka Journal* felt *Triple-A Plowed Under* demonstrated Democratic partisanship—"if the Republicans were in power the Biltmore Theatre would doubtless witness a different [play]"—while an editorial in an Indianapolis paper read, "Those who see the New York play are subtly invited to become convinced that permanent joy and happiness, peace and prosperity would have come to the home of every American farmer had the supreme court decided for the administration."[10]

Critics of the FTP also claimed that theater wasted public money, particularly when the nation faced an economic crisis. In other words, tangible products such as buildings, bridges, and ditches were considered useful; theater considered a luxury. The reviewer from the *Oneonta Star* (New York) felt that "spending public money to educate our citizenry on a delicate political problems [*sic*] via the dramatic stage [is] revolting and impertinent."[11] Failing to recognize theater as (dignified) work, the writer calls the FTP: "scatterbrain extravagance." A Milwaukee reviewer, however, framed attendance to *Triple-A Plowed Under* as a civic duty by asserting that "actors and actresses are being saved from hunger and idleness and demoralization."[12] This argument articulates citizens' rights to food provided through work and champions the WPA for providing that opportunity. While these reviewers differ about whether the government should subsidize theater, their perspectives exemplify the contradictions between productivity and value that also structure rights to food and recognition of citizenship.

Like the protests examined throughout this book in which citizens proved their rights by theatricalizing consumption or production, FTP theater artists experienced the same burden of proof, just as the story of *Triple-A Plowed Under* reinforced this paradigm. Yet commercial artists further diminished FTP artists' productivity by demeaning them as "amateurs"; here, unemployment status was used as proof of a lack of talent or skill. In his memoir about his work as an FTP dramatist, Tony Buttitta recalled that members of Actors Equity, the professional actors' union, initially did not want their names printed in FTP programs and resented having to work with nonunion actors. Professional actors' anxiety about their reputations was fueled by powerful commercial producers who belittled the FTP productions as lowering professional standards that "do more harm than good to the theater as an institution."[13] In the essay "Plow the Plays Under," written for *Stage,* screenwriter William De Mille, the older brother of Cecile B. De Mille, criticized the anti-free-market tenets of the FTP by satirically proposing that it follow the model of the AAA itself. He suggested that the government stem the overproduction of theater and the glutting of the market with more artists than it can handle by paying playwrights not to write plays:

> Why should the poor playwright be discriminated against when the poor farmer is being treated like the teacher's pet? The playwright cannot lease land from an Indian for two dollars an acre and then get seven dollars for not raising wheat on it. Of course, under the plan I suggest, a producer might lease a play from an author for a nominal sum, and then receive thousands for not producing it; but producers are much too high minded to do this sort of thing, and anyway they would not dare to try to get paid for not producing an unwritten play. For, once we admit that any expansion of this principle is practicable, the audience would expect to get paid for not going to see the unwritten play which the manager did not produce.[14]

From each of these perspectives, FTP employees, regarded simultaneously as artists and relief recipients, failed to produce or consume "properly." Critics of the FTP rendered theater and its artist-laborers "surplus."

The Aesthetic of the Living Newspaper and *Triple-A Plowed Under*

The new living newspaper genre was very fertile ground for alleging politicking (read: manipulative pretense) because it *dramatized actual* current events—a combination that confirmed theater's infamy as "a maker of counterfeits that look like the truth."[15] Nevertheless, the Living Newspaper Unit cast *Triple-A Plowed Under* and subsequent living newspapers as fair and impartial, "Flash News in the Flesh," by drawing on conventions of journalistic narrative, scope, and layout.[16] *Triple-A Plowed Under* includes historical figures; contemporary political figures such as Henry Wallace, National Recovery Administration (NRA) head General Hugh Johnson, AAA administrator Chester A. Davis, Farmers' Holiday Association President Milo Reno; and rural and urban everyman types—"workers," "farmers," and "consumers." The play advances chronologically from 1917 to the immediate moment in the theater through a combination of documented and fictional scenes. It depicts the nation's economic decline into the Depression, farmers' and workers' growing desperation, the enactment of the AAA, and the legislation's complications and implications. All scenes were framed as authentic news objects regardless whether a scene was derived from a documented event and reproduced an individual's words verbatim or was imagined.

A male voice amplified over a loudspeaker introduced many scenes in a style that mimicked the tenor of print headlines and the announcements in *March of Time* newsreels. This disembodied character, the "Voice of the Living Newspaper" (VLN), set scenes by date and place and provided a brief exposition or statistics. These introductions balanced news headlines' sensationalism and factuality. The content identified a scene's emotional, political, or informational significance, while it also situated the VLN as outside the narrative and so an "objective" voice.

Federal Theatre Magazine, a vehicle for communication between regional units of the FTP, attributed the living newspaper form to the demands of press reporting, asserting that artistic personnel were "subject to the newspaper rules—brevity, simplicity, clearness."[17] The range of stories represented in *Triple-A Plowed Under,* its inclusivity of constituencies, and its quick juxtapositions of scenes taking place in very distant locales rehearsed the front page by bringing together a range of topics beyond audiences' regular field of vision. Many roles (around a hundred) and scenes that featured crowds of people created the sense of an American panorama; for example, the Chicago production commenced with forty-one people onstage.[18] It took only forty-five to fifty-five minutes to perform the twenty-six scenes in the play; each scene tended to last less than one minute, and many took no more than twenty seconds.[19] The terse dialogue and the blackouts ending each scene reproduced the episodic structure of news reports. In many of the scenes, the use of projections and backlit scrims to cast actors in massive silhouette expressed the incidents' newsworthy magnitude. These scenic devices also materialized the economic crisis or news-style range of coverage and allegorized producer and consumer characters as American everymen and everywomen. The rhythm and imagery produced in the productions occupied reviews; scenes described as "lighting-like flashes" impressed critics.[20] The *Survey Graphic* listed the various effects used, describing them as "ingenious"; showing characters in silhouette made the actors appear to the reviewer "like drawings, shadow pictures."[21] *Billboard* enumerated the use of a "fast peppering of blackouts, interspersed with graphs thrown on a scrim drop" and compared the play both to newspaper headlines and *March of Time*.[22] Overall narrative swiftness, diversity, and sparse language combined with the visual scale of scenes to call to mind a news sensibility in size, sound, image, and stakes. At the same time and despite its claims to reproduction rather than interpretation of current events, in the speed of *Triple-A Plowed Under*'s progression from beginning to end, historical phenomena and discrete incidents became tightly linked. The play and its productions aimed at the social functions of the morality play by giving concrete facts and current events "universal" significance. Unlike a newspaper, it asked audiences to infer meaning from the totality and make a moral judgment.

However, a number of cultural and theater critics, who felt that theater should instruct its audience, expressed dissatisfaction with the play's lack of an overarching viewpoint on the contemporary situation. Even the play's title, *Triple-A Plowed Under,* stood as a contradiction by holding in tension the AAA's "wastefulness" with the Supreme Court decision that killed the 1933 legislation. Mark Randall, writing for the *Brooklyn Ridgewood Times,* implied that the ending caused a sort of paralysis: "With the problem still unsolved, as is still the cast [sic] today, the curtain is drawn and the audience left to ponder on what happens next." The critic for *Variety* criticized *Triple-A Plowed Under*'s lack of a solution: "Where the dramatic effort falters is that it fails to clearly show just how this miracle is to be brought about." *Billboard* determined that the play's failure to provide an answer stemmed from its aping of newspapers: "It really is a muddled presentation, giving several viewpoints—which is just what most newspapers do." The *New York Sun* concurred: "It was far too impartial for drama; it gave too much to all sides." A few reviewers, however, recognized the ambiguity as inherent to the national drama of agriculture. Frank Mittauer, reviewing the Los Angeles production, concluded, "If it leaves its audience bewildered as it ends, it is only because, as the play ably demonstrates, our efforts under compulsion to repair our faltering economic system do not make very good sense viewed in retrospect." On the one hand, the critique that the play's failure as a drama was its lack of a solution or viewpoint points to the belief that theater's purpose is social and political. On the other hand, the fact that theater, a plaything, might influence society and politics was regarded by some critics as the danger of theatricalizing the "real world"—that is, documentary drama is a cultural oxymoron.[23]

Playbills for the New York and Chicago productions of *Triple-A Plowed Under* augmented the living newspaper's journalistic frame (see figure 5.1). These programs included articles about the process of creating a living newspaper, detailing research and editing methods. For example, the Chicago program includes an article on *Triple-A Plowed Under* titled "Dramatized News Now Offered in Famous Play." It discusses the forty researchers' work on the play's topic and how fifteen dramatists turned news incidents into scenes.[24] The New York programs, which were updated with new stories each week of the performance, offered a bibliography listing the articles, government reports, and books from which *Triple-A Plowed Under*'s scenes derived. Programs also featured stories of critical praise for the living newspaper, the successes of other Federal Theatre productions, and promotions for upcoming shows. The programs' headlines, captions, and photos positioned *Triple-A Plowed Under* as a document of the times that dramatized citizens' real lives, leaders' real words, and the problems with which the nation struggled.

Although the Milwaukee, Cleveland, and Los Angeles productions of *Triple-A Plowed Under* used conventional playbills, every program featured scene titles. They functioned similarly to the titling of acts in revue or news headlines, indicating the narrative independence of each scene

NOW AT AIR CONDITIONED CIVIC THEATRE

WACKER DRIVE at WASHINGTON   Phone State 7887

| LIVING DRAMA | The Living Newspaper | SPOT NEWS |

Vol. I.   No. 1.   GREAT NORTHERN THEATRE   Opened July 6, 1936

"TRIPLE A PLOWED UNDER"

SILHOUETTE

One of the Many Spectacular Scenes in "Triple A Plowed Under"
Now Playing at the Great Northern Theatre.

DRAMATIZED NEWS NOW OFFERED IN FAMOUS PLAY

An entirely new form of theatrical production, live news enacted by living actors, is being given for the first time in Chicago, by the presentation at the Great Northern of the New York success "Triple A Plowed Under," under the auspices of the Federal Theatre. This production marks a unique and spectacular departure for the stage by offering a thrilling series of dramatized news events, with a large cast of actors in a series of swiftly moving scenes.

A good description of this new stage form is conveyed by its secondary title, The Living Newspaper. To achieve it, the abilities of many newspaper men and women, dramatists, actors, directors, scenic designers and other stage technicians were employed. In all, the work of 200 persons, including 100 actors and actresses, has gone into the production, with the staging being done by H. Gordon Graham, who also staged the New York edition of the same play.

One of the biggest jobs connected with producing the show was the editing. The first step was to choose which of thousands of news events to present on the stage.

News Subjects Sifted

Preliminary scanning of newspaper files resulted in the choice of about 100 events as of sufficient importance and lending themselves to dramatization. From these the editors of THE LIVING NEWSPAPER finally selected the most important connected with the main subject,—that of Triple A.

The forty research workers, for the most part experienced newspaper workers, on the staff of THE LIVING NEWSPAPER were then sent out to gather material on the selected subjects. Their reports were voluminous, in some instances running to more than 5,000 words on a single subject.

With this material they picked out about 30 events that could be presented vividly on the stage. They also kept in mind that the production should be balanced; that as wide as possible a variety of subjects should be included.

Still More Sifting

When the dramatic versions of the remaining happenings were turned in by the fifteen dramatists on the project there was more editing. The technical difficulties of staging some of the episodes made their presentation impractical. Some were too long. The show was not to run for more than an hour.

Even after the rehearsals were started, various scenes were re-written—often several times—or were discarded and replaced by others. Those who saw the early rehearsals scarcely recognize the production as it is now presented.

In this way "Triple A Plowed Under" finally took form and after weeks of rehearsing was ready to make its bow to the public.

Draw of Federal Theatre
Goes Over Best Expectations

Results Prove Public Is Eager For Plays

New York City.
Fed Shows Do Top Biz!
Which is the way that our theatrical neighbor, "Variety," might hint at the fact that a handful of WPA Federal Theatre productions in New York recently played to more customers than many commercial productions on Broadway.

This is neither a boast nor idle fancy. It does not prove that the Federal Theatre is undermining commercial production, for the box-office scale, from 25 to 55 cents, can hardly be considered important money competition for the commercial managers. Moreover, about twenty per cent of the audiences have occupied free seats, since certain nights are free to WPA workers and persons on relief—and they make the most of it!

What it does indicate is that the recent batch of New York WPA productions has offered superb entertainment meriting a high degree of public acceptance. That it has kept a body of actors, writers and theatre workers constructively busy is almost too obvious to note.

Fine Record

Here is the record. From its opening on March 14, "Triple A Plowed Under," THE LIVING NEWSPAPER'S first production, played to over 40,000 people in 85 perform-

ances—two a night—in a small theatre. "Murder in the Cathedral," at the Manhattan, served an even larger number of playgoers, in a week's less run with one performance a night, 38 curtains in all. "Murder" topped them all in audiences and money business, and was a sellout when reluctantly closed on May 2.

And so it goes. The Experimental Theatre's "Chalk Dust," first to open and showing for eight weeks, the longest run of any, brought 21,000 persons to Daly's Theatre in its 51 performances.

The Bard a Hit

"Macbeth," the Negro Theatre's amazing hit at the Lafayette in Harlem, proved consistent in doing capacity business of 7,400 seats a week in the early part of its run. With the Lafayette having a slight edge on the Manhattan Theatre in seating capacity, Shakespeare topped T. S. Eliot in attendance (both were sell-outs) and drew

(Continued on Page 3)

Don't forget! "Triple A" is given twice nightly, at 8:30 and 9:40 p. m. sharp. Be prompt so as not to miss any of the twenty-five exciting scenes. There are no matinees and no Sunday performances.

as well as its content. Titles created a timeline and demonstrated which episodes from the nation's recent past and present would be depicted. For example, the Cleveland production titled scenes 11 through 21 as "Birth of Triple A," "Payments," "Gruel," "Wine," "Drought," "Prayer," "Cotton Patch," "Sharecroppers," "Housewives Rebel," "Sherwood Case," and "Triple A Killed."[25] A preshow glance over the scenes would have provided an audience with adequate information to predict the well-known narrative's unfolding, especially as these were current events. Playbills of different productions reveal the various ways in which these titles colored the same narrative and similarly staged scenes. For instance, in New York, scene 10 was titled, "Crops Burned"; Los Angeles used the title "Farmer vs. Worker"; and in Chicago, it was called "Worker and Farmers' Families."[26] Emphasis on conflict or mutuality framed the subsequent action and helped shape the play's central thesis: (re)connecting farmers and consumers will restore moral American capitalism.

The Controversial Origins of the Living Newspaper

Triple-A Plowed Under is an early instance of the "space stage" aesthetics developed by the Living Newspaper unit. This style drew upon theatrical techniques associated with various politically affiliated forms: the conservative March of Time, the Group Theatre's social realism, the agit-prop forms of European communist theaters such as the Soviet Blue Blouses and those used in American workers' theaters such as the Theatre Union. The unit created "space stage" as an explicit alternative to realism's psychological portraits in order to represent materialist analysis of systemic and institutional "forces that motivated the act." Living Newspaper dramatists stated that the conventional three-act drama was inadequate for communicating the news's "many component parts." Instead, they incorporated direct-address dialogue into the short scenes, à la Clifford Odets's Waiting for Lefty (1935), because it enabled a "direct sharing of a problem with the audience."[27] Actors complained that the dramaturgy precluded realistic acting technique; most characters had names like "Unemployed" or "Farmer," and each character also had very little stage time.[28] In the place of idiosyncratic characters, the style aimed to represent the effects of political-economic forces on citizens' lives. According to the living newspaper dramatists, contemporary stage design's elaborate realism was also too "decadent." The living newspaper unit utilized the new stagecraft techniques of Edward Gordon Craig and Adolphe Appia as the "abstract technique, which widened the scope of action and mood." Sparse and suggestive scenery was also in line with the FTP's budgetary constraints. As a work relief program, the bulk of the funding was allocated for salaries, not scenery, costuming, or other equipment.[29]

The origins of this dramatic form, the attribution of stylistic choices to Odets's famous labor play, and the unit's antirealist stance aligned the living newspaper form with leftist and radical theater groups and was used by New Deal critics to support allegations against the FTP as a fundamentally un-American enterprise. Critics also cited as evidence the travels and theater training of Hallie Flanagan and FTP stage director Joseph Losey (director of the New York City production of *Triple-A Plowed Under*) in the Soviet Union. Writers and personnel on the Living Newspaper Unit countered these claims by asserting that the form developed out of the need to "encompass the wide scope of present-day events."[30] Similarly, the New York City program for *Triple-A Plowed Under* credits the New York Newspaper Guild with the "idea of living dramatization of current news events."[31] In a 1938 *Theatre Arts Monthly* article, Arthur Arent, lead writer for living newspapers, both noted "the possibility of a whole avalanche of predecessors" *and* "[denied] their influence." Arent concedes minor indebtedness to revue and the *March of Time,* but he imagines an interminable drawing-room debate about its lineage:

> Soon the air is heavy with scholarly references to the Blue Blouses, the commedia dell' arte, to Bert Brecht, and the March of Time.
> What are the sources of this technique? As far as I know, there aren't any. At least if there are, we didn't know about them. Among those immediately concerned—author, director, producer, designer, technician, and composer—each had ideas as to what could be done in his particular orbit, and we all had a healthy respect for the opportunity for experimentation that the Federal Theatre offered.[32]

Of course, three years of red-baiting by anti-New Deal press and government officials suggests the impossibility for FTP personnel to acknowledge indebtedness to left-wing or radical aesthetic movements without jeopardizing the project. Indeed, Arent's article appeared one month

before Hallie Flanagan defended the Americanness of the Federal Theatre Project in her testimony before the Congressional Committee on
Un-American Propaganda Activities.

Triple-A Plowed Under in Production

The following entails an analysis of primarily the New York City pre-
miere production of *Triple-A Plowed Under*. The manuscript of the play
is my source for the narrative and stage directions. I also employ the New
York City production notes, which contain property and costume lists;
scenery, sound and light cues; and plots denoting light and scenery placement. Additionally, photographs, narrative reports, programs, and production bulletins from the various productions assist in reconstructing
the New York City mise-en-scène and provide a comparative basis for the
play as performed in Los Angeles, Milwaukee, Cleveland, and Chicago.

The History of the Paradox: Scenes 1, 2, and 3

In the first three scenes of *Triple-A Plowed Under*, eighteen years elapse,
from World War I to the midst of the Great Depression in 1935. These
first few minutes make clear the reasons for the contemporaneous glutting of agricultural markets, ecological problems, and national economic
crisis: spurred on by ideological machinations used to conscript farmers into the war effort, the farmer bought more land, clear-cut forest to
make fields, and produced "more." In the New York production, actors
appeared behind a scrim in silhouette. Following the VLN's introduction "1917—Inflation," at stage left, a red light highlighted a continuous
march of soldiers; the volume of their trek into bloody battle increased
as the scene progressed. On stage right, three silhouettes towered above
shadows of farmers. These looming speakers appeal to farmers' revered
position by barraging them with short, morally charged statements:

FIRST SPEAKER. The fate of our country rest upon the farmer.

FIRST SPEAKER. Do you want our land invaded?

SECOND SPEAKER. Do you want your daughters ravaged by Huns?

WOMAN. Farmer, save the Nation! (Trumpet)[33]

These lines stress farmer's obligation and ability to stave off the threat to women, land, and U.S. civilization by increasing food production: "Every bushel of barley is a barrel of bullets" and "Every hand with a spade is a hand-grenade." These martial metaphors, complete with memorable alliteration and rhyme, recall the wartime propaganda of the Wilson administration. Amid appeals to masculine duty, the significance of "Woman" multiplies. She is mother, wife, land, and democracy. A trumpet punctuated each of her entreaties, in which the streams of solicitations culminate. Woman repeatedly beseeches the farmer to "save" "our boys," "democracy," "our honor," "civilization," "our flag." Silhouettes erased Speakers and Woman as individual characters; their daunting shadows signaled the ubiquity and intensity of the moral imperatives put to farmers to produce "More! More! More!" to, ultimately, in Woman's words, "SAVE THE WORLD."[34] In doing so, the scene places culpability for the 1930s agricultural crisis on the Wilson administration by both expressing the enormous pressure on farmers and defending farmers' actions as motivated by patriotism and selflessness. The scene resonates with the Milk Pool's strike poem (see Chapter 2) in the elision of agricultural profits and elevation of the farmer to heroic proportions. By historicizing the "paradox" in this way, the play dismisses any inclination an urban audience might have to blame farmers for the agricultural crisis, while it involves them intimately in the present situation.

Scenes 2 and 3 ushered the 1936 audiences of *Triple-A Plowed Under* into the recent past. Scene two consists of three brief vignettes representing "The 1920s. Deflation." The scenes illustrate the domino effect of foreign markets' decline following the armistice: while large exporters refuse shipments, pressure for loan repayment increases from large lenders to country banks and from these banks to farmers, resulting in the "paradox of want amid plenty." Farmer's inability to sell the wheat rotting in his fields dumbfounds him:

> Well, hell, people still need to eat, don't they. And they can't tell me there aren't people who couldn't eat what's lying out in my fields now. My son, Jim, in New York says he can't walk down the street without having hungry men beg him for money.[35]

Scene 3's brief statistical account of the fall in farm income and rise in unemployment from 1920 to 1935 shows the economic interdependence of Farmer, Dealer, Manufacturer, and Worker. In the New York production, each actor stood facing the audience in a straight line from stage right to stage left (Farmer far SR, then Dealer and Manufacturer, and Worker far SL). Four different spotlights isolated the characters from each other. The actors remained motionless; when they spoke, they turned only their heads to look at the character immediately to the left. Following each line, the spot lighting the speaker went dark.[36] One-line statements about each man's inability to participate economically combined with receding illumination and movement from stage right to stage left to culminate in focusing on Worker, who speaks directly to the audience:

FARMER. I can't buy that auto.

DEALER. I can't take that shipment.

MANUFACTURER. I can't use you any more.

WORKER. I can't eat. (Count one, two, light out.)[37]

The singular movement, a head turn, linked each man to the next and ultimately to the audience. The scene begins with Farmer's inability to purchase industrial products but does not end with Worker's lack of purchasing power. The head turns from Farmer to Dealer to Manufacturer to Worker to the audience symbolize the grinding circle of the persistent downturn. Though the VLN's introduction set this scene in the "troubled 15 years, 1920 to 1935," subsequent scenes muddied the timeline of political events to give the impression that the AAA quelled rural disorder. This plotting paints farmers' protests as pre-Roosevelt administration phenomena.

The Years before AAA: Scene 4 to Scene 10

Scenes 4 through 10 represent farmers' increasing desperation as occurring in the years prior to the passage of the AAA. These scenes show the violent and extralegal means farmers turned to in the absence of government intervention and attack food processors and distributors via middlemen characters. Here, and throughout the play, middlemen are depicted as making nothing and consuming nothing, while siphoning farmers' earned profit and diminishing consumers' purchasing power. At the same time, these scenes characterize farmers as deeply moral and motivated by altruism rather than economics.

Scene 4 begins a narrative thread used to justify farmers' violence by alleging that the committee of Commission Merchants bribed Farmers' Holiday President Milo Reno to call off the national strike. Scene 5 depicts price gouging as an outcome of Reno's actions that motivates farmers' decision to dump milk in scenes 6 and 7. VLN introduces scene 5 with the words "Milk flows to market." Though not the only food subject to price gouging, milk's cultural significance amplifies the scene's depiction of injustice and immorality, while the incidents surrounding Reno and the dairy industry lend veracity to the fictional exchange. On the Biltmore stage in New York City, Middleman, in a business suit, sat at a desk; Farmer and Consumer stood on each side of him. Middleman offers Farmer three cents for his quart of milk. His "Take it or Leave it" offer epitomizes his control over Farmer's livelihood. With no other outlet for his product, Farmer sells his milk. Middleman then poured the milk from Farmer's can into a bottle and offered it to the female consumer at the selling price of fifteen cents. Consumer, of course, cannot leave the milk because of its necessity to her family's well-being, so, despite the astronomical price, she states, "I'll take it." Middleman then took her money without remorse and patted his pockets as the scene went to blackout.[38]

Middleman's placement between producer and consumer literalized both his character and the advantage he takes of his position in the food system. The nearness of Farmer, who initially held the tin of milk, to Consumer, who, at scene's end, clutched her newly purchased milk bottle, visualized Middleman's dispensability. Unlike Farmer, Middleman has not labored for his profit. Also, Consumer's responsibility for an entire family, connoted by her gender, strikingly contrasts with Middleman's masculinity, framed in the scene as a lack of familial obligation. Theater critic Burns Mantle wrote of this scene's galvanizing moral force: "The picture of an arrogant middleman buying milk for 3 cents ... and selling it for 15 cents ... on a 'take it or leave it' basis is eloquent of a situation that cannot be effectively driven home in headlines."[39] As staged, the scene materialized belief in farmers' rights to cost of production plus profit and consumers' rights to a reasonable cost of living. It belies the idea widely held by contemporary anthropologists and social scientists that, "unlike non-capitalist societies where food exchanges reduce social distance and solidify relationships . . . in our [U.S.] capitalist society, food is a commodity, an object whose exchange creates distance and differentiation."[40] That is to say, this scene does not recognize as problematic the commercialization of food or capitalism per se. Rather, it imagines the potential of capitalist exchange to create producer-consumer solidarity and scapegoats middlemen for the imbalance and the injustice in the capitalist market.

VLN's announcement opening scene 6 aimed to generate empathy for farmers by integrating audiences into the action: "Sioux City—September 18th, 1932—Farmers organize Relief Conference in theatre."[41] Dispersed among the audience, five actors playing farmers breached the fourth wall and debated directly across the footlights with the conference Chairman seated at center stage, until finally:

> CHAIRMAN. (Holding up hand for silence) Friends. There's a great deal to be done. Yesterday fourteen of our men were shot down on the picket line in Cherokee County . . . We want our rights. . . . We want relief. . . . and we will get it.
> (Thunderous roar greets him. Cries of "strike" "dump the milk" and "Turn over the trucks.")
>
> FIFTH SPEAKER. (From audience) Men!—we've got to save ourselves, with or without Milo Reno—and the only way to do that is to dump every truck and spill every can of milk we can lay our hands on—let's stop talking and do something! (Tremendous roar)[42]

This staging treats the entire audience as farmers. It exemplifies the Living Newspaper Unit's objective to reimagine performance space and, so, the audience's relationship to the narrative and characters: "[The dramatist] should often conceive of the entire theater as a single unit, as opposed to the concept of a stage separated from its audience. . . . In most theatres the audience has paid to attend and watch the spectacle of a group of characters. . . . The characters may have the sympathy of the audience but there is a conscious effort to retain their own identity as something separate from the observers."[43] In the New York production, the transition from scene 6 into scene 7 furthered the effect of immersion. Sound effects transformed the conventional theatrical darkness between scenes, which pauses a narrative, into night on a Midwestern rural road. In the darkness, Farmers' cries of "strike" faded into "an ominous musical undercurrent" created by violins. VLN announced, "The challenge echoes through Wisconsin, Ohio, Iowa, Indiana. Over the middle West embittered farmers act." The lack of light obscured the spatial differentiation between audience and stage, while ambient noise surrounded spectators. Motor sounds and lighting mimicking headlights simulated a vehicle's approach in the night. When the light fully illuminated an onstage rock, it revealed farmers lying in wait for the truck. They indicated their readiness to attack. When the moment to strike came, the actors ran off stage, the sound of screeching brakes played, and off-stage a voice yelled, "Get down off that truck." Offstage shouts of "Dump the milk!" and crashing sounds effected the chaos of milk being thrown from a truck. A riotous directive to overturn the truck was heard, lights swirled, and the sounds of a "final terrific crash" ended the scene.[44]

Scene 8 depicts another instance of extralegal means farmers used to survive: the penny auction. This type of protest sustained and symbolized community by protecting against the seizure of family-owned farms by corporations, banks, and insurance companies. When a farm was foreclosed and put up for auction, the community would gather, prevent large bids on the land from outsiders (often through physical intimidation), and offer bids of mere cents for hundreds of acres of land and machinery. The new "owners" of the farm would then transfer ownership back to the original owner. The auction staged in scene 8 is set in Wisconsin, the heart of the dairy industry. Though the auctioneer values the farm and its capital equipment at thirty thousand dollars, in the end it is sold for thirteen cents.

Scene 9 brings the audience to the final months of the Hoover administration when farmers held the International Farmers' Conference in Washington, DC, to outline legislative demands to the incoming administration. VLN introduces Lem Harris as "your secretary"; the sound of applause and use of direct address continued to involve the audience as farmers. The scene does not acknowledge Harris's membership in the Communist Party USA. It reproduces the excerpts of Harris's speech, focused on the degradation of farmers as "surplus," the "fallacy" of over-production, and farmers' interest in consumers' well-being:

> The three quarters of the farmers which economists consider as surplus, cannot really be considered as such. Neither can they consider their crops as surplus when they know that there are millions of unemployed who lack the very things which they produce and cannot sell. It was the recognition of this ironical situation which led the farmers of Iowa to give milk to the unemployed of Sioux City during the farm strike there.[45]

Scene 10 stages the nation at the breaking point, as if on the cusp of revolution, to represent the need of the AAA for farmers as well as consumers. The scene consists of a fictional meeting between a Nebraskan farm family and a New York City worker's family. Over the loudspeaker, VLN describes capitalism's dysfunction through the lens of the "paradox": "As our economic system works, the greater the surplus of wheat on Nebraska farms, the larger are the breadlines in New York City."[46] Silhouetted in blue, figures in cowboy hats, bonnets, and derbies replaced individuality with iconicity, creating rural and urban everymen and everywomen.[47] The families faced one another in lines behind their patriarch, literalizing their opposition. Each family consisted of husband, wife, two sons, and a daughter; this mirroring signals their economic interdependence, which, nevertheless, has pitted consumer against farmer. As they talk back and forth, becoming increasingly incensed or despondent, it becomes clear that their troubles reflect one another's. The situation seems irreconcilable, and this leads the farmer to an act of hopeless destruction:

> WORKER. We have been evicted from our homes.
>
> FARMER'S WIFE. And we from our land.
>
> FARMER. We plough our sweat into the earth.
>
> FARMER'S WIFE. And bring forth ripe provender.
>
> WORKER. We starve.
>
> FARMER. The wheat stands high in our fields.
>
> FARMER'S WIFE. Our fields no longer.
>
> WORKER'S DAUGHTER. Feed us.
>
> FARMER'S FIRST SON. Pay us.
>
> WORKER'S FAMILY. Feed us.
>
> FARMER. The wheat is better destroyed. I say, burn it.[48]

The blue light turned to a wash of red to signify fields ablaze, the violent effects of revolution, and the threat of communism, while a massive
shadow holding a pitchfork loomed over both families. Farmer raised his
hand in a gesture of camaraderie with the radical shadow; Worker asks,
"Why?" and his family members reached out to one another in horror.[49]
Then, the represented voice of General Hugh Johnson, administrator
of Roosevelt's NRA, warns that the crisis will end in an overthrow of the
government: "Something is depriving one third of our population of the
God-given right to earn their bread by the sweat of their labor. That
single ugly fact is an indictment under which no form of government can
long continue. For slighter causes than that we revolted against British
rule, and suffered the bitterest civil war in history." Both families turned
toward the origin of the voice and together disdain mere "Words!"[50]
They call for action, for the government to fulfill its obligation to farmers
and consumers. In doing so, the scene sets up the AAA as the Roosevelt
Administration's response to the people's call to end the crisis.

AAA in Action: Scenes 11 to 19

The "Birth of Triple A," scene 11, immediately follows. On the one hand,
this dramaturgical arrangement prompts an audience to interpret the
AAA as the measure that averted national insurrection. Yet scene 11's
characterization of the act calls into question the morality of the measures taken by the Roosevelt administration to boost the agricultural
economy, and subsequent scenes question whether the AAA actually
benefits farmers and consumers. The *New Leader*, a socialist cultural
magazine, recognized the play's critical depiction of the AAA and interpreted it as objective: "Triple A tried to bring back prosperity by artificially creating high prices—which profited only the capitalist. . . . And
high prices created by Triple A, themselves created triple distress."[51]
   In scene 11, an actor representing Secretary of Agriculture Wallace
quotes Wallace's description of the AAA, which explained how farmers'
increased purchasing power would positively affect industrial employment levels. As the lights faded on Wallace in the New York performance,
massive projections disclosed his rhetoric of "organized control" as the
destruction of vital foodstuffs. A "staccato" voice spouted statistics re-

garding decreased production and price increases, while a projection showed an image of small pigs labeled "1934" in front of an image of large pigs labeled "1933." This faded into a projection of two equal-sized bread loaves to indicate consumer price increases due to wheat acreage reduction from 1933 to 1934. The projections, ostensibly only illustrations of agricultural production statistics, reformulated Wallace's careful, technical language about what the AAA program entailed to illustrate its troubling details.

Scenes 12 through 15 portray federal failure to curb exploitation and suggest that the AAA compounded farmers', consumers', and workers' already dire circumstances. Scenes in which men, women, and children suffer hunger are juxtaposed with those in which profiteers indulge in an excess of refined foods. Unfolding in quick succession, these scenes are framed by VLN's announcement at the start of scene 12: "Triple A pays out four million dollars a day." First, Farmer receives his AAA subsidy, but, when he attempts to buy a shirt, he finds that the price has increased by 25 percent because of higher cotton prices. Next, traders buy and sell at a furious pace as agricultural stock values fluctuate volatilely. During this, VLN intermittently announces "Fair and Warmer," portending dust storms and drought. Then, a man at a lunch counter learns that the bowl of oatmeal that cost him two cents yesterday is now three cents and unaffordable.[52] In the New York production, a brief blackout separated this character's inability to pay for the most humble foodstuff from a tuxedoed man and his date, stylishly attired in an evening gown with a corsage, dining at a table dressed in white linens while Strauss's elegant *Blue Danube* waltz plays. Man orders expensive menu items—"Imported Beluga Caviar. Broiled Roual Squab. Grilled Mushrooms"—and offers a champagne toast to "Wheat." In response to his date's inquiry about whether he has been "affected by these new processing taxes," Man picked up a dinner roll to explain how he fleeces farmers and consumers: "it's the man who eats it who pays for it." To him, the dinner roll is nothing more than a prop, while previous scenes make clear that workers, consumers, and farmers pay the price for his extravagant meal, as well as the new car and fur that the man pledges to buy his date.[53]

Cultural historian Barbara Melosh argues that the latter two scenes aim to "incite indignation about an economy where one class produces so that another may consume" by using "food to represent consumption . . . associating it with the two poles of consumption," which she refers to as "nonnegotiable subsistence" and "conspicuous" consumption, respectively.[54] This split scene angered critic John Mason Brown of the *New York Post*. Brown, however, interpreted the restaurant scene as an attack on capitalism designed to propagate communism: "Is [a federally funded] project justified in implying in the regulation manner of a Communist script, that any one who wears a Tuxedo or orders the kind of good meals that all of us would occasionally like to order, is a villain?"[55] Though the scene's critique is directed at and limited to the AAA, Mason read the stage action through its relationship to the WPA. Moreover, what was particularly incendiary about these scenes, for Mason and others, was that, in distinction from Melosh's assertion, food onstage did not stand for something else in the interest of making an abstract argument. The moral struggle over food, determining whether the right to it is innate or earned—whether we all deserve a good meal—was at the center of both the dramatic and actual conflict.

In the dramatic narrative and in the contemporaneous moment, this problem was further complicated by natural phenomena. Throughout scenes 16, 17, and 18, the weather forecast is incessantly reported over the loudspeaker, and it is always the same: "Fair and warmer." The depictions of the 1934 drought include a farmer finding his land turned to "Dust!"; a rural congregation praying for divine intervention as a projection displays images of dying cattle; and traders quoting climbing agricultural commodity prices as the temperature gauge on a giant thermometer rises and a clock ticks away the summer months. The arrangement of scenes, which focus on the combined effects of natural disaster and agricultural legislation for consumers and farmers, repeats the confusion experienced during the first years under the AAA.[56]

Drought and Dust Storms in the Los Angeles Production

In the New York, Cleveland, Chicago, and Milwaukee productions, the drought sequence functioned as one of many snapshots of distress under agricultural adjustment; three scenes were devoted to drought, and then the narrative shifted to the "Southern" problem of sharecropper evictions. Los Angeles FTP writer Edward Lynn extended the drought sequence by five scenes for the July-August 1936 Los Angeles production.[57] This number is notable by many measures of artistic practice, but given *Triple-A Plowed Under*'s unique narrative brevity and the national scope of its story, five additional scenes centered on this one facet of the agricultural crisis throws into relief the pressing regional concerns of drought and dust storms for Californians, crystallizing during 1936. Stage manager Walter Clyde stated, "We expect a lot of heat . . . but it's a cinch we'll pack 'em in. There's some hot stuff in 'Triple-A' that will shake the town." Clyde gave as an example one of these added scenes, titled "Hunger."[58]

Beginning with the onset of the dust storms, by 1940, 250,000 people had migrated from the Great Plains to California in search of work.[59] Released in 1936, Woodie Guthrie's song "Do Re Mi" disabused migrants of the notion that Californians would welcome them and of the false promises of corporate-owned farms, which had been recruiting displaced farmers and unemployed men with handbills advertising the need for farm laborers. Once in California, Dust-bowl refugees received cut-rate wages due to the huge influx of laborers, and many lived in "ditch bank" camps created along irrigation ditches or in company camps. If lucky, migrant families secured a spot in a Farm Security Administration camp; these were set up to provide clean water, other sanitation measures, and safe living space. In October 1936, the *San Francisco News* published John Steinbeck's seven-part series "Harvest Gypsies." His exposé on these migrants' lives was just as much an indictment of "speculative farmers" and corporate-held land as it was a warning against treating this new class of migrants in the same manner that Mexican, Filipino, Chinese, and Japanese immigrants had been treated (exploitation that Steinbeck also vehemently condemned):

> The earlier foreign migrants have invariably been drawn from a peon class. This is not the case with the new migrants. They are small farmers who have lost their farms, or farm hands who have lived with the family in the old American way. They are men who have worked hard on their own farms and have felt the pride of possessing and living in close touch with the land. They are resourceful and intelligent Americans who have gone through the hell of the drought, have seen their lands wither and die and the top soil blow away; and this, to a man who has owned his land, is a curious and terrible pain. . . . It should be understood that

with this new race the old methods of repression, of starvation wages, of jailing,
beating and intimidation are not going to work; these are American people.
Consequently we must meet them with understanding and attempt to work out
the problem to their benefit as well as ours.[60]

The added scenes in the Los Angeles production of *Triple-A Plowed
Under* offer sympathetic representations of the victims of drought and
dust storms that, much like Steinbeck's reportage, operate through producerist discourse. Titled "The Drought," "Hunger v. Plenty," "Burial
Scene," "Drought Relief," and "Exodus," these scenes show how those
who work the land are resigned to survive off items culturally deemed
not food, while profiteers feed off farm women and men. In the first two
scenes, VLN repeatedly intones, "Fair and Warmer." First, a father and
mother, described in the script as sickly looking, can give only black
water to their coughing child. Next, a split scene shows a young rural
couple caring for their invalid mother and "an enormously fat woman"
served by a slew of waiters. Lacking food to feed their dying mother,
the rural woman shoots her husband's ailing horse for its meat. Simultaneously, the fat woman, clad in jewels, pantomimes "very haughty"
attitudes, refusing each of the more and more elegant meals presented to
her. Only the appearance of a roast pig—an indispensible food perverted
into a luxury—satisfies her. The scene blacked out as VLN's voice rang,
"Fair and warmer, wheat is rising." This scene is followed by a woman
denouncing a minister's sermon that the death of her son was God's divine choice, insisting that he was "Murdered!!! ... by DUST!" Then comes
an announcement by an actor portraying Harry Hopkins, former head
of the Federal Emergency Relief Administration and current head of the
Works Progress Administration, that "We are prepared and we intend to
take care of the people in the drought area," during which a drum beat
marks the march of rural men and women west and farmers fiercely debate if they should trust in the government's relocation program or if it
is a plot to steal farm land.

The Los Angeles production unit transformed the performance of
Triple-A Plowed Under into an event that addressed the tensions between
native Californians and its mass of rural migrants by nightly screening
Pare Lorentz's short documentary film *The Plow That Broke the Plains*
(1936) prior to each performance of the play. Produced by the Resettle-

ment Administration, the film examines the dust storms in the Great Plains and the resultant migration of hundreds of thousands of farm families to California. In the same vein as *Triple-A Plowed Under*, the film blames the Wilson administration's agricultural programs during and after World War I, which encouraged farmers to clear-cut grasslands and plant wheat and gave away land to returning servicemen. It opens with declamations of propagandistic government slogans while images of tanks merge with images of armies of farmers on tractors. The film culminates in a portrayal of the Roosevelt administration as savior of the farmer and the plains to argue that all hope is not lost for Midwestern and Great Plains farmers, or for Californians, because of the Resettlement Administration's sixty-five land projects, designed to rebuild the soil and resettle farmers onto better agricultural lands.[61] Together, the play and the film suggested that California as the haven for Dustbowl refugees was a temporary arrangement.

Southern Problems on Northern Stages: "Cotton Patch" and Scene 19

On April 8, 1936, sharecroppers Reverend E. B. McKinney (an African American man) and Walter Moskop (a white man), both representatives of the Southern Tenant Farmers' Union, gave a preperformance talk to New York City audiences in which they discussed conditions for sharecroppers throughout the South. McKinney and Moskop had been touring northern states together to speak on the subject throughout 1935–36.[62] In the days before their appearance at the Biltmore Theatre, these men and Odis Sweeden, an Oklahoma sharecropper, were interviewed at the socialist League for Industrial Democracy. When asked about what the men were going to do about their physical and economic exploitation, Sweeden answered, "We aim to fight it. . . . We just been to Washington and they gave us what you people call the run around. Mr. Wallace, the secretary of agriculture, he didn't seem to think he could do anything, and the WPA people wouldn't even see us, when we went to beg for relief for our evicted people and them others that ain't eatin'."[63] I have not discovered the content of McKinney's and Moskop's lecture, yet their appearance would have certainly heightened the reality of the exploitation of sharecroppers under the AAA by introducing that evening's audience to the real-life counterparts of the "sharecroppers" in scene 19.

Triple-A Plowed Under included two scenes about the USDA's marginalization of sharecroppers and landowners' abuse of AAA. The first of the two scenes, "Cotton Patch," was cut from the production after the first week of the New York City run (a couple of weeks before McKinney and Moskop's lecture) by the production's director, Joseph Losey, because "it was impossible to get actors to play it with the necessary simplicity."[64] "Cotton Patch" regards the contradictions of federal resettlement programs for sharecroppers. Over the course of the scene, "Sam, a Negro farmer" is left without a means to work his new land when the Sheriff takes Sam's mule in lieu of a tax payment. Sam is written in minstrel style that is incongruent with Triple-A Plowed Under's austere dramaturgy; the character not only speaks in a racist dialect but also sings. Losey did not mention stylistic inconsistency as a reason for cutting the scene and, in fact, offered staging advice to the other regional FTP production teams. "Cotton Patch" was used in the Los Angeles, Chicago, Cleveland, and Milwaukee productions and appears in the published version of Triple-A Plowed Under.[65] Immediately following "Cotton Patch," scene 19 portrays the interracial Southern Tenant Farmers' Union and argues for croppers' rights to payment under AAA legislation by depicting the power dynamics between plantation owners and landless farmers:

> FARMER. . . . You git you stuff together and git. The Guv'ment ain't wantin' me to plant the land you been workin'.
>
> THIRD CROPPER. Wait a minute. The guv'ment's payin' you not to plant, and it says here . . . (waves a paper) . . . that you're supposed to pay us.
>
> FARMER. Every durn one of you owes me money, and I ain't sayin' nothin' if you git.[66]

These croppers, then, determine to join the union, echoing the sentiments expressed by E. B. McKinney that, despite almost certain violent reprisal from planters, he would "fight for the union until he dies because it's his only chance."[67]

From the little evidence available about the production history of "Cotton Patch," it seems that, while Losey may have been struggling to articulate an inclusive conception of citizenship that minstrelsy did not accommodate, the artists in the other regional units seem unable to recognize Sam as a condescending representation incompatible with a documentary drama. Nor, it seems, did these artists recognize the contradictions between this character and the dignified portrayal of sharecroppers in scene 19. While scene 19 suggests a kind of solidarity in unionization that diminishes racial boundaries, at least between the landless croppers, "Cotton Patch" suggests the inability to reject those boundaries when imagining and representing the iconic American farmer. For while, the character Sam embodies the American ethic of producerism—he has used a government loan to raise a crop—racism institutionalized in theatrical conventions depicts the African American character *playing at* farmer, never a "real" one:

> SAM. Long time since I drive a purty mule like yo'. I'se goin' call you Guv'ment. Yeah, man! Dey's whe' yo' come from an' dats what I call yo'. Ol' Guv'ment say, "Sam, yo' take dis money and buy yo'self a play an' a mule an' raise yo' a crop."[68]

AAA *Undone: Scenes 20, 21, and 22*

The dissolution of the AAA is delivered in three scenes, in which the gendered role of "consumer" aids in bringing the crisis to a climax. Beginning with the dramatization of the Women's Committee boycott in Hamtramck (referred to as "Detroit" in the play), the hog slaughter, again, becomes the reference point for the damage wrought by the AAA and the questionable moral vision of the New Deal government. In the New York production, a chart indicating the gross escalation in beef, pork, wheat, corn, and cotton prices during 1935 hung above a storefront drop as women actors "picketed" (see figure 5.2). The FTP dramatists took the scene's action and dialogue almost verbatim from the Associated Press report "Buyers Trampled by Meat Strikers," published in the *New York Times,* so that, when the leader of the women is questioned during the heat of the women's attacks on fellow consumers, she states, "Maybe they started it by killing the little pigs and cattle. We don't know and we don't care. But we're not going to pay such high prices for meat and that's all there is to it!" The scene titillated with the spectacle

Figure 5.2. Meat Strike, Scene Twenty, *Triple-A Plowed Under,* Biltmore Theatre, New York City, 1936. Courtesy National Archives, Photo no. 69-TC-NYC-186-10.

of women engaged in violence to amplify the urgent conditions driving women to such "unladylike" behavior. The shift from a focus on rural plight to an urban incident also seized upon its audiences' first-hand knowledge for the "final moments" of the AAA. This well-crafted complication gained the crisis intensity by virtue of audiences' association with their onstage counterparts, and it framed the ensuing scene about infanticide as consumers' unbearable (lack of) options in this economic struggle.

Based on a *Daily News* article, scene 21 accounts for Dorothy Sherwood's decision to murder her child as caused by political-economic forces, not psychosis (see figure 5.3). In New York, lights came up on a woman bearing the body of a small child to uniformed police officers, as VLN announces, "Newburgh, New York: August 20th, 1935. Mrs. Dorothy Sherwood." The character Sherwood then explains to police officers

Figure 5.3. Mrs. Sherwood Confessing, Scene Twenty-One, *Triple-A Plowed Under,* Biltmore Theatre, New York City, 1936. Courtesy National Archives, Photo no. 69-TC-NYC-186-3.

that she drowned her son because she "couldn't feed him, and . . . couldn't bear to see him hungry." Lights faded on the officers and the scenery, while an overhead spotlight illuminated the childless mother. A voice, heard over the loudspeaker, asks her questions:

VOICE. Why did you do it?

MRS. SHERWOOD. I couldn't feed him. I had only five cents.

VOICE. Your own child. Did you think you were doing the right thing?

MRS. SHERWOOD. I just thought it had to be done, that's all. It was the best thing to do.

VOICE. How could a mother kill her own child?

MRS. SHERWOOD. He was hungry. I tell you. Hungry, hungry, hungry, hungry, <u>hungry</u>. (As her voice mounts it is blended with that of another which commences in a progression of nine voices crying 'guilty'. . .)[69]

The character's/Mrs. Sherwood's explanation, inarticulate with anguish as it is, suggests the inability to comprehend her action outside the context of the AAA. The contention is profound, particularly in its specificity. Unlike many of the other scenes, which, in Living Newspaper lead dramatist Arthur Arent's words, were "typical but non-factual representations of the effect of these news events on the people," Dorothy Sherwood was not a type but a woman who declared hunger to be at the root of her crime.[70]

Numerous New York critics of the play, and of theater as a legitimate political venue, decried this scene's depiction of hunger as pernicious theatrical illusion. A photograph of the scene appeared in the *New York American* with the caption "Here the Soviet Bait That Consumers Are the Victims of 'Capitalistic Speculators' Caused by High Bread Prices due to Drought and AAA Crop Reduction, Is Emphasized as the Woman Hands the Baby She Has Killed because She Says She Couldn't Buy It Food."[71] Garet Garrett, writing for the *Saturday Evening Post*, questioned inclusion of the Sherwood scene, stating that it "had no more relation to AAA than any other case of psychopathic infanticide." Garrett expressed wariness about the application of high-caliber artistic "skill and technique" to political issues because "the amount of suggestion sometimes evoked by a scene lasting only two or three minutes was extraordinary." He was most alarmed that talk and scenes of hunger dominated the play from beginning to end, believing as he did that crying "hunger" was a favorite tactic of communists. The Sherwood scene serves as the dramatic equivalent of hunger parades for Garrett; he states that, while antihunger protesters carry signs with slogans like "Abolish Starvation, or, These Babies Want Food," they are dressed warmly in "the height of bourgeois comfort."[72] Much like the opponents of the Hamtramck housewives and the Missouri sharecroppers, Garrett deployed antitheatrical rhetoric as the means to dispense with the circumstance of hunger as a political-economic phenomenon. Further, Garrett's "proof" that antihunger marchers were acting offers another instance in which the conventions of theatrical representation reinforced certain embodiments as "hungry" or "American" to the exclusion of others.

On the Biltmore stage, the climatic demise of the AAA was bolstered by the monumental scale and symbolism of the scenic design. Silhouettes of historic and contemporary political figures threw shadows on a massive projection of the U.S. Constitution. The scene portrayed the majority and minority opinions of Supreme Court justices on the AAA and contained extensive excerpts from the speeches and writings of prominent political figures. It staged not just the ruling of AAA as unconstitutional but also a larger debate on the powers of the judiciary over Congress. Thomas Jefferson's opinion that the people are the true "arbiter" of a law's constitutionality concludes the debate and is followed by VLN's stating what the people want: "Farmers voted, by more than 6 to 1, for continuance of Triple A."[73] (This line is the only mention of the farmers' approval of the AAA.) A processional of disenchanted Americans who do not know how they will survive the winter completes the lament over the death of the AAA.

This scene caused controversy even before the play premiered because it included the opinion of Earl Browder, president of the Communist Party USA, among those of men considered great Americans. Actors in *Triple-A Plowed Under*, calling themselves the Federal Theatre Veterans League, announced that they would strike if the representation of Browder remained in the play: "as loyal Americans, we regard as an insult the placing of Earle [*sic*] Browder on a level with our patriotic forefathers, Thomas Jefferson and Abraham Lincoln, and our distinguished fellow citizen Alfred E. Smith [an anti-New Deal democrat]." On the day *Triple-A Plowed Under* premiered, newspapers ran the strike story under headlines such as "Veterans in U.S. Play 'Insulted' by Role of Browder: 'War Slacker'," "WPA Living Show Threatened Again: Opposition Develops on Role of Communist—2 Plays Previously Banned," and "Actors Resent Red in Scene." Due to this threat, police were ordered on patrol for the first performance. A photograph of opening night patrons under the marquee, however, conveys a lax atmosphere: groups cluster in conversation, mill about, smoke, and wait to enter the theater; in the street, a single mounted officer looks down to speak with an officer on the sidewalk.[74] Forty years later, Philip Barber, director of the New York City Federal Theatre Project, recalled police officers' bewilderment at the situation:

> there was a threat because among various people commenting on the Supreme
> Court decision [in the play] of course there was Earl Browder.... At any rate word
> spread that on the opening night there was going to be violence.... the plan was
> to storm the back of the theatre and pull off the lights and destroy the scenery
> and so forth.... we got about 20 police in.... the Police Captain said, "Don't you
> worry Mr. Barber, we won't let this play open not at all we'll shut it right down...."
> He never got over being confused about that cause it was the only time in his life
> that he ever heard of the police being called out to keep a play open.[75]

During the performance, an audience member protested the representation of Browder by standing and singing the national anthem; police
removed him from the theater and the performance continued. Representation of Browder became prime fodder for critics, claiming the
FTP was, at best, "boondoggling" and, at worst, a communist enterprise
unwittingly sponsored by U.S. taxpayers. The hullabaloo surrounding
Browder's depiction followed the play to subsequent production sites—
the Los Angeles unit tried to garner favor with audiences by publicizing
that it cut Browder from the play—and into the 1939 Congressional
Hearings on Un-American Propaganda Activities.

The Contemporary Moment: Scenes 23, 24, and the Finale

The final scenes of *Triple-A Plowed Under* located its audience in the
"contemporary." Performance theorist David Román uses this term to
describe the sense of community created during a theatrical performance: "the present [becomes] a time in which an audience imagines
itself within a fluid and nearly suspended temporal condition, living in
a moment not yet in the past and not yet in the future, yet a period we
imagine as having some power to shape our relation to both history
and futurity."[76] *Triple-A Plowed Under*'s culmination in national events-
still-unfolding magnified the suspension of the audience in the present.
Scene 23, called "The Big 'Steal,'" reproduced Wallace's inflammatory
statements against the Supreme Court, in which he claimed that returning the monies from the processing tax portion of the AAA to processors and manufacturers, who had shown uninterrupted profits since the
Depression's beginning, was the "greatest legalized steal in American
history!"[77] Scene 24 showed AAA administrator Chester A. Davis de-
vising a replacement for the AAA. As scripted, Davis exhibits growing

excitement as it dawns on him that the Soil Conservation and Domestic Allotment Act's (SCDAA) land acquisition and soil conservation provisions for farmers resemble the AAA's subsidies for production curtailment. That this new legislation's implications were not yet clear and that the audience was truly in the midst of the crisis presented onstage is evident in the play's finale.

The play ends in the present, in the theater, directing the audience to take action.[78] The finale begins at a national Farmers' Convention, as announced by the VLN and signified by farmers holding signs featuring the names of Midwestern states. At the Biltmore, they stood in a straight line across the front of the stage demanding that the new SCDAA provide farmers with "cost of production" in order that they obtain a "decent standard of living." Curtains then opened to reveal the full stage. The actor playing Henry Wallace stood center-stage, elevated above actors portraying the unemployed, who were positioned on a stage right ramp, and actors playing farmers, who were clustered stage left. Distanced from the "People," the wealthy profiteer and woman in evening clothes stood upstage left. Consumers, farmers, and workers reiterated the problems depicted throughout the play. They directed their complaints to Wallace and the profiteer. Short lines and choral responses escalate the impasse dividing farmers, the unemployed, and consumers:

ALL UNEMPLOYED. . . . We need a decent standard of living.

ALL FARMERS. So do we.

A FARMER. Then all our problems are the same.

ALL UNEMPLOYED. Then all our problems are the same.

WOMAN IN EVENING CLOTHES. All must be helped, John.

FARMER, UNEMPLOYED, AND WOMEN. No charity!

AN UNEMPLOYED. Jobs!

ALL UNEMPLOYED. Jobs!

A FARMER. Help.

AN UNEMPLOYED. We need a state that permits no man to go hungry.

. . .

ONE FARMER. We can't harvest.

ALL FARMERS. We can't harvest.

ONE WOMAN. We can't buy.

ALL WOMEN. We can't buy.

ONE UNEMPLOYED. We can't eat!

ALL UNEMPLOYED. We can't eat![79]

Over the loudspeaker, VLN announces recent farm-labor coalitions. Actors playing farmers and the unemployed moved together and extended their arms to the audience as their chorus intensified toward an urgent "We need you."[80] *Triple-A Plowed Under*'s final gesture is indicative of the moment of its performance and the belief in the possibility of moral capitalism based in a farmer-consumer connection. Yet its desire for an America "that permits no man to go hungry" also locates the value of humanity in productivity, narrowing the scope of moral obligation from every person to socially recognized "good" citizens.

Triple-A Plowed Under finally and purposefully scoffs at the alleged binary between "real" and "theater" by obliging its audiences to act outside the theater. And from their anxious disavowals of political theater, it is clear that politicians and cultural critics feared the power of theater in the "real world." Yet there is very little evidence that offers insight into what audiences in the five cities that produced the play thought about its closing directive.[81] Critics rarely mentioned audiences in their reviews; those that did describe a split between admiration and condemnation signaled to them by boos, cheers, and applause throughout the course of a performance.[82] The same is true for the internal reports between regional units and Flanagan's office. George Kondolf, reporting on early response to the Chicago production, wrote, "The whole thing seemed to genuinely stir the audience. The majority was definitely on the cheering side. That, however, may be explained by the fact that it was largely composed of our own friends. It is still too early to really know just what we have."[83] The production bulletin from Los Angeles reported disagreement among the audience: "wither [sic] enthusiastically liked it, or noisily didn't like it; there were few who did not feel impelled to voice an emphatic opinion either one way or the other."[84] The nature of these responses may be less important than audiences' demonstrated investment in the play.

Triple-A Plowed Under drew people. The New York City production enjoyed huge popularity, so much so that the scheduled two-week run was repeatedly extended until it had played for three months to nearly thirty-eight thousand people.[85] Theater critic Stark Young observed that the New York audience engaged with the play: "they clapped and booed, loved and hated."[86] The play also ran for many weeks in Chicago, and reports from Los Angeles stated that it "was well attended during its entire run," playing to roughly eighty-three hundred people in its fifteen performances.

Roughly forty years after the production, Norman Lloyd, who performed a number of roles in *Triple-A Plowed Under*, reflected on why these urban audiences cared about rural issues:

> I'm surprised when we talk about it that New York audiences were so moved considering it was a Midwest and Southwest problem, but they were, whatever it was. Of course, the world was a raw nerve in those days. People were, because of the Depression, were on such an edge. They really didn't know where they were going to be the next day in regard to where they were going to live or eat. And they were ready for anything, and I think the play sort of touched it.[87]

In his 1979 interview, Philip Schrager, assistant stage manager of the New York City production, put it more succinctly: "When we all realized, as we did, that there weren't isolated sectors of the country . . . that felt the terrible impact of the Depression that . . . all of a sudden we were all in the same pot, literally."[88] *Triple-A Plowed Under* represented the limitations of federal regulation of agriculture and rendered the relationship between struggling consumers and farmers one of mutuality. Whether or not audiences agreed with the politics of the portrait, immediate identification of the exclusions and inclusions of the U.S. food system occurred through the characters' and the FTP artists' social statuses vis-à-vis food and productivity.

Epilogue

I tell you frankly that it is a new and untrod path, but I tell you with equal frankness that an unprecedented condition calls for the trial of new means to rescue agriculture. If a fair administrative trial of it is made and it does not produce the hoped-for results I shall be the first to acknowledge it and advise you.

—Franklin D. Roosevelt, Message to Congress on the
Agricultural Adjustment Act, March 16, 1933

We've got to restore the idea of opportunity for all people—the idea that
no matter who you are, what you look like, where you came from, how you
started out, what your last name is, you can make it if you're willing to work
hard and take responsibility. That's the idea at the heart of this country.
That's what's at stake right now. That's what we've got to work on.

—Barack Obama, remarks at signing of the Farm Bill, February 7, 2014

AS I WRITE THIS, WE ARE, ONCE AGAIN, IN THE MIDST OF A BATTLE over agriculture, making my act of conclusion ironically appropriate to the acts driven by uncertainty during the New Deal. The Agricultural Adjustment Act was an experiment devised out of urgent distress in the interest of restoring the economy and salvaging the livelihoods of one-quarter of Americans. Today, its most basic programs—price supports, conservation, U.S. food assistance, and federal purchase of surplus commodities tied to global hunger relief—are both integral to the American food system and under fire from diverse social movements and political groups. The central interests of these activist groups tend to involve the promotion of local and organic foods, sustainable farming practices, and non-GMO foods. Many of these groups are also implicitly and explicitly opposed to industrial farming and processed food products, which receive federal support via current agricultural policy. There are also antiobesity and antihunger movements that hold food processors and corporate (fast-) food giants accountable for health and hunger issues nationwide.

For all these social and political concerns, there are American theater artists staging performances throughout the United States. Much of the food theater in this country is community based and noncommercial, involving collaborations between artists and local citizens. These companies are invested in dispelling the misperception that theater is an isolated art form, and they are committed to changing public policy. Sometimes, a food politics play is a single piece in an activist company's repertoire, such as *If You Can Stand the Heat: The History of Women and Food* by Guerilla Girls On Tour! (2010); or contemporary farming is the subject of an individual study by a playwright, as in Greg Kotis's *Pig Farm* (2006) about the degraded lives of farm men and women compelled by economies of scale to run massive livestock operations. In other cases, a theater's investment in food politics is sustained. Granted almost $350,000 from ArtPlace in June 2012, the Cornerstone Theatre Company has embarked on a six-year play series in Los Angeles on hunger, food, and food equity called *The Hunger Cycle*. There are also a handful of companies like Double Edge Theatre (Massachusetts) that create with community members, feed audiences as part of their performances, and work a farm where the artists live and perform.

Meanwhile, activists and documentary filmmakers have produced slews of films and popular press publications concerned with food politics. Daniel Imhoff's primer *Food Fight: The Citizen's Guide to the Next Food and Farm Bill* (originally published in 2008) was revised and released in time to advocate for changes to agricultural policy in 2012, when agricultural legislation was set to expire. In it, Imhoff first sets out to disillusion citizens of the idea that farm subsidies go to American farm men and women: "Many Americans believe . . . that the tens of billions of dollars the government spends on agriculture primarily support farms where a husband and wife work from dawn to dusk growing crops, with roosters crowing from fence posts, and cows grazing on rolling pastures.

The real picture is not so idyllic."[1] Imhoff alerts his readers to how corporate entities profit from the illusion that rural America is still the cradle of morality. With its cover image of a raised hand gripping a fork in defiance, Imhoff's *Food Fight* repurposes the revolutionary gesture seen in *Triple-A Plowed Under*, transferring the power over the food system from the farmer's hands into consumers'. The gesture, which is the symbol of the "Vote with Your Fork" movement, like the protests and performances of the New Deal-era, calls for people to unite against corporate control of agriculture. Consumers are empowered to restore "real" farmers and farming to America by supporting local, organic growers that use sustainable practices. It is an impressive goal that suggests the staying power of the promise of a farmer-consumer connection. "Vote with Your Fork" politicizes and theatricalizes consumption; consumers choose how and from whom they will purchase food. Largely a movement of upper-middle-class consumers, who can afford to participate, local foods restaurants, groceries, and farmers' markets have become major sites of political performance.

The USDA has responded to contemporary consumer movements, and consumers' impressive political-economic power, with the "Know Your Farmer, Know Your Food" initiative (KYF2). Its mission is "to support the critical connection between farmers and consumers and to strengthen the USDA's support for local and regional food systems." KYF2 frames local foods, land stewardship, healthy eating, and community-based economic development as moral commitments of the federal government, sharing many goals with activist groups that oppose current U.S. agricultural policy. But like its adversarial counterparts, KYF2's audience is economically secure citizens; mitigating systemic causes of hunger is not included in its ambitions. Whether KYF2 will stimulate (or is even interested in) deep institutional change or is a band-aid solution to the very problems that the farm bill perpetuates is not yet clear. Regardless, the initiative, once again, represents the USDA as the facilitator of farmer-consumer connectedness in the interest of a better America.[2]

In the months leading up to the September 30, 2013, expiration date of the 2008 "Farm Bill," formally titled the "Food, Conservation, and Energy Act of 2008," activists and politicians fought over the bill's most controversial aspect: the Supplemental Nutritional Assistance Program (SNAP). The September date actually marked the expiration of the temporary extension passed in January 2013, after the 2008 legislation had officially expired in September 2012, because Congress was at an impasse over SNAP (or so-called food stamps), which comprised almost 80 percent of costs and had reached record-high enrollment: forty-seven million (or one in seven) Americans. In 2013, the Republican-controlled House proposed to cut $40 billion (close to 50 percent) from the program, while the Democrat-controlled Senate had passed a version that decreased allocations to SNAP by $4.5 billion (around 10 percent). Senator Debbie Stabenow (Democrat-Mich.), chairwoman of the Agriculture Committee, stated emphatically, "The House bill will not see the light of day in the Senate," and President Barack Obama threatened to veto the House version of the bill, if it reached his desk.[3] At the center of the debate was the character of SNAP recipients. Both sides staged performances and protests that invoked the producer ethic to determine citizens' rights to food.

Senate majority leaders Bob Dole (Republican-Kans.) and Tom Daschel (Democrat-S.D.) wrote the op-ed piece "Stop Playing Politics with Hunger," published in the Los Angeles Times on September 16, 2013. The piece itself was a protest performance against partisanship written to persuade the House to "do the right thing and follow the Senate's lead." Dole and Daschel based the morality of the Senate's plan not only on the obligations related to the nation's blessing of agricultural abundance but on the economic fact that "every $1 spent to fight hunger has resulted in $1.70 in economic activity." With this statistic, Dole and Daschel aimed to counter representation of SNAP participants as nonproductive Americans or "the 47 percent," a derogatory term now used publicly by SNAP opponents. In 2012, the use of "the 47 percent" was a source of embarrassment. Recorded while speaking at a $50,000-a-plate campaign fundraising dinner, Republican presidential candidate Mitt Romney stated, "All right, there are 47 percent who are with him [President Barack Obama], who are dependent upon government, who believe that they are victims, who believe that government has a responsibility to care for them, who believe that they are entitled to health care, to food, to housing, to you name it. That that's an entitlement. And the government should give it to them."[4] Comedian Stephen Colbert, playing himself as an ultraconservative cable newsman, "defended" Romney's comments: "Finally a candidate with the courage to say half of all Americans are free-loaders, who believe they are entitled to food. What do they think: food grows on trees? No. We job creators know there is no such thing as a free lunch. Lunch is $50,000 a plate."[5] Colbert targets the moral contradictions innate to treating food as a commodity, arguing that food is, indeed, an entitlement of citizenship and humanity. Much like his satirical predecessor Eleanor Roosevelt, Colbert throws into relief how the ideology of performance-based citizenship is used to mitigate rights to food. And like Roosevelt, Colbert too implies a consequent moral obligation of those with power to create opportunities for economic and social inclusion.

Nevertheless, the summary paper on the House's proposed farm bill, titled "Nutrition Reform and Work Opportunity Act," prepared by the Office of Majority Whip Kevin McCarthy (Republican-Cal.), outlined seven major "problems" with SNAP. The bullet-pointed list included the number of Americans receiving aid, federal "recruitment" of enrollees, benefits to people with incomes above designated cut-off levels, and the following:

- The number of able-bodied adults under the age of 50 without children enrolled on the program grew by 163.7% from 2007 to 2011.
- And while this is the very group that is supposed to be subject to a work requirement, the requirement has been waived in almost every state.
- Newscasts tell stories of young surfers who aren't working, but cash their food stamps in for lobster.
- Costing taxpayers $80 billion a year, middle class families struggling to make ends meet themselves foot the bill for a program that has gone well beyond a safety net for children, seniors, and the disabled.[6]

In this document, McCarthy's office tried to kindle the anger of the middle class at "wasteful" government spending via an image of the athletic, blond-haired, blue-eyed stereotype indulging in "the kind of good meals that all of us would occasionally like to order."[7] "He" is the embodiment of a morally irresponsible America. The surfer is both an example of "shiftlessness" and a new-style profiteer. This figure is also the "ideal" American man; by predominating cultural configurations, he is the most natural producer. Yet this figure lacks any sense of obligation to his nation, while he feeds off of the already cash-strapped hard-working (or want-to-be-working) middle-class family, that is, contemporary everymen.[8] USDA statistics regarding which citizens participate in SNAP, unemployment figures, and SNAP recipients' personal testimonies that have been blasted, published, and broadcast via the Internet and broadcast and print media during the past years tell a different story.[9]

Throughout the summer of 2013, a handful of activist groups staged protests against proposed cuts. In Newburgh, New York, on June 17, a group called Citizens Voices Heard Power! formed "Maloney's Soup Line" outside Congressman Sean Patrick Maloney's office; at the center of the scene was a table with a large soup pot; children and adults held signs that read "You call it reform, we call it breakfast."[10] On September 18, in Spokane, Washington, the group Washington Now held a rally against cuts to SNAP.[11]

Beginning in August 2013 and ending in winter 2014, fast-food workers across the country staged a series of one-day strikes for a living wage. They carried signs that read "We are worth more." These workers were not engaged in a fight to preserve SNAP. However, many of them argued for an increase in the minimum wage based on their need for food stamps despite working full-time. In this case, opponents of raising the minimum wage plainly devalue these citizens' contributions to the nation. They argue that, in a free market, laborers are compensated based on skill level and education, as well as the market value of that skill, though these two factors are not acknowledged to be potentially at odds. These citizens also asserted that fast food jobs are meant to be "stepping stones" or "fun money" for teens, not careers. Finally, as *McClatchy-Tribune* (Washington) columnist James Sherk put it in his guest editorial for the *Seattle Times*, "Competition forces businesses to pay workers according to their productivity.... For better or worse, fast-food jobs are relatively low-productivity positions, typically filled by inexperienced workers. Most fast-food customers want a quick, inexpensive meal. They will not regularly pay premium prices for a burger and fries."[12] This final point in defense of the current minimum wage conflates skill with experience and productivity and collapses the market and cultural value of the food produced by the worker with the worker him- or herself.

In June, twenty-six members of Congress, all Democrats, took the Food Stamp Challenge, eating on $4.50 a day for seven days, in protest of Republicans depiction of SNAP as wasteful spending on the "dependency class." On the House floor, Hank Johnson (Democrat-Ga.) unloaded a single shopping bag with groceries that included bacon, waffles, a one-quart milk bottle, bananas, oatmeal, ramen noodles, hot dogs, and tea. The congressman said he "splurged" on this last item for some comfort. These "low" foods, and the insufficient amounts of the nutritious ones, materialized Democrats arguments about the impossibility of getting by, the lack of choice, and the indignity of consumption on this limited budget, in an attempt to viscerally impress on opponents and the public the dire effects of lessening this meager provision on the lives of low-income Americans (for example, fast-food workers). In an interview with Al Sharpton, Congressman Johnson suggested that, while the Food Stamp Challenge was leaving him feeling weak, he could barely comprehend the mental, physical, and emotional strain of living with hunger because his challenge was temporary and by choice— a performance.[13] One political commentator wrote of the Democrats' protest performance: "while the food-stamp play by Democratic politicians may be little more than political *threater* [sic], the cuts proposed by Republicans and the potential damage of those cuts are very real."[14] I like to think of that pundit-blogger's typographical error as the inevitable, if threatening, slip between the "real" and the "theatrical" that comprises politics.

When President Barack Obama arrived at Michigan State University—the first agricultural land-grant institution chartered by a state— to sign the "Farm Bill," he entered a scene that, ironically and unwittingly, revealed the contradictions of contemporary American agriculture. A massive tractor, an enormous American flag, and bushels of fruits formed the backdrop to the speakers' platform, symbolizing both the overwhelming power of corporate agribusiness and bucolic American abundance. These tensions persisted in the speeches celebrating the bill.

A Michigan fruit farmer named Ben, who described his "farm at home [as] a lot like yours across the country," enjoyed the privilege of introducing the president.[15] President Obama then identified the legislation's beneficiaries as owner-tillers like Ben and American consumers, implying that the producer-consumer connection is the moral basis of American capitalism. He also talked about the increase in agricultural exports worldwide, the support for agricultural research, and the jobs that the bill provides, evading the unsavory implications of these economic achievements. SNAP was the final item highlighted by the president. As Obama praised the bipartisan spirit of the legislators, who worked together in a contentious political environment, his rhetorical efforts to include SNAP recipients as part of the American citizenry illustrates the fact that, even though the legislation is in place, the ideological struggle remains unresolved: "[F]or a lot of families, a crisis hits, you lose your job, somebody gets sick, strains on your budget—you have a strong work ethic. . . . They're not looking for a handout, these folks, they're looking for a hand up."[16] Despite the compromise reached—$8.6 billion cut to SNAP—political parties and the public remain deeply divided over what constitutes productivity, what is a valuable contribution to the nation, and who has *earned* the right to food.

NOTES

INTRODUCTION

1. Henry A. Wallace, *New Frontiers* (New York: Reynal and Hitchcock, 1934), 180.

2. "Exhibit Effectiveness Studies 1940–1941," Exhibits Effectiveness Study—The Effectiveness of Selected Exhibits, [Office of Information] Records Relating to Exhibitions and Expositions, 1889–1949, Records of the Office of the Secretary of Agriculture, 1839–1981, Record Group 16, National Archives and Records Administration, College Park, MD (hereafter cited as [Office of Information] Records Relating to Exhibitions, RG 16).

3. "Beans, Bacon and Gravy," in *Early American Folk Music and Songs*, performer Clark Jones, Smithsonian Global Sound for Libraries (New York: Folkways, 1982).

4. Janet M. Fitchen, "Hunger, Malnutrition, and Poverty in the Contemporary United States," *Food and Culture: A Reader*, ed. Carole Counihan and Penny Van Esterik (London and New York: Routledge, 1997), 389.

5. Franklin Roosevelt, nomination address to the Democratic Convention, Chicago, July 2, 1932, accessed May 5, 2011, http://newdeal.feri.org/speeches/1932b.htm.

6. John Simpson, quoted in Jean Choate, *Disputed Ground: Farm Groups That Opposed the New Deal Agricultural Program* (Jefferson, NC: McFarland and Company, Inc., 2002), 134.

7. "Wallace Tells $55,000,000 Aid for Corn Belt," *Chicago Daily Tribune*, August 19, 1933.

8. Reprinted in *Chicago Daily Tribune*, September 14, 1933, and quoted in George T. Blakey, "The Ham That Never Was: The 1933 Emergency Hog Slaughter," *Historian* 30.1 (1967): 53.

9. Janet Poppendieck, *Breadlines Knee-deep in Wheat: Food Assistance in the Great Depression* (New Brunswick, NJ: Rutgers University Press, 1986), 114.

10. "Resolutions of National Farmers' Holiday Association," January–June 1934, Wisconsin Cooperative Milk Pool Records, 1925–43, Wisconsin Historical Society-Madison (hereafter cited as Wisconsin Cooperative Milk Pool Records).

11. On the FSRC, see Roger C. Lambert, "Slaughter of the Innocents: The Public Protests to AAA Killing of Little Pigs," *Midwest Quarterly* 14.3 (1973): 247–56; Janet Poppendieck argues that "In lieu of a major means of redistributing the nation's abundance to those in need, it [the FSRC] became a sort of safety valve in a program designed to reduce the abundance to profitable levels, to restore scarcity," *Breadlines Knee-deep in Wheat*, xvi.

Poppendieck has written several books on the history of food assistance and problems stemming from the USDA's administration of these programs. These include *Sweet Charity? Emergency Food and the End of Entitlement* (New York: Viking, 1998) and *Free for All: Fixing School Food in America* (Berkeley: University of California Press, 2010).

12. "Mr. Wallace's Plan for Corn," editorial, *Chicago Daily Tribune,* August 21, 1933.

13. Roger C. Lambert, "The Drought Cattle Purchase, 1934–1935: Problems and Complaints," *Agricultural History* 45.2 (1971): 85–93.

14. This estimate appears in William Winders, *The Politics of Food Supply: U.S. Agricultural Policy in the World Economy* (New Haven, CT: Yale University Press, 2009), 66.

15. See Daniel O. Hastings, "Battle of November," *Today* II (1934), in *The New Deal: A Documentary History,* ed. William E. Leuchtenburg (Columbia: University of South Carolina Press, 1968), 194.

16. "Wallace Defines His Farm Policy: Economy of Scarcity Denied by Secretary in Speech at Seattle," *Spartanburg* [SC] *Herald-Journal,* July 19, 1935.

17. Theodore Saloutos and John D. Hicks, *Agricultural Discontent in the Middle West, 1900–1939* (Madison: University of Wisconsin, 1951), 506.

18. Wallace fought repayment to processors into the 1940s. By 1938, the USDA had also granted cotton, tobacco, and potato processors refunds, but Wallace continued to oppose refunds to hog processors because he felt they had received higher prices as a direct result of AAA. In 1941, a bill to refund hog processors passed in the Senate but failed to make it out of the committee in the House. See Choate, *Disputed Ground,* 106–15.

19. John L. Shover, *Cornbelt Rebellion: The Farmers' Holiday Association* (Urbana: University of Illinois Press, 1965). Michael W. Schuyler also identifies the many benefits farmers received from the various programs of the AAA, in "New Deal Farm Policy in the Middle West: A Retrospective View," *Journal of the West* 33.4 (1994): 52–63. Gary Libecap demonstrates that the AAA was the foundation of U.S. agricultural policy until the late-twentieth century in "The Great Depression and the Regulating State: Federal Government Regulation of Agriculture, 1884–1970," in *The Defining Moment: The Great Depression and the American Economy in the Twentieth Century,* ed. Michael D. Bordo, Claudia Goldin, and Eugene N. White, 181–224 (Chicago: University of Chicago Press, 1998).

20. Pete Daniel, *Breaking the Land: The Transformation of Cotton, Tobacco, and Rice Cultures since 1880* (Urbana: University of Illinois Press, 1985), 175.

21. Robin Kelley discusses the efforts of the Southern Tenant Farmers' Union to obtain rights for tenant farmers and croppers in *Hammer and Hoe: Alabama Communists during the Great Depression* (Chapel Hill: University of North Carolina Press, 1990). Theodore Saloutos describes the controversy regarding the evictions of tenants and croppers, the Agricultural Adjustment Administration's efforts to secure tenant-owner agreements despite AAA acreage reduction, and the firings of officials over tenants' rights in his definitive history of Agricultural Adjustment Acts, *The American Farmer and The New Deal* (Ames: Iowa State University Press, 1982), 99–122.

22. Henry Wallace, secretary of agriculture, to Eleanor Roosevelt, first lady, June 7, 1939; Eleanor Roosevelt to Henry Wallace, June 15, 1939, Tenancy, 1939, General Correspondence of the Office of the Secretary of Agriculture, 1906–1970, Records of the Office of the secretary of agriculture, 1839–1981, Record Group 16, National Archives and Records Administration, College Park, MD (hereafter cited as General Correspondence of the Office of the Secretary of Agriculture, RG 16).

23. I am deeply indebted to food historians, to food studies scholars, and to anthropologists who have produced a vast literature that elaborates the centrality of food's social, cultural, political, and economic functions in distinct societies and in various historical periods.

24. Daniel Miller, *Stuff* (Cambridge: Polity Press, 2010), 50.

25. In 1969, theater scholar Lee Baxandall set forth a foundational dramaturgical paradigm for political performance in "photo-analyses of the performance of history in terms of the essential dramatic ingredient" from the French Revolution to Fascist Germany to the Vietnam-era of United States, in "Spectacles and Scenarios: A Dramaturgy of Radical Activity," TDR: *The Drama Review* 13.4 (1969): 53. More recent examinations of protest as performance that are not otherwise cited in this book include: Fernando Calzadilla, "Performing the Political: Encapuchados in Venezuela," TDR: *The Drama Review* 46.4 (2002): 104–25; Victor Emeljanow, "The Events of June 1848: the 'Monte Cristo' Riots and the Politics of Protest," *New Theatre Quarterly* 19.1 (2003): 23–32; Kirk W. Fuoss, *Striking Performances / Performing Strikes*, (Jackson: University of Mississippi Press, 1997); Silvija Jestrovic, "Theatricalizing Politics / Politicizing Theatre," *Canadian Theatre Review* 103 (2000): 42–46; Rebekah J. Kowal, "Staging the Greensboro Sit-Ins," TDR: *The Drama Review* 48.4 (2004): 135–54; Claudia Orenstein, "Agitational Performance, Now and Then," *Theater* 31.3 (2001): 139–51; Rebecca Schneider, "It Seems As If . . . I Am Dead: Zombie Capitalism and Theatrical Labor," TDR: *The Drama Review* 56.4 (2012): 150–62; Diana Taylor, "'You Are Here': The DNA of Performance," TDR: *The Drama Review* 46.1 (2002): 149–69.

26. James M. Jasper, *The Art of Moral Protest: Culture, Biography, and Creativity in Social Movements* (Chicago: University of Chicago Press, 1997) 80, 234.

27. Baz Kershaw, *The Radical in Performance: Between Brecht and Baudrillard* (London: Routledge, 1999), 97–99. Susan Leigh Foster, "Choreographies of Protest," *Theatre Journal* 55.3 (2003): 395–412. I am also indebted to Ric Knowles's model of "materialist semiotics" for performance analysis, in which he stresses the importance of historic contingency to reception in *Reading the Material Theatre* (Cambridge: Cambridge University Press, 2004).

28. "Media may well play into the hands of people creating the events." Kershaw, *Radical in Performance*, 97.

29. Peter R. R. White, "Media Objectivity and the Rhetoric of a News Story Structure," in *Discourse and Community: Doing Functional Linguistics*, ed. Eija Ventola (Tübingen: Narr, 2000), 370.

30. Emphasis added, Michael Kazin, *The Populist Persuasion: An American History*, rev. ed. (Ithaca, NY: Cornell University Press, 1998), 13. In a recent popular press piece, Kazin remarked that the U.S. producerist ethic differed from Marxist European configurations focused on the proletariat: "While many producers were wage-earners, producerism as a concept cast a broad moral net over society instead of dissecting it with a scalpel. A producer could be a craftsman, a teacher, a small merchant, a farmer with hired hands, a homemaker. To qualify for the honor, one simply had to do something useful for society and not prosper from the labor or weaknesses of others," in "The Producers," *New Republic*, February 8, 2012, accessed April 4, 2014, http://www.newrepublic.com/article/politics/magazine/100526/producers-middle-class-income-inequality-occupy#.

31. Emphasis added, Catherine McNicol Stock, *Rural Radicals: Righteous Rage in the American Grain* (Ithaca, NY: Cornell University Press, 1996), 16.

32. Barbara Melosh, *Engendering Culture: Manhood and Womanhood in New Deal Public Art and Theater* (Washington, DC: Smithsonian Institution Press, 1991), 53.

33. For the history of competing economic theories and the shift from classical liberal thought to modern American liberalism by the mid-twentieth century, a culture in which Roosevelt could promise "freedom from want," see Kathleen G. Donohue, *Freedom from Want: American Liberalism and the Idea of the Consumer* (Baltimore: The John Hopkins University Press, 2003). For the related rise of consumer-citizenship and activism in the early-twentieth century, see Gary Cross, *An All-Consuming Century: Why Commercialism Won in Modern America* (New York: Columbia University Press, 2000); Meg Jacobs, *Pocketbook Politics: Economic Citizenship in Twentieth-Century America* (Princeton, NJ: Princeton University Press, 2005); Annelise Orleck, *Common Sense and a Little Fire: Women and Working-class Politics in the United States, 1900–1965* (Chapel Hill: University of North Carolina Press, 1995); and Mary E. Triece, *On the Picket Line: Strategies of Working-class Women during the Depression* (Urbana: University of Illinois Press, 2007).

34. Roxworthy recounts the nation-state's and media's use of this myth to exclude Japanese Americans from citizenship, showing how the discourse aimed to distance the U.S. program of internment from fascist Europe in the same breath that it justified the internment of these citizens for "suspicious behavior." She also documents internees' resistance to the "two-faced promise of American citizenship" through performances that staged both faces simultaneously. *The Spectacle of Japanese American Trauma: Racial Performativity and World War II* (Honolulu: University of Hawaiʻi Press, 2008), 13.

35. Harvey A. Levenstein, *The Paradox of Plenty: A Social History of Eating in Modern America* (New York: Oxford University Press, 1993), 59.

36. Alice O'Connor, *Poverty Knowledge: Social Science, Social Policy, and the Poor in Twentieth-Century U.S. History* (Princeton, NJ: Princeton University Press, 2001), 72.

37. Charles Cunningham, "*Life* Magazine and the Mythology of Rural Poverty in the Depression," *Journal of Narrative Theory* 29.3 (1999): 285.

38. Judith Butler defines "performative" as the constitution of the gendered social subject through the unconscious repetition of a set of codified practices and discourses that "precede, constrain, and exceed the performers." Society recognizes individuals as proper men or women based on these norms (or individuals are only legible within society through these norms). See Butler, *Bodies That Matter: On the Discursive Limits of "Sex"* (London: Routledge, 1993), 234. Scholars of race and performance have applied Butler's theory of gender performativity to the process of racialization. Shannon Jackson describes racialized subjectivity as internalized: "[Racism] maintains itself by being unregistered. . . . its performers (both dominant and marginalized) are less aware of the ways its production depends upon their own repetitions." Jackson, *Professing Performance: Theatre in the Academy from Philology to Performativity* (Cambridge: Cambridge University Press, 2004), 183. Emily Roxworthy also notes this pervasive internalization, understanding its impact as a way of (literally) seeing to explicate the exclusion of Japanese Americans from citizenship, despite their patriotic performances. She construes Butler's conception of racial performativity as "a conditioned mode of perceiving visual evidence that spectacularizes the other—in other words, the unconscious (or even conscious) enactment of codified acts would seem to have little impact because race will be predetermined through the reading practices of the interracial observer"; *Spectacle of Japanese American Trauma*, 12.

1. THE NEW DEAL VISION FOR AGRICULTURE

1. An earlier version of this chapter appeared as "Performing the Promise of Plenty in the USDA's 1933–34 World's Fair Exhibits," special issue, "Food and Performance, Food as Performance," *Text and Performance Quarterly* 29.1 (2009): 22–43.

2. C. W. Warburton, USDA director of extension work, to Henry Wallace, secretary of agriculture, October 24, 1933, CC-Chicago WF 1933, General Correspondence of the Office of the Secretary of Agriculture, RG 16.

3. Richard Schechner, *Performance Studies: An Introduction* (New York: Routledge, 2002), 35.

4. David Potter, *People of Plenty: Economic Abundance and the American Character* (Chicago: University of Chicago Press, 1954), 79, 91.

5. Franklin D. Roosevelt, "Inaugural Speech of Franklin Delano Roosevelt," March 4, 1933, *History and Politics Out Loud*, accessed April 15, 2014, http://www.hpol.org/fdr/inaug/.

6. Burton Benedict, *The Anthropology of World's Fairs: San Francisco's Panama Pacific International Exposition of 1915* (Berkeley, CA: Lowie Museum of Anthropology in association with Scolar Press, 1983), 15; Eilean Hooper-Greenhill, *Museums and the Interpretation of Visual Culture* (London: Routledge, 2000), 113; "Chicago's Fair: Heavenly Gestures to Open Century of Progress on Beam from Arcturus," *Newsweek*, May 27, 1933, 8, 10. Architectural historian John Findling surmises, "The raw modernism of the buildings and the bright colors used to paint them seemed to combine with the carnival spirit present in all expositions to recreate a mood that had disappeared with the stock market crash," in *Chicago's Great World's Fairs* (New York: St. Martin's Press, 1994), 79. *The New World's Fair of 1934*, folder 16-172, Century of Progress Records, Special Collections and University Archives, Richard J. Daley Library, University of Illinois-Chicago, (hereafter cited as Century of Progress Records).

7. JMR, "Food," press release, A Century of Progress Publicity Office, May 25, 1934, folder 14-169; *Official Guidebook of the Fair 1933* (Chicago: A Century of Progress International Exposition, 1933); HTB, "Foods and Agriculture Building," press release, A Century of Progress Publicity Office, June 20, 1934, folder 14-156; and "Food at the New Fair," *Commerce* (May 1934): 17, folder 16-129, Century of Progress Records.

8. The 1.4 million attendees who registered in 1933 show nationwide attendance, and, though the bulk of citizens came from Midwestern, near-Eastern, and Western states, Californians (9 percent) attended in greater numbers than Midwesterners such as Iowans, Kentuckians, and Michiganders. "Where They Came From," *Commerce* (April 1934): 16, folder 16-129; and press release, A Century of Progress Publicity Office, January 15, 1934, folder 14-148, Century of Progress Records. Only a handful of international exhibitors participated in addition to those that sponsored "villages," including China, Czechoslovakia, Italy, Japan, and Mexico. Century of Progress president Rufus C. Dawes expressed disappointment about this: "Although it is true . . . that we experienced some benefits as a direct result of the depression . . . our invitations for the participation of foreign governments were not presented at a time favorable for their reception"; Dawes, *Report of the President of a Century of Progress to the Board of Trustees* (Chicago: Century of Progress, 1936), 68.

9. Robert Rydell, *World of Fairs: The Century of Progress Exhibitions* (Chicago: University of Chicago Press, 1993), 7.

10. Ibid., 21–22.

11. Dawes, *Report of the President,* 28.

12. James O'Donnell Bennett, "Reporter Sees the Glories of Our Own Land," *Chicago Daily Tribune,* June 6, 1933, Charges Criticism—Chicago World's Fair 1933, General Correspondence of the Office of the Secretary of Agriculture, RG 16.

13. "A Perfect Setting for a Great National Jubilee," *Chicago Daily Tribune,* May 27, 1933.

14. Dawes, *Report of the President,* 51.

15. Robert W. Rydell, Kimberley Pelle, and John Findling describe the fair as "a vision of a planned future where technology and science, wedded to corporate capitalism, made social and economic problems seemingly disappear," in *Fair America: World's Fairs in the United States* (Washington, DC: Smithsonian Institution Press, 2000), 136. Folke T. Kihlstedt concurs: "Visitors saw a vision of a future in which democracy, capitalism, and consumerism were affirmed by science and technology"; "Utopia Realized: The World's Fairs of the 1930s," in *Imagining Tomorrow: History, Technology and the American Future,* ed. Joseph J. Corn (Cambridge, MA: Massachusetts Institute of Technology Press, 1986), 97.

16. Sidney Mintz, *Tasting Food, Tasting Freedom: Excursions into Eating, Culture, and the Past* (Boston: Beacon Press, 1996), 82–83.

17. "The Pedigree of Food," *Official World's Fair Weekly,* for the week ending May 27, 1933, 8–9, folder 16-134, Century of Progress Records.

18. Kyla Wazana Tompkins investigates the representation during the nineteenth century of the black subject as edible in relation to the consolidation of a white body politic in *Racial Indigestion: Eating Bodies in the Nineteenth Century* (New York: New York University Press, 2012).

19. Lois Scharf, *To Work and to Wed: Female Employment, Feminism, and the Great Depression* (Westport, CN: Greenwood Press, 1980), 157.

20. Richard Osborn Cummings shows that 25 percent of farm women in 1915 ordered food from catalogues, in *The American and His Food: A History of Food Habits in the United States,* rev. ed. (Chicago: University of Chicago Press, 1941), 108; Harvey A. Levenstein, *Paradox of Plenty: A Social History of Eating in Modern America* (New York: Oxford University Press, 1993), 27–28.

21. Lois Johnson Hurley, "The Human Side of the World's Fair," *Wisconsin Agriculturist and Farmer,* July 9, 1933, 8.

22. HDJ, "Wilson," press release, A Century of Progress Publicity Office, May 30, 1934, folder 14-156, Century of Progress Records.

23. Eve Jochnowitz concludes that a "feminized vision of the future" was vital to manufacturers' promotion of processed food at the 1939–40 New York World's Fair; these exhibits tried to appeal to women because women controlled family food choices. See Jochnowitz, "Feasting on the Future: Foods of the World of Tomorrow at the New York World's Fair of 1939–40," *Performance Research* 4.1 (1999): 110–20.

24. "America's Food Supply," *Commerce,* May 1934, 40, folder 16-129, Century of Progress Records.

25. For studies regarding women's employment as an "issue" in the Great Depression, see Scharf, *To Work and to Wed;* Eileen Boris, "Regulating Industrial Housework: The Triumph of 'Sacred Motherhood,'" *Journal of American History* 71.4 (1985): 745–63; Ruth Milkman, "Women's Work and the Economic Crisis: Some Lessons from the Great Depression," in *A Heritage of Her Own: Toward a New Social History of American Women,* ed. Nancy F. Cott and Elizabeth H. Pleck, 507–41 (New York: Simon and Schuster, 1979); and Landon Storrs, *Civilizing Capitalism: The National Consumers' League, Women's*

Activism, and Labor Standards in the New Deal Era (Chapel Hill: University of North Carolina Press, 2000).

26. See Daniel Miller, *Stuff* (Cambridge: Polity Press, 2010), for a discussion of the socio-political power of objects due to their seemingly obvious meanings. Many museum studies scholars have written about the institutional power of the museum to differentiate cultures and to distinguish art. An excellent volume on these issues is Ivan Karp and Steven D. Lavine, eds., *Exhibiting Cultures: The Poetics and Politics of Museum Display* (Washington, DC: Smithsonian Institution Press, 1991).

27. Hooper-Greenhill, *Museums,* 112.

28. For elaborations of this idea, see Jane Ferry, *Food in Film: A Culinary Performance of Communication* (New York: Routledge, 2003); Kathleen LeBesco and Peter Naccaratto, eds., *Edible Ideologies: Representing Food and Meaning* (Albany: State University of New York Press, 2008); and the essays in three journals: *Performance Research* 4.1 (1999), spec. issue "On Cooking"; *Text and Performance Quarterly* 29.1 (2009), spec. issue "Food and Performance, Food as Performance"; and *Women and Performance* 21.3 (2011), spec. issue "Food Legacies."

29. Unless otherwise noted, descriptions of this exhibit are taken from "Dairy Products Build Superior People," folder 16-261, Century of Progress Records.

30. Spectacle entails "(1) the primacy of visual sensory and symbolic codes, (2) monumentality and an aggrandizing ethos, (3) . . . presentational action set in opposition to passive spectating, and (4) dynamism in the presentation that engenders excitement in the audience." This is Margaret Drewal's précis of John MacAloon's definition in "From Rocky's Rockettes to Liberace: The Politics of Representation in the Heart of Corporate America," *Journal of American Culture* 10.2 (1987): 71. See also John MacAloon, "Olympic Games and the Theory of Spectacle in Modern Societies," in *Rite, Drama, Festival, Spectacle: Rehearsals toward a Theory of Cultural Performance,* ed. John MacAloon, (Philadelphia: ISHI, 1984), 241–80.

31. For an explanation of processes by which individuals are indoctrinated into ideologies and social and political subjectivity is constituted, see Louis Althusser, "Ideology and Ideological State Apparatuses (Notes towards an Investigation)," in *Lenin and Philosophy and Other Essays* (New York: Monthly Review Press, 1972), 127–86. Here, Drewal weds Victor Turner's concept of "ideological *communitas*" to MacAloon's elaboration of spectacle, in "From Rocky's," 71.

32. Exodus 3:8; Proverbs 27:27; 1 Peter 2:2.

33. Leslie Goddard, "'Something to Vote for': Theatricalism in the U.S. Women's Suffrage Movement," PhD diss., Northwestern University, 2001, 94.

34. *Milk for You and Me,* Motion Picture Films, ca. 1915–ca. 1959, Records of the Extension Services, 1888–1996, Record Group 33, National Archives and Records Administration, College Park, MD (hereafter cited as Records of Extension Services, RG 33); Cummings, *The American and His Food,* 152–53.

35. Hi'ilei Hobart, "'The Milk Problem': The New York Milk Station and Surveys of the Immigrant Body, 1906–1912," paper presented at "Food Networks: Gender and Foodways: An Interdisciplinary Conference," Gender Studies Program, Notre Dame, IN, January 26–28, 2012.

36. Bridget Heneghan, *Whitewashing America: Material Culture and Race in the Antebellum Imagination* (Jackson: University of Mississippi Press, 2003). At the federal level, the Children's Bureau, whose primary purpose was to ensure American children's

welfare, could not keep up with the demand for its pamphlet "Child Care and Milk: The Indispensable Food for Children," underscoring Americans belief in milk's vitality. See Robyn Muncy, *Creating a Female Dominion in American Reform, 1890–1935* (New York: Oxford University Press, 1991), 55–56.

37. U.S. Department of Labor, Children's Bureau, "Why Drink Milk? Milk Is the Indispensable Food for Children," folder no. 3, rev. ed., November 1931.

38. P. S. Lucas, "Milk—The Ideal Food," USDA Extension Bulletin No. 140, reprint, August 1934.

39. Cummings, *The American and His Food*, 181, 206.

40. Levenstein, *The Paradox of Plenty*, 59.

41. E. Melanie DuPuis, *Nature's Perfect Food: How Milk Became America's Drink* (New York: New York University Press, 2002), 105.

42. H. E. Van Norman, president, Century Dairy Exhibit, Inc., foreword to "Dairy Products Build Superior People," September 15, 1933, folder 16-261, Century of Progress Records.

43. In her history of the home economics movement and the USDA Bureau of Home Economics, Carolyn M. Goldstein defines "rational consumption" as the transference of production efficiencies onto consumption in an attempt to shape consumer culture toward middle-class values. See Goldstein, *Creating Consumers: Home Economists in Twentieth-Century America* (Chapel Hill: University of North Carolina Press, 2012).

44. Allan D. Albert, *Official View Book, A Century of Progress Exhibition* (Chicago: Reuben H. Donnelley Corp., 1933), folder 16-201, Century of Progress Records.

45. Herford Cowling and Burton Holmes, *A Century of Progress Exposition: Around the Fair with Burton Holmes*, reel 1, 1933, FLA 225, Cowling Collection, Library of Congress Motion Picture Collection, Library of Congress.

46. Photograph no. NWDNS-016-EX-51-014, Photographic Prints of USDA Exhibits and Other Exhibits, 1900–1953, Records of the Office of the Secretary of Agriculture, 1839–1981, Record Group 16, National Archives and Records Administration, College Park, MD (hereafter cited as Photographic Prints of USDA Exhibits, RG 16).

47. *Light Art Lumia: A Site about the Pioneering Work of Thomas Wilfred with Images and Information from the Eugene and Carol Epstein Collection*, accessed April 1, 2014, http://www.lumia-wilfred.org/.

48. Emphasis added, "The Dairy Industry at a Century of Progress," *Hoard's Dairyman*, May 25, 1933, 194.

49. Drewal, "From Rocky's Rockettes," 71.

50. Unless otherwise noted, descriptions of this exhibit are taken from the Meat and Livestock Industry Exhibit Brochure, untitled, folder 16-268, Century of Progress Records.

51. Barbara Kirschenblatt-Gimblett, *Destination Culture: Tourism, Museums, and Heritage* (Berkeley: University of California Press, 1998), 3–4.

52. Tracy C. Davis, "Performing and the Real Thing in the Postmodern Museum," TDR: *The Drama Review* 39.3 (1995): 15–40.

53. Roger Horowitz, *Putting Meat on the American Table: Taste, Technology, Transformation* (Baltimore, MD: Johns Hopkins University Press, 2005); Levenstein, *Paradox of Plenty*, 74.

54. Megan J. Elias, *Food in the United States, 1890–1945* (Santa Barbara, CA: Green Wood Press, 2009), 14–17.

55. C. B. Stanford, *The Hunting Apes: Meat Eating and the Origins of Human Behavior* (Princeton, NJ: Princeton University Press, 2001), 210; Barbara Willard, "The American Story of Meat: Discursive Influences on Cultural Eating Practice," *Journal of Popular Culture* 36.1 (2002): 108–10.

56. Katharina Vester, "Regime Change: Gender, Class, and the Invention of Dieting in Post-bellum America," *Journal of Social History* 44.1 (2010): 43–44. See also E. Melanie DuPuis, "Angels and Vegetables: A Brief History of Food Advice in America," *Gastronomica* 7.3 (2007): 34–44.

57. Cummings, *The American and His Food,* 138–59.

58. Willard, "The American Story of Meat," 113.

59. *Official Guidebook of the Fair 1933,* 74, Century of Progress Records.

60. Photograph no. NWDNS-016-EX-52-29382-C, Photographic Prints of USDA Exhibits, RG 16.

61. Potter critiques this "frontier hypothesis" as a valid explanation of the American character; in doing so, he demonstrates its prevalence; *People of Plenty,* 151–52.

62. A. W. Bitting, "Report on the Food and Agriculture Exhibits," November 10, 1933, Charges Criticism—Chicago World's Fair 1933, General Correspondence of the Office of the Secretary of Agriculture, RG 16.

63. Michael Owen Jones, "What's Disgusting, Why, and What Does It Matter?" *Journal of Folklore Research* 37.1 (2000): 63.

64. Bitting, "Report on the Food," General Correspondence of the Office of the Secretary of Agriculture, RG 16.

65. "Report of Exhibit of United State Department of Agriculture at A Century of Progress Exposition Chicago, Illinois May 27–November 12, 1933," 55, Egypt/Fairs and Expositions—Report of Exhibit (A Century of Progress Exposition), [Office of Information] Records Relating to Exhibitions, RG 16.

66. Stanton B. Garner, *Bodied Spaces: Phenomenology and Performance in Contemporary Drama* (Ithaca, NY: Cornell University Press, 1994), 99.

67. United States Congress, "A Century of Progress Exposition in Chicago, 1933," Joint Letter from the Secretary of State, the Secretary of Agriculture, and the Secretary of Commerce as Members of the Chicago World's Fair Centennial Commission, 73rd Congress, 2nd Session, April 17, 1934 (Washington DC: United States Government Printing Office), 48.

68. Photo no. NWDNS-016-EX-52-007, Photographic Prints of USDA Exhibits, RG 16.

69. *Official Guidebook of the Fair, 1933,* 74, Century of Progress Records.

70. D. S. Burch, "The Effectiveness of Various Types of Agricultural Exhibits," October 1933: 5–6, 8, Exhibits Effectiveness Study—The Effectiveness of Selective Exhibits, [Office of Information] Records Relating to Exhibitions, RG 16.

71. Ibid., 5–6, 9.

72. United States Congress, "A Century of Progress Exhibition in Chicago," 85.

73. Rydell, *World of Fairs,* 150.

74. *Official Guidebook of the Fair 1933,* 85, Century of Progress Records.

75. Ibid., 73.

76. Photograph No. NWDNS-016-EX-52-29485-C, Photographic Prints of USDA Exhibits, RG 16.

77. Photograph of a woman and a girl standing next to a cake, Events-Exhibits-Illinois-Chicago-Century of Progress, Century of Progress Records.

78. Kirschenblatt-Gimblett, *Destination Culture*, 21.

79. *Official World's Fair Weekly*, for week ending August 6, 1933, 6, Century of Progress Records.

80. Goldstein, *Creating Consumers*, 105–111.

81. United States Congress, "A Century of Progress Exhibition in Chicago," 47. I have not be able to locate a photograph of this portion of the installation in the records of the exhibit at National Archives in College Park, MD, University of Illinois-Chicago, or at the Chicago Historical Society.

82. Milton Danziger, "A Critique of the United States Department of Agriculture Exhibits at A Century of Progress, Chicago, 1933," 5–6, Effectiveness Studies—Official Pictures in Color (A Century of Progress), [Office of Information] Records Relating to Exhibitions, RG 16.

83. Hooper-Greenhill, *Museums*, 106.

84. Michael Belcher, *Exhibitions in Museums*, ed. Susan Pearce (Leicester and Washington, DC: Leicester University Press and Smithsonian Institution Press, 1991), 122.

85. "Federal Agriculture," press release, A Century of Progress Publicity Office, 10 August 1934, folder 15-137, Century of Progress Records.

86. Joseph Hiscox, chief officer of exhibits, to Dr. C. W. Warburton, contact officer, Century of Progress Exhibition, July 5, 1933, Charges Criticism—Chicago World's Fair 1933, General Correspondence of the Office of the Secretary of Agriculture, RG 16.

87. Michael Baxandall, "Exhibiting Intention: Some Preconditions of Visual Display of Culturally Purposeful Objects," in *Exhibiting Cultures: The Poetics and Politics of Museum Display*, ed. Ivan Karp and Steven D. Lavine (Washington, DC: Smithsonian Institution Press, 1991), 34.

88. Barbara Kirschenblatt-Gimblett, "Playing to the Senses: Food as a Performance Medium," *Performance Research* 4.1 (1999): 3.

89. Helen Iball, "Melting Moments: Bodies Upstaged by the 'Foodie Gaze,'" *Performance Research* 4.1 (1999): 74.

90. United States Congress, 42. This report states that a motion picture was shown here, which "presented the Department's field of service beneath a statement by the Honorable Henry A. Wallace." However, photographs do not show any apparatus on which to show a film.

91. Photograph No. NWDNS-16-EX-29451-C, Photographic Prints of USDA Exhibits, RG 16.

92. "Report of Exhibit of United States Department of Agriculture," 8–9, [Office of Information] Records Relating to Exhibitions, RG 16.

93. A small stereopticon box sits atop the map in Photograph no. NWDNS-016-EX-29374-C, Photographic Prints of USDA Exhibits, RG 16. USDA and congressional reports do not mention the use of slides in the exhibit. However, the Extension Service's film slide, "Prepared by the Department of Agriculture Washington, D.C.," is visible in photographs. This exhibit would have been an appropriate venue for use of slides from *The Agricultural Crisis*, a film produced in 1933, Motion Picture Films, ca. 1915–ca.1959, Records of Extension Services, RG 33.

94. Hiscox to Warburton, 3, General Correspondence of the Office of the Secretary of Agriculture, RG 16.

95. Lewis Holloway and Moya Kneafsey, "Producing-Consuming Food: Closeness, Connectedness and Rurality in Four 'Alternative' Food Networks," in *Geographies of Rural Cultures and Societies,* ed. Lewis Holloway and Moya Kneafsey (Burlington, VT: Ashgate, 2004), 271.

96. Arthur P. Chew, "Science Serving Agriculture" (Washington, DC: United States Government Printing Office, 1933), 1, folder 16-367, Century of Progress Records.

97. Ibid.

98. "Farm Week at the Fair," *Official World's Fair Weekly,* for week ending August 19, 1933, 14, Century of Progress Records; "Wallace Makes Farm Plea at Fair Tomorrow," *Chicago Daily Tribune,* August 17, 1933; Earl Mullin, "Farmer Throng at Fair to Hear Wallace Today," *Chicago Daily Tribune,* August 18, 1933; Earl Mullin, "Fair Ceremony Pays Tribute to U.S. Farm Women," *Chicago Daily Tribune,* August 16, 1933; "Farm Woman is 9,000,000th Visitor at Fair," *Chicago Daily Tribune,* August 15, 1933.

99. "Federal Farm Program Lags, Dairymen Told," *Chicago Daily Tribune,* August 16, 1933.

100. Earl Mullin, "Farmer Throng at Fair to Hear Wallace Today," *Chicago Tribune,* August 18, 1933; "Wallace Tells $55,000,000 Aid for Corn Belt," *Chicago Tribune,* August 18, 1933.

101. "Wallace Seeks Ways to Boost Farm Revenues," *Chicago Daily Tribune,* August 18, 1933.

102. Franklin D. Roosevelt, Sound Picture Address, May 27, 1934, folder 14-227, Century of Progress Records.

103. C. W. Warburton, USDA director of extension work, to Colonel W.B. Causey, assistant commissioner, A Century of Progress, December 6, 1934, included in "Report of Exhibit of United States Department of Agriculture," 1 [Office of Information] Records Relating to Exhibitions, RG 16. A third addition consisted of adding samples of "pasture and forage crops" to the plant industry exhibit; these crops were promoted as restoratives for farmland.

104. Rexford G. Tugwell, "Agriculture and the Consumer" (Washington, DC: U.S. Government Printing Office, 1934), folder 16-368, Century of Progress Records.

105. Warburton to Causey, 1 [Office of Information] Records Relating to Exhibitions, RG 16.

106. Photograph no. NWDNS-016-EX-51-29510-C, Photographic Prints of USDA Exhibits, RG 16.

107. Warburton to Causey, 2 [Office of Information] Records Relating to Exhibitions, RG 16.

108. C. W. Warburton, director of extension work, USDA, to Henry Wallace, secretary of agriculture, November 23, 1934; and Henry Wallace, secretary of agriculture to secretary of state, U.S. Commission to a Century of Progress, December 18, 1934, Charges Criticism—Chicago World's Fair 1933, General Correspondence of the Office of the Secretary of Agriculture, RG 16.

109. "Renovation of Department Exhibits at a Century of Progress to Make Them Suitable for Use at State Fairs, 1934," Charges—Chocolate, General Correspondence of the Office of the Secretary of Agriculture, RG 16.

110. "Exhibit Effectiveness Studies 1940–1941," 7 [Office of Information] Records Relating to Exhibitions, RG 16.

111. Holloway and Kneafsey, "Producing-Consuming Food," 271.

2. MILK DUMPING ACROSS AMERICA'S DAIRYLAND

1. Protesters, authorities, and journalists almost exclusively referred to these acts of milk destruction as "dumping." I have discovered only a few instances in which the term "spill" appears in headlines or photo captions representing the Milk Pool strike, and no instances that imply a variation of the proverb "don't cry over spilled milk." I note the phrase because it suggests the pointlessness of regret or the futility of worrying about things one cannot change; in uttering it, the speaker dismisses the subject's concerns. Thus, using "spill" would belie news editors' attempts to win public sentiment through "objective" accounting or trivialize consumers' and farmers' concerns. "Dumping" indicates the serious attitude taken toward the action and evokes the act's profound wastefulness.

2. Jon Robert Adams, *Male Armor: The Soldier-Hero in Contemporary American Culture* (Charlottesville: University of Virginia Press, 2008), 2.

3. The February strike was announced as probable on February 8, 1933, and quickly staged one week later on February 15, 1933. According to William Rubin, attorney for the Milk Pool, its hasty staging contributed to its failure. The October strike was called by the National Farmers' Holiday Association and came as something of a surprise to the Milk Pool. October standoffs at dairy corporations by Milk Pool and Holiday Association members conveyed a different character. First, it was a national collective action; the Milk Pool was just one of many farm groups. The October strike was also distinct from the May protest in terms of its symbolic rendering of milk. In October, milk was one of numerous commodities withheld by farmers. In October, the Milk Pool waited to make sure that the National Farmer's Holiday Association would follow through. It did. However, shortly after the pool joined the strike, the association called off the strike in Wisconsin and the Milk Pool continued its strike unaided. The October strike was very violent, and the governor threatened to call out the National Guard once again, a precedent he had set during the May 1933 strike; see Herbert Jacobs, "The Wisconsin Milk Strikes," *Wisconsin Magazine of History* 35.1 (1951): 35.

4. Patrick Mooney and Scott Hunt, "A Repertoire of Interpretations: Master Frames and Ideological Continuity in U.S. Agrarian Mobilization," *Sociological Quarterly* 37.1 (1996): 183.

5. Report of Meeting of Farmers relative to Wisconsin Milk Pool, Marshfield, Wisconsin, May 17, 1933, 2–3, Ralph M. Immell Papers, 1908–1960, Wisconsin Historical Society-Madison, (hereafter cited as Immell Papers).

6. See Tim Yuan-Shiao Kung, "Spilt Milk: Dairy Farmer Rhetoric and Actions during the Wisconsin Milk Strikes of 1933," Master's thesis, University of Wisconsin-Madison, 1996, 1.

7. "Address of Mr. Harry Jeck [sic] of Outagamie County, Wisconsin," May 17, 1933, Immell Papers.

8. Strike poem attached to Resolutions of National Farmers' Holiday Association, n.d., 1934 January–June, Wisconsin Cooperative Milk Pool Records.

9. Cory Bernat, overview of poster exhibit, "Beans Are Bullets and Of Course I Can! An Exhibit of War-era Food Posters from the National Agricultural Library," www.good-potato.com.

10. H. H. Jack, and H. F. Dries, "A Declaration and Petition," November 11, 1932, Wisconsin Cooperative Milk Pool Records.

11. Federal Writers' Project of the Works Progress Administration, *The WPA Guide to Wisconsin* [1941], introduction by Norman K. Risjord (St. Paul: Minnesota Historical Society Press, 2006), 73.

12. U.S. Census of Population and Housing, 1930, *Historical Census Browser Geospatial and Statistical Data Center,* University of Virginia Library, accessed April 29, 2014, http://mapserver.lib.virginia.edu/.

13. Federal Writers' Project of the Works Progress Administration, *The WPA Guide to Wisconsin,* 91, 75.

14. *State of Wisconsin Blue Book 2003–2004,* accessed July 30, 2006, http://www.legis.state.wi.us/lrb/bb/03bb.

15. A.G. Schmedeman, Wisconsin governor, to H. F. Dries, secretary-treasurer, Wisconsin Cooperative Milk Pool, Appleton, Wisc., November 25, 1932, Wisconsin Cooperative Milk Pool Records.

16. Address of Governor Schmedeman, Eighty-fifth Anniversary, Immell Papers.

17. William Rubin to A. R. Sanna, Federal Surplus Relief Corporation, April 7, 1934, William Benjamin Rubin Papers, 1908–1950, Wisconsin Historical Society-Milwaukee, (hereafter cited as Rubin Papers).

18. Abraham Lincoln, February 12, 1861, National Park Service, accessed November 23, 2011, www.nps.gov/home/historyculture/presquotes.htm.

19. E. Melanie DuPuis, *Nature's Perfect Food: How Milk Became America's Drink* (New York: New York University Press, 2002), 147–48.

20. Theodore Saloutos, *The American Farmer and the New Deal* (Ames: Iowa State University, 1982), xv.

21. In urban settings, recreational athletics substituted for agricultural and frontier labor, while education was perceived to civilize rural ruggedness. Because middle-class men lacked the opportunity to realize proprietary autonomy in the corporate workplace, they conducted themselves toward success by "perfecting body, mind, and presentability"; Michael Kimmell, *Manhood in America: A Cultural History* (New York: Free Press, 1996), 143. Hollywood star Gary Cooper epitomized the modern urban man. He embodied the ideal transformation from rural to urban man, having moved from a ranch to Los Angeles. He was depicted as practical, rugged but self-possessed, with a sexualized athleticism; see Steven T. Sheehan, "'Costly Thy Habit as Thy Purse Can Buy': Gary Cooper and the Making of the Masculine Citizen-Consumer," *American Studies* 43.1 (2002): 101–25.

22. Earl Young, Melrose, Wisc., to Henry Wallace, May 3, 1933, Strikes, General Correspondence of the Office of the Secretary of Agriculture, RG 16.

23. Harry Bragarnick to Daniel W. Hoan, mayor of Milwaukee, Milwaukee, Wisc., n.d., Bragarnick Papers, 1930–1960, Wisconsin Historical Society-Milwaukee (hereafter cited as Bragarnick Papers).

24. Jacobs, "The Wisconsin Milk Strikes," 30–35.

25. The Wisconsin Cooperative Milk Pool used the Sioux City strike and the 1910s protests by the New York Dairymen's League as evidence of the economic efficacy of withholding and destroying agricultural products. In fact, the 1933 Milk Pool's milk dumpings represent a few of many acts of food destruction by farmers during the Great Depression. Oscar Ameringer, an Oklahoma activist, testified before Congress in 1932 about farmers' desperate efforts to raise prices through produce and crop destruction;

these actions, however, were not carried out as public protest but were efforts to reduce surplus; see Janet Poppendieck, *Breadlines Knee-deep in Wheat* (New Brunswick, NJ: Rutgers University Press, 1986), xii. In the summer of 1933, Stanley Piseck led ten thousand New York milk producers in a strike involving milk dumping; see Paul Abrahams, "Agricultural Adjustment during the New Deal Period, The New York Milk Industry: A Case Study," *Agricultural History* 39.2 (1965): 92–101. More recent acts of food destruction during farmers' protests include the National Farmers Organization's (NFO) actions during the 1960s, and, very recently, Confédération paysanne (France) and Farmers for Action (Britain) have employed this tactic. See Luther Tweeten, *Terrorism, Radicalism, and Populism in Agriculture* (Ames: Iowa State University Press, 2003); Michael Woods, "Politics and Protest in the Contemporary Countryside," in *Geographies of Rural Cultures and Societies,* ed. Lewis Holloway and Moya Kneafsey (Burlington, VT: Ashgate, 2004), 103–25; and F. W. Groves, "Twentieth Century Farm Strikes: A Comment," *Agricultural History* 39.4 (1965): 217–19.

26. Rubin was trying to persuade Milo Reno, president of the Farmers' Holiday Association, to come to Wisconsin by flattering Reno that the pool needed "a man of [his] experience in Executive Session to lay down certain lines of activity," February 24, 1933, Rubin Papers.

27. The announcement of a February 14, 1933, meeting was sent on February 13, 1933, and the strike began on February 15. "To the Presidents of Various Locals in Ozaukee County," Appleton, Wisc., February 13, 1933, Wisconsin Cooperative Milk Pool Records.

28. "This Strike's Not a Picnic, Milwaukee Cops Still Tough," unlabeled newspaper clipping, Wisconsin Cooperative Milk Pool Records.

29. Milo Reno to William Rubin, February 27, 1933, Rubin Papers.

30. "Resolutions by the Various Co-Operative Organizations of Wisconsin," Madison, Wisc., February 22, 1933, vol. 1, Wisconsin Cooperative Milk Pool Records.

31. Minutes of meeting of Governor Schmedeman's Dairy Committee, March 21, 1933, Madison, Wisc., Wisconsin Cooperative Milk Pool Records.

32. "Why Milk Business Is Sound," *Wisconsin Agriculturist and Farmer,* January 7, 1933.

33. Albert G. Schmedeman, "Address of Governor Albert G. Schmedeman of Wisconsin, before the President's Conference of Governors," Washington, DC, March 6, 1933, Immell Papers.

34. "To our fellow citizens in Wisconsin," n.d., Wisconsin Cooperative Milk Pool Records.

35. "Reporter Learns View of Farmers on Strike," *Wisconsin State Journal,* May 13, 1933.

36. "Governor A.G. Schmedeman's legislative message on relief," n.d., folder 19-122, William Theodore Evjue Papers, 1880–1969, Wisconsin Historical Society-Madison.

37. Daniel R. Block, "Public Health, Cooperatives, Local Regulation and the Development of Modern Milk Policy: The Chicago Milkshed, 1900–1940," *Journal of Historical Geography* 35.1 (2009): 128–53. Daniel R. Block and E. Melanie DuPuis, "Making the Country Work for the City: Von Thunen's Ideas in Geography, Agricultural Economics and the Sociology of Agriculture," *American Journal of Economics and Sociology* 60.1 (2001): 79–98.

38. "City Assured of Milk for School Children and Sick," *Marshfield News-Herald,* May 11, 1933.

39. "County Crisis in Strike May Come Tonight," *Daily Northwestern*, May 14, 1933; "Milk Supply for Needy to be Permitted," *Sheboygan Press*, May 6, 1933; "Koehler Named to Route Milk for Ill, Needy," *Milwaukee Leader*, May 9, 1933; Milk Strike, January 29–May 26, 1933, Bragarnick Papers; Singler quoted in "Madison Area Milk Embargo Will End within Few Hours," *Wisconsin State Journal*, May 12, 1933.

40. "Milk Supply for Needy to be Permitted," *Sheboygan Press*, May 6, 1933.

41. Susan Leigh Foster, "Choreographies of Protest" *Theatre Journal* 55.3 (2003): 395–412.

42. "Strike Proclamation," *Marshfield News-Herald*, May 11, 1933.

43. "State Controls Farm Strike in Wisconsin," *Daily Northwestern*, May 12, 1933.

44. "'Peaceable Picketing' Defined by Finnegan," *Daily Northwestern*, May 15, 1933; "Picketing to Be Permitted," *Marshfield News-Herald*, May 12, 1933.

45. "State's Plans Are Complete," *Marshfield News-Herald*, May 12, 1933.

46. "Singler Calls for Picketing," *Milwaukee Sentinel*, May 13, 1933.

47. Shane Hamilton, *Trucking Country: The Road to America's Wal-Mart Economy* (Princeton, NJ: Princeton University Press, 2008), 29. Fluid milk dairymen invested in improving herds in order to produce safe, high-quality milk. They blamed the poverty of cheese and butter dairymen on their inefficient operations and their deliberate production of milk that was safe only for processed products. Cheese farmers did produce lower-grade milk. Each spring, however, fluid milk farmers flooded the markets for cheese and other processed dairy products when their cows produced surpluses of milk and drove down prices even further.

48. "Will Attempt Mediation at Milwaukee Round Table," *Plymouth Review*, April 17, 1933; "Farmer Won't Need Strike, Is Assertion," *Milwaukee Leader*, April 20, 1933; "Probable Need for National Guard in Farm Strike Seen," *News Beloit*, April 21, 1933; "National Guard May Be Called for Milk Strike," *Sheboygan Press*, April 21, 1933, Bragarnick Papers.

49. Harry Bragarnick to President Franklin D. Roosevelt, April 22, 1933; "Hoan Cautions Farm Strikers," *Milwaukee Sentinel*, April 29, 1933; "Hoan's Milk Speech Irks Strike Chief" and "National Dairy Parley Ahead," *Milwaukee Sentinel*, April 30, 1933, Bragarnick Papers.

50. "Farm Session Attracts 2,000," *Des Moines Tribune*, May 8, 1933, Bragarnick Papers.

51. Emphasis added. Radio address delivered by Dr. S. K. Pollask, in behalf of Mr. Harry Bragarnick, over station WTMJ, May 9, 1933, from 8:15 to 8:30 PM, Bragarnick Papers.

52. "Strike Proclamation," *Marshfield News-Herald*, May 11, 1933.

53. "Madison Farmers Prepare Petition to Halt Strike," *Milwaukee Sentinel*, May 11, 1933. A May 11 *Wisconsin State Journal* article, "Madison Farmers Prepare Petition to Halt Strike," was subtitled "Decision Left to Farmers" and "Majority to Rule." The *Milwaukee Sentinel* implied that farmers' inability to store milk was a central reason behind petition signing in "Non-Strikers Ride with Milk Trucks and Fight Off Pickets; Two Rioting Warrants Issued," *Milwaukee Sentinel*, May 14, 1933.

54. "Appleton Unit Is Opposed to Farm Strike" and "Do Not Believe Strike Will Affect Sheboygan," *Sheboygan Press*, May 12, 1933; "Many Groups Oppose Strike," *Marshfield News-Herald*, May 12, 1933.

55. "Dairy Defies Order," *Milwaukee Sentinel*, May 13, 1933. On May 14, the Winnebago County sheriff telephoned Immell regarding the Carver Creamery's refusal to close. It was still open on the evening of May 15, 1933. From Port Washington on May 16, 1933,

the district attorney reported, "Farmers are getting sore, saying that dairy companies were violating the Governor's orders," Report of Activities of the Adjutant General's Office May 13–18, 1933, Immell Papers.

56. "Petitions not Public Record," *Marshfield News-Herald*, May 13, 1933; "State Checks on Milk 'Leaks,'" *Milwaukee Sentinel*, May 13, 1933.

57. "Schmedeman Orders Milk Outlets Shut," *Daily Northwestern*, May 13, 1933.

58. Joseph Roach, *It* (Ann Arbor: University of Michigan Press, 2007), 180.

59. Michael Managan, in *Staging Masculinities: History, Gender, Performance* (New York: Palgrave Macmillan, 2003), reproduces the list of masculine attributes that Ian M. Harris used in his foundational sociological study. Managan analyzes the contradictions within the taxonomy itself and the anxieties potentially produced in men who recognize their own conformance to and divergence from the list.

60. "Youths Emulate Walter Singler," *Sheboygan Press*, May 17, 1933; Jacobs, "The Wisconsin Milk Strikes," 31.

61. William Rubin to Harry A. Jung, American Vigilant Intelligence Federation, March 10, 1933, Rubin Papers.

62. "The Answer to a Letter to Mr. Singler," Peoples Forum, *Hartford Times*, clipping, Wisconsin Cooperative Milk Pool Records.

63. Roach, *It*, 8.

64. "Milk Strike Leader Is Back Home," *Marshfield News-Herald*, May 29, 1933, 7.

65. Roach, *It*, 6, 8.

66. "Peace Parley Called to Halt Farm Holiday." *Milwaukee Sentinel*, April 8, 1933.

67. "Plan Resumption of Milk Strike May 10, Says Pool President," *Milwaukee Sentinel*, April 10, 1933, Wisconsin Cooperative Milk Pool Records.

68. Arthur M. Evans, Reports to Adjutant General, May 13–17, 1933, Immell Papers.

69. "1,000 Pickets Stone Deputies in Battle," *Wisconsin State Journal*, May 15, 1933.

70. "Bryan! Bryan!! Bryan!!! Bryan!!!!" *Fortune Magazine*, January 1934, 64.

71. The poem is written from the perspective of a sixteen-year-old boy, enamored with Bryan and Populism, who is heartbroken at the orator's defeat: "Defeat of the wheat. / Victory of letterfiles /And plutocrats in miles / With dollar signs upon their coats, / Diamond watchchains on their vests and spats on their feet. / Victory of custodians, Plymouth Rock, / And all that inbred landlord stock.... / Defeat of the young by the old and the silly." Accessed April 4, 2014, http://php.indiana.edu/~rotella/aeh/bryan1.htm.

72. Charlotte Canning, *The Most American Thing in America: Circuit Chautauqua as Performance* (Iowa City: University of Iowa Press, 2005), 160.

73. The article implicitly represents Singler as an uncanny repetition of Bryan and his historical fate. Of Bryan, Canning concludes, "It is easy to see Bryan on the losing side of history ... and the rise of contemporary corporate culture as inevitable. Even though that agrarian vision had limited political suasion into the twentieth century, it was because of a broad range of forces, most of them outside a single party's control, not because Bryan and his allies were promoting a hopelessly naïve view of American society, politics, and economics"; *The Most American Thing in America*, 157.

74. Roosevelt was only the third Democratic presidential candidate to carry Wisconsin since the Civil War. In 1932, he won the popular vote in sixty-nine of seventy-one counties. See Wayne Elmer Laufenberg, "The Schmedeman Administration in Wisconsin: A Study of Missed Opportunity," Master's thesis, University of Wisconsin-Madison, 1965, 4, 55.

75. Albert G. Schmedeman, speech, January 5, 1933, Juneau, Wisconsin, folder "Personal Correspondence," January–February 28, 1933, box 1, Papers of Albert G. Schmedeman, 1907–1934, Wisconsin Historical Society–Madison.

76. Schmedeman reduced maximum interest rates on loans and delinquent taxes, extended the collection on foreclosures to three years, and exempted milk checks from garnishment.

77. Laufenberg, "The Schmedeman Administration," 48.

78. Ibid., 11. Jonathan Kasparek draws similar conclusions in "FDR's 'Old Friends' in Wisconsin: Presidential Finesse in the Land of La Follette," *Wisconsin Magazine of History* 84.4 (2001): 16–25. Kasparek argues that the 1934 political situation in Wisconsin was awkward for Roosevelt. The press anticipated the delicate negotiations that FDR would have to undertake ostensibly to assist Schmedeman's gubernatorial campaign as a fellow Democrat, without endorsing the governor's conservative agenda or his actions during the Milk Pool and Koehler strikes. Progressive Republicans were more in line with New Deal policies, and FDR supported Congressman Robert La Follette but was concerned about a third-party rivalry if Philip La Follette won the governorship. After Schmedeman lost the 1934 governor's race, Roosevelt appointed him federal housing administrator for Wisconsin. The May 1933 strike affirmed the suspicions of an elderly Milk Pool member, C. B. Ballard, about the entire Democratic Party. Ballard's letter to the editor blamed President Wilson for farmers' ruin and the death of his sons during the Great War: "I never knew anything but trouble to come from a democratic administration and am not surprised to see our election returns coming in," *Wisconsin Dairymans News* 2.1 (November 1933).

79. William F McIlrath, "Move to Oust Singler Defeated," *Wisconsin State Journal,* June 2, 1933.

80. Stuart L. Weiss, *The President's Man: Leo Crowley and Franklin Roosevelt in Peace and War* (Carbondale: Southern Illinois University Press, 1996), 7.

81. The figure of 11,283 comes from William Hoglund, "Wisconsin Dairy Farmers on Strike," *Agricultural History* 35.1 (January 1961): 26. The figure of 24,000 comes from "Wisconsin News Items," *Wisconsin Agriculturist and Farmer,* June 10, 1933. The *Wisconsin Agriculturist and Farmer* was a Milk Pool publication.

82. "Singler Calls on Pool to Continue Fight," *Sheboygan Press,* June 1, 1933, 1; "Singler Does Not Want to Be Reelected," *Marshfield News-Herald,* May 23, 1933, 1.

83. "Nation-Wide Holiday Is Off," *Marshfield News-Herald,* May 13, 1933.

84. *Aristotle's Poetics,* trans. S. H. Butcher (New York: Hill and Wang, 1961), 70, 73.

85. Minutes of Executive Committee, May 16, 1933, Wisconsin Cooperative Milk Pool Records.

86. William H. McIlrath, "Singler Off for Trout as Strike Opens," *Wisconsin State Journal,* May 12, 1933.

87. "Trouble Ahead Singler States," *Daily Northwestern,* May 13, 1933. Singler denied making this statement in a phone conversation he had with Adjutant General Immell during the strike, in Report of Activities of the Adjutant General's Office, May 13–18, 1933, Immell Papers.

88. Herbert Jacobs, "The Wisconsin Milk Strikes," 34.

89. Report of Activities of the Adjutant General's Office May 13–18 1933, 15, Immell Papers.

90. Edward F. Schmidt, Shawano, Shiocton, and Milwaukee, May 17–19, 1933; and Fred J. Mattingly, commanding troops in Waukesha County, May 16–19, 1933, Report

of Activities of the Adjutant General's Office, May 13–18, 1933, 2, 41, Immell Papers. Following the strike, the *Appleton Post-Crescent* published a letter to the editor from an Ontagamie County resident that described special deputies' crass behavior: "When it is our misfortune to have to use means by which to gain our ends, those who are deputized to keep peace and order at least can refrain from vile and profane remarks. . . . Surely, it is a citizen's right to be able to walk through the streets of your city without being subject to remarks common among such men." Despite this citizen's antistrike attitude, the letter expresses the violation of moral standards by the special deputies, whom the citizen calls "jail birds" and "detriments to human welfare." Letter to *Appleton Post-Crescent* editor, reprinted in *Wisconsin Dairyman's News* 1.8 (June 1933): 7.

91. William A. Holden, Colonel 128th Infantry, Suspension of Otto Druckery, sheriff of Shawano County, Report to the Adjutant General, Wisconsin National Guard 128th Infantry Headquarters, Wisconsin Veterans Home, Wisconsin, May 31, 1933, 15, Immell Papers.

92. "Striker Hurt in Fight at Shawano," *Sheboygan Press*, May 17, 1933.

93. "Ready for Showdown in Shawano," *Milwaukee Journal*, May 17, 1933; "Deputies Move to Front," *Milwaukee Sentinel*, May 17, 1933; "On Milk Strike Front," *Milwaukee Sentinel*, May 15, 1933.

94. Photographers were embedded alongside filmmakers to document the Great War, which enabled still-image makers to photograph bodies on battlefields and present war in the epic mode. Richard Abel's argument that the popularity of documentary Great War films in the 1910s demonstrates audiences' desire to "be there" complements both Jon Robert Adams's assertion that civilians use the performance of men at war in novels and fictional films to gauge a nation's strength and Sontag's observation that Western societies have trained spectators to perceive glory in artistic representations (and photographic reproductions) of war. They all conclude that civilians have been taught to want to look at this kind of suffering, as it offers one way through which a nation proves its righteousness and bravery to itself. Richard Abel, "Charge and Countercharge: Documentary War Pictures in the USA, 1914–1916," *Film History: An International Journal* 22.4 (2010): 366–88, http://muse.jhu.edu.proxy1.cl.msu.edu/journals /film_history/v022/22.4.abel.html; Susan Sontag, *Regarding the Pain of Others* (New York: Picador, 2003); Adams, *Male Armor*.

95. In 1929, Wisconsin provided 30 percent of Chicago's milk supply. By 1940, it provided 49 percent; Block, "Public Health," 146. I discovered the cartoon among newspaper clippings from the May strike in the Wisconsin Cooperative Milk Pool Papers, which I take as an indication that Milk Pool members also associated the image with their actions. The cartoon's publication date, September 18, 1933, aligns with a short-lived strike by dairymen in McHenry and Kane counties in Wisconsin. These strikers opposed the plan for the Chicago milkshed designed by Wallace and the Pure Milk Association because the proposal included only Illinois dairymen and Wisconsin farmers stood to lose their place in the Chicago milk market.

96. "Determined Strikers Face Deputies at Shawano," photograph, *Milwaukee Sentinel*, May 17, 1933, Wisconsin Cooperative Milk Pool Papers.

97. There are two known incidents of milk destruction by contamination. Protesters poured kerosene into vats at the H. Christman Dairy in Johnson Creek and nearby in Farmington at the Christians Creamery. These acts occurred in the presence of plant workers and deputies. There is no evidence to support the allegation that protesters

wished to harm consumers; see "Parade at Lake Mills," *Sheboygan Press,* May 16, 1933; "Lake Mills Guard Doubled as Officials Hear Threats to Poison Milk, Bomb Plant," *Wisconsin State Journal,* May 16, 1933. Authorities arrested eight men in Shawano County because they threatened to dump kerosene into milk vats, Charles E. Lafferty, captain 57th F. A. Brigade, Report of Activities of Battery during the Recent Emergency, Whitefish Bay, Wisc., May 27, 1933, Immell Papers. Additionally, the commander of the Racine Co. deputies heard rumors that protesters were going to poison milk, Report of Company K to General Immell, n.d., 1, Immell Papers.

98. "Four Counties Remain Closed," *Marshfield News-Herald,* May 17, 1933.

99. Glenn Kuehn, "How Can Food Be Art?" in *The Aesthetics of Everyday Life,* ed. Andrew Light and Jonathan M. Smith (New York: Columbia University Press, 2005), 210.

100. "State Acts to Prevent Red Control of Strike," *Wisconsin State Journal,* May 17, 1933.

101. "Angry Crowd of 150 Storms into the Courthouse," *Daily Northwestern,* May 18, 1933.

102. "Senate Avoids Interference in Wisconsin Milk Strike," *Sheboygan Press,* May 16, 1933.

103. "Residents Are Irate," *Milwaukee Sentinel,* May 19, 1993; "Gas Bombs, Bayonets Flash in Milk Battles," *Wisconsin State Journal,* May 18, 1933.

104. "Gas Bombs," *Milwaukee Sentinel,* May 18, 1933.

105. "Woman Defies Barricade," *Milwaukee Sentinel,* May 15, 1933.

106. "Bomb Squad in Action Road Blocked Milk Goes into Ditch," *Milwaukee Sentinel,* May 15, 1933.

107. "1,000 Pickets Stone, Club Deputies in Wild Battle; Six Farmers Arrested," *Wisconsin State Journal,* May 15, 1933.

108. William A. Holden, colonel 128th Infantry, Suspension of Otto Druckery, sheriff of Shawano County, Report to the Adjutant General, Wisconsin National Guard 128th Infantry Headquarters, Wisconsin Veterans Home, Wisconsin, May 31,1933, 2, Immell Papers.

109. Report of Activities of the Adjutant General's Office, May 13–18, 1933, 21, Immell Papers.

110. Nicholas M. Schantz, Lt. Co., A.G.D., Wisconsin Nation Guard, Assistant Adjutant General, Report on Milk Strike, May 23, 1933, Immell Papers.

111. Report of Activities of the Adjutant General's Office, May 13–18, 1933, 26, Immell Papers.

112. "On Milk War Front," *Wisconsin State Journal,* May 17, 1933, 1, 4. One, albeit superficial, explanation for Menominee men's participation as deputies is that deputies were promised payment. The participation of Native Americans was remarkable enough to merit mention in the press, but it was treated as incidental. Perhaps this contradictory treatment was due to the fact that Native Americans' participation interrupted the neat frame of World War I. While this is one of two examples—the other mentioned below— of alternate configurations of power and citizenship, the representation of this fact operates to dismiss this possibility. And the absence of evidence about the participation of distinct Native American tribes on different sides of the protest aids this occlusion.

113. Emphasis added, Report of Activities of the Adjutant General's Office, May 13–18, 1933, 22, 33–35, Immell papers. Throughout the strike, there were a few rumblings that "foreign" elements instigated violence. In these communications with Immell,

commanding guards and sheriffs reported three separate accounts of outsiders, including "city hoodlums" and communists, damaging property and participating in affrays. Herbert Jacobs also recollected that some "jobless city sympathizers" joined the Milk Pool's efforts; "The Wisconsin Milk Strikes," 34.

114. CN causes eye irritation, tearing, burning pain, and respiratory discomfort. DM causes vomiting. According to the U.S. Army Center for Health Promotion and Preventive Medicine, DM gas "proved to be too drastic for use against civilian mobs; it was banned for use against civilian populations in the 1930s in the Western nations." "Detailed Facts about Vomiting Agent Adamsite (DM)," *U.S. Army Center for Health Promotion and Preventive Medicine,* last accessed February 26, 2006, http://chppm-www.apgea .army.mil/dts/docs/detdm.pdf. I am grateful to Lt. Colonel James Storey, USMC Ret., for directing me to this information.

115. Report of Activities of the Adjutant General's Office, May 13–18, 1933, 27, Immell Papers.

116. "Farmer Is Run Down by Truck," *Marshfield News-Herald,* May 18, 1933.

117. Edgar C. Barnes to Adjutant General Immell, May 18, 1933, Immell Papers.

118. Like the above example, the archive does not disclose the motivations of the Oneida men who joined the Milk Pool strikers. While Native Americans' participation as strikers suggests complicated racial politics of collectivism, I have found no evidence that explains the specific dynamics at work in the Milk Pool strike. Though Native Americans played an integral part in Wisconsin's history of radical activism, particularly in the lumber strikes of the late nineteenth and early twentieth centuries, the state, the Milk Pool, and the press did not associate the 1933 strikes with this history.

119. "Jail 250 in Shawano Fight," *Milwaukee Sentinel,* May 18, 1933; "Milk Strikers Routed by Gas in Battle," photo caption, *Marshfield News-Herald,* May 19, 1933.

120. Wilbert E. Ryan, Comdg. 32nd Tank Co., Wisconsin National Guard, Janseville, Wisc., Report of Activities 32nd Tank Co. and attached troops of 121st F.A. Band, Janseville, Wisc., Waukesha County, May 16, 1933, 2, Immell Papers.

121. "Terms of Pool Accepting Truce in Farm War," *Milwaukee Sentinel,* May 19, 1933.

122. "Boys, I'm Glad to See All of You," photo caption, *Wisconsin State Journal,* May 19, 1933.

123. "Thousands Journey Here for Celebration," *Wisconsin State Journal,* May 19, 1933.

124. "5,000 of Milk Pool Drive to State Capital," *Daily Northwestern,* May 19, 1933; "Farmers Gather at Capital Today," *Marshfield News-Herald,* May 19, 1933.

125. "State Senate Stays Neutral in Milk Strike," *Wisconsin State Journal,* May 19, 1933; "Officials War over Use of Cops in Strike," *Milwaukee Sentinel,* May 19, 1933.

126. William Rubin to Alex McDonald, June 27, 1934, Rubin Papers.

127. Postcard to William T. Evjue, February 14, 1938; and M. J. Donovan to William T. Evjue, August 6, 1946, Tomah, Wisc., Evjue Papers.

128. "Crowds Clutter Up Roads Seeking Strike Excitement," *Milwaukee Sentinel,* May 15, 1933.

129. On the evening of May 16, a Racine deputy fired two shots at a car, injuring teenaged spectator Russell Helding. In one report, the car in which Helding was riding roused deputies' suspicion because of its slow, repeated passes around an area where strikers had gathered. The commanding officer told the driver to stop, but when he failed to do so, the officer ordered a deputy to "get that car"; "Farm Youth Shot during Gifford Riot," *Sheboygan Press,* May 17, 1933.

130. "Strike's First Bullet Victim Is Near Death," *Milwaukee Sentinel*, May 18, 1933. After a fight between authorities and protesters at Woodlawn Cemetery in Shawano County on May 17, the *Sheboygan Press* reported that police released several spectators from custody after they "established their innocence as 'bystanders.'" On May 18, gas bombs, which deputies had thrown into protesters' trucks, affected the hundreds of spectators at a battle between 350 deputies and 1,000 strikers in Appleton; "Thousand Pickets Routed after Furious Fight," *Wisconsin State Journal*, May 18, 1933.

3. PLAYING "HOUSEWIFE" IN POLONIA

1. "Business & Finance: Butcher Boycott," *Time*, June 10, 1935, Accessed April 30, 2014. http://content.time.com/time/subscriber/article/0,33009,883492,00.html.

2. "Average American Income of $412 in 1934: A.A.A. Statistics Set National Total at Highest Point since 1931; Soaring Prices Forecast," *Los Angeles Times*, February 16, 1935; "Food Prices in City Soar Sharply over Last Year," *Los Angeles Times*, March 16, 1935.

3. "New Deal in Hamtramck," *Detroit Free Press*, July 29, 1935; "MEAT: Butchers Blame God and Government for Higher Prices," *NewsWeek*, August 17, 1935.

4. On the United Conference against the High Cost of Living, see Tracey Deutsch, *Building a Housewife's Paradise: Gender, Politics, and American Grocery Stores in the Twentieth Century* (Chapel Hill: University of North Carolina Press, 2010), 110–15. Denise Lynn, "United We Spend: Communist Women and the 1935 Meat Boycott," *American Communist History* 10.1 (2011): 45.

5. From the *Polish Daily News*, clipping, Mary Zuk, Polish American Labor History, Don Binkowski Papers, 1920–2008, Walter P. Reuther Library, Wayne State University, (hereafter cited as Binkowski Papers). All translations of articles from *Polish Daily News*, *Voice of the People*, and *Workers' Tribune* are by Magdalena Kopacz.

6. Annelise Orleck's account of the 1935 meat strikes is recognized by women's historians as the foundational history of the national movement; *Common Sense and a Little Fire* (Chapel Hill: University of North Carolina Press, 2007). Mary Triece argues that the 1930s housewives' movement "de-sentimentalized domesticity thereby politicizing women's experiences"; *On the Picket Line* (Urbana: University of Illinois Press, 2007), 64. Barbara Melosh, writing on gendered artistic representations during the New Deal, asserts that the movement "recognize[d] consumption as part of women's unpaid work and as a site of social action"; *Engendering Culture* (Washington, DC: Smithsonian Institution Press, 1991), 198. See also Mimi Abramovitz, "Learning from the History of Poor and Working-Class Women's Activism," *Annals of the American Academy of Political and Social Science* 577 (2001): 118–30; and Lynn, "United We Spend."

7. Annelise Orleck, "'We are that mythical thing called the public': Militant Housewives during the Great Depression," *Feminist Studies* 19.1 (1993): 149.

8. Odai Johnson, *Absence and Memory in Colonial American Theatre: Fiorelli's Plaster* (New York: Palgrave Macmillan, 2006), 3.

9. Mary Elizabeth Perry, "Finding Fatima, a Slave Woman of Early Modern Spain," *Contesting Archives: Finding Women in the Sources*, ed. Nupur Chaudhuri, Sherry J. Katz, and Mary Elizabeth Perry, 3–19 (Urbana: University of Illinois Press, 2010).

10. Temma Kaplan, "Female Consciousness and Collective Action: The Case of Barcelona, 1910–1918," *Signs: Journal of Women in Culture and Society* 7.3 (1982): 545.

11. Meg Jacobs, *Pocketbook Politics* (Princeton, NJ: Princeton University Press, 2008).

12. "Buyers Trampled by Meat Strikers," *New York Times,* July 28, 1935.

13. *New York Times,* April 25, 1935, in Grace Hutchins, "Millions for Meat Barons; Beans for the Unemployed," *Working Woman,* June 1935, 14.

14. The statistics regarded "A.M.U.s" or "American male units" and their "families." Adult women were included within the category of "family," and attention to nutritional deficits focused on the categories of "children" and "men," not "women"; Dorothy G. Wiehl, "Diets of Low-Income Families in New York City," *The Milbank Memorial Fund Quarterly* 11.4 (1933): 322.

15. Dorothy G. Wiehl, "Diets of Urban Families with Low Incomes: An Analysis of Weekly Food Budgets of 472 Families in Baltimore, Cleveland, Detroit, Pittsburgh, and Syracuse in April-May, 1933," *The Milbank Memorial Fund Quarterly* 12.4 (1934): 362.

16. Hutchins, "Millions for Meat Barons," 14.

17. Ibid.

18. Eugene E. Obidinski and Helen Stankiewiscz Zand, *Polish Folkways in America: Community and Family* (Lanham, MD: University Press of America, Inc. 1987), 86–87.

19. Patrick McGann, "Eating Muscle: Material-Semiotics and a Manly Appetite," in *Revealing Male Bodies,* ed. Nancy Tuana et al (Bloomington: Indiana University Press, 2001), 88.

20. This man asserted that he might go the whole summer without meat just to show that he could do it; "Meatless Day Follows Strike in Hamtramck," *Detroit Free Press,* July 29, 1935.

21. "Women Close Meat Markets in Hamtramck," *Detroit Free Press,* July 28, 1935.

22. "Meatless Day Follows Strike in Hamtramck," *Detroit Free Press,* July 29, 1935.

23. Deutsch, *Building a Housewife's Paradise,* 17–18.

24. Arthur Evans Wood, *Hamtramck Then and Now* (New York: Bookman Associates, 1955), 230.

25. Laetitia Conrad, "Some Effects of the Depression on Family Life," *Social Forces* 15.1 (1936): 80.

26. Sam Lewisohn, "New Aspects of Unemployment Insurance," *Political Science Quarterly* 50.1 (March 1935): 4.

27. Alexis Jetter, Annelise Orleck, and Diana Taylor, eds., *The Politics of Motherhood: Activist Voices from Left to Right* (Hanover, NH: University Press of New England, 1997).

28. Rebecca Jo Plant, *Mom: The Transformation of Motherhood in Modern America* (Chicago: University of Chicago Press, 2010), 5. Plant's study demonstrates the unraveling of this construction of motherhood from the Progressive Era to the 1960s. In the 1920s and 1930s, home economists and social scientists began to question women's authority and expertise; so too did progressive women, though for different reasons. Yet the traditional view of motherhood, which I quote above, was the dominant understanding of motherhood.

29. Lois Kershen, *American Proverbs about Women: A Reference Guide* (Westport, CN: Greenwood Press, 1998) 22.

30. Paul Allain and Jen Harvie, *The Routledge Companion to Theatre and Performance* (London: Routledge, 2006), 127.

31. The title character of *Craig's Wife* (1936), Harriet Craig, serves as McHugh's exemplar of the pervasiveness of this discourse because critics characterized Harriet as a

well-known type of *actual* woman and the story as a useful cautionary tale. See Kathleen Anne McHugh, *American Domesticity: From How- to Manual to Hollywood Melodrama* (New York: Oxford University Press, 1999), 116.

32. See Eileen Boris on the NRA's ban of industrial homework, in "Regulating Industrial Homework: The Triumph of 'Sacred Motherhood,'" *Journal of American History* 71.4 (1985): 745–63; Lois Scharf, *To Work and to Wed* (Westport, CN: Greenwood Press, 1980); Ruth Milkman, "Women's Work and the Economic Crisis: Some Lessons from the Great Depression," in *A Heritage of Her Own: Toward a New Social History of American Women*, ed. Nancy F. Cott and Elizabeth H. Pleck, 507–41 (New York: Simon and Schuster, 1979); and Suzanne Mettler, *Dividing Citizens: Gender and Federalism in New Deal Public Policy* (Ithaca, NY: Cornell University Press, 1998).

33. Milkman, "Women's Work," 524.

34. "Woman's Place in the United States Today—Is It in the Home?" *Working Woman*, April 1935, 3.

35. Baz Kershaw, "Curiosity or Contempt: On Spectacle, the Human, and Activism," *Theatre Journal* 55.4 (2003): 592.

36. Susan Leigh Foster, "Choreographies of Protest," *Theatre Journal* 55.3 (2003): 396.

37. "Crowd Storms Police Station; Wives Freed," *Chicago Tribune*, August 4, 1935.

38. Orleck, "'We are that mythical thing,'" 159.

39. Gladys H. Kelsey, "Consumers Widen Boycott in Detroit," *New York Times*, August 11, 1935.

40. For an elaboration of "performative utterances" and how speech constitutes action, see J.L. Austin, *How to do Things with Words*, 2nd ed. (Oxford: Oxford University Press, 1975), 5.

41. See pledge card for the United States Food Administration in "Meatless Mondays, Wheatless Wednesdays: Home Economists and World War I," Digital Exhibit, Albert R. Mann Library, Cornell University, curated by Ashley Miller, accessed April 5, 2014, http://exhibits.mannlib.cornell.edu/meatlesswheatless/meatless-wheatless.php?content=two_a.

42. Celia M. Kingsbury, "'Food Will Win the War': Food and Social Control in World War I Propaganda," in *Edible Ideologies: Representing Food and Meaning*, ed. Kathleen LeBesco and Peter Naccarato (Albany: State University of New York Press, 2008): 45–46.

43. Bruce A. McConachie, *Melodramatic Formations: American Theatre and Society, 1820–1870* (Iowa City: University of Iowa Press, 1992).

44. Wood, *Hamtramck*, 18–24.

45. Frank Serafino, *West of Warsaw* (Hamtramck, MI: Avenue Publishing Co., 1983), 40.

46. Wood, *Hamtramck*, 20.

47. Federal Writers' Program of the Work Projects Administration in the State of Michigan, *Michigan: A Guide to the Wolverine State* (New York: Oxford University Press, 1941), 284.

48. Wood, *Hamtramck*, 28.

49. The local Socialist Polish-language paper, the *Workers' Tribune*, also aimed to get women organized during this time because women's earlier attempts had been too disorganized to take effect; see "Only a Strike on Meat Will Lower Prices," July 18, 1935, Binkowski Papers.

50. "City Council Condemns the Disorder during the Meat Strike," *Polish Daily News,* July 31, 1935, Binkowski Papers; "Meat Strike Revived Today," *Hamtramck Citizen,* August 3, 1935.

51. Shelley Scott, *The Violent Woman as a New Theatrical Character Type: Cases from Canadian Drama* (Lewiston, NY: Edwin Mellen Press, 2007).

52. Lynn, "United We Spend," 48.

53. "Buyers Trampled by Meat Strikers," *New York Times,* July 28, 1935.

54. Section Organizer, Section 8, District 7, *Party Organizer* 8, no. 9 (September 1935): 16, Binkowski Papers.

55. Serafino, *West of Warsaw,* 83–86.

56. Unidentified newspaper, clipping, Binkowski Papers.

57. The term "Negro removal" was used by U.S. District Judge Damon Keith, who presided over the case against the city.

58. "Fourth Week of Meat Strike in Detroit," *Worker's Tribune,* August 17, 1935, Binkowski Papers.

59. "20th Commission of Polish Women's Alliance Condemns Behavior of Mary Zuk," *Polish Daily News,* n.d., Binkowski Papers.

60. John Dingell was the child of Polish immigrants; his original surname was Dzieglewicz. Rep. Dingell was a significant contributor to the New Deal. He helped craft the Social Security Act, which would be signed into law in August 1935. Dingell held his office as U.S. representative from 15th Congressional district from 1933 until his death in 1955.

61. "Belated Relief on Meat Seen," *Detroit Free Press,* August 2, 1935.

62. Clarence Cannon, "The Meat Strike in Detroit," H. R., August 17, 1935, 172 Cong. Rec., Appendix H 14,181, Binkowski Papers.

63. Nan Enstad, "Fashioning Political Identities: Cultural Studies and the Historical Construction of Political Subjects," *American Quarterly* 50.4 (1998): 772–73.

64. Deirdre Clemente, "Striking Ensembles: The Importance of Clothing on the Picket Line," *Labor Studies Journal* 30.4 (2006): 5.

65. Cannon, "The Meat Strike in Detroit," 14, 182, Binkowski Papers.

66. "Meat Strikers Train Guns on Processing Tax," *Chicago Daily Tribune,* August 18, 1935; "Detroit Women Lay Down Law To Congressman," *Chicago Daily Tribune,* August 21, 1935.

67. "The News of the Week Passes in Review," *Washington Post,* August 25, 1935; "Women Ask Packer Quiz," *Los Angeles Times,* August 20, 1935.

68. Elizabeth Marshall, "Stripping for the Wolf: Rethinking Representations of Gender in Children's Literature," *Reading Research Quarterly* 39.3 (2004): 262.

69. Jane Gaines, "The Showgirl and the Wolf," *Cinema Journal* 20.1 (1980): 53–67.

70. Amber Day, *Satire and Dissent: Interventions in Contemporary Political Debate* (Bloomington: Indiana University Press, 2011), 73.

71. "Meat: Women Want Big Bad A A A to Let the Little Pigs Alone," *Newsweek,* August 31, 1935. See also "Wallace Flees Women Protesting Meat Price," *Washington Post,* August 20, 1935.

72. Otis B. Johnson, secretary of Federal Trade Commission, to Mary Zuk, Binkowski Papers.

73. Central Committee of Action against the High Cost of Living, "For the Ongoing Fight for Lower Prices on Food," Binkowski Papers.

74. "Butchers Defy Picketers," *Hamtramck Citizen,* August 9, 1935.

75. "The Radio Speech by Mrs. Maria Zuk," Binkowski Papers.

76. "Detroit Hints Meat Boycott Backed by Reds," *Washington Post,* August 7, 1935; "Reds Blamed for Housewives' Meat Boycott," *Chicago Daily Tribune,* August 7, 1935.

77. "The Communist Activity over the Radio," *Polish Daily News,* n.d., clipping, Binkowski Papers.

78. "Mary Zuk, Labor Candidate Wins Strong Support," *Farm-Labor Challenge,* April 1936, Binkowski Papers.

79. "Woman Leader of Food Strike Wins Election," *Chicago Daily Tribune,* April 10, 1936.

80. S. T. Holland, "Hundreds Attend Michigan Branch of the National Negro Congress," *Pittsburgh Courier,* February 1, 1936; "Celebration of Formation of Polish Local in the Union of Auto Workers," Polish Local, handwritten document, trans. Magdalena Kopacz; "From the Ceremony of the Polish Local of Automobile Union," *Voice of the People,* October 23, 1936; "The Epidemic of the Seated Strike Is Spreading Rapidly in Detroit," *Polish Daily News,* February 21, 1937; and "1,000 People at Meeting in Hamtramck," *Voice of the People,* February 22, 1937, Binkowski Papers.

81. "Councilwoman Zuk Admits Communist Charge," *Hamtramck Citizen,* August 21, 1936.

82. *Detroit Free Press,* April 10, 1936; Orleck cites Zuk's words as evidence of the "politicization of motherhood and family," in "'We are that mythical thing,'" 164.

83. "Mrs. Mary Zuk Councilwoman," *New Deal,* April 10, 1936.

84. "Husband Gives in; Divorce Certain," *Hamtramck New Deal,* May 28, 1936, Binkowski Papers.

85. "Night Life," Newspaper source unknown, most likely *Hamtramck Citizen* due to adjacent announcements, Binkowski Papers.

86. "Mary Zuk, Meat Striker," circa May–June 1937(?); unidentified newspaper clipping, Binkowski Papers.

87. Lou Tendler, "Voters Rebel at a 'High Hat,'" *Detroit News,* n.d., Binkowski Papers.

88. Don Binkowski, email correspondence with author, September 27, 2010.

89. The Michigan Women's Historical Center and Hall of Fame, "Michigan Women's Historical Center and Hall of Fame," http://www.michiganwomenshalloffame.org. As of January 7, 2014, the timeline includes women's accomplishment from 1702–2007.

90. Don Binkowski, email correspondence with author, November 12, 2008.

4. HUNGER ON THE HIGHWAY IN THE COTTON SOUTH

1. An earlier version of this chapter appeared as "Starving Where People Can See: The 1939 Bootheel Sharecroppers' Demonstration," *TDR: The Drama Review* 55:4 (2011): 14–32.

2. Highway Captain Sheppard quoted in Aubrey Williams, National Youth Administration, Report to President Roosevelt, January 19, 1939, Tenant Farming, 1933–1944, President's Official File 1650, Franklin D. Roosevelt Presidential Library, Hyde Park, NY. (hereafter cited as President's Official File 1650).

3. Ben Morris Ridpath, "The Case of the Missouri Sharecroppers," *Christian Century,* February 15, 1939, 174.

4. Jarod Roll, *Spirit of Rebellion: Labor and Religion in the New Cotton South* (Urbana: University of Illinois Press, 2010), 144.

5. "Roadside Campers Removed by Highway Patrol to Former Homes," *Sikeston Herald,* January 19, 1939.

6. "Evicted Sharecroppers Roam Highways Homeless," *Cleveland Call and Post,* January 19, 1939.

7. W. F. Baxter, "Farmers en Route," *Christian Advocate,* June 22, 1939, 592, Newspaper and Magazine Clippings, January 1939–June 1939, reel 22, lot 12024, U.S. Office of War Information, Overseas Picture Division Washington Sections, FSA-OWI Written Records, 1935–1946, Library of Congress (hereafter cited as FSA-OWI Written Records).

8. Michel de Certeau, *The Practice of Everyday Life,* trans. Steven Randall (Berkeley: University of California Press, 1988), xiv–xv.

9. Ibid., xv.

10. Rufus Lark, to Southern Tenant Farmers' Union, 19 February 1939, reel 10, Southern Tenant Farmers' Union Papers, 1934–1970 (NC: Microfilming Corporation of America, 1971) (hereafter cited as STFU Papers).

11. Federal Emergency Relief Administration report quoted in Pete Daniel, *Breaking the Land: The Transformation of Cotton, Tobacco, and Rice Cultures since 1880* (Urbana: University of Illinois Press, 1985), 86.

12. "Investigation concerning the Sharecropper Situation in Southeast Missouri," memorandum for the Attorney General, February 11, 1939, Federal Bureau of Investigation, United States Department of Justice, Washington, DC, HD 1527.M8, University of California Library, Berkeley, CA (hereafter cited as "Investigation").

13. Max R. White, Douglas Ensminger, and Cecil L. Gregory, "Rich Land—Poor People," Research Report No.1, USDA Farm Security Administration Region III, Indianapolis, January 1938, Supplementary Reference Files 1193–1197, reel 17, lot 12024, FSA-OWI Written Records, 45.

14. Ibid.," 5.

15. "Farm Tenancy," a message from the President of the United States transmitting The Report of the Special Committee on Farm Tenancy, 75th Congress, 1st Session, House Document No. 149, February 16, 1937 (Washington, DC: United States Government Printing Office, 1937), 7.

16. Jacqueline Jones, *The Dispossessed: America's Underclasses from the Civil War to the Present* (New York: Basic Books, 1992), 106.

17. "Investigation," 12, 28.

18. Farm Security Administration, "La Forge Farms," October 5, 1940, attached to memorandum for Mr. Russell Lord from John Fischer, Chief Information Division, May 5,1941, 2, Southeastern Missouri Projects, Project Records, 1935–1940, Records of the Farmers Home Administration, 1918–1975, Record Group 96, National Archives and Records Administration, College Park, MD (hereafter cited as Records of FHA, RG 96).

19. Anna M. Emerson to J. R. Butler, president, Southern Tenant Farmers' Union, January 26 1939; J. R. Butler to Anna M. Emerson, February 4, 1939, reel 10, STFU Papers.

20. Robin D. Kelley, *Hammer and Hoe: Alabama Communists during the Great Depression* (Chapel Hill: University of North Carolina Press, 1990), 54.

21. "Government Programs Lesson One: The Agricultural Adjustment Act," Reel 16, STFU Papers.

22. Daniel, *Breaking the Land,* 101.

23. S. B. Bledsoe, assistant director of information, USDA, to Henry Wallace, secretary of agriculture, March 9, 1939, Agricultural Adjustment Act, General Correspondence of the Office of the Secretary of Agriculture, RG 16.

24. "Farm Tenancy," 25.

25. For a complete explanation of the effects of 1933 AAA and cotton contracts on tenants and croppers see Daniel, *Breaking the Land,* and Theodore Saloutos, *The American Farmer and the New Deal* (Ames: Iowa State University Press, 1982).

26. Bledsoe to Wallace, March 9, 1939, RG 16.

27. Thad Snow, "Missouri Roadside Sit-Down Is Dramatization of One of America's Biggest Social Problems," *St. Louis Post-Dispatch,* March 5, 1939.

28. Farm Security Administration, "La Forge Farms," 2, 10, Records of FHA, RG 96.

29. Mississippi County Prosecuting Attorney James Haw sent a letter to Senator Clark warning that a deputy sheriff would have plenty of "work" if the project was established, April 14, 1937; John T. Clark, executive secretary, Urban League, to Bennett C. Clark, U.S. Senate, May 4, 1937; John T. Clark, executive secretary, Urban League, to Henry A. Wallace, secretary of agriculture, June 4, 1937; and R. C. Smith, regional director, Resettlement Administration, to W. W. Alexander, Resettlement Administration administrator, "Subject: Report on Proposed Negro Resettlement Project in Southeastern Missouri," May 4, 1937, Southeastern Missouri, Attitude of Citizens toward Project, Southeastern Missouri Projects, Project Records, 1935–1940, Records of FHA, RG 96.

30. Resolution adopted by the farmers of Mississippi Co., Mo., at Charleston, Mo., January 12, 1939, in "Additional Facts about So-called Tenant and Sharecropper Uprising in Southeast Missouri," Extension of Remarks of Hon. Orville Zimmerman of Missouri in the House of Representatives, January 18, 1939, Supplementary Reference File 1207, Lot 12024, FSA-OWI Written Records.

31. "Sharecropper Eviction," January 18, 1939, reprinted in "What Others Say about the Sharecropper Problem," *Enterprise-Courier,* January 19, 1939.

32. Mildred G. Freed, "Ten Million Sharecroppers," *Crisis* (December 1939): 367.

33. F. A. Behymer, "Southeast Missouri Sharecroppers Transformed into Self-sustaining Farmers by Federal Project, with Decent Homes Replacing Shacks," *St. Louis Post-Dispatch Everyday Magazine,* January 6, 1939, 3D.

34. Report attached to memo from Secretary Wallace to Attorney General Murphy, January 24, 1939, Telephone to Tenancy 1939, Records of the Office of the Secretary of Agriculture, RG 16. Original report from Aubrey Williams, National Youth Administration, to President Roosevelt January 19, 1939, President's Official File 1650.

35. Case No. 51, Case No. 46, and Case No. 45, January 17, 1939, President's Official File 1650; "Letters Written on Backs of Survey Blanks," reel 10, STFU Papers; "Investigation," 23.

36. Owen H. Whitfield, "Letter to All Locals in Missouri Southern Tenant Farmers' Union," February 5, 1939, reel 10, STFU Papers.

37. Owen Whitfield to H. L. Mitchell, December 1, 1939, reel 9, STFU Papers. The STFU would later deny any foreknowledge of the sharecropper protest. In his 1939 "Report of the Secretary," Mitchell wrote, "The National Office of the Southern Tenant Farmers' Union, although it had received no word of the proposed roadside demonstration went into action immediately," Sixth Annual STFU Convention, Blytheville, AK., January 5–7, 1940, reel 14, STFU Papers.

38. Thad Snow, *From Missouri* (Boston: Houghton Mifflin Company, 1954), 246–47, 250.

39. "Sharecroppers Evicted, Camp along Highways," *St. Louis Post-Dispatch,* January 10, 1939, 1.

40. "Investigation," 28.

41. de Certeau, *The Practice of Everyday Life,* xiv–xv.

42. Roll, *Spirit of Rebellion,* 128.

43. Cedric Belfrage, "Cotton-Patch Moses," *Harper's* (November 1948): 94.

44. Ridpath, "The Case of the Missouri Sharecroppers," 147.

45. "Snow Increases Distress among Sharecroppers," *St. Louis Post-Dispatch,* January 13, 1939.

46. "Missouri Farm Laborers are Persuaded to Leave Homes by CIO Leaders," *Sikeston Herald,* January 12, 1939.

47. John Lofland, *Protest: Studies in Collective Behavior and Social Movements* (New Brunswick, NJ: Transaction Books, 1985), 266.

48. Ike Tripp, Case No. 72, January 17, 1939, President's Official File 1650.

49. Ernest Lindley, "Missouri Farm Tenant Problem," *Des Moines Register,* January 19, 1939, 6.

50. de Certeau, *The Practice of Everyday Life,* 36–37.

51. Jarod Roll, "Road to the Promised Land: Rural Rebellion in the New Cotton South, 1890–1945," PhD diss., Northwestern University, 2006, 306–7. Roll elaborates the uneasy alliance between "juke men" and leaders in the African Methodist Episcopal Church, in *Sprit of Rebellion,* 142.

52. Bonnie Stepenoff, *Thad Snow: A Life of Social Reform in the Missouri Bootheel* (Columbia: University of Missouri Press, 2003), 93; H. L. Mitchell, secretary, Southern Tenant Farmers' Union, Press Release, January 23, 1939, reel 10, STFU Papers.

53. de Certeau, *The Practice of Everyday Life,* xix.

54. Barbara Kirschenblatt-Gimblett, *Destination Culture: Tourism, Museums, and Heritage* (Berkeley: University of California Press, 1998), 3–4, 47.

55. Ibid., 55.

56. Roger A. Hall, *Performing the American Frontier, 1870–1906* (Cambridge: Cambridge University Press, 2001), 141.

57. Amma Y. Ghartey-Tagoe Kootin, "Lessons in Blackbody Minstrelsy: Old Plantation and the Manufacture of Black Authenticity," *TDR: The Drama Review* 57.2 (2013): 102–22.

58. Diana Taylor, "A Savage Performance: Guillermo Gómez-Peña and Coco Fusco's *Couple in the Cage,*" *TDR: The Drama Review* 42.2 (1998): 163.

59. Contemporary performance artists have staged private and banal activities to critique the objectification of women and colonial processes. For example, Lián Amaris Sifuentes, in her exhibition *Fashionably Late for the Relationship,* dressed and put on makeup in New York City's Union Square (2007). Famously, in *Two Undiscovered Amerindians Visit the West,* Coco Fusco and Guillermo Gómez-Peña (1992) placed themselves in a cage at natural history museums, costumed in a mismatch of "traditional" garb of colonized peoples, and engaged in activities such as watching television.

60. Steve Durland examines this idea in relation to Greenpeace protest actions in "Witness: The Guerilla Theatre of Greenpeace," *Radical Street Performance: An International Anthology,* ed. Jan Cohen-Cruz (London: Routledge, 1998), 68.

61. Taylor, "A Savage Performance," 163.

62. Kirschenblatt-Gimblett, *Destination Culture,* 55.

63. Samuel D. Warren and Louis D. Brandeis, "The Right to Privacy," *Harvard Law Review* 4.5 (1890), accessed April 7, 2014, http://groups.csail.mit.edu/mac/classes/6.805 /articles/privacy/Privacy_brand_warr2.html.

64. Ibid.

65. Jacqueline Jones was one of the first historians to recognize the Bootheel women as activists: "together with their families, Missouri 'Bootheel' women made national headlines when they camped out along a roadside in the Winter of 1939"; Jones, *Labor of Love, Labor of Sorrow: Black Women, Work and the Family from Slavery to the Present* (New York: Basic Books, 1985), 204.

66. "A Project Home Management Supervisor Answers Any and All Calls to Aid the Project Farm Woman," attached to Farm Security Administration Southeast Missouri Project, New Madrid County, La Forge, Missouri, Southeastern Missouri Projects, Project Records, 1935–1940, Records of the FHA, RG 96.

67. Newsreel footage from *Oh Freedom after While,* produced by Candace O'Connor and Lynn Rubright, directed by Steven John Ross (St. Louis and Memphis: Webster University and the University of Memphis: California Newsreel, 1999).

68. Nick Kaye, *Site-Specific Art: Performance, Place and Documentation* (London: Routledge, 2000), 11.

69. Kirschenblatt-Gimblett, *Destination Culture,* 55; Michel Foucault, *Discipline and Punish: The Birth of the Prison,* trans. Alan Sheridan (New York: Pantheon Books, 1977).

70. Elisabeth Angel-Perez and Alexandra Poulain, "Introduction," in *Hunger on the Stage,* ed. Elisabeth Angel-Peres and Alexandra Poulain (Newcastle: Cambridge Scholars Publishing, 2008), ix.

71. Elaine Scarry, *The Body in Pain: The Making and Unmaking of the World* (New York: Oxford University Press, 1985). Theater scholar Enzo Cozzi writes that "hunger [cannot] easily be simulated and hunger cannot even be represented," in "Hunger and the Future of Performance," *Performance Research* 4.1 (1999): 122.

72. This idea is commonplace among political-economic anthropologists who study consumption practices and food security. See, for instance, Mary Douglas, ed., *Food in the Social Order: Studies of Food and Festivities in Three American Communities* (New York: Russell Sage Foundation, 1984); Ron Scapp and Brian Seitz, eds., *Eating Culture* (Albany: State University of New York Press, 1998); Carole Counihan and Penny Van Esterik, eds., *Food and Culture: A Reader* (New York: Routledge, 1997); Sidney Mintz, *Sweetness and Power: The Place of Sugar in Modern History* (New York: Viking, 1985); Jane Dusselier, "Understandings of Food as Culture," *Environmental History* 14.2 (2009): 331–38; E. N. Anderson, *Everyone Eats: Understanding Food and Culture* (New York: New York University Press, 2005).

73. "Rain, Snow Defied by Sharecroppers," *New York Times,* January 12, 1939; "Fear of Disease Haunts Camp of Sharecroppers," *Chicago Daily Tribune,* January 12, 1939; "Evicted Campers on Roads Await Food from State," *St. Louis Post-Dispatch,* January 11, 1939; "Evicted Farmers Short of Food in Road Camps," *St. Louis Post-Dispatch,* January 12, 1939.

74. *Oh Freedom after While.*

75. Kootin, "Lessons in Blackbody Minstrelsy," 104.

76. "Sharecroppers, Ordered Evicted, to Camp on Road," *St. Louis Post-Dispatch,* January 8, 1939.

77. Eric Lott, *Love and Theft: Blackface Minstrelsy and the American Working Class* (New York: Oxford University Press, 1993), 20, 32.

78. Nicholas Natanson, *The Black Image in the New Deal: The Politics of FSA Photography* (Knoxville: University of Tennessee Press, 1992), 116–17.

79. "Evicted Missouri Sharecroppers," *St. Louis Post-Dispatch*, Pictures sec., January 15, 1939.

80. "Evicted Campers on Roads Await Food from State," *St. Louis Post-Dispatch*, January 11, 1939. Barbara Kirschenblatt-Gimblett uses the term "unmediated encounter" to describe the impression of the "real thing" unfolding before an audience's eyes, in *Destination Culture*, 55.

81. Donald Bogle, *Toms, Coons, Mulattoes, Mammies, and Bucks: An Interpretive History of Blacks in American Films*, 3rd ed. (New York: Continuum, 1994), 4–6.

82. Josephine Johnson, "Among the Evicted Sharecroppers," *St. Louis Post-Dispatch*, January 15, 1939.

83. "Evicted Croppers ???," *Enterprise-Courier*, January 12, 1939.

84. "Rain, Snow Defied by Sharecroppers," *New York Times*, January 12, 1939.

85. "Move to End Trek by Sharecroppers," *New York Times*, January 14, 1939.

86. Farm Security Administration, "Southeast Missouri: A Laboratory for the Cotton South," December 30, 1940, Supplementary Reference Files 1193–1197, reel 17, lot 12024, FSA-OWI Written Records.

87. "Landowners Ask Probe: Check Shows Campers not Sharecroppers," *Southeast Missourian*, January 13, 1939.

88. "Croppers Make Camp on Highway: 'Evicted' Families Stage Demonstration Planned by Preacher," *Southeast Missourian*, January 10, 1939.

89. "Sharecropper Eviction Hoax," editorial, *St. Louis Globe-Democrat*, January 18, 1939.

90. H. L. Mitchell, press release, January 14, 1939, reel 10, STFU Papers.

91. Maud Ellmann, *The Hunger Artists: Starving, Writing, and Imprisonment* (Cambridge, MA: Harvard University Press, 1993), 21.

92. On January 14, 1939, the *Daily Worker* article "Sharecropper Dies in Missouri Fight against Evictions" vilified the Red Cross's official position: "A state Red Cross director from St. Louis came down, sniffed over the situation, and declared that 'A state of emergency does not exist.'" I have not discovered evidence that substantiates the headline. Mildred G. Freed, quoted Whitfield's conversation with Red Cross officials: "Red Cross they said they cain't help 'cause this is a man-made disaster," in "Ten Million Sharecroppers," *Crisis* 46.12 (1939): 367–68.

93. Colonel Franklin, chief of staff, 7th Corps Area, confidential memorandum to General Craig, War Department chief of staff, January 13, 1939, President's Official File 1650.

94. Arthur Rothstein, FSA photographer, to Roy Stryker, director FSA photography, January 16, 1939, Correspondence Photocopies (Group III) Rothstein/Stryker 1939, Roy Emerson Stryker Papers, 1934–1964, Archives of American Art, Washington, DC.

95. "Sharecroppers Evicted, Camp along Highways," *St. Louis Post-Dispatch*, January 10, 1939.

96. J. R. Butler, president, STFU, to Harry H. Woodring, secretary of war, and Lloyd C. Stark, Missouri governor, January 11, 1939; Lloyd C. Stark telegram to J. R. Butler, January 12, 1939, reel 10, STFU Papers.

97. General Craig, War Department chief of staff, memorandum to M. H. McIntyre, secretary to the president, January 13, 1939, President's Official File 1650. In late February, J. R. Butler sent letters to Eleanor Roosevelt and Secretary Woodring again; he was appealing for tents to shelter displaced families who had not yet found farm arrangements. Butler informed the first lady that the STFU's continued attempts to obtain authorization from the secretary of war to distribute National Guard tents "met with failure because of false statements of Missouri officials that all people are adequately sheltered." Written on the same day, Butler recounted to Secretary of War Harry H. Woodring the false statements of Missouri's officials, which he thought resulted in a reversal of Woodring's order to release National Guard tents to the protesters. Butler was properly informed that certain Missouri officials had reported that adequate relief was being provided to the sharecroppers. However, it seems that Butler was misinformed regarding the War Department's intention to assist the demonstrators, February 20, 1939, reel 10, STFU Papers.

98. Adjutant General Means, Missouri National Guard, confidential memorandum to General Craig, War Department chief of staff, January 13, 1939, President's Official File 1650.

99. "Seeking Aid," *St. Louis Post-Dispatch,* January 11, 1939.

100. "Reds Linked with Sharecroppers," *St. Louis Globe-Democrat,* January 14, 1939.

101. "State Police Clear Roads of Squatters," *St. Louis Globe-Democrat,* January 15, 1939; "Farm Laborers Persuaded to Leave Homes by CIO Leaders," *Sikeston Herald,* January 12, 1939.

102. "Sharecropper Campers Greet Future with Smiles," *Southeast Missourian,* January 12, 1939.

103. "Rain, Snow Defied by Sharecroppers," *New York Times,* January 12, 1939; "Ragged Sharecroppers Keep Protest Vigil in Raging Snowstorm," *Philadelphia Inquirer,* January 13, 1939.

104. "Sharecroppers Face Weather," *St. Louis Post-Dispatch Everyday Magazine,* January 13, 1939.

105. Mr. and Mrs. David A. Horowitz, record slip of correspondence, Mr. and Mrs. David A. Horowitz, Philadelphia, Penn., with Department of Justice, March 14, 1939, class numbers (Interfield): 95-01-20 (5/14/41) to 95-64-0 (11/16/39), record slips, 1910–1967, General Records of the Department of Justice Central Files and Related Records, 1790–1989, Record Group 60, National Archives and Records Administration, College Park, MD.

106. Elizabeth Telfer, *Food for Thought: Philosophy and Food* (London: Routledge, 1996), 7.

107. "State Police Clear Roads of Squatters," *St. Louis Globe-Democrat,* January 14, 1939.

108. Herbert Little, transcript of telephone conversation with Aubrey Williams, National Youth Administration administrator, January 15, 1939, President's Official File 1650.

109. Aubrey Williams, National Youth Administration administrator, report to President Roosevelt, January 19, 1939; Case No. 45, January 17, 1939, President's Official File 1650.

110. "Sharecropper Campers Forced to Move Again," *St. Louis Post-Dispatch,* January 19, 1939.

111. "Roadside Campers Removed by Highway Patrol to Former Homes," *Sikeston Herald,* January 19, 1939.

112. "Flood of Checks Ordered Stopped Pending Probe by Federal Agents," *Enterprise-Courier,* February 9, 1939.

113. "Brakes Applied to FSA Emergency Relief Grants," *Sikeston Herald,* February 9, 1939.

114. Lloyd C. Stark, Missouri governor, to Henry Wallace, secretary of agriculture, January 16, 1939, Tenancy, 1939, General Correspondence of the Office of the Secretary of Agriculture, RG 16.

115. Orville Zimmerman, "Additional Facts about So-called Tenant and Sharecropper Uprising in Southeast Missouri," House of Representatives, January 18, 1939, supplementary reference file 1207, reel 17, lot 12024, FSA-OWI Written Records.

116. "Investigation," 17–18.

117. Gary Alan Fine, *Difficult Reputations: Collective Memories of the Evil, Inept, and Controversial* (Chicago: University of Chicago Press, 2001), 10–11.

118. Report attached to memo from Henry Wallace, secretary of agriculture, to Frank Murphy, attorney general, January 24, 1939, Tenancy, 1939, General Correspondence of the Office of the Secretary of Agriculture, RG 16. The STFU also wanted an investigation. On January 16, H. L. Mitchell sent a telegram to Frank Murphy requesting an investigation into landowners' and highway troopers' violations of croppers' civil liberties. The complaint stated that individuals "have been escorted across state lines by Missouri Police when they attempted to aid members of this organization [STFU] secure—relief. Attempts have also been made to prevent distribution of food and clothing contributed by members of other labor unions." H. L. Mitchell, secretary, STFU, to Frank Murphy, attorney general, January 16, 1939, reel 10, STFU Papers.

119. "Southern Tenant Farmers Union activities may have had some part in organizing the protest, although the persons interviewed in many cases were apparently unacquainted with the organization," in report attached to memo from Henry Wallace, secretary of agriculture, to Frank Murphy, attorney general, General Correspondence of the Office of the Secretary of Agriculture, RG 16. Original report from Aubrey Williams, National Youth Administration administrator, to President Roosevelt, January 19, 1939, President's Official File 1650.

120. "Investigation," 32.

121. Franklin D. Roosevelt, president, to Henry Wallace, secretary of agriculture, January 19, 1939, President's Official File 1650. That same day, FSA administrator Will Alexander reported to the White House that "Surplus commodities had been shipped to the region so that there is no lack of food available to meet immediate need" and that the only complaints regarding subsistence distribution came from "certain citizens in the area who think no relief should be given these families by the Federal Government," Dr. Will Alexander, FSA administrator, to Mr. Henry Kannee, the White House, January 19, 1939, attached to memorandum from Will Alexander to Secretary Wallace, Tenancy, 1939, General Correspondence of the Office of the Secretary of Agriculture, RG 16.

122. Jarod Roll gives the most comprehensive account of croppers' gains from 1939–40s. Roll also shows the organizational struggles between various unions that affected these achievements and the vision of the sharecroppers' movement, in *Spirit of Rebellion.* See also, Louis Cantor, *A Prologue to the Protest Movement: The Missouri Sharecropper Roadside Demonstration of 1939* (Durham, NC: Duke University Press, 1969); and Carey McWilliams, *Ill Fares the Land: Migrants and Migratory Labor in the United States* (Boston: Little, Brown and Company, 1942), 291–95; P. G. Beck, FSA regional director,

Region III, to J. R. Butler, president Southern Tenant Farmers' Union, January 16, 1940, reel 14, STFU Papers.

123. Owen Whitfield to F. R. Betton, Cotton Plant, Ark., n.d. reel 14, STFU Papers.

124. Roll, *Spirit of Rebellion*, 157.

125. Cantor, *A Prologue to the Protest Movement*.

126. Baxter, "Farmers en Route," 592.

5. STAGING THE AGRICULTURAL ADJUSTMENT ACT

1. Hallie Flanagan, *Arena* (New York: Duell, Sloan and Pearce, 1940), 66.

2. David Potter, *People of Plenty: Economic Abundance and the American Character* (Chicago: University of Chicago Press, 1954), 91.

3. Cedric Larson, "The Cultural Projects of the WPA," *Public Opinion Quarterly* 3.3 (1939): 494.

4. Flanagan, *Arena*, 362.

5. Theater and cultural historians have paid substantial attention to the Federal Theatre Project as synecdoche and scapegoat of tensions apparent in government patronage of theater in the United States. Further, much of this discussion has been focused on the living newspaper and how the genre epitomizes this political and cultural issue. There are also numerous studies that examine the economic, artistic, and bureaucratic structures of the FTP, as well as its local-national politics and its gender and race politics. Recent studies that are not otherwise cited in this book include Elizabeth Osborne, *Staging the People: Community and Identity in the Federal Theatre* (New York: Palgrave Macmillan, 2011); Susan Manning, *Modern Dance, Negro Dance* (Minneapolis: University of Minnesota Press, 2004); Bonnie Nelson Schwartz, *Voices from the Federal Theatre* (Madison: University of Wisconsin Press, 2003); Barry Witham, *The Federal Theatre Project: A Case Study* (Cambridge: Cambridge University Press, 2003); Mark Franko, *The Work of Dance: Labor, Movement, and Identity in the 1930s* (Middletown, CN: Wesleyan University Press, 2002); Rena Fraden, *Blueprints for a Black Federal Theatre, 1935–1939* (Cambridge: Cambridge University Press, 1994); and Barry Witham, "The Economic Structure of the Federal Theatre Project," in *The American Stage: Social and Economic Issues from the Colonial Period to the Present*, ed. Ron Engel and Tice Miller, 200–214 (Cambridge: Cambridge University Press, 1993). Older studies not otherwise cited include Jane DeHart Mathews, *The Federal Theatre, 1935–1939: Plays, Relief, and Politics* (Princeton, NJ: Princeton University Press, 1967); John O'Connor and Lorraine Brown, *Free, Adult, Uncensored: The Living History of the Federal Project* (Washington, DC: New Republic Books, 1978); Stuart Cosgrove, "From Shock Troupe to Group Theatre," in *Theatres of the Left 1880–1935*, ed. Stuart Cosgrove, Raphael Samuel, and Ewan MacColl, 259–79 (London: Routledge and Kegan Paul, 1985); John O'Connor, "The Federal Theatre Project's Search for an Audience," in *Theatre for Working-Class Audiences in the United States, 1830–1980*, ed. Bruce MacConachie and Daniel Friedman, 171–83 (Westport, CN: Greenwood Press, 1985); and George Kazacoff, *Dangerous Theatre: The Federal Theatre Project as a Forum for New Plays* (New York: Peter Lange Publishing, 1989). Michael Denning's theory of the "Cultural Front" explains how Federal Arts programs enabled cultural work to be seen as labor and stimulated increased unionization of artists in *The Cultural Front: The Laboring of American Culture in the Twentieth-Century* (London: Verso, 1996).

Editorial Staff of the Living Newspaper Federal Theatre Project for New York City, "Triple-A Plowed Under," Publication No. 35 (1936; reprint New York: Works Progress Administration, National Service Bureau, 1938), 2, Triple-A Plowed Under Production Record NYC, Production Title File, 1934–39, Production Records, 1934–43, Federal Theatre Collection, Library of Congress, Washington, DC, (hereafter cited as "Triple-A Plowed Under").

6. *Brooklyn Eagle,* April 6, 1936, Triple-A Plowed Under—Living Newspaper Publicity, Production Title File, 1934–39, Production Records, 1934–43, Federal Theatre Collection, Library of Congress, Washington, DC (hereafter cited as Triple-A Publicity, Federal Theatre Collection).

7. "McDermott on WPA Play," *Cleveland Plain Dealer,* March 30, 1936, Scrapbooks Compiled by the Department of Information, NYC Office, Feb.–June 1936, Work Projects Administration Records of the Federal Theatre Project, Record Group 69, National Archives and Records Administration, College Park, MD (hereafter cited as Scrapbooks, RG 69).

8. "WPA to Stage New Red Play," *New York American,* March 17, 1936, Triple-A Plowed Under—NYC—News clippings, SW—TR, Vassar Collection of Programs and Promotion Materials, 1935–39, Work Projects Administration Records of the Federal Theatre Project, Record Group 69, National Archives and Records Administration, College Park, MD (hereafter cited as Vassar Collection, RG 69).

9. "'Living Newspaper' in Trouble Again on Charge of Radicalism," *Variety,* March 18, 1936, Triple-A Publicity, Federal Theatre Collection.

10. The *Topeka Journal* article is referring to the January 1936 Supreme Court ruling of the AAA processing tax as unconstitutional. Bernard Macfadden, "Inciting to Riot," *Liberty Magazine,* May 23, 1936; "State Theater," *Survey Graphic,* May 1936; "The Living Newspaper Finally Gets under Way with 'Triple A Plowed Under,'" [*New York?*] *Times*), March 16, 1936; J. H. Pollack, "Two Significant Plays," *Pennsylvanian,* April 6, 1936; "Uncle Sam as Producer," *Topeka Journal,* March 21, 1936; "Federal Plays," *Indiana News,* March 27, 1936, Triple-A Publicity, Federal Theatre Collection.

11. *Oneonta Star,* March 28, 1936, Triple-A Publicity, Federal Theatre Collection.

12. *Milwaukee Leader,* June 23, 1936, in "Narrative Report Covering June 16–30," Wisc., April–September 1936, NC–Wisc., Narrative Reports, 1935–1939, Work Projects Administration Records of the Federal Theatre Project, Record Group 69, National Archives and Records Administration, College Park, MD (hereafter cited as Narrative Reports, RG 69).

13. Tony Buttitta and Barry Witham, *Uncle Sam Presents: A Memoir of the Federal Theatre 1935–1939* (Philadelphia: University of Pennsylvania Press, 1982), 15.

14. William De Mille, "Plow the Plays Under," *Stage,* June 1, 1933, Scrapbooks, RG 69.

15. Jonas Barish, *The Anti-Theatrical Prejudice* (Berkeley: University of California Press, 1981), 7.

16. Playbill for *Triple-A Plowed Under,* New York City Biltmore Theatre, March 14–16, 1936, Triple-A Plowed Under Playbills, The Tailor Becomes a Storekeeper to The Vinegar Tree, Federal Theatre Collection, Library of Congress, Washington, DC (hereafter cited as Playbills, Federal Theatre Collection).

17. "Editing the Living Newspaper: It's Not so Simple as It Seems," *Federal Theatre,* April 1936, 17; 1.4.17 Federal Theatre [Magazine] Vol. 1, No. 5 Apr. 1936, Nov. 1935–Dec.

1936, Publications File, 1935–39, Administrative Records, 1935–42, Federal Theatre Collection, Library of Congress, Washington, DC.

18. Playbill for *Triple-A Plowed Under,* Chicago Great Northern Theatre, July 6, 1936, Playbills, Federal Theatre Collection.

19. This estimate is based on newspaper reviews. However, the short duration between the two nightly performances (8:30 PM and 9:40 PM) at the Great Northern Theatre in Chicago suggests that *Triple-A Plowed Under* may have been performed in less than fifty minutes. The production report from the Wisconsin production states that, at the final rehearsal, the show was timed at forty-three minutes, "Narrative Report Covering June 16–30," Narrative Reports, RG 69.

20. W. Ward Marsh, "Federal Theater Opens with Sensational Melo of the Farmers' Woes," *Cleveland Plain Dealer,* June 3, 1936, Scrapbooks, RG 69.

21. *Survey Graphic,* May 1936, Triple-A Publicity, Federal Theatre Collection.

22. Paul Denis, "Two Smash Hits Scored by Federal Theater Project," *Billboard,* March 28, 1936, Vassar Collection, RG 69.

23. Mark Randall, *Brooklyn Ridgewood Times,* April 24, 1936; "'Triple-A Plowed Under,'" *Variety,* March 18, 1936; *Billboard,* March 28, 1936; and "The Stage in Review: Terrors of Impartiality," *New York Sun,* March 21, 1936, Triple-A Publicity, Federal Theatre Collection; Frank Mittauer, "Federal Propaganda," *Evening News,* August 3, 1936, J. Howard Miller Papers, Theatre of the Thirties, Federal Theatre Project Collection, Fenwick Library, Special Collections and Archives Department, George Mason University, Fairfax, VA, (hereafter cited as Miller Papers).

24. Playbill for *Triple-A Plowed Under,* Chicago, Great Northern Theatre, July 6, 1936, Playbills, Federal Theatre Collection.

25. Playbill for *Triple A Plowed Under,* Cleveland, Carter Theater, May 29, 1936, Playbills, Federal Theatre Collection.

26. Playbill for *Triple-A Plowed Under,* New York City, Biltmore Theatre, March 14–16, 1936; and Playbill for *Triple-A Plowed Under,* Chicago, Great Northern Theatre, July 6, 1936, Playbills, Federal Theatre Collection; Playbill for *Triple-A Plowed Under,* Los Angeles, Mayan Theatre, Triple A Plowed Under (L.A.), Production Title File, 1934–39, Production Records, 1934–43, Federal Theatre Collection, Library of Congress, Washington, DC.

27. "Writing the Living Newspaper," n.d., 8–12, Living Newspaper "Writing the Living Newspaper" 25.8, Lighting—Theatre Construction, Technical Studies File, 1935–39, Federal Theatre Collection, Library of Congress (hereafter cited as "Writing the Living Newspaper").

28. Philip Barber, New York City FTP administrator, stated in a 1975 interview, "It was an awful job to get the actors to agree to continue and to appear on stage in the Living Newspapers 'cause they were sure they were going to be ridiculed for it, 'cause 'who ever heard of a play? . . . 'who's the heroine?,'" interview by Diane Bowers, Lorraine Brown, and others, November 11, 1975, Fairfax, VA, Oral History New Deal Culture, Federal Theatre Project Collection, George Mason University, Fairfax, VA (hereafter cited as Oral History.) The director's note in the Los Angeles production report reads, "In 'Triple-A Plowed Under' an unusual problem confronts the director. Primarily it involves a new form not very well known by the majority of our acting personnel, a form in which the actor becomes secondary both to the content and the mechanics. . . . it was difficult to impress the actor with the importance of the play since their relationship to it was to them

rather vague," "Triple A Plowed Under Production Bulletin 1936," Bureau of Research and Publications, Georgia S. Fink, regional director, Cyrilla P. Lindner, regional research supervisor, Federal Theatre Projects Region V, Los Angeles, CA, Triple-A Plowed Under Plowed Under (L.A.), Production Title File, 1934–39, Production Records, 1934–43, Federal Theatre Collection, Library of Congress, Washington, DC.

29. "Writing the Living Newspaper," 12.

30. Ibid., 2.

31. "Guild Sponsors Living Newspaper," Playbill for *Triple-A Plowed Under,* New York City Biltmore Theatre, March 14–16, 1936, Playbills, Federal Theatre Collection.

32. Arthur Arent, "The Techniques of the Living Newspaper," *Theatre Arts Monthly,* November 1938, 280. In interviews conducted in the late 1970s and 1980s as part of George Mason University's oral history project on the Federal Theatre, participants offered different answers about the origins of the living newspaper. Philip Barber stated that the living newspaper form derived from a Viennese theater company that "improvise[d] on the day's news" and that the idea for a Federal Theatre Project version was Elmer Rice's, an expressionist playwright and the original director of New York City FTP, interview by Diane Bowers, Lorraine Brown, and others, November 11, 1975, Fairfax, VA, Oral History. Norman Lloyd, an actor in *Triple-A Plowed Under,* told interviewers that Vsevolod Meyerhold and Sergei Eisenstein influenced living newspaper aesthetics, stating that these techniques "lent to the quickest telling of that story in the most direct way," interview by John O'Connor, Hollywood, CA, January 5, 1976, Oral History.

33. "Triple-A Plowed Under," 2.

34. Ibid., 3.

35. Ibid., 6.

36. Set and light plots, Technical Dept. Living Newspaper W.P.A. 486–1B Theatre, Triple A Plowed Under—NYC Stage Sets, SW—TR, Vassar Collection, RG 69.

37. "Triple-A Plowed Under," 9.

38. Ibid., 13.

39. "They Boo and Cheer Living Newspaper at the Biltmore Theatre," *New York Daily News,* March 18, 1936, Triple-A Publicity, Federal Theatre Collection.

40. Carole Counihan, "Food Rules in the United States: Individualism, Control and Hierarchy," *Anthropological Quarterly* 65.2 (1992): 55.

41. "Triple-A Plowed Under," 15.

42. Ibid., 16.

43. "Writing the Living Newspaper," 11–12.

44. "Triple-A Plowed Under," 18–19; Triple-A Plowed Under Production Notes [New York], Production Title File, 1934–1939; Production Records, 1934–43, Federal Theatre Collection, Library of Congress, Washington, DC; Photograph of "farmers" upstage of rock, 69-TC-NYC-186, Federal Theatre Project Central Files, Records of the Work Projects Administration, 1922–1944, Record Group 69, National Archives and Records Administration, College Park, MD (hereafter cited as FTP Central Files, RG 69).

45. "Triple-A Plowed Under," 25.

46. Ibid., 27.

47. In the Los Angeles production, the silhouette effect was not used; however, the basic blocking was maintained. Farmer families occupied the ramp from downstage right to center stage, and Worker families stood on the opposing ramp. The actors took on stoic postures that reflect those of prayer: arms at sides, palms facing up, choral

three-quarter turn out to the audience. Photograph No. P588-CA-LA-1, Episode 4 Item 2 "Farmer v. Worker," Triple-A Plowed Under-California-Los Angeles, Photographic Prints File, 1934–39, Federal Theatre Collection, Library of Congress, Washington, DC.

48. "Triple-A Plowed Under," 28.

49. Photograph of actors in silhouette, 69-TC-NYC-186, FTP Central Files, RG 69.

50. "Triple-A Plowed Under," 29.

51. "American Living Newspaper Scores a Social Beat," *New Leader,* March 21, 1936, Triple-A Publicity, Federal Theatre Collection.

52. "Triple-A Plowed Under," 36, 38.

53. "Triple-A Plowed Under," 38–41, and Triple-A Plowed Under Production Notes [New York], Production Title File, 1934–1939, Production Records, 1934–43, Federal Theatre Collection, Library of Congress, Washington, DC.

54. Barbara Melosh, *Engendering Culture: Manhood and Womanhood in New Deal Public Art and Theater* (Washington, DC: Smithsonian Institution Press, 1991), 196, 195.

55. "'The Living Newspaper' Acted at the Biltmore: 'Triple A Plowed Under,' A Vig-, orous Federal Theatre Experiment which Raises Some Ethical Questions," *New York Post,* March 16, 1936, Triple-A Publicity, Federal Theatre Collection.

56. "Triple-A Plowed Under," 41–47.

57. These five scenes do not appear in the version of *Triple-A Plowed Under* published in *Federal Theatre Plays* (1938). The added scenes are attributed to Edward Lynn in the Los Angeles program, and his notes appear throughout his script, which is mislabeled in the archive as "Chicago version," 52093(1), Playscripts File, 1936–39, Federal Theatre Collection, Library of Congress, Washington, DC.

58. Lyle Downing, "Dynamite-Packed Revue of Theatre Project Expected to Rock L.A. July 13," clipping, newspaper unknown, Miller Papers.

59. "Dust Bowl Migration," *Rural Migration News* 14.4 (October 2008), online edition, https://migration.ucdavis.edu/rmn/more.php?id=1355_0_6_0, accessed May 7, 2014.

60. John Steinbeck, "Harvest Gypsies," *San Francisco News,* October 5-October 12, 1936, accessed March 20, 2013, via New Deal Network, Roosevelt Institute, http://newdeal.feri.org/nchs/docs02.htm.

61. The film explicitly mentions four programs: Soil Conservation Service, Civilian Conservation Corps, Resettlement Administration, and Forest Service. *The Plow That Broke the Plains,* Records of the Farmers Home Administration, 1918–1975, Record Group 97, National Archives at College Park, College Park, MD.

62. *New York Herald Tribune* and *New York Post,* April 8, 1936, Triple-A Publicity, Federal Theatre Collection.

63. "'Starve or Face Guns,' Is Sharecroppers' Story," *Milwaukee Journal Sentinel,* April 2, 1936.

64. "Triple-A Plowed Under," 48. I examine the vexing production history of this scene in light of Losey's stated reasons for cutting it in "Page 48: Vaudeville of a Historian," special issue "A Tyranny of Documents: The Performing Arts Historian as Film Noir Detective, Essays Dedicated to Brooks McNamara," ed. Stephen Johnson, *Performing Arts Resources* 28 (2011): 243–51.

65. Pierre de Rohan, ed. *Federal Theatre Plays: Triple-A Plowed Under by the Staff of the Living Newspaper; Power: A Living Newspaper by Arthur Arent; Spirochete: A History by Arnold Sundgaard* (New York: Random House, 1938).

66. "Triple-A Plowed Under," 52.

67. "'Starve or Face Guns,' Is Sharecroppers' Story," *Milwaukee Journal Sentinel*, April 2, 1936.

68. "Triple-A Plowed Under," 49.

69. Ibid., 57.

70. Arent, "The Techniques of the Living Newspaper," 280.

71. "U.S. Contributes to Reds through Theatre Project," *New York American*, March 21, 1936, Miller Papers.

72. Garet Garrett, "Federal Theatre for the Masses," *Saturday Evening Post*, June 20, 1936.

73. "Triple-A Plowed Under," 60–61.

74. "Actors Resent Red in Scene," *New York Sun*, March 14, 1936; "Veterans in U.S. Play 'Insulted' by Role of Browder: 'War Slacker'," *New York World-Telegram*, March 14, 1936; T. P. Headen, "wpa Living Show Threatened Again: Opposition Develops on Role of Communist—2 Plays Previously Banned," *New York Post*, March 14, 1936, Triple-A Publicity (4); Photograph of Biltmore marquee, 69-tc-nyc-186, ftp Central Files, rg 69.

75. Phillip Barber, interview by Diane Bowers, Lorraine Brown, and others, November 11, 1975, Fairfax, VA, Oral History.

76. David Román, *Performance in America: Contemporary Culture and the Performing Arts* (Durham, NC: Duke University Press, 2005), 11.

77. "Triple-A Plowed Under," 63.

78. Multiple scholars have examined the dramaturgical techniques used in living newspapers to stimulate the audiences to take action. In her discussion of the living newspaper as an example of the "vernacular" aesthetics and content of 1930s political theater, Ilka Saal argues that the genre "critique[s] American capitalism and calls for change, while at the same time affirming the very system it criticizes"; *New Deal Theater: The Vernacular Tradition in American Political Theater* (New York: Palgrave Macmillan, 2007), 134. See also Laura Browder, "Finding a Collective Solution: The Living Newspaper Experiment," *Prologue* 30.2 (1998): 87–97; Loren Kruger, *The National Stage: Theatre and Cultural Legitimation in England, France, and America* (Chicago: University of Chicago Press, 1992).

79. "Triple-A Plowed Under," 68.

80. Ibid., 73; Photograph of ensemble with U.S. state signs, 69-tc-nyc-186, ftp Central Files, rg 69.

81. For its subsequent plays, the ftp solicited information such as "opinion of play," knowledge of theater, and demographics using the survey "The Audience Is the Best Critic," Audience Survey, Administrative Records, 1935–42, Card File, 1935–42, Federal Theatre Collection, Library of Congress, Washington, DC.

82. In "Boos, Cheers Greet Federal Farm Drama," the reviewer wrote, "the house [was] evenly divided between approval and dissension as the character Earl Browder . . . denounced the [Supreme Court's] move as unconstitutional," *New York News*, March 16, 1936, Triple-A Publicity, Federal Theatre Collection. The evening J. H. Pollack saw the production the audience booed New Deal opponents, while applauding for Wallace, Jefferson, and Browder, "Two Significant Plays," *Pennsylvanian*, April 6, 1936, Triple-A Publicity, Federal Theatre Collection.

83. George Kondolf, July 10, 1936, IL—Kondolf, George—dramatic director, Illinois, Correspondence of the National Office with the Regional Offices, 1935–39, Work Proj-

ects Administration Records of the Federal Theatre Project, RG 69, National Archives and Records Administration, College Park, MD.

84. "Triple A Plowed Under Production Bulletin 1936," Bureau of Research and Publications, Georgia S. Fink, regional director, Cyrilla P. Lindner, regional research supervisor, Federal Theatre Projects Region V, Los Angeles, CA, Triple-A Plowed Under Plowed Under (L.A.), Production Title File, 1934–39, Production Records, 1934–43, Federal Theatre Collection, Library of Congress, Washington, DC.

85. Ibid.; NYC 3 Month Reports—December 1935—March 1936, and March-May 1936, NY-NYC, Narrative Reports, RG 69.

86. Stark Young, "Expressionistic," *New Republic*, April 1, 1936, Triple-A Publicity, Federal Theatre Collection.

87. Norman Lloyd, interview by John O'Connor, Hollywood, CA, January 5, 1976, Oral History.

88. Philip Schrager, interview by Karen Wicke, The Drama Lab, Torpedo Factory, Alexandria, VA, February 28, 1979, Oral History.

EPILOGUE

1. Daniel Imhoff, *Food Fight: The Citizen's Guide to the Next Food and Farm Bill*, 2nd ed. (Healdsburg, CA: Watershed Media, 2012), 25.

2. *Know Your Farmer, Know Your Food*, accessed April 10, 2014, http://www.usda .gov/wps/portal/usda/usdahome?navid=KYF_MISSION.

3. Ron Nixon, "Anti-Hunger Advocates Put Pressure on Lawmakers over Food Stamp Bill," *New York Times*, September 18, 2013, accessed April 10, 2014, http://www.nytimes .com/2013/09/19/us/politics/anti-hunger-advocates-put-pressure-on-lawmakers-over -food-stamp-bill.html?_r=0.

4. Mojo News Team, "Full Transcript of the Mitt Romney Secret Video," accessed April 10, 2014, http://www.motherjones.com/politics/2012/09/ full-transcript-mitt-romney-secret-video.

5. Stephen Colbert, "The Colbert Report," September 18, 2012, accessed April 10, 2014. http://www.colbertnation.com/the-colbert-report-videos/419186/september-18-2012 /mitt-romney-s-secret-video.

6. Kelly A. Dixon, deputy floor director for Majority Whip Kevin McCarthy, "Nutrition Reform and Work Opportunity Act," accessed April 10, 2014, http://www.hagstrom report.com/assets/2013/2013_0903_NutritionReformIntro.pdf.

7. "'The Living Newspaper' Acted at the Biltmore: 'Triple A Plowed Under,' A Vigorous Federal Theatre Experiment which Raises Some Ethical Questions," *New York Post*, March 16, 1936, Triple-A Publicity (4).

8. This figure is based on Jason Greenslate, a SNAP participant, who was featured on the August 10, 2013, *Fox News Insider* investigation, "The Great Food Stamp Binge." The interview paired shots of Greenslate pulling a lobster off of a grill with his comments about how steady work just was not for him.

9. According to the most recent report prepared by the USDA as of this writing, 45 percent of SNAP participants are children and "9 percent are age 60 years or older"; 31 percent of participants had some income, and 42 percent "lived in households with earnings"; 7 percent were Temporary Assistance for Needy Families (TANF, or "welfare") recipients; 18 percent had gross income above the poverty line. "Characteristics

of Supplemental Nutrition Assistance Program Households: Fiscal Year: 2012—Summary," USDA Office of Research and Analysis, February 2014, accessed April 30, 2014,http://www.fns.usda.gov/sites/default/files/2012CharacteristicsSummary.pdf.

10. "CVH Power Protests Rep Maloney Food Stamp Vote," accessed April 10, 2014, cvhpower.org/hudson-valley-99-2/maloney-food-stamp.

11. Casey Lund, "Spokane Residents Protest Against Food Stamp Cuts," KXYL.com, September 18, 2013.

12. James Sherk, "Instead of Increasing Wage, Fast-food Can Use Robot Workers," *Seattle Times,* September 20, 2013.

13. Hank Johnson, interview by Al Sharpton, *PoliticsNation with Al Sharpton,* MSNBC, June 13, 2013, accessed April 10, 2014, http://tv.msnbc.com/2013/06/14/democrats-take -food-stamp-challenge-to-highlight-gops-proposed-cuts/.

14. Emphasis added, Joshua De Leon, "Politicians Go on Food Stamps in Protest of Farm Bill," *Ring of Fire,* June 14, 2013, accessed April 10, 2014, http://www.ringoffire radio.com/2013/06/politicians-go-on-food-stamps-in-protest-of-farm-bill/#.

15. Ben LaCross, introduction of President Barack Obama, Michigan State University, East Lansing, MI, February 2, 2014, accessed May 2, 2014, http://www.c-span.org /video/?317673-1/president-signs-farm-bill.

16. Barack Obama, "Remarks by the President at Signing of the Farm Bill—MI," Michigan State University, East Lansing, Michigan, February 7, 2014, accessed May 2, 2014, http://www.whitehouse.gov/the-press-office/2014/02/07/remarks-president -signing-farm-bill-mi.

BIBLIOGRAPHY

MANUSCRIPT COLLECTIONS

Berkeley, California

University of California Library
"Investigation Concerning the Sharecropper Situation in Southeast Missouri." Memorandum for the Attorney General. February 1939. Federal Bureau of Investigation, United States Department of Justice, Washington, DC. HD 1527.M8.

Chicago, Illinois

Richard J. Daley Library, University of Illinois-Chicago
  Century of Progress Records

College Park, Maryland

National Archives and Records Administration
  Records of the Extension Services, 1888–1996. Record Group 33
  General Records of the Department of Justice Central Files and Related Records,
    1790–1989. Record Group 60
  Records of the Farmers Home Administration, 1918–75. Record Group 96
    Project Records, 1935–40
  Records of the Office of the Secretary of Agriculture, 1839–1981. Record Group 16
    General Correspondence of the Office of the Secretary of Agriculture, 1906–70
    [Office of Information] Records Relating to Exhibitions and Expositions, 1889–1949
    Photographic Prints of USDA Exhibits and Other Exhibits, 1900–53
  Work Projects Administration Records of the Federal Theatre Project. Record
    Group 69
    Federal Theatre Project Central Files
    Federal Theatre Project State Files
    Vassar Collection of Programs and Promotion Materials, 1935–39

Detroit, Michigan

Walter P. Reuther Library, Wayne State University
  Don Binkowski Papers, 1920–2008

Evanston, Illinois

Northwestern University Library
  Southern Tenant Farmers' Union Papers, 1934–70. NC: Microfilming Corporation
    of America, 1971.

Fairfax, Virginia

Fenwick Library, George Mason University
  Federal Theatre Project Collection
      Oral History New Deal Culture
      Theatre of the Thirties

Hyde Park, New York

Franklin D. Roosevelt Presidential Library
  President's Office File 1650

Madison, Wisconsin

Wisconsin Historical Society
  Ralph M. Immell Papers, 1908–60
  William Theodore Evjue Papers, 1880–1969
  Wisconsin Cooperative Milk Pool Records, 1925–43

Milwaukee, Wisconsin

Wisconsin Historical Society
  Harry Bragarnick Papers, 1930–60
  William Benjamin Rubin Papers, 1908–50

Washington, DC

Archives of American Art
  Roy Emerson Stryker Papers, 1934–64
Library of Congress
  Cowling Collection
  Farm Security Administration—Office of War Information, Written Records, 1935–46
  Federal Theatre Collection

PUBLISHED PRIMARY AND CONTEMPORARY WORKS
AND GOVERNMENT DOCUMENTS

Arent, Arthur. "The Techniques of the Living Newspaper." *Theatre Arts Monthly,* November 1938, 280–82.
"Beans, Bacon and Gravy." In *Early American Folk Music and Songs,* performer Clark Jones, Smithsonian Global Sound for Libraries. New York: Folkways, 1982.
Bernat, Cory. "Beans Are Bullets and Of Course I Can! An Exhibit of War-Era Food Posters from the National Agricultural Library." 2010. Accessed September 7, 2013. http://www.good-potato.com.
Colbert, Stephen. *The Colbert Report.* September 18, 2012. Accessed April 10, 2014. http://thecolbertreport.cc.com/videos/dsvsbf/mitt-romney-s-secret-video.

Conrad, Laetitia. "Some Effects of the Depression on Family Life." *Social Forces* 15.1 (1936): 76–81.

Cummings, Richard Osborn. *The American and His Food: A History of Food Habits in the United States.* Rev. ed. Chicago: University of Chicago Press, 1941.

CVH Power. "CVH Power Protests Rep Maloney Food Stamp Vote." Accessed September 29, 2013. http://cvhpower.org/hudson-valley-99-2/maloney-food-stamp.

Darrow, Clarence. Address delivered at the Henry George Congress, Chicago, Illinois, September 1933. Reprinted from *Land and Freedom,* November–December 1933. Accessed July 2, 2011. http://www.cooperativeindividualism.org/darrow-clarence _roosevelts-new-deal-a-critical-appraisal-1933.html.

Dawes, Rufus. *Report of the President of a Century of Progress to the Board of Trustees.* Chicago: Century of Progress, 1936.

De Rohan, Pierre, ed. *Federal Theatre Plays: Triple-A Plowed Under by the Staff of the Living Newspaper; Power: A Living Newspaper by Arthur Arent; Spirochete: A History by Arnold Sundgaard.* New York: Random House, 1938.

Dixon, Kelly A. "Nutrition Reform and Work Opportunity Act." Accessed April 10, 2014. http://www.hagstromreport.com/assets/2013/2013_0903_NutritionReformIntro.pdf.

"Farm Tenancy." A Message from the President of the United States transmitting the Report of the Special Committee on Farm Tenancy, 75th Congress, 1st Session, House Document No. 149, February 16, 1937. Washington: United States Government Printing Office, 1937.

Federal Writers' Program of the Work Projects Administration in the State of Michigan. *Michigan: A Guide to the Wolverine State.* New York: Oxford University Press, 1941.

Federal Writers' Project of the Works Progress Administration. *The WPA Guide to Wisconsin.* Wisconsin Library Association and New York: Duell, Sloan and Pearce, 1941. Rpt. Introduction by Norman K. Risjord. St. Paul: Minnesota Historical Society Press, 2006.

Flanagan, Hallie. *Arena.* New York: Duell, Sloan and Pearce, 1940.

Freed, Mildred G. "Ten Million Sharecroppers." *Crisis* 46.12 (1939): 367–68.

"The Great Food Stamp Binge." *Fox News Insider.* August 10, 2013. Accessed April 10, 2014. http://foxnewsinsider.com/tag/great-food-stamp-binge.

Hastings, Daniel O. "Battle of November." *Today* II (1934). In *The New Deal: A Documentary History,* edited by William E. Leuchtenburg, 194. Columbia: University of South Carolina Press, 1968.

Hutchins, Grace. "Millions for Meat Barons; Beans for the Unemployed." *Working Woman,* June 1935, 14.

Imhoff, Daniel. *Food Fight: The Citizen's Guide to the Next Food and Farm Bill.* 2nd ed. Healdsburg, CA: Watershed Media, 2012.

Johnson, Hank. Interview by Al Sharpton. *Politics Nation with Al Sharpton.* MSNBC. June 13, 2013. Accessed April 10, 2014. http://tv.msnbc.com/2013/06/14/democrats -take-food-stamp-challenge-to-highlight-gops-proposed-cuts/.

LaCross, Ben. Introduction of President Barack Obama. Michigan State University, East Lansing, MI. February 7, 2014. Accessed May 2, 2014. http://www.c-span.org /video/?317673-1/president-signs-farm-bill.

Larson, Cedric. "The Cultural Projects of the WPA." *Public Opinion Quarterly* 3.3 (1939): 491–96.

Lewisohn, Sam. "New Aspects of Unemployment Insurance." *Political Science Quarterly* 50.1 (1935): 1–14.

Lincoln, Abraham. February 12, 1861. "Presidential Quotes about the Homestead Act." *National Park Service.* Last updated September 18, 2012. Accessed April 10, 2014. http://www.nps.gov/home/historyculture/presquotes.htm.

Lindsay, Vachel. *Bryan, Bryan, Bryan, Bryan.* 1919. Accessed April 10, 2014. http://php .indiana.edu/~rotella/aeh/bryan1.htm.

Lucas, P.S. "Milk—The Ideal Food." USDA Extension Bulletin No. 140, Reprint, August, 1934.

McWilliams, Carey. *Ill Fares the Land: Migrants and Migratory Labor in the United States.* Boston: Little, Brown and Company, 1942.

Mojo News Team. "Full Transcript of the Mitt Romney Secret Video." Accessed April 10, 2014. http://www.motherjones.com/politics/2012/09/full-transcript-mitt-romney -secret-video.

Obama, Barack. "Remarks by the President at Signing of the Farm Bill—MI." Michigan State University, East Lansing, Michigan. February 7, 2014. Accessed May 2, 2014. http://www.whitehouse.gov/the-press-office/2014/02/07/remarks-president-signing -farm-bill-mi.

Roosevelt, Franklin. "Inaugural Speech of Franklin Delano Roosevelt." March 4, 1933. *History and Politics Out Loud.* Accessed April 10, 2014. http://www.wyzant.com/Help /History/HPOL/fdr/inaug/.

———. Message to Congress on the Agricultural Adjustment Act. March 16, 1933. Accessed April 10, 2014. *The American Presidency Project.* http://www.presidency.ucsb .edu/ws/?pid=14585

———. "Roosevelt's Nomination Address." Chicago, Illinois, July 2, 1932. Accessed April 10, 2014. *New Deal Network, Roosevelt Institute.* http://newdeal.feri.org/speeches /1932b.htm.

Snow, Thad. *From Missouri.* Boston: Houghton Mifflin Company, 1954.

State of Wisconsin Blue Book 2003–2004. July 30, 2006. Accessed April 10, 2014. http:// www.legis.state.wi.us/lrb/bb/03bb.

Steinbeck, John. "Harvest Gypsies." *San Francisco News,* October 5–12, 1936. Accessed April 10, 2014. *New Deal Network, Roosevelt Institute.* http://newdeal.feri.org.

U.S. Census of Population and Housing 1930. *Historical Census Browser Geospatial and Statistical Data Center.* University of Virginia Library. Accessed April 29, 2014. http:// mapserver.lib.virginia.edu/.

U.S. Congress. "A Century of Progress Exposition in Chicago, 1933." Joint Letter from the Secretary of State, the Secretary of Agriculture and the Secretary of Commerce as Members of the Chicago World's Fair Centennial Commission. 73rd Congress, 2nd Session. April 17, 1934. Washington DC: United States Government Printing Office.

U.S. Department of Agriculture. "Characteristics of Supplemental Nutrition Assistance Program Households: Fiscal Year: 2011—Summary." USDA Office of Research and Analysis. November 2012. Accessed April 10, 2014. http://www.fns.usda.gov/sites /default/files/2011CharacteristicsSummary.pdf.

———. *Know Your Farmer, Know Your Food.* Last modified August 19, 2013. Accessed April 10, 2014. http://www.usda.gov/wps/portal/usda/usdahome?navid=KYF_MISSION.

U.S. Department of Labor, Children's Bureau, "Why Drink Milk? Milk Is the Indispens- able Food for Children," Folder No. 3. Rev. ed. November, 1931.

U.S. Food Administration. "Pledge Card for United States Food Administration." "Meatless Mondays, Wheatless Wednesdays." Digital Exhibit. Albert R. Mann Library, Cornell University. Accessed April 10, 2014. http://exhibits.mannlib.cornell .edu/meatlesswheatless/meatless-wheatless.php?content=two_a.

Wallace, Henry A. *New Frontiers*. New York: Reynal and Hitchock, 1934.

Warren, Samuel D., and Louis D. Brandeis. "The Right to Privacy." *Harvard Law Review* 4.5. (1890). Accessed April 10, 2014. http://groups.csail.mit.edu/mac/classes/6.805 /articles/privacy/Privacy_brand_warr2.html.

Wiehl, Dorothy. "Diets of Low-Income Families in New York City." *The Milbank Memorial Fund Quarterly* 11.4 (1933): 308–24.

———. "Diets of Urban Families with Low Incomes: An Analysis of Weekly Food Budgets of 472 Families in Baltimore, Cleveland, Detroit, Pittsburgh and Syracuse in April-May, 1933." *The Milbank Memorial Fund Quarterly* 12.4 (1934): 343–69.

"Woman's Place in the United States Today—Is It in the Home?" *Working Woman*, April 1935, 3.

SECONDARY SOURCES

Abel, Richard. "Charge and Countercharge: 'Documentary' War Pictures in the USA, 1914–1916." *Film History: An International Journal* 22.4 (2010): 366–88.

Abrahams, Paul. "Agricultural Adjustment during the New Deal Period, The New York Milk Industry: A Case Study." *Agricultural History* 39.2 (1965): 92–101.

Abramovitz, Mimi. "Learning from the History of Poor and Working-class Women's Activism." *Annals of the American Academy of Political and Social Science* 577 (2001): 118–30.

Adams, Jon Robert. *Male Armor: The Soldier-Hero in Contemporary American Culture*. Charlottesville: University of Virginia Press, 2008.

Allain, Paul, and Jen Harvie. *The Routledge Companion to Theatre and Performance*. London: Routledge, 2006.

Althusser, Louis. *Lenin and Philosophy and Other Essays*. New York: Monthly Review Press, 1972.

Anderson, E. N. *Everyone Eats: Understanding Food and Culture*. New York: New York University Press, 2005.

Angel-Perez, Elisabeth, and Alexandra Poulain. "Introduction." In *Hunger on the Stage*, edited by Elisabeth Angel-Perez and Alexandra Poulain, ix–xii. Newcastle: Cambridge Scholars Publishing, 2008.

Aristotle's Poetics. Translated by S. H. Butcher. Introduction by Francis Fergusson. New York: Hill and Wang, 1961.

Austin, J. L. *How to do Things with Words*. 2nd ed. Oxford: Oxford University Press, 1975.

Barish, Jonas. *The Anti-Theatrical Prejudice*. Berkeley: University of California Press, 1981.

Baxandall, Lee. "Spectacles and Scenarios: A Dramaturgy of Radical Activity." *TDR: The Drama Review* 13.4 (1969): 52–71.

Baxandall, Michael. "Exhibiting Intention: Some Preconditions of Visual Display of Culturally Purposeful Objects." In *Exhibiting Cultures: The Poetics and Politics of Museum Display*, edited by I. Karp and S. D. Lavine, 33–41. Washington, DC: Smithsonian Institution Press, 1991.

Belcher, Michael. *Exhibitions in Museums*. Edited by Susan Pearce. Leicester and Washington, DC: Leicester University Press and Smithsonian Institution Press, 1991.

Benedict, Burton. *The Anthropology of World's Fairs: San Francisco's Panama Pacific International Exposition of 1915*. Berkeley, CA: Lowie Museum of Anthropology in association with Scolar Press, 1983.

Blakey, George T. "The Ham That Never Was: The 1933 Emergency Hog Slaughter." *Historian* 30.1 (1967): 41–57.

Block, Daniel R. "Public Health, Cooperatives, Local Regulation and the Development of Modern Milk Policy: The Chicago Milkshed, 1900–1940." *Journal of Historical Geography* 35.1 (2009): 128–53.

Block, Daniel R., and E. Melanie DuPuis. "Making the Country Work for the City: Von Thunen's Ideas in Geography, Agricultural Economics and the Sociology of Agriculture." *American Journal of Economics and Sociology* 60.1 (2001): 79–98.

Bogle, Donald. *Toms, Coons, Mulattoes, Mammies, and Bucks: An Interpretive History of Blacks in American Films*. 3rd ed. New York: Continuum, 1994.

Boris, Eileen. "Regulating Industrial Housework: The Triumph of 'Sacred Motherhood.'" *Journal of American History* 71.4 (1985): 745–63.

Browder, Laura. "Finding a Collective Solution: The Living Newspaper Experiment." *Prologue* 30.2 (1988): 87–97.

Butler, Judith. *Bodies That Matter: On the Discursive Limits of "Sex."* London: Routledge, 1993.

Buttitta, Tony, and Barry Witham. *Uncle Sam Presents: A Memoir of the Federal Theatre 1935–1939*. Philadelphia: University of Pennsylvania Press, 1982.

Calzadilla, Fernando. "Performing the Political: Encapuchados in Venezuela." *TDR: The Drama Review* 46.4 (2002): 104–25.

Canning, Charlotte. *The Most American Thing in America: Circuit Chautauqua as Performance*. Iowa City: University of Iowa Press, 2005.

Cantor, Louis. *A Prologue to the Protest Movement: The Missouri Sharecropper Roadside Demonstration of 1939*. Durham, NC: Duke University Press, 1969.

Choate, Jean. *Disputed Ground: Farm Groups That Opposed the New Deal Agricultural Program*. Jefferson, NC: McFarland, 2002.

Clemente, Deirdre. "Striking Ensembles: The Importance of Clothing on the Picket Line." *Labor Studies Journal* 30.4 (2006): 1–15.

Cosgrove, Stuart. "From Shock Troupe to Group Theatre." In *Theatres of the Left 1880–1935*, edited by Stuart Cosgrove, Raphael Samuel, and Ewan MacColl, 259–79. London: Routledge and Kegan Paul, 1985.

Counihan, Carole. "Food Rules in the United States: Individualism, Control and Hierarchy." *Anthropological Quarterly* 65.2 (1992): 55–66.

Counihan, Carole, and Penny Van Esterik, eds. *Food and Culture: A Reader*. New York: Routledge, 1997.

Cozzi, Enzo. "Hunger and the Future of Performance." *Performance Research* 4.1 (1999): 121–29.

Cross, Gary. *An All-Consuming Century: Why Commercialism Won in Modern America*. New York: Columbia University Press, 2000.

Cunningham, Charles. "*Life* Magazine and the Mythology of Rural Poverty in the Depression." *Journal of Narrative Theory* 29.3 (1999): 278–302.

Daniel, Pete. *Breaking the Land: The Transformation of Cotton, Tobacco, and Rice Cultures since 1880.* Urbana: University of Illinois Press, 1985.

Davis, Tracy C. "Performing and the Real Thing in the Postmodern Museum." *TDR: The Drama Review* 39.3 (1995): 15–40.

Day, Amber. *Satire and Dissent: Interventions in Contemporary Political Debate.* Bloomington: Indiana University Press, 2011.

de Certeau, Michel. *The Practice of Everyday Life.* Translated by Steven Randall. Berkeley: University of California Press, 1988.

De Leon, Joshua. "Politicians Go on Food Stamps in Protest of Farm Bill." *Ring of Fire,* June 14, 2013. Accessed April 10, 2014. http://www.ringoffireradio.com/2013/06/politicians-go-on-food-stamps-in-protest-of-farm-bill/#.

Denning, Michael. *The Cultural Front: The Laboring of American Culture in the Twentieth-Century.* London: Verso, 1996.

"Detailed Facts about Vomiting Agent Adamsite (DM)." 218-17-1096. *U.S. Army Center for Health Promotion and Preventive Medicine.* Last accessed February 26, 2006. http://chppm-www.apgea.army.mil/dts/docs/detdm.pdf.

Deutsch, Tracey. *Building a Housewife's Paradise: Gender, Politics, and American Grocery Stores in the Twentieth Century.* Chapel Hill: University of North Carolina Press, 2010.

Donohue, Kathleen G. *Freedom from Want: American Liberalism and the Idea of the Consumer.* Baltimore, MD: The Johns Hopkins University Press, 2003.

Douglas, Mary, ed. *Food in the Social Order: Studies of Food and Festivities in Three American Communities.* New York: Russell Sage Foundation, 1984.

Drewal, Margaret. "From Rocky's Rockettes to Liberace: The Politics of Representation in the Heart of Corporate America." *Journal of American Culture* 10.2 (1987): 69–82.

DuPuis, E. Melanie. "Angels and Vegetables: A Brief History of Food Advice in America." *Gastronomica* 7.3 (2007): 34–44.

———. *Nature's Perfect Food: How Milk Became America's Drink.* New York: New York University Press, 2002.

Durland, Steve. "Witness: The Guerilla Theatre of Greenpeace." In *Radical Street Performance: An International Anthology,* edited by Jan Cohen-Cruz, 67–73. London: Routledge, 1998.

Dusselier, Jane. "Understandings of Food as Culture." *Environmental History* 14.2 (2009): 331–38.

"Dust Bowl Migration." *Rural Migration News* 14.4 (2008). Accessed April 10, 2014. https://migration.ucdavis.edu/rmn/more.php?id=1355_0_6_0.

Elias, Megan J. *Food in the United States, 1890–1945.* Santa Barbara, CA: Greenwood Press, 2009.

Ellmann, Maud. *The Hunger Artists: Starving, Writing, and Imprisonment.* Cambridge, MA: Harvard University Press, 1993.

Emeljanow, Victor. "The Events of June 1848: The 'Monte Cristo' Riots and the Politics of Protest." *New Theatre Quarterly* 19.1 (2003): 23–32.

Enstad, Nan. "Fashioning Political Identities: Cultural Studies and the Historical Construction of Political Subjects." *American Quarterly* 50.4 (1998): 745–82.

Ferry, Jane. *Food in Film: A Culinary Performance of Communication.* London: Routledge, 2003.

Findling, John. *Chicago's Great World's Fairs.* New York: St. Martin's Press, 1994.

Fine, Gary Alan. *Difficult Reputations: Collective Memories of the Evil, Inept, and Controversial.* Chicago: University of Chicago Press, 2001.

Fitchen, Janet. "Hunger, Malnutrition, and Poverty in the Contemporary United States." In *Food and Culture: A Reader,* edited by Carole Counihan and Penny Van Esterik, 384–401. New York: Routledge, 1997.

Foster, Susan Leigh. "Choreographies of Protest." *Theatre Journal* 55.3 (2003): 395–412.

Foucault, Michel. *Discipline and Punish: The Birth of the Prison.* Translated by Alan Sheridan. New York: Pantheon Books, 1977.

Fraden, Rena. *Blueprints for a Black Federal Theatre, 1935–1939.* Cambridge: Cambridge University Press, 1994.

Franko, Mark. *The Work of Dance: Labor, Movement, and Identity in the 1930s.* Middletown, CN: Wesleyan University Press, 2002.

Fuoss, Kirk W. *Striking Performances/Performing Strikes.* Jackson: University of Mississippi Press, 1997.

Gaines, Jane. "The Showgirl and the Wolf." *Cinema Journal* 20.1 (1980): 53–67.

Garner, Stanton B., Jr. *Bodied Spaces: Phenomenology and Performance in Contemporary Drama.* Ithaca, NY: Cornell University Press, 1994.

Goddard, Leslie. "'Something to Vote for': Theatricalism in the U.S. Women's Suffrage Movement." PhD diss., Northwestern University, 2001.

Goldstein, Carolyn M. *Creating Consumers: Home Economists in Twentieth-Century America.* Chapel Hill: University of North Carolina Press, 2012.

Groves, F.W. "Twentieth Century Farm Strikes: A Comment." *Agricultural History* 39.4 (1965): 217–19.

Hall, Roger A. *Performing the American Frontier, 1870–1906.* Cambridge: Cambridge University Press, 2001.

Hamilton, Shane. *Trucking Country: The Road to America's Wal-Mart Economy.* Princeton, NJ: Princeton University Press, 2008.

Heneghan, Bridget. *Whitewashing America: Material Culture and Race in the Antebellum Imagination.* Jackson: University of Mississippi Press, 2003.

Hobart, Hi'ilei. "'The Milk Problem': The New York Milk Station and Surveys of the Immigrant Body, 1906–1912." Paper presented at "Food Networks: Gender and Foodways: An Interdisciplinary Conference," Gender Studies Program, Notre Dame, IN, January 26–28, 2012.

Hoglund, William. "Wisconsin Dairy Farmers on Strike." *Agricultural History* 35.1 (1961): 24–35.

Holloway, Lewis, and Moya Kneafsey. "Producing-Consuming Food: Closeness, Connectedness and Rurality in Four 'Alternative' Food Networks." In *Geographies of Rural Cultures and Societies,* edited by Lewis Holloway and Moya Kneafsey, 262–81. Burlington, VT: Ashgate, 2004.

Hooper-Greenhill, Eilean. *Museums and the Interpretation of Visual Culture.* London: Routledge, 2000.

Horowitz, Roger. *Putting Meat on the American Table: Taste, Technology, Transformation.* Baltimore, MD: The Johns Hopkins University Press, 2005.

Iball, Helen. "Melting Moments: Bodies Upstaged by the 'Foodie Gaze.'" *Performance Research* 4.1 (1999): 70–81.

Jackson, Shannon. *Professing Performance: Theatre in the Academy from Philology to Performativity.* Cambridge: Cambridge University Press, 2004.

Jacobs, Herbert. "The Wisconsin Milk Strikes." *Wisconsin Magazine of History* 35.1 (1951): 30–35.

Jacobs, Meg. *Pocketbook Politics: Economic Citizenship in Twentieth-Century America.* Princeton, NJ: Princeton University Press, 2008.

Jasper, James M. *The Art of Moral Protest: Culture, Biography, and Creativity in Social Movements.* Chicago: University of Chicago Press, 1997.

Jestrovic, Silvija. "Theatricalizing Politics/Politicizing Theatre." *Canadian Theatre Review* 103 (2000): 42–46.

Jetter, Alexis, Annelise Orleck, and Diana Taylor, eds. *The Politics of Motherhood: Activist Voices from Left to Right.* Hanover, NH: University Press of New England, 1997.

Jochnowitz, Eve. "Feasting on the Future: Foods of the World of Tomorrow at the New York World's Fair of 1939–40." *Performance Research* 4.1 (1999): 110–20.

Johnson, Odai. *Absence and Memory in Colonial American Theatre: Fiorelli's Plaster.* New York: Palgrave Macmillan, 2006.

Jones, Jacqueline. *The Dispossessed: America's Underclasses from the Civil War to the Present.* New York: Basic Books, 1992.

———. *Labor of Love, Labor of Sorrow: Black Women, Work and the Family from Slavery to the Present.* New York: Basic Books, 1985.

Jones, Michael Owen. "What's Disgusting, Why, and What Does It Matter?" *Journal of Folklore Research* 37.1 (2000): 53–71.

Kaplan, Temma. "Female Consciousness and Collective Action: The Case of Barcelona, 1910–1918." *Signs: Journal of Women in Culture and Society* 7.3 (1982): 545–66.

Karp, Ivan, and Steven D. Lavine, eds. *Exhibiting Cultures: The Poetics and Politics of Museum Display.* Washington, DC: Smithsonian Institution Press, 1991.

Kasparek, Jonathan. "FDR's 'Old Friends' in Wisconsin: Presidential Finesse in the Land of La Follette." *Wisconsin Magazine of History* 84.4 (2001): 16–25.

Kaye, Nick. *Site-Specific Art: Performance, Place and Documentation.* London: Routledge, 2000.

Kazacoff, George. *Dangerous Theatre: The Federal Theatre Project as a Forum for New Plays.* New York: Peter Lange Publishing, 1989.

Kazin, Michael. *The Populist Persuasion: An American History.* Rev. ed. Ithaca, NY: Cornell University Press, 1998.

———. "The Producers." *New Republic,* February 8, 2012. Accessed April 10, 2014. http://www.newrepublic.com/article/politics/magazine/100526/producers-middle-class-income-inequality-occupy#.

Kelley, Robin D. *Hammer and Hoe: Alabama Communists during the Great Depression.* Chapel Hill: University of North Carolina Press, 1990.

Kershaw, Baz. "Curiosity or Contempt: On Spectacle, the Human, and Activism." *Theatre Journal* 55.4 (2003): 591–611.

———. *The Radical in Performance: Between Brecht and Baudrillard.* London: Routledge, 1999.

Kershen, Lois. *American Proverbs about Women: A Reference Guide.* Westport, CN: Greenwood Press, 1998.

Kihlstedt, Folke T. "Utopia Realized: The World Fairs of the 1930s." In *Imagining Tomorrow: History, Technology and the American Future,* edited by Joseph J. Corn, 97–118. Cambridge: Massachusetts Institute of Technology Press, 1986.

Kirschenblatt-Gimblett, Barbara. *Destination Culture: Tourism, Museums, and Heritage.* Berkeley: University of California Press, 1998.

———. "Playing to the Senses: Food as a Performance Medium." *Performance Research* 4.1 (1999): 1–30.

Kimmell, Michael. *Manhood in America: A Cultural History.* New York: Free Press, 1996.

Kingsbury, Celia M. "'Food Will Win the War': Food and Social Control in World War I Propaganda." In *Edible Ideologies: Representing Food and Meaning,* edited by Kathleen LeBesco and Peter Naccarato, 53–72. Albany: State University of New York Press, 2008.

Knowles, Ric. *Reading the Material Theatre.* Cambridge: Cambridge University Press, 2004.

Kootin, Amma Y. Ghartey-Tagoe. "Lessons in Blackbody Minstrelsy: Old Plantation and the Manufacture of Black Authenticity." *TDR: The Drama Review* 57.2 (2013): 102–22.

Kowal, Rebekah J. "Staging the Greensboro Sit-Ins." *TDR: The Drama Review* 48.4 (2004): 135–54.

Kruger, Loren. *The National Stage: Theatre and Cultural Legitimation in England, France, and America.* Chicago: Chicago University Press, 1992.

Kuehn, Glenn. "How Can Food Be Art?" In *The Aesthetics of Everyday Life,* edited by Andrew Light and Jonathan M. Smith, 194–212. New York: Columbia University Press, 2005.

Kung, Tim Yuan-Shiao. "Spilt Milk: Dairy Farmer Rhetoric and Actions during the Wisconsin Milk Strikes of 1933." Master's thesis, University of Wisconsin-Madison, 1996.

Lambert, Roger C. "The Drought Cattle Purchase, 1934–1935: Problems and Complaints." *Agricultural History* 45.2 (April 1971): 85–93.

———. "Slaughter of the Innocents: The Public Protests to AAA Killing of Little Pigs." *Midwest Quarterly* 14.3 (1973): 247–56.

Laufenberg, Elmer Wayne. "The Schmedeman Administration in Wisconsin: A Study of Missed Opportunity." Master's thesis, University of Wisconsin-Madison, 1965.

LeBesco, Kathleen and Peter Naccaratto, eds. *Edible Ideologies: Representing Food and Meaning.* Albany: State University of New York Press, 2008.

Levenstein, Harvey A. *The Paradox of Plenty: A Social History of Eating in Modern America.* New York: Oxford University Press, 1993.

Libecap, Gary. "The Great Depression and the Regulating State: Federal Government Regulation of Agriculture, 1884–1970." In *The Defining Moment: The Great Depression and the American Economy in the Twentieth Century,* edited by Michael D. Bordo, Claudia Goldin, and Eugene N. White, 181–224. Chicago: University of Chicago Press, 1998.

Light Art Lumia: A Site about the Pioneering Work of Thomas Wilfred with Images and Information from the Eugene and Carol Epstein Collection. Accessed April 10, 2014. http:// www.lumia-wilfred.org/.

Lofland, John. *Protest: Studies in Collective Behavior and Social Movements.* New Brunswick, NJ: Transaction Books, 1985.

Lott, Eric. *Love and Theft: Blackface Minstrelsy and the American Working Class*. New York: Oxford University Press, 1993.

Lund, Casey. "Spokane Residents Protest against Food Stamp Cuts." KXYL.com. September 18, 2013. Accessed April 10, 2014. http://downtownspokane.kxly.com/news/news/107911-spokane-residents-protest-against-food-stamp-cuts.

Lynn, Denise. "United We Spend: Communist Women and the 1935 Meat Boycott." *American Communist History* 10.1 (2011): 35–52.

MacAloon, John J. "Olympic Games and the Theory of Spectacle in Modern Societies." In *Rite, Drama, Festival, Spectacle: Rehearsals toward a Theory of Cultural Performance*, edited by John J. MacAloon, 241–80. Philadelphia: ISHI, 1984.

Managan, Michael. *Staging Masculinities: History, Gender, Performance*. New York: Palgrave Macmillan, 2003.

Manning, Susan. *Modern Dance, Negro Dance*. Minneapolis: University of Minnesota Press, 2004.

Marshall, Elizabeth. "Stripping for the Wolf: Rethinking Representations of Gender in Children's Literature." *Reading Research Quarterly* 39.3 (2004): 256–70.

Mathews, Jane DeHart. *The Federal Theatre, 1935–1939: Plays, Relief, and Politics*. Princeton, NJ: Princeton University Press, 1967.

McConachie, Bruce A. *Melodramatic Formations: American Theatre and Society, 1820–1870*. Iowa City: University of Iowa Press, 1992.

McGann, Patrick. "Eating Muscle: Material-Semiotics and a Manly Appetite." In *Revealing Male Bodies*, edited by Nancy Tuana, William Cowling, Maurice Hamington, Greg Johnson, and Terrance MacMullen, 83–99. Bloomington: Indiana University Press, 2001.

McHugh, Kathleen Anne. *American Domesticity: From How- to Manual to Hollywood Melodrama*. New York: Oxford University Press, 1999.

Melosh, Barbara. *Engendering Culture: Manhood and Womanhood in New Deal Public Art and Theater*. Washington, DC: Smithsonian Institution Press, 1991.

Mettler, Suzanne. *Dividing Citizens: Gender and Federalism in New Deal Public Policy*. Ithaca, NY: Cornell University Press, 1998.

"Michigan Women's Historical Center and Hall of Fame." *The Michigan Women's Historical Center & Hall of Fame*. Accessed April 10, 2014. http://www.michiganwomenshalloffame.org.

Milkman, Ruth. "Women's Work and the Economic Crisis: Some Lessons from the Great Depression." In *A Heritage of Her Own: Toward a New Social History of American Women*, edited by Nancy F. Cott and Elizabeth H. Pleck, 507–41. New York: Simon and Schuster, 1979.

Miller, Daniel. *Stuff*. Cambridge: Polity Press, 2010.

Mintz, Sidney. *Sweetness and Power: The Place of Sugar in Modern History*. New York: Viking, 1985.

———. *Tasting Food, Tasting Freedom: Excursions into Eating, Culture, and the Past*. Boston: Beacon Press, 1996.

Mooney, Patrick H., and Scott A. Hunt. "A Repertoire of Interpretations: Master Frames and Ideological Community in U.S. Agrarian Mobilization." *Sociological Quarterly* 37.1 (1996): 177–97.

Muncy, Robyn. *Creating a Female Dominion in American Reform, 1890–1935*. New York: Oxford University Press, 1991.

Natanson, Nicholas. *The Black Image in the New Deal: The Politics of FSA Photography.* Knoxville: University of Tennessee Press, 1992.

Obidinski, Eugene E., and Helen Stankiewicz Zand. *Polish Folkways in America: Community and Family.* Lanham, MD: University Press of America, Inc, 1987.

O'Connor, Alice. *Poverty Knowledge: Social Science, Social Policy, and the Poor in Twentieth-Century U.S. History.* Princeton, NJ: Princeton University Press, 2001.

O'Connor, John. "The Federal Theatre Project's Search for an Audience." In *Theatre for Working-Class Audiences in the United States, 1830–1980,* edited by Bruce MacConachie and Daniel Friedman, 171–83. Westport, CN: Greenwood Press, 1985.

O'Connor, John, and Lorraine Brown. *Free, Adult, Uncensored: The Living History of the Federal Project.* Washington, DC: New Republic Books, 1978.

Oh Freedom After While. Produced by Candace O'Connor and Lynn Rubright. Directed by Steven John Ross. St. Louis and Memphis: Webster University and the University of Memphis: California Newsreel, 1999. DVD.

Orenstein, Claudia. "Agitational Performance, Now and Then." *Theater* 31.3 (2001): 139–51.

Orleck, Annelise. *Common Sense and a Little Fire: Women and Working-class Politics in the United States, 1900–1965.* Chapel Hill: University of North Carolina Press, 2007.

———. "'We are that mythical thing called the public': Militant Housewives during the Great Depression." *Feminist Studies* 19.1 (1993): 147–72.

Osborne, Elizabeth. *Staging the People: Community and Identity in the Federal Theatre.* New York: Palgrave Macmillan, 2011.

Perry, Mary Elizabeth. "Finding Fatima, a Slave Woman of Early Modern Spain." In *Contesting Archives: Finding Women in the Sources,* edited by Nupur Chaudhuri, Sherry J. Katz, and Mary Elizabeth Perry, 3–19. Urbana: University of Illinois Press, 2010.

Plant, Rebecca Jo. *Mom: The Transformation of Motherhood in Modern America.* Chicago: University of Chicago Press, 2010.

Poppendieck, Janet. *Breadlines Knee-deep in Wheat: Food Assistance in the Great Depression.* New Brunswick, NJ: Rutgers University Press, 1986.

———. *Free for All: Fixing School Food in America.* Berkeley: University of California Press, 2010.

———. *Sweet Charity? Emergency Food and the End of Entitlement.* New York: Viking, 1998.

Potter, David. *People of Plenty: Economic Abundance and the American Character.* Chicago: University of Chicago Press, 1954.

Roach, Joseph. *It.* Ann Arbor: University of Michigan Press, 2007.

Roll, Jarod. "Road to the Promised Land: Rural Rebellion in the New Cotton South, 1890–1945." PhD diss., Northwestern University, 2006.

———. *Spirit of Rebellion: Labor and Religion in the New Cotton South.* Urbana: University of Illinois Press, 2010.

Román, David. *Performance in America: Contemporary Culture and the Performing Arts.* Durham, NC: Duke University Press, 2005.

Roxworthy, Emily. *The Spectacle of Japanese American Trauma: Racial Performativity and World War II.* Honolulu: University of Hawai'i Press, 2008.

Rydell, Robert W. *World of Fairs: The Century of Progress Exhibitions.* Chicago: University of Chicago Press, 1993.

Rydell, Robert W., Kimberley Pelle, and John Findling. *Fair America: World's Fairs in the United States*. Washington, DC: Smithsonian Institution Press, 2000.

Saal, Ilka. *New Deal Theater: The Vernacular Tradition in American Political Theater*. New York: Palgrave Macmillan, 2007.

Saloutos, Theodore. *The American Farmer and the New Deal*. Ames: Iowa State University Press, 1982.

Saloutos, Theodore, and John D. Hicks. *Agricultural Discontent in the Middle West, 1900–1939*. Madison: University of Wisconsin, 1951.

Scapp, Ron, and Brian Seitz, eds. *Eating Culture*. Albany: State University of New York Press, 1998.

Scarry, Elaine. *The Body in Pain: The Making and Unmaking of the World*. New York: Oxford University Press, 1985.

Scharf, Lois. *To Work and to Wed: Female Employment, Feminism, and the Great Depression*. Westport, CN: Greenwood Press, 1980.

Schechner, Richard. *Performance Studies: An Introduction*. New York: Routledge, 2002.

Schneider, Rebecca. "It Seems as If . . . I Am Dead: Zombie Capitalism and Theatrical Labor." *TDR: The Drama Review* 56.4 (2012): 150–62.

Schuyler, Michael W. "New Deal Farm Policy in the Middle West: A Retrospective View." *Journal of the West* 33.4 (1994): 52–63.

Schwartz, Bonnie Nelson. *Voices from the Federal Theatre*. Madison: University of Wisconsin Press, 2003.

Scott, Shelley. *The Violent Woman as a New Theatrical Character Type: Cases from Canadian Drama*. Lewiston, NY: Edwin Mellen Press, 2007.

Serafino, Frank. *West of Warsaw*. Hamtramck, MI: Avenue Publishing Co., 1983.

Sheehan, Steven T. "'Costly Thy Habit as Thy Purse Can Buy': Gary Cooper and the Making of the Masculine Citizen-Consumer." *American Studies* 43.1 (2002): 101–25.

Shover, John L. *Cornbelt Rebellion: The Farmers' Holiday Association*. Urbana: University of Illinois Press, 1965.

Sontag, Susan. *Regarding the Pain of Others*. New York: Picador, 2003.

Stanford, C. B. *The Hunting Apes: Meat Eating and the Origins of Human Behavior*. Princeton, NJ: Princeton University Press, 2001.

Stepenoff, Bonnie. *Thad Snow: A Life of Social Reform in the Missouri Bootheel*. Columbia: University of Missouri Press, 2003.

Stock, Catherine McNicol. *Rural Radicals: Righteous Rage in the American Grain*. Ithaca, NY: Cornell University Press, 1996.

Storrs, Landon. *Civilizing Capitalism: The National Consumers' League, Women's Activism, and Labor Standards in the New Deal Era*. Chapel Hill: University of North Carolina Press, 2000.

Taylor, Diana. "A Savage Performance: Guillermo Gómez-Peña and Coco Fusco's *Couple in the Cage*." *TDR: The Drama Review* 42.2 (1998): 160–75.

———. "'You Are Here': The DNA of Performance." *TDR: The Drama Review* 46.1 (2002): 149–69.

Telfer, Elizabeth. *Food for Thought: Philosophy and Food*. London: Routledge, 1996.

Tompkins, Kyla Wazana. *Racial Indigestion: Eating Bodies in the Nineteenth Century*. New York: New York University Press, 2012.

Triece, Mary C. *On the Picket Line: Strategies of Working-class Women during the Depression*. Urbana: University of Illinois Press, 2007.

Tweeten, Luther. *Terrorism, Radicalism, and Populism in Agriculture.* Ames: Iowa State Press, 2003.

Vester, Katharina. "Regime Change: Gender, Class, and the Invention of Dieting in Post-bellum America." *Journal of Social History* 44.1 (2010): 39–70.

Weiss, Stuart L. *The President's Man: Leo Crowley and Franklin Roosevelt in Peace and War.* Carbondale: Southern Illinois University Press, 1996.

White, Ann Folino. "Page 48: Vaudeville of a Historian," "A Tyranny of Documents: The Performing Arts Historian as Film Noir Detective, Essays Dedicated to Brooks McNamara." Special issue, edited by Stephen Johnson. *Performing Arts Resources* 28 (2011): 243–51.

White, Peter R. R. "Media Objectivity and the Rhetoric of a News Story Structure." In *Discourse and Community: Doing Functional Linguistics,* edited by Eija Ventola, 379–400. Tübingen: Narr, 2000.

Willard, Barbara. "The American Story of Meat: Discursive Influences on Cultural Eating Practice." *Journal of Popular Culture* 36.1 (2002): 105–18.

Winders, William. *The Politics of Food Supply: U.S. Agricultural Policy in the World Economy.* New Haven, CT: Yale University Press, 2009.

Witham, Barry. "The Economic Structure of the Federal Theatre Project." In *The American Stage: Social and Economic Issues from the Colonial Period to the Present,* edited by Ron Engel and Tice Miller, 200–214. Cambridge: Cambridge University Press, 1993.

———. *The Federal Theatre Project: A Case Study.* Cambridge: Cambridge University Press, 2003.

Wood, Arthur Evans. *Hamtramck Then and Now.* New York: Bookman Associates, 1955.

Woods, Michael. "Politics and Protest in the Contemporary Countryside." In *Geographies of Rural Cultures and Societies,* edited by Lewis Holloway and Moya Kneafsey, 103–25. Burlington, VT: Ashgate, 2004.

INDEX

Italicized references refer to illustrations.

ANN FOLINO WHITE is Assistant Professor of Theatre Studies in
the Department of Theatre at Michigan State University, where she
teaches performance theory, theater history, and stage directing.
Dr. Folino White's scholarship on American drama and performance
has appeared in *American Drama, Text and Performance Quarterly,
Women and Performance: A Journal of Feminist Theory, Performing Arts
Resources,* and TDR: *The Drama Review.*